LOWER CANADA
1791-1840

FERNAND OUELLET

LOWER CANADA
1791-1840

SOCIAL CHANGE AND
NATIONALISM

Translated and adapted by Patricia Claxton

The Canadian Centenary Series

McClelland and Stewart

Copyright © 1980 McClelland and Stewart Limited

Reprinted in paperback 1983

CANADIAN CATALOGUING IN PUBLICATION DATA

Ouellet, Fernand, 1926-
  Lower Canada, 1791-1840

(The Canadian centenary series; [8])

Translation, abridgement, and adaptation of Le Bas-
Canada, 1791-1840.

Bibliography: p.
Includes index.
ISBN 0-7710-6921-9 (bound) ISBN 0-7710-6922-7 (pbk.)

1. Quebec (Province) – Economic conditions – To 1867. *
2. Quebec (Province) – History – 1791-1841. *
3. Quebec (Province) – Social conditions.   I. Title
II. Series.

HC117,Q408513   330.9'714'03   C79-094596-7

McClelland and Stewart Limited
The Canadian Publishers
25 Hollinger Road
Toronto

Acknowledgements

The map of the parishes of Quebec was prepared by
R. Chabot, *M.A. Français*, *M.A. Histoire*, and J.-Y.
Julien, *Lic. Géographie,* with cartography by J.-Y.
Julien.

Printed and bound in Canada

A History of Canada

W.L. Morton, EXECUTIVE EDITOR

D.G. Creighton, ADVISORY EDITOR

Ramsay Cook, EXECUTIVE EDITOR, 1983

VOLUMES STARRED ARE PUBLISHED

†ALSO AVAILABLE IN PAPERBACK

CONTENTS

LOWER CANADA 1791-1840
Social Change and Nationalism

à ma femme

The Canadian Centenary Series

Half a century has elapsed since *Canada and Its Provinces*, the first large-scale co-operative history of Canada, was published. During that time, new historical materials have been made available in archives and libraries; new research has been carried out, and its results published; new interpretations have been advanced and tested. In these same years Canada itself has greatly grown and changed. These facts, together with the centenary of Confederation, justify the publication of a new co-operative history of Canada.

The form chosen for this enterprise was that of a series of volumes. The series was planned by the editors, but each volume will be designed and executed by a single author. The general theme of work is the development of those regional communities which have for the past century made up the Canadian nation; and the series will be composed of a number of volumes sufficiently large to permit adequate treatment of all the phases of the theme in the light of modern knowledge.

The Centenary History, then, was planned as a series to have a certain common character and to follow a common method but to be written by individual authors, specialists in their fields. As a whole, it will be a work of specialized knowledge, the great advantage of scholarly co-operation, and at the same time each volume will have the unity and distinctive character of individual authorship. It was agreed that a general narrative treatment was necessary and that each author should deal in a balanced way with economic, political, and social history. The result, it is hoped, will be an interpretative, varied, and comprehensive account, at once useful to the student and interesting to the general reader.

The difficulties of organizing and executing such a series are apparent: the overlapping of separate narratives, the risk of omissions, the imposition of divisions which are relevant to some themes but not to others. Not so apparent, but quite as troublesome, are the problems of scale, perspective, and scope, problems which perplex the writer of a one-volume history and are magnified in a series. It is by deliberate choice that certain parts of the history are told twice, in different volumes from different points of view, in the belief that the benefits gained outweigh the unavoidable disadvantages.

With this volume Fernand Ouellet brings to the Canadian Centenary Series his demographic skills and his own particular historical scholarship. The Series is enriched thereby. The volume was originally commissioned by and written for the Series. After its publication in French, by permission, it has been skillfully and painstakingly adapted for the Series by the translator, Patricia Claxton. The author has added a new Conclusion for this volume.

W.L. MORTON,
Executive Editor

The translation and adaptation of an important and complex historical work raises a host of interesting problems which require much research, both linguistic and historical. Professor Ouellet has given generous attention to many points during the consultations necessary to ensure that his analysis and interpretation are accurately and clearly conveyed. Professor Morton has lent the benefit of his vast knowledge of Canadian history to the solution of a number of problems, particularly regarding terminology and original English quotations.

Many problems are technical, and most of these are minor. Thus, the measures *minot* and *arpent* are only roughly equivalent to "bushel" and "acre," and it would be fallacious to translate them. A number of French terms, such as *habitant*, are not translated because they have a specific sense in the historical context. Terms that have no real equivalent in English are italicized or not according to custom or editorial decision: "seigneur," for instance, is in roman and is spelled as in French, although in contemporary English quotations it often appears as "seignior," a curious half-anglicized spelling which has been abandoned in present scholarly usage; *censitaire*, a much less familiar word, is italicized. Terms that are italicized in the body of the text are in roman when they occur inside a quotation originally in French. Theoretically, that is; for whatever rules one sets, once in a while circumstance seems to require that they be broken.

The conceptual parameters of certain French terms can confound the search for entirely satisfactory yet concise equivalents in English. An example is *mentalité*, used in a sociological sense; "group mentality," which seems to be the closest English equivalent, needs to be understood as encompassing an entire pattern of thinking, values, and attitudes common to a social group, moulded by and inseparable from everything in the group's social and cultural context, past and immediate. The French word in italics would convey none of this, and would invite a simplistic identification with its English double. A number of potentially puzzling terms are briefly clarified or placed in perspective in the text.

Most intriguing for a translator are the "intangibles," those things which transcend mere meaning—atmosphere, irony, certain metaphors, archaic or personal language style, *et cetera*. Contemporary quotations are often rich with intangible content: Bishop Plessis's fire-and-brimstone, for instance. In direct and paraphrased quotations and throughout the text, every effort has been made to recreate the flavour of the original French.

In many original English quotations there is authentic quaintness. There are also authentic errors and clumsiness, as in statements by the Hungarian exile Fratelin. Diligence in tracking down the exact original versions of English quotations has sometimes gone unrewarded; in such cases the Chapter Note indicates retranslation.

Contemporary newspapers reported public speeches by indirect quotation, often rather garbled. Occasionally such a report brings the translator a very human picture of an harrassed nineteenth-century journalist being jostled by a crowd as he strives to record some barnstorming politician's oratory, which may have been less than perfectly coherent in the first place. Contemporary English newspaper reports of French speeches are sometimes literal, embarrassingly bad renditions into English.

Monetary values, given usually in pounds but sometimes in *livres*, reflect the lack of a uniform currency. In this period there was not even uniformity in pounds, which were the legal tender; in relation to sterling, local English pounds were overvalued, but not equally everywhere or for all purposes. Transactions and account-keeping were further complicated by a chronic shortage of specie, of which there was a bewildering variety, pre- and post-Conquest and from several countries. Discussions of elections and voting patterns need to be read in knowledge of the fact that most ridings elected two members to the legislative assembly; each elector therefore had two votes in general elections, one in by-elections to replace one member.

The statistical tables at the back of the book are presented and titled as uniformly as possible to facilitate consultation. Their salient features have been incorporated in the body of the text, with parenthetic table references.

PATRICIA CLAXTON

The present book derives primarily from my study *Histoire économique et sociale du Québec: 1760-1850: structures et conjoncture* (Montreal, Fides, 1966) and is an adaptation of my more recent book *Le Bas-Canada: 1791-1840: changements structuraux et crise* (Ottawa, Presses de l'Université d'Ottawa, 1976). In *Histoire économique*, social development is seen as the product of a plurality of influences—economic, demographic, military, religious, ideological, and political. In *Le Bas-Canada* and in this book, while my overall perspective remains the same, the emphasis is placed on social and political change. The voluminous documentation assembled on political movements and the revolution of 1837-38 for the earlier study has been supplemented by further research on these subjects. An analysis of the various poll books has enabled an examination of the interrelations among political movements, socio-ethnic change, and economic and demographic problems. Socio-ethnic structure has also received special attention; analysis of the censuses for 1831 and 1842 has provided a sufficiently accurate appreciation of the equilibria between social groups and ethnic groups.

Since 1966 the history of Lower Canada has attracted the attention of many historians and engendered much controversy. I note here the thesis by Pierre Tousignant entitled "La genèse et l'avènement de la constitution de 1791," which defines the reform movement before 1791 as one led by the English and French middle classes in opposition to the seigneurial aristocracy; also the provocative questions raised by Professors J.-P. Wallot and G. Paquet, who have concentrated on the beginning of the nineteenth century as a major turning point. Studies by Professors J.-P. Bernard and P.-A. Linteau on Montreal in the nineteenth century examine urban life in Lower Canada and also the changes perturbing the popular strata of the society after 1830. The growing interest in social history is further reflected by the work on the clergy by R. Chabot. Even this short list will amply show the rapid progress of research on this segment of Canadian history.

The interpretative approach conceived for *Histoire économique* has proven valid in the light of further research on demography, economic evolution, and particularly the rural economy, and is reaffirmed in the present work as in *Le Bas-Canada*, despite criticism from Professors Wallot and Paquet. The economic crisis and the demographic pressures taking form in the early nineteenth century were the principal fuels of the rural discontent which found expression through the Canadian and *patriote* party, and subsequently in an insurrectional movement led by the French-Canadian middle classes.

While writing *Le Bas-Canada* I have incurred a number of debts. My gratitude is due first to Richard Chabot who assembled the data on tithing and on sums collected in the parishes through that other yardstick of rural productivity, the Quête de l'Enfant-Jésus. I would like to express my gratitude also to Carleton University, which for ten years provided me with a calculator and a microfilm reader and sometimes financial assistance. The Canada Council has been generous in providing the funds needed for research. I must finally thank Patricia Claxton who has assumed the difficult task of translating and adapting *Le Bas-Canada* for the Canadian Centenary Series.

FERNAND OUELLET

LOWER CANADA
1791~1840

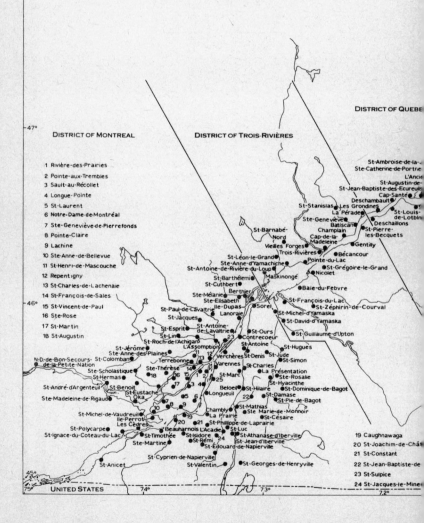

THE PARISHES OF QUEBEC
1615-1840

DISTRICT OF QUEBEC

DISTRICT OF MONTREAL

DISTRICT OF TROIS-RIVIÈRES

1 Rivière-des-Prairies
2 Pointe-aux-Trembles
3 Sault-au-Récollet
4 Longue-Pointe
5 St-Laurent
6 Notre-Dame-de-Montréal
7 Ste-Geneviève-de-Pierrefonds
8 Pointe-Claire
9 Lachine
10 Ste-Anne-de-Bellevue
11 St-Henri-de-Mascouche
12 Repentigny
13 St-Charles-de-Lachenaie
14 St-François-de-Sales
15 St-Vincent-de-Paul
16 Ste-Rose
17 St-Martin
18 St-Augustin

19 Caughnawaga
20 St-Joachim-de-Châ
21 St-Constant
22 St-Jean-Baptiste-de
23 St-Sulpice
24 St-Jacques-le-Mine

St-Ambroise-de-la-
Ste-Catherine-de-Portne
L'Anci
St-Augustin-de-
St-Jean-Baptiste-des-Ecureuls
Cap-Santé
Deschambault
St-Louis-
de-Lotbini
St-Stanislas Les Grondines
La Pérade
Ste-Geneviève
Batiscan
Champlain
Deschaillons
St-Pierre-
les-Becquets
St-Barnabé-
Nord
Cap-de-la-
Madeleine
Vieilles Forges
Gentilly
St-Léon-le-Grand
Bécancour
Trois-Rivières
Ste-Anne-d'Yamachiche
Pointe-du-Lac
St-Antoine-de-Rivière-du-Loup
St-Grégoire-le-Grand
St-Barthélemi
Maskinongé
Nicolet
St-Cuthbert
Baie-du-Febvre
Berthier
Ste-Mélanie
St-François-du-Lac
St-Elisabeth
St-Zéphirin-de-Courval
Île-Dupas
Sorel
St-Paul-de-Lavaltrie
Lanoraie
St-Michel-d'Yamaska
St-Jacques
St-David-d'Yamaska
St-Esprit
St-Antoine-
de-Lavaltrie
St-Lin
St-Ours
St-Guillaume-d'Upton
St-Roch-de-l'Achigan
Contrecoeur
L'Assomption
St-Jérôme
St-Hugues
Ste-Anne-des-Plaines
Verchères
St-Denis
St-Jude
N-D-de-Bon-Secours-
St-Colomban
Terrebonne
St-Antoine
St-Simon
de-la-Petite-Nation
Varennes
St-Charles
Ste-Scholastique
Ste-Thérèse
St-Marc
La Présentation
St-Hermas
Ste-Rosalie
St-André-d'Argenteuil
St-Benoit
St-Hyacinthe
Beloeil
St-Dominique-de-Bagot
St-Eustache
St-Hilaire
Ste-Madeleine-de-Rigaud
Oka
Longueuil
St-Damase
St-Pie-de-Bagot
St-Michel-de-Vaudreuil
Île-Perrot
Chambly
St-Mathias
Les Cèdres
Ste Marie-de-Monnoir
La Prairie
Ste-Césaire
St-Polycarpe
Beauharnois
L'Acadie
St-Phillippe-de-Laprairie
St-Ignace-du-Coteau-du-Lac
St-Timothée
St-Isidore
St-Athanase-d'Iberville
St-Rémi
St-Jean-d'Iberville
Ste-Martine
St-Édouard-de-Napierville
St-Cyprien-de-Napierville
St-Anicet
St-Valentin
St-Georges-de-Henryville

UNITED STATES

75°   74°   73°   72°
48°
47°
46°
45°

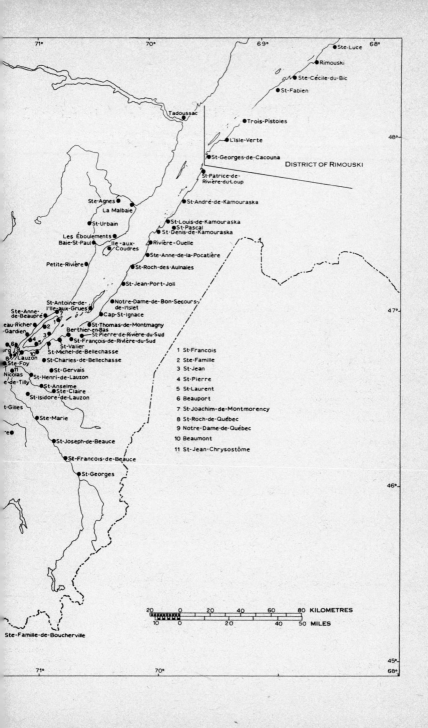

Lower Canada in 1791

In 1791, the people of the St Lawrence Valley were granted a new constitution giving them representative government and dividing their territory into two distinct entities.

This was a major political change which can hardly be interpreted as a response to popular demand in the wake of economic and social revolution. On the contrary, in certain respects it ran counter to geographic and economic imperative. The St Lawrence River was still as strong a binding force as ever between the West and the lands toward the Gulf. The fur trade was still a vital element of the colony's economic structure and one of the principal sources of commercial profit. The English-speaking bourgeoisie objected strenuously to the division into two provinces; even the French Canadians who had been advocating constitutional change had not wanted the colony fragmented in this way, for they too were active in the fur trade and hence necessarily involved with the West. The upper country, the Pays d'En Haut, even for those who never went there, was part of an integral economic area unified by the St Lawrence. Only a particular reading of the demands of Loyalist immigrants and implications of ethnic diversity can have prompted the creation of a new province.

The promoters of representative government had been the English-speaking and the French-Canadian middle classes. The old seigneurial families and the clergy (for all the latter's apparent neutrality) had wanted the Quebec Act of 1774 preserved. The peasant masses, who were pressured from both sides, certainly did not instigate the constitutional innovation; for them it was largely a puzzling abstraction, perhaps a nefarious device for imposing taxes on them.

I Stability of Economic Structure

In the long-term economic evolution of the St Lawrence Valley, the slow pace of change in the eighteenth century is striking. The structural framework within which the economy developed remained basically the same throughout the century,[1] weathering such momentous events as the conquest of 1760 and the American Revolution. The mother country would draw raw materials from the colony and then sell its manufactured products to it. During the French Régime the principal attraction was furs, and the fur trade was therefore the colony's leading commercial activity. Competition with New England and the Hudson's Bay Company necessitated rapid expansion toward the West, with enormous investments in military power even in peacetime. After the conquest of 1760 these lines of force remained intact. The mother country was now another, but as long as its interests were thus served it still provided an outlet for the colony's raw materials. The fur trade now no longer needed such prodigious military protection and was still the leading commercial activity. Even the competitors were the same, that is to say, New England and the Hudson's Bay Company. The American Revolution, while it cast a shadow over the future of the trade in beaver, for the time being did not affect the predominance of the fur trade. In 1791 the cession of Great Lakes posts to the Americans under the treaty of 1783 was still no more than theoretical, largely because the Americans were not yet ready to compete aggressively. Between 1786 and 1788 the fur trade accounted for 57 per cent of total exports. The volume of fur exports in fact continued to rise, following the trend since the beginning of the century. Average annual shipments of beaver skins were as follows: 98,181 from 1763 to 1772; 111,155 from 1773 to 1782; 125,481 from 1784 to 1786; 148,212 from 1793 to 1802.

The fur trade had long been dominated by isolated entrepreneurs, either individuals or small groups, but most of the time they had operated independently of one another. Beginning with the American Revolution, however, economic, political, and military conditions stimulated some efforts at pooling; the increasingly far-flung territory to be covered in search of furs had greatly inflated the cost of transport, forcing attempts at cost-cutting and greater efficiency. Domestic competition and a labour shortage due to commercialization in agriculture had already had ruinous effects, and now there were signs of greater competition from outside. It was imperative for small entrepreneurs to band together into larger organizations. In the northwest, greater urgency resulted in a stronger tendency toward combination than in the southwest.

The first sign of this tendency had appeared in 1775, when McGill, Frobisher, and Blondeau, on their arrival at Grand Portage, agreed to pool their interests with those of their principal competitors. About this time contemporaries began to talk of the North West Company. In 1779, eight rival groups combined, thus extending their control over the northwest. Four years later when the traders of the northwest and of the southwest were staking out their territories, the North West Company, with leadership from the McTavish-Frobisher team, concluded agreements which once more enlarged its membership. But the movement toward a major monopoly strong enough to compete with the Hudson's Bay Company ran afoul of powerful interests among the Montreal merchants. Opposition polarized around Gregory, Pangman, Ross, Mackenzie, McLeod, and Leroux. The ensuing struggle appears to have been so bitter and so disastrous for all that in 1787 the North West Company was reorganized yet again to take in the rival elements. Three years later, after a further structural overhaul, there was no longer any doubt; there was now a powerful monopoly focused on the resources of the northwest. In the southwest there was a similar if less pronounced development. All of which was setting the stage for a vigorous expansionary thrust.[2]

This broadening of base led to a sharp reduction in the number of permits issued, and traders operating alone were gradually pushed out of the picture. The small traders could not keep pace with the intensified climate of competition and many who were not content to tap the marginal areas left to them entered the employ of their former competitors. The French Canadians seem to have been the most severely affected. This, the period between the start of the American Revolution and 1790, saw the beginning of what was later termed the commercial inferiority of the French Canadians, which was soon apparent in the other sectors of the economy as well. In 1787, the English-speaking colonists estimated their own non-landed wealth at 1,017,333 pounds (currency of the day), or, it was said, nineteen-twentieths of the total,[3] though this was an exaggeration. The fur trade accounted for at least a third. By 1784 disparities could already be seen as well in the ownership of seigneurial lands; English-speaking individuals owned 26 per cent of the seigneuries but received 43 per cent of revenues deriving from them[4] (see Table 1).

Clearly the most profitable businesses were in English hands. Even the four most lucrative seigneuries had English-speaking owners: Jacob Jordan, 1,500 pounds; James Cuthbert, 1,700 pounds; Alexander Grant, 1,500 pounds; Henry Caldwell, 1,250 pounds. The top-ranking French-speaking owner was only fifth overall: Juchereau Duchesnay, 1,000 pounds.

Can this be attributed simply to different group mentalities? It can hardly be supposed that the English-speaking had achieved such commercial power merely by profiting from the American Revolution and the resultant increase in imports, or from the lion's share of patronage. It is clear, however, that the merchants of the two groups had sprung from very different milieux, the French-Canadian merchant coming from an increasingly rural North American society and the English-speaking immigrant from a society which was already well on the way to industrialization. This and other differences in educational institutions and values are the more significant factors, each affecting group mentality.

Agriculture played a major role in this lop-sided economy. In 1790, 81 per cent of the population was rural. There were villages in many parishes, but the proportion of their inhabitants not involved with agriculture was still negligible. In occupations, landowner-farmers dominated by far. Occupational diversification had begun but was still very limited, as was local marketing. A large number of farmers were seasonally active in the fur trade as well.

Agriculture played first and foremost a subsistence role. Since bread was the basic food, wheat was the leading staple. A normal harvest around 1790 was 60 to 75 per cent wheat and 12 to 20 per cent oats, followed by potatoes, corn, barley, and buckwheat. The Bishop of Quebec's report on tithing for 1784, covering some hundred parishes, confirms the dominant status of wheat; 69 per cent of the harvest was in wheat and 31 per cent in oats and peas.[5] The average *habitant* also raised a few cattle, sheep, and hogs; he did not normally use horses as work animals though there were many in the colony. Efforts to increase the cultivation of flax had had some success, but attempts to implant widespread production of hemp had met with dismal failure. The focus of subsistence dictated that each farm provide first the necessities of life in food and clothing. The *habitant*, however, had long since acquired a taste for imported European fabrics and for linens and woollens in general, and as conditions worsened, sheep-raising and flax-growing expanded. And yet money in rural hands was not necessarily reflected in a greater number of farm animals.

Preoccupation with subsistence imposed dangerous uncertainties on the farmer. Besides providing for his family's immediate needs, he had to produce enough for his next sowing and for his tithe (one-twenty-sixth of his harvest) and earn enough to pay his share of religious expenses (church-building and repairs, pew rental, collections, masses, baptisms, marriages and burials, and various other services) and his seigneurial dues (*cens et rentes, banalité, lods et ventes,* and hunting and fishing dues). A poor or even mediocre crop would leave him in debt. It was natural for the curés, *Fabriques* ("parish councils"), and seigneurs to be creditors, but the problem was often compounded by the existence, since the seventeenth century, of a class of speculative merchants who would take advantage of the sequence of good and bad crops, buying when harvests were plentiful and prices low and selling in times of scarcity and inflated prices.

Surplus production which fell into the hands of gentlemen landowners supplied the urban centres, and also the rural districts in times of shortage. Because of slow urban growth in the eighteenth century, however, Quebec and Montreal provided only limited outlets for agricultural produce, and an agricultural élite would therefore never emerge on the strength of domestic marketing alone. During the French Régime the prospects for export had also been dim, for France itself was a wheat producer, and New France could look for markets for its surpluses only to the fishing areas and the French West Indies, where there was competition from New England. Some wheat was exported before the Seven Years' War, but the colony's agricultural products began to hold their own in the export market only after 1760, first in southern Europe, perhaps because of conflict between England and her North American colonies. Access to the market in England itself remained difficult. The Corn Laws were restricting, and the full effects of the English agricultural revolution were still to be felt in grain production. The chronic English wheat shortage materialized only later. It was not until around 1790 that the English market really opened up for North American wheat. In any event, from that time on wheat appears to have become a second staple trade alongside furs. Wheat export and flour-milling began to attract investment. In 1788 Allsopp's Jacques Cartier River mill, the biggest, converted 65,000 *minots* of wheat into flour (see Table 2). The commercialization of agriculture led the merchant bourgeoisie to acquire seigneuries for profit as well as social prestige. While the large landowners and merchants benefited most from the increasing agricultural activity, as in the fur trade a proportion of the profit found its way into the hands of the humbler folk as well.

For all that, was there really an agricultural revolution under way? Many farmers certainly perceived the possibilities offered by an enlarged market. There is no doubt that production increased, but it would be rash to attribute this to a radical transformation in agricultural techniques, at least among the vast majority of farmers. More likely it was due to the abundance of fertile virgin land in the St Lawrence Valley, which, with incentive, was cleared and put to the plow to provide additional acreage—both extensions of existing farmland and more productive new farms.

The importance of agriculture and furs tends to overshadow other sectors which were by no means negligible in the development of the

economy. The lumber trade was resumed after 1760, though it did not
expand significantly until the first decade of the nineteenth century.
Owing to heavy transportation costs, England, like France before it,
obtained its lumber more cheaply from northern Europe and even
New England. Outlets for Canadian lumber, apart from the slim possibilities of sales to the West Indies in competition with New England,
were therefore largely restricted to the domestic marker, and what
growth there was depended on increase in local demand. Shipbuilding,
too, despite high hopes and heroic efforts during the French Régime,
remained a secondary industry serving only the domestic market until
after 1787, when it began to obtain some modest orders from Britain;
its centre of greatest activity was Quebec. In fishing there was no
extensive development; a few merchants won a place for themselves in
the highly competitive international market, but most were content to
sell domestically. The colony's sole major manufacturing enterprise
was the Forges du Saint-Maurice, an ironworks which employed a
great many craftsmen and woodsmen in and around Trois-Rivières.
After 1760 there were attempts at establishing local manufacturing of
various kinds, including distilleries, particularly in view of the disappointingly small market for grains, but the innovations were exceedingly modest in scope.

The commercial sectors which obtained the best results, it should be
noted, were those which were dominant during the French Régime.
The manufacturing sector remained the weakest. The mercantile system
no doubt worked against it, but this was not the sole determining factor.
Suffice it to say that had conditions been healthier, either mercantile
policies would have been softened or the colony's business community
would have been up in arms. That manufacturing failed to develop
seems largely attributable to the small size of the local market, and
perhaps to a shortage of labour resulting from the easy availability of
farmland, but most of all to the attractions of the fur trade. The latter
might indeed have been expected to stimulate activity in distilling and
other local manufacturing. For the fur trade, however, a vital factor was
a labour force which in general was active in agriculture as well, thus
enriching the coffers of the numerous merchants who invested in land
and traded in grain. Altogether, the fur trade appears to have been a poor
stimulant for industrial development.

So the colony continued to import the manufactured goods it
needed, as it had during the French Régime: from the West Indies,
rum (replacing brandy), molasses, sugar, and coffee; from Britain,
woollens and other textiles and manufactured goods in general; even
tobacco was imported. With a certain time-lag, export movements in
wheat and furs were reflected in import volumes. In time of war,

greater activity in the domestic market stimulated import demand. Thus, from 1760 to 1791, growth in the traditional commercial sectors accounted for an orderly export-import activity. So simple was the economic structure that there was little pressure for the creation of credit establishments, or for improved transportation. The key instrument of the fur trade was still the canoe (the flat-bottomed *bateau* being an innovation), and colonization continued on or near the shores of the St Lawrence.

In business circles, understandably, hopes were founded on a commercial type of economy. The old concept of a triangular trade pattern still had considerable allure, but gaining a foothold in the British and West Indian markets would require greater and more regular agricultural surpluses, even if it meant augmenting them from certain American sources. After the American Revolution, the Montreal and Quebec merchants therefore demanded that agricultural and forest products imported by inland routes be exempt from duty and considered Canadian. The legislative council, to which the imperial government referred the question, concurred readily in 1787.[6]

Though the merchants were realistic about their chances in the British market, they cherished the hope of gaining control of the West Indies market, particularly with the advent of American independence. Such control would demand diversified and stable agricultural production in greater volume, well-established forest operations, and aggressive fish marketing. But the post-war years brought disappointment. Until 1785, crop yields were poor and supplementation from American sources proved impossible. Further negative factors were the winter closing of the St Lawrence and competition from Nova Scotia and the United States.

The creation of Upper Canada in 1791, then, was not justified by the imperatives of economic development. The economic unity of the colony was strengthened by the dominance of the fur trade, rivalries with the Americans and disputes over Great Lakes posts, and the agricultural colonization begun by the Loyalists. In the legislative assembly, Adam Lymburner expressed widely shared misgivings: he had not heard that "this violent measure" was "the general wish of the loyalists," and it was assuredly not desired "by the Inhabitants of the Lower Parts of the Country"; the plan could have "the most fatal consequences, while the apparent advantages ... are few, and of no great moment...." On the contrary, he asserted, the people of the country "... from local situation were certainly designed by Nature to remain united as one."[7] In the motivation behind the major political decision, however, there emerges a clear line of connection linking economic expansion, immigration, and the growing influence of groups calling for representative government.

II The New Demographic Balance

With the American Revolution the demographic balance in the colony began to change. Loyalist immigration introduced a new element in a structure which had been stable since the beginning of the eighteenth century: a demographic accident brought about by political and military circumstances. It was to have an impact both within the colony and in Britain, for British policy, though concerned with economic, military, and strictly political matters, seems to have been very sensitive to the social factors inherent in the numerical relationship between the colony's linguistic groups. When he wrote to London in 1780, Governor Haldimand, without the slightest shadow of doubt, still considered "the [French] Canadians the people of this country."

In 1791, the French-Canadian population was growing as it had in the early eighteenth century. Studies by Jacques Henripin show an exceptionally high birth rate in comparison to Europe, and a remarkably low death rate, doubling the population every twenty-five to twenty-seven years, a growth rate which continued until about 1850. In this respect the conquest of 1760 had had no real effect at all, despite the conclusions of certain historians that the event had launched the "revenge of the cradle" movement. Mason Wade, for instance, writes: "But their survival was not dependent upon either British magnanimity or the force of circumstances; for French Canada possessed an indomitable will to live, witnessed in the first decade after the conquest by the attainment of the highest birthrate (63.3 per 1000) ever recorded for any white people."[8]

While the birth rate was indeed consistently high (over 50 per 1,000), it was subject as much as other demographic variables to short-term fluctuation according to varying circumstances. Logically enough, war had the effect of increasing mortality and also postponing marriages, resulting in decreased birth rates; and cessation of hostilities occasioned increased marriages and a subsequent temporary swelling of birth rates. Similarly, mortality increased with crop failures and epidemics. The Seven Years' War, poor harvests, and epidemics all had such effects in this period; in 1765 for instance, the death rate rose from 25 per 1,000 to 39, and in 1784 from 22 per 1,000 to 45. These accidents from year to year do not invalidate the basic structural trend. The conquest neither slowed nor accelerated the rate of increase over the long term. In 1765 the population of Quebec was 70,000; in 1790 it was 161,311. This growth is the more significant in that it was little influenced by immigration (see Table 3).

New France had not attracted immigrants, and the reason appears to have been its sluggish economic development. British authorities both

in Canada and England at the time of the conquest were convinced that
feudalism and poor administration had been to blame, and foresaw radical economic changes that would bring immigrants flocking to the St
Lawrence Valley from the British Isles and even New England. These
hopes were quickly belied, for the colony, having become English, exerted no greater attraction on immigrants than before. The first three
English governors proposed policies which recognized these economic
and demographic realities. Carleton wrote in 1768, "considering that
we can look only to the Canadian race to increase the population, it
appears that the best policy to pursue is the preservation of the customs
of this province."[9] Between the conquest and the American Revolution
there was so little immigration that the English-speaking element remained a tiny minority consisting of merchants and civil servants and, to
a lesser extent, skilled craftsmen. Their numbers, however, were not the
true measure of their importance in the commercial and social life of the
colony.

The coming of the Loyalists was to change many things. In contrast
to the previous trickle of immigrants, 1778 brought 855 loyalists to
Quebec by way of Lake Champlain and the flow reached its peak in
1783; the following year a census of Loyalists ordered by Haldimand
counted 4,764 persons.[10] Another thousand or so probably came more
or less independently between 1775 and 1783 and missed being enu-
merated; these were no doubt of the upper social classes, mostly merchants, but the mass of the refugees represented a broad range of
occupations. A survey of 482 of them[11] shows that 6.8 per cent were
merchants, 0.4 professionals, 8.1 skilled tradesmen, 81.4 farmers, and
3.3 per cent practitioners of other occupations. The wealth they
claimed to have left behind is also interesting; 50.8 per cent declared
losses of 100 pounds and less, 37.4 between 101 and 500 pounds, 6.8
between 501 and 1,000 pounds and 4.7 per cent over 1,000 pounds.
Despite the large majority of farmers, the percentage of merchants and
skilled tradesmen among the Loyalists was much greater than in most
of Quebec's rural parishes at that time, in other words quite disproportionate for an agricultural colony. Just as significantly, if the sampling
is valid, most of the Loyalists do not appear to have been accustomed
to economic deprivation.

Instead of gravitating to the cities, the Loyalists became country-
dwellers. The authorities at first gathered them together in a number
of localities already settled by French Canadians: St-Jean, Chambly,
Yamachiche, Pointe Claire, Sorel, Gaspé, St-Armand, Noyan, Fou-
cault, and Montreal. At the time, Haldimand had reasons for feeling
that the Eastern Townships should be kept for the French Canadians.
"It seems to me good policy," he said, "to have the frontier settled

with people professing a different religion, speaking a different language and accustomed to different laws from those of our enterprising neighbours of New England." He also saw the Upper St Lawrence as the ideal location for the Loyalists who would soon, he predicted, transform the region into Quebec's breadbasket. The Loyalists seemed to be of the same mind, for by 1784 most of them had settled in the region which was to become Upper Canada.

Surprisingly enough, the advent of the Loyalists, massive though it was, does not seem to have aroused any great fear or hostility in the French Canadians. If indeed there had been widespread fears expressed among the rural folk, surely they would have been translated in political terms, with the French Canadians advocating constitutional change and particularly the formation of two separate provinces, one of which should serve then and in the future as an outlet for British immigration. That there was no such reaction may be attributed to the feeling that there was plenty of land for all in the St Lawrence Valley. The French-Canadian merchant bourgeoisie calling for representative government was too much involved with the fur and grain trades to want an economically dangerous political division. The Loyalists, because of their number and their misfortunes, in fact brought strong support to the reformists.

The English-speaking proportion of the population rose abruptly, from 4 to 9 per cent, and gradually the conviction grew that this was only the beginning of a major demographic change in the colony, with, in the minds of some, a shift in migratory patterns. The newcomers aroused admiration and sympathy, but they were not prepared simply to settle down and accept things as they found them. They objected strenuously to the seigneurial régime and the French civil law. They demanded not only English law but grants of land in English freehold tenure.

The Loyalists' views regarding the creation of a new province were not clearly expressed, except in the petition of April 15, 1787. In any event, Grenville, then secretary of state for war and the colonies, saw the situation in the St Lawrence Valley as similar to that in the Maritimes preceding the creation of New Brunswick, and he envisaged similar solutions.[12] He rejected the view of the English-speaking merchants, who were proposing only the creation of a new judicial district, for in his mind social considerations were uppermost; the border between Upper and Lower Canada would separate the two societies and prevent ethnic conflict.

III Social Structure

One of the major characteristics of eighteenth-century Quebec, due to the relationship between population growth and economic structure, was that the society was an increasingly rural one. The fur trade could not alone provide employment for the rapidly growing population, and besides it attracted largely seasonal labour. Great value was attached to land ownership and land was abundantly available. Not surprisingly, therefore, the majority of the people were drawn to agriculture and the rural population grew much more rapidly than the urban in the eighteenth century and indeed until the advent of industrialization. Increasing commercialization in agriculture spurred the tendency and led to a degree of occupational diversification, which in turn gave birth to a myriad of small villages. Rural attitudes so dominated the society that they permeated even the urban milieu; education was held to be of small account, and in general schools were not considered an essential part of the social scene. The family was the basic institution, followed by the seigneury and the parish. It was not a society entirely describable through "staple approach" concepts, or "folk society" or "frontier thesis" models. It seems to have related more to what Labrousse calls *l'Ancien Régime Social*, the "old social régime."

The institutional framework of the Old Régime inherited from New France was maintained by the new rulers, and the British, with their monarchist and aristocratic traditions, were not averse to nurturing its values. The relationship between church and state in Britain was not necessarily at variance with French church traditions. In the St Lawrence Valley a Catholic Church united with a Protestant state ceased to be regarded as a contradiction. The preservation of Catholic Church privileges and functions appeared to be justified by the circumstances. The circumstances were also, it seems, favourable for assuring the survival of the seigneurial system through which, by division of land revenues, economic maintenance was provided for an authoritative clerical class and a landed lay aristocracy. In this context, the clergy and the aristocracy were situated together at the top of the social pyramid, without either having precedence over the other.

The aristocracy, a mixture of authentic nobles and bourgeois with pretensions rather than real titles, lived a precarious existence after 1760. Their economic base was weakened, for the government patronage which had channelled a portion of fur trade revenues into their hands was less generous, forcing them to depend more on the management of their fiefdoms. Population increase raised hopes of greater seigneurial revenues, but rising prices and agricultural commercialization, the extravagant habits of many members of the class, and the fragmentation of fiefs through inheritance took their toll. The new government, furthermore, seemed little inclined to recognize the nobles' traditional military role. And then, since 1760 there had been pressure from the merchants for representative government, which would not only raise the status of the merchants but would even make a *censitaire* ("tenant") the political equal of his seigneur. These were disturbing prospects for the old aristocracy.

The aristocrats certainly regarded the Quebec Act as a guarantee of their rights and therefore of their survival, since it formally confirmed the preservation of the seigneurial system and French civil law, both of which had been endangered by the Royal Proclamation of 1763. At the time of the American Revolution, a time of peril for Quebec, they rejoiced in the opportunity to demonstrate their military role and un-swerving loyalty to the monarchy, not, it must be said, without an eye to a possible resurgence of government munificence toward them. Their attitude was that their class, after all, was the mainstay of the monarchical state, even in a colonial milieu. In this period they be-haved with consummate arrogance toward the peasantry and particu-larly the merchant classes.

The security of the landed aristocracy was eroded not only by their own prodigality but also by the economic crisis and the peasants' refu-sal to take sides at the time of the American invasion of 1775. With hostilities over, furthermore, reformist pressures made it clear that the merchant classes were bent on obtaining a share of social and political power. But the aristocrats held firm to their conception of society as divided into three orders: the aristocracy, the clergy, and the third estate. In 1786, Pierre-Amable De Bonne declared on behalf of the seigneurs:

> In all civilized realms, the people are and can only be validly repre-sented by what is known as the Three Estates; which is to say, the clergy, the aristocracy and the bourgeoisie; and if you are wise, you will agree to nothing as may be proposed to you, except as you perceive unanimity in at least the majority of these several bodies.[13]

To the aristocrats the very idea of representative government which would give the bourgeoisie and perhaps even the peasantry the right to change social institutions was anathema. They attacked the merchant community of both language groups for daring to assume a representa-tive role. They accused the French-speaking merchants of being the pawns of their English-speaking counterparts.

A handful of young merchants of the Capital, most of them in debt to British Merchants, modestly accepting the title of Leading Citizens, as they deign to call themselves, and considering nowadays that they too have that right, have acceded to their proposals that there be recognized a small number of Merchants of our city, [all] equally unworthy of consideration.[14]

The English-speaking merchants they painted as ambitious, power-hungry rogues determined to impose taxes on landed property. What they really dreaded was the abolition of the seigneurial system and the law that upheld it. When they deplored the lot of the peasantry, their concern was really more for their own future. They knew the intense dislike of taxes among the peasantry and played on it, being fully aware that a state property tax could jeopardize seigneurial dues and tithing, and foreseeing a possible peasant revolt against the institutions of the Old Régime. Preservation of the Quebec Act in its entirety, on the other hand, would guarantee survival of the social structure of the Old Régime. Hence their resistance to other proposals. Their resort to nationalistic themes was only a front, for long after 1800 any nationalistic approaches to the problems of Lower Canada were to find them more doggedly opposed than any other group. In short, their attitudes were motivated by fear.

The aristocracy, it must be said, did not comprise the entire seigneurial class. Seigneurial property, besides being the principal stepping-stone to aristocracy, had also become a real investment proposition and attracted many merchants and professionals. For some of these, the investment value outweighed the concomitant social prestige, and for others the reverse. The landed aristocracy was not a caste, for it was not closed to newcomers, who generally came to adopt the attitudes and behaviour of the group, though there were individuals who maintained their bourgeois activities and mentality. There was in fact a taste for aristocracy among both the French- and the English-speaking, more markedly among the former, and more visibly in 1790 than by 1820. The long decline of the old aristocracy continued, accelerating toward the end of the century.

The power of the church also had long-established roots. During the French Régime the Catholic Church was the only established one and there was real religious unity. The church was joined to the state in the manner recognized by Gallican precepts, which is to say that it bowed to the state in all that was not strictly religious. While enjoying the protection of the state it was expected to work to ensure its stability. Its belief in the theory of monarchy by divine right and in aristocratic society was a cornerstone of the politico-religious ideology of the time. By virtue of its status as the established church, it had certain exclusive responsibilities in the social order: religious observances, teaching, and ministration to the sick and the poor. So that it might fulfil them and maintain its élite status, it was assured of certain revenues. Religious communities and institutions had been granted many seigneuries by the state. Parish curés had the right, supported by law, to collect tithes of one-twenty-sixth of all grain harvested and received further revenues in the form of fees and collections to finance parish activities. Clerics also received financial support from the king during the French Régime.

In the first years of the British régime there were many uncertainties hanging over the future of the church. Material damage caused by the war, the prohibition of relationships with Rome, the abolition of tithing in 1763, the precariousness of the seigneurial régime, problems in ensuring episcopal continuity, and the looming threat of Protestantism in general might have been enough to engender the blackest pessimism. And yet there quickly evolved a system of relationships very like that which had existed in New France. The small number of Protestants and the diversity of their allegiances, together with the weakness of the Anglican clergy, prevented the Anglican Church from becoming a true social force for many years. Life went on as though the Catholic Church were to become the sole state church, in fact if not in name. Much later Bishop Jacob Mountain was to express outrage at this situation, which had evolved along with the society as a whole. When Bishop Briand declared, "they are our masters and we owe them what we owed the French when they were the same," he was simply expressing the continuity of ideology between the Old Régime and the new.

The Quebec Act of 1774 confirmed the status of the clergy in the colonial milieu as an élite class in the sense of the Old Régime. Uncertainties persisted, to be sure, from which specific interests even drew advantage. The rapid growth of the population and expansion in agriculture swelled the revenues of the ecclesiastical seigneurs and of the curés and *Fabriques*, strengthening the clergy's position in the society. The Canadianization of the clergy, to use Professor Marcel Trudel's term, in other words the training of priests within the colony, had not yet become a prime objective for the Canadian church. When two parish councillors failed in their mission to England requesting permission to bring priests from France, the church authorities adopted a very cautious attitude toward the reform movement. In effect they shelved their hostility toward representative government, having concluded that British refusal to allow the importation of French priests would only be overcome by the existence of an assembly in which Catholics were in the majority. Monseigneur Plessis's later explanation reveals the neutrality of the clergy on the constitutional question:

Upon the expulsion in 1783 of Messrs Capel and Ciquard [Coquard], a plan was made to send delegates to England in the persons of Messrs Adhémar and Delisle, not on behalf of the Marguilliers but of the people of the country and those of Montreal in particular, to beseech the government to give more protection than it has done thus far to the Catholic Religion. Their instructions were to ask for the liberty to bring priests from France and to establish a bishop in Montreal. This I have found in the letters of Montgolfier and Mr Gravé. The mission was without success; the delegates reported that above all there must be an Assembly Chamber, through which all else might be obtained from the government. This was given as the opinion of Lord North, then Secretary of State for the colonies, and in consequence the following year there was prepared and sent to England a request for the constitution which was granted us in 1791; which constitution is ill-conceived for the mentality of Canadians and has had the effect only of rendering the governed insolent toward their governors. The spirit of democracy and independence has penetrated the people, and passed from them to the clergy, and now you see the fruits.[15]

In 1791 the clergy of Quebec were not the principal leading class; the French Canadians had not yet laid their fate in their hands. In the society of those days power was theoretically shared by an aristocracy which was showing signs of increasing decadence and a clergy which was having great difficulty maintaining its numbers. Both were fully aware of their position in the society, but power was not theirs alone. The merchants were claiming a share of political power by virtue of their economic strength.

Agitation for representative government came with the rise of the middle classes. The constitution of 1763 had promised the establishment of an assembly at such time as circumstances should allow. In the minds of the English-speaking merchants who had come from other British colonies and from Britain, this was a perfectly normal institution even for a colony. The governors and their advisers, however, took it upon themselves to judge and interpret the circumstances. They not only refused to summon an assembly but recommended to London that the absolutist traditions of the French Régime be maintained, giving as their reasons the small number of English-speaking merchants and the economic and social continuities inherited from the Old Régime by the new, which lent weight to the position taken by the seigneurial aristocracy and the clergy. They drew arguments of considerable cogency as well from the mother country's conflict with her colonies on the Atlantic coast. While the Quebec Act of 1774 confirmed the existence of political absolutism and the status of the seigneurs and clergy, the merchants, seeing an elected assembly as an instrument of their own economic, social, and political advancement, were eager to see the fulfilment of the constitution of 1763. The French-speaking merchants supported their English-speaking counterparts in most of their goals but were reticent on the subject of representative government because aristocratic propaganda had successfully persuaded them that the Test Oath would be rigidly administered to all elected representatives, which would exclude Catholics from the assembly.[16] Thus, while the business community was in conflict with the governors and their entourage, it was divided within itself largely on religious grounds. It was not until 1773 that the English-speaking merchants clarified their views on this matter. A year later the Quebec Act effectively nullified any religious impediment to political activity, which would probably have occurred in any event had a legislative assembly been summoned earlier.

With the end of the American War of Independence, to the despair of Governor Haldimand who continued to see the problems before him in the light of past situations, the English-speaking merchants resumed their agitation. They also quickly realized the importance of Loyalist immigration to their cause, for by and large the newcomers were in favour of representative government. Despite the sizeable Loyalist reinforcement, however, the reformists were perhaps still not in a position, numerically and otherwise, to refute the arguments of Haldimand and his predecessors: "... we must consider the feelings and outlook of 60,000 men rather than those of 2,000, three quarters of whom are merchants and cannot really be regarded as the people of this province."[17] The English-speaking merchants countered by making much of their economic power and the permanence of their ties with Quebec. Their influence, they argued, with figures in support, extended to all economic sectors including landed property. In their view representative government would assure the future of the economy, enabling the merchant classes to define economic policies in response to the needs of the country. In 1791, Adam Lymburner declared in London:

> There are now, among the Mercantile Gentlemen of the Province, those whose moveable fortunes are perhaps equal, if not superior to any of the Seigneurial Estates; and who, from the Employment and Support they give to thousands of the people, have infinitely more influence in the country than the Seigneurs.... This Honourable House must perceive, from the very small value of the landed fortunes, that the only means of accumulation in that country must be

by the operations of Trade and Commerce.... That it is more probable in twenty years, perhaps in ten years, a new set of men may come forward, who may have acquired and realized fortunes much superior to any now in that country; and, it is natural to suppose, will possess a proportional degree of Political Power and Influence.[18]

This statement is an excellent summation of the aspirations of the English-speaking merchants at this time. So sure were they of the importance of their role as a class that they did not doubt their ability to manipulate the new institutions to their own ends. They were confident of controlling representation from the cities and perhaps even from the country districts to some extent. Yet the English-speaking comprised less than 25 per cent of the urban population and an infinitesimal minority in the country parishes. Clearly the English merchants expected the popular vote to favour merchant candidates, whether French- or English-speaking, at the expense of the aristocracy's representatives. Loyalist ridings certainly figured large in their expectations.

The English-speaking merchants saw themselves primarily in opposition to the seigneurial aristocracy, in which they were sure of support from their French counterparts for whom economic and social considerations outweighed the ethnic. That direct or indirect action by the clergy might perturb the political balance they were hoping for seemed not to worry them greatly. To them a merchant was first a merchant, whatever his origins, and the business community was the most important in the society, though these sentiments did not imply republican or revolutionary leanings. They visualized an elected legislative assembly to be counterbalanced by a legislative council with direct representation of aristocratic and landholding interests. They were contesting neither the institutions of monarchy nor the colonial system.

By 1783 the English-speaking merchants had the full support of the French-Canadian middle classes. The petition of November 24, 1784, was the fruit of efforts of the two groups combined, bearing the signatures of 2,300 individuals, 37 per cent of whom were English-speaking. The extent of French-Canadian participation in the reform movement has been well documented by Pierre Tousignant in his study "La Genèse et l'avènement de la constitution de 1791."[19] French-Canadian merchants and professionals, particularly if they were seigneurs, obtained the support of certain elements among the humbler urban and rural folk. On Île Bizard, the merchant seigneur Pierre Foretier obtained forty-four signatures for the petition. The seigneur's counterpetition, which bore 2,400 signatures, showed the strength of the landed gentry when pushed to win at least the appearance of peasant support. The merchants and the handful of professionals who were lead-ing the reform movement among French Canadians, despite the aristo-crats' disdain, were possessed of a keen social and political conscience. The members of the French-Canadian committee wrote as follows to a committee of friends in London:

> The ministers must not take it into their heads to try to divert us with palliatives and lenitives. We will be content only when Parlia-ment has responded to our claims by giving us the same rights and privileges as the English; and why not? We are English subjects just as they are. The ministers will fancy perhaps that ours is not the voice of Canada but only talk from a few factious partisan hotheads. Well then, we shall be charmed to be tested so that we may en-lighten them. During the summer we shall be at work in order to have the petition signed by the generality of the parishes of Canada, except for a few nobles and ambitious individuals who crave office and the pay and perquisites thereof, and to that end grovel before the great, but by whom we will not be duped.... Freedom, Gentle-men, Freedom at all cost....[20]

With such calls for freedom the reformists were not attacking the seigneurial régime and the Coutume de Paris. They believed an elected legislative assembly should take whatever decisions corre-sponded with the opinion of the people at large on these points. They were more determined, English- and French-speaking alike, to see English commercial law entrenched in the new constitution. Wrote the French-Canadian merchants:

> The prosperity of this country depends on commerce...; nothing would contribute so much to its advantage than laws founded on the spirit and essence of trade in general. We have considered the matter and deem that England is the leading commercial kingdom in the world and its laws on such questions being the result of several centuries of experience, they ought certainly to be prefer-able to all others.... Besides which all our commercial liaisons have their termination in England; it is therefore the more advantageous and suitable that we should have those laws.[21]

The reform of 1791 would no doubt have been impossible without the active participation of an important segment of the French-Canadian society in the reform movement. Both this segment and the aristocrats claimed to be making the voice of Canada heard in London. The reform movement was the first manifestation of the rise of the merchant classes, supported by certain elements among the professionals. The latter were still too small in number and too uncohesive as a group to make their own distinctive impression on the movement; the majority still lived in the shadow of the old élite classes, though certain of them rallied enthusiastically to the side of the business community. Outside these groups, the movement found support among the Loyalists and perhaps an élite of French-Canadian tradesmen and farmers.

In this basically Old Régime society, without directly challenging the institutions underlying the status and power of the traditional élite, the notion of social reform was not entirely absent in the minds of the reformists. Once the merchant classes had achieved control of an assembly, the reasoning went, the reform of institutions would follow without disruption. This seems to have been more the assumption of the English-speaking than the French-speaking.

A similar attitude appears to have prevailed regarding the colonial system as applied in the St Lawrence Valley. Since 1760 the society had indeed remained a fundamentally colonial one. Power was exercised on behalf of the mother country by a bureaucratic and military apparatus headed by a governor, assisted by an executive council. In this sense the French Régime was thus carried over into the British. The governors and their advisers sought their support among the colonial élite, the aristocrats, and the clergy, rather than among British immigrants or the merchant classes in general. The Quebec Act provided striking confirmation of this relationship, which was at variance with English colonial tradition elsewhere. Opposition from the merchants cannot be interpreted as condemnation of the colonial system in itself, for merchant interests were very much tied to the empire. The opposition was to a colonial conception that justified political absolutism and denied the merchants a share in the exercise of power. On this point there is no reason to suppose that the French-Canadian merchants' objectives differed from those of the English. The French-Canadian middle classes were not yet entertaining the idea of an elected assembly as a great institution charged with upholding the values of the French-Canadian collectivity.

The élite of both sides, for and against representative government, claimed to have popular support or to be expressing the more-or-less recognized desires of the masses. Only close scrutiny of the names attached to the petitions allows any kind of accuracy in assessing how much support, neutrality, or opposition the reform movement attracted. Much could no doubt be said about pressure tactics used to obtain signatures. The government in London, however, was certainly not forced to yield by overwhelming pressure originating in the urban and rural masses.

In the cities, conditions for skilled craftsmen and labourers were relatively stable. After the war there was a period of serious economic recession, true enough, but there followed a new period of expansion. Though urban growth was slow, conditions for the common folk seem to have been steadily improving over the long term. But with the vast majority being illiterate and of traditional mentality, it is difficult to imagine a sudden and broad-based political awareness among these groups. Such as did emerge occurred among a small and select élite of skilled tradesmen. In the country districts, with their overwhelmingly peasant population, a succession of disappointing harvests between 1780 and 1785 followed by the famine of 1789 doubtless aided the aristocratic-seigneurial propaganda, which was calculated to enflame rural hostility toward possible land taxes. On the other side of the coin, this was also a period in which certain seigneurs were raising their seigneurial dues. Population growth also led to the creation of new parishes, which meant there were new churches and presbyteries to be built. All of which engendered discontent among the peasantry, though not to the point where rural folk began to question the seigneurial régime or the economic privileges of the church. The introduction of representative government was certainly not viewed by the peasantry as the first step in the abolition of seigneurial dues and tithing. Continuing rural acceptance of the seigneurial institution is indicated by the list of elected representatives in 1792; more than 50 per cent were seigneurs. In 1791 the institution of monarchy and the absolutist tradition were firmly rooted in the popular mentality. If the message of the French Revolution had reached any of the Canadian farmers, they were unable to spread it for lack of listeners.

In summation, the constitution in 1791 granting representative government appears to have been the product of local pressures, specifically demands from a rising merchant class and Loyalist elements. Loyalist claims were responsible for the introduction of English civil law and English land tenure in certain areas. The division of the colony into two provinces was prompted by a particular analysis of the wishes of the Loyalists, following the precedent set in Nova Scotia. Yet all cannot be laid to local pressures, for interpretations of the local situation were made and compromises effected by the authorities in London, with particular attention being paid to averting the possibility of another American Revolution. In the creation of two provinces, economic considerations were outweighed by the linguistic, the intention being not to rectify a situation of ethnic conflict but to prevent one from developing. Perhaps all that was achieved was to create a framework in which such a situation would evolve.

IV Political Reform

The new constitution, which received royal assent on June 10, 1791, was in large measure the brainchild of William Grenville, secretary of state for the colonies. In 1789, working with information received from the colony, he devised a plan. This plan was adopted with modifications which appeared minor at the time but which were to have a major influence in the evolution of the political system: an increase in the number of elected representatives, a reduction in the financial qualifications of electors, and elections every four years instead of every seven. Thus, this constitution bore as close a resemblance as possible to the English. Its prime objective was to implant the concept of "British liberty" in Canada.

Chief Justice Smith, a man of wide-ranging vision, also had a plan, at the core of which was a large political unit encompassing all the North American colonies. Though this plan was a preview of what was realized in 1867, it lacked foundation in the economic realities of the day, for the commercial ties between the Maritimes and the St Lawrence Valley were insubstantial to say the least. The authorities in London, for their part, envisaged fragmentation rather than unity, as demonstrated by the creation of New Brunswick. This was central in Grenville's thinking with respect to Quebec, and it led him to underestimate the importance of economic determinants. In his eyes, Quebec in 1789 was composed of two elements; one was French-Canadian, Catholic, bound to the seigneurial régime and the Coutume de Paris, and concentrated in the east of the colony; the other was Loyalist, firmly attached to British institutions, and destined to increase numerically in the west.

The new province of Upper Canada, then, was to enable the Loyalists and British immigrants and their descendants to live in an entirely English context, with English civil law, free and common socage, and British political institutions. Grenville certainly did not wish to see it fall under American economic domination. But he forgot that the new province would have no access to the sea; that it would be at the mercy of Lower Canada in that respect, economically dependent on it, and particularly on the commercial centres of Quebec and Montreal. Compounding the dependence, Quebec City was the port of entry for imports, where import duties were collected, the major source of revenue for both provinces. But the implications were constitutional as well as financial. Under the new constitution only the legislature of Lower Canada was empowered to impose import duties, which meant limitation of the constitutional freedoms of Upper Canadians and the revenues of their government. While England had given up its right of taxation, the colonists of Lower Canada would reap the lion's share of the benefit. The division of customs revenues was to become a source of discord and resentment. In creating a new province, the constitution of 1791 in effect bestowed a colony on Lower Canada. The relationship between the Canadas from 1791 to 1840 cannot be fully understood without an appreciation of this fact.

With the Loyalist problem settled, Grenville turned his attention to the French-Canadian problem, but the solution he proposed took no account of the position taken by the merchant classes. Nor did he foresee that, with the rapid increase of the French-Canadian population, the day would come when the seigneurial framework would become restricting. As far as he was concerned, the seigneurial system and the French customary law in which it was rooted, along with the status of the Catholic Church, had been guaranteed by the Quebec Act and must be reconfirmed by the new constitution. Any change in these institutions must be left to the decision of the majority in Lower Canada. The British minority living in seigneurial territory must fit themselves into the institutional framework. He had indeed considered the introduction of English commercial law as the merchants wished, but abandoned the idea because of the difficulties of codifying it.

But Grenville's thinking went further. Haldimand's idea had been to reserve the lands between the seigneuries and the American border for overflow French-Canadian population in order to create a cultural barrier between the United States and Quebec. Grenville, however, saw this region as ideal for absorbing British immigrants. For several reasons he proposed that land outside the seigneuries be conceded according to English custom, which implied that English civil law would apply in those locations. With British settlement, an English landed aristocracy should emerge to match the seigneurs. Aristocratic institutions, particularly the legislative council, would thus be progressively strengthened. The establishment of crown and clergy reserves was inspired by similar preoccupations. Crown reserves were seen as a source of revenue outside the control of the legislative assembly. Clergy reserves, it was hoped, would establish a balance between the Catholic Church, which controlled 26 per cent of seigneurial lands, and the Anglican Church, whose status as established church was more theoretical than real. Grenville was not unaware that progress in these matters would depend on immigration.

The freezing of seigneurial territory mattered little over the short term; there was still plenty of land available within the seigneuries and immigration had fallen back to where it had been before the American Revolution. After the turn of the century, however, Grenville's policy on this question was to have resounding consequences.

In the design of this constitution we also see the mark of hindsight, of reaction to the American Revolution and to certain tendencies apparent in the French Revolution. English statesmen blamed the revolt of the American colonies more on the weakness of monarchy and of the landed aristocracy in America than on the strength of popular assemblies. The British liberty they were so anxious to bring to Lower Canada was to be the fruit of a felicitous equilibrium among the three traditional principles of government: monarchy, aristocracy, and democracy. Democratic-minded elements in the political system were to be counterbalanced by strong executive power and an important role for the landed aristocracy. Thus it was a balance of powers, not the supremacy of the legislative assembly, which in theory was to make the political machinery work. The authorities in London firmly believed that suppression of democratic tendencies would be just as harmful as allowing them totally free rein. Ministerial responsibility was a notion yet to evolve.

The powers given the executive by the constitution were very broad. At its head was the governor, with the lieutenant-governors of the two provinces directly under him; he was the king's representative, the embodiment of the principle of monarchy, and as such assured the colony's political dependence on the mother country. His degree of prestige and authority as civil and military leader was a direct function of the colony's economic dependence and the strength of monarchical sentiment in the minds of the people. It was he who had control of patronage, in particular the power to appoint or suggest the appointment of civil servants. In his executive function he was assisted by an executive council which, in 1792, was composed of nine members, four of them French Canadians. On this first council the aristocracy, seigneurs, and merchants were all well represented; no great differences arose, in fact, between this council and the assembly. Generally speaking the governor played the role of arbiter among opposing factions and guardian of the political balance. In principle he was not entitled to take sides with any political group or interfere in elections, but some governors disregarded the principle on the pretext of redressing political imbalance. Ordinarily the governors, when they wished to correct a situation which could lead to change in the nature of the political system, would exercise their right to suggest appointments to the two councils, executive and legislative. In their choice of legislative councillors, they always considered the social, ethnic, and partisan composition of the assembly with a view to maintaining the desired balance. Where the higher interests of the empire or the prerogatives of the crown were at stake, they could also veto a bill or set it aside for sanction or rejection by the king himself. In last resort they could dissolve the assembly and appeal directly to the people, though in so doing they would run the risk of public repudiation. Clearly, for the system to work, the governors needed to handle their powers with great dexterity.

The constitution of 1791 rested, of course, on a kind of aristocratic pipe dream. The aristocracy being the monarchy's best support and the best possible curb on the excesses of popular assemblies, the legislative council, composed of aristocrats, was supposed to play the same role as the House of Lords in England. This was how even the French-Canadian reformists had envisioned it. According to Grenville's plan, legislative council membership would eventually become hereditary. Charles James Fox, knowing the weakness of the Canadian aristocracy, had suggested that in preference the British parliament provide for a legislative council elected from and by the major landowners. Grenville won out, and the constitution was adopted with a provision for hereditary peerages for legislative councillors, though it was never implemented. In 1791 the old aristocracy still possessed enough vigour and influence to play its assigned politico-social role, but with its progressive decline and the social evolution in the colony the nature of the legislative council was to change. In any event, on the first council (composed of sixteen members of whom seven were French Canadians) aristocratic, seigneurial, and imperial interests were more than amply represented: a council the governor could depend on.

In the circumstances, the expressions of the democratic tendencies in the system, to which the constitution had given voice and form through an elected legislative assembly, might be expected to be severely curbed, but the British government and the opposition both considered that dangerous. Having little understanding of Canadian conditions, they considered the English system of adjustable financial qualifications for voters appropriate to the Canadas, too. Using a similar procedure, the French constitution of 1790 gave the vote to only 50,000 persons out of a population of 24 million.[22] On the eve of the final passage of England's Reform Bill in 1832, Lord John Russell estimated the number of English electors at 100,000, and proposed raising the number to close to 500,000.[23] Grenville's original plan for enfranchisement in the Canadas would have been onerous: an income of five pounds sterling in the country districts, and in the cities, property of a value of 100 pounds. The opposition, however, forced simple exportation of the English qualifications to the Canadas.

In the country districts, the right of vote was granted to owners of land and buildings returning an annual income of two pounds, which meant almost all landowners; in 1791 farms were so large and land so easy to acquire that the great majority of rural heads of families were enfranchised. The peasant vote was therefore preponderant; in the five elections from 1824 to 1836 in the riding of Dorchester, it varied between 83 and 98 per cent of the total. But change was afoot in these districts, for with diversification of occupations, division of landholdings among progeny, and an increasing shortage of farmland, there was a growing class with no land and therefore no vote.[24] By 1831, 30 per cent of heads of families were in this category.

In the cities, owners of buildings or land returning an annual income of five pounds and tenants who paid an annual rent of ten pounds were enfranchised. These qualifications were easily met by the military, civil servants, professionals, merchants and even skilled tradesmen. In the Lower Town of Quebec in 1832, 51 per cent of the vote was cast by skilled tradesmen. In the Upper Town their vote was 40 or 41 per cent in the five elections from 1824 to 1836.[25] Between 1831 and 1842, the proportion of this class in Quebec City rose from 41 to 42 per cent of heads of families. Those denied the vote were mostly domestics and labourers, who rarely owned property and paid little or no rent, and yet they were a growing class: 15 per cent of heads of families in Quebec City in 1792 and 20 per cent in 1831. Still, in the Upper Town in the period 1824 to 1836, the labourer vote was between 4 and 8 per cent of the total.[26] The constitution of 1791 also imposed an overall residence requirement of twelve months.

English franchise qualifications as applied in Lower Canada, where income and access to landed property was differently structured, led to an exceptional extension of the suffrage; at least one out of every eight inhabitants was qualified to vote. Assuming that they had the right to anything not expressly excluded by the constitution, moreover, the Lower Canadians applied these provisions logically. Indians qualified along with others, as shown by the poll records for 1827 and 1834 in the riding of Quebec.[27] The clergy too had the right to vote; the Protestant clergy used it but the Catholic clergy generally seems to have abstained, though occasionally some rural curés voted. City and rural women who qualified could also vote. In 1820, Bédard wrote to Neilson: "Mr. Ogden and Badeaux were elected by the men and women of Trois-Rivières. For you should know that here the women vote as the men, excepting only where they are married and the husband is living."[28] The women's vote seems to have followed the major trends, which suggests that women were swayed by pressure from the candidates. The election records of 1832 for Montreal West are the most revealing; of the 225 women who registered at the poll, 95 voted for Tracey, 104 for Bagg, and 26 did not vote.[29] There was soon dissent over a woman's right to vote, Andrew Stuart probably being the first to register an objection, "in consequence of her sex."[30] The feminine vote appears to have been disadvantageous to the reformists and the *patriotes*, for the law disqualifying women was passed in 1834 with enthusiastic support from Papineau and the members of his party.

The constitution's qualifications for candidates were even more liberal than those for voters. Admission to the English House of Commons was governed by an act passed in 1710, which established categories for candidature with landed property requirements ranging from 300 to 600 pounds, though this criterion had not been rigidly respected. In Lower Canada, a member of the assembly had only to be at least twenty-one years old and not a member of the clergy. The constitution's silence on the subject of Jews allowed Ezekiel Hart to be elected in 1807 as the member for Trois-Rivières. Anachronistically, he was twice declared ineligible by his supposedly liberal adversaries in the assembly, while his conservative confrères and Governor Craig countered with calls for a liberal interpretation of the constitution. In any event, in Lower Canada the doors of the legislative assembly were open to all social and religious classes, in contrast with England, where financial qualifications and religious discrimination restricted the choice of representatives to a narrow range of the social spectrum.

From the beginning, the legislative assembly of Lower Canada seems to have reflected more accurately the élite structures and the changes taking place in the society than did the English House of Commons. Farmers did not necessarily vote for peasant candidates, and the same attitude prevailed in the cities, where skilled tradesmen composed over 40 per cent of the population (see Table 4).

The general election of 1792 and a by-election brought fifty-one representatives to the assembly for the period 1792-96.[31] The average age was 44.2, which was close to the average in England for the period 1734-1832, but older than the average age of entry to the House of Commons, or 34.6.[32] Pierre Bédard and Pierre-Amable De Bonne were respectively thirty and thirty-four years of age, but Jean-Antoine Panet and Joseph Papineau were both over forty. The introduction of representative government therefore did not immediately open career opportunities for large numbers of ambitious young men. Nor did it attract a large contingent of illiterate peasants and tradesmen to the assembly; only three members could be classed as such. No fewer than thirty (58 per cent) were merchants, most of them in the fur trade. Next came the military and aristocracy, nine in number (17 per cent), demonstrating their persisting influence (see Table 7). They were not an isolated minority in the assembly, either, for no less than 50 per cent of the members were seigneury owners. There were also nine professionals, who in 1792, though a rising class, were not yet attracting wide popular support. The English-speaking members numbered sixteen (31 per cent), eight elected by rural ridings and eight by urban (out of a total of eleven urban representatives). From a purely demographic point of view, the English-speaking were over-represented, though the imbalance rather accurately reflected the socio-economic disparities between the ethnic groups which were soon to become a source of resentment in French-Canadian circles. The growth of the liberal professions was to prove a vital factor in this.

The constitution, then, though it laid the ground for the eventual emergence of political parties and popular government, in 1792 served the interests of the current ruling classes eminently well. The aristocrats dominated the executive and legislative councils and their interests were well protected in the assembly, both by members of their own class and by merchant seigneurs, some of whom had marked aristocratic aspirations. The merchant bourgeoisie was present on the two councils and dominated the assembly. It was foreseeable that in the division of power the scales were very shortly to tip in favour of the merchant classes. From an ethnic point of view, imbalance was apparent only in the ratio of representatives to the population; on the two councils the proportion of French Canadians to English-speaking members was eleven to fourteen, and in the assembly thirty-four to sixteen.

The shortcomings of the political régime established in 1791 could hardly be apparent to the ruling classes of the day. Legislation was the joint responsibility of the assembly and the legislative council, and each had the power to block any bill potentially detrimental to its interests and aspirations. It is therefore untrue that the assembly was impotent. It did not in fact have control over all public funds, but it could impose taxes and raise revenues sufficient to cover the colony's expenses. It is true also that the constitution did not recognize the principle of ministerial responsibility, but in 1791 this was not yet considered important. The weaknesses of the political system eventually came to light with economic, ideological, and social change. Money supply and ministerial responsibility emerged as issues when a new social élite with a sense of leadership began to aspire to political power. The political conflicts of the first decade of the nineteenth century arose not from the imperfections of the constitution of 1791 but from changes in the social fabric. In 1791-92, the aristocracy and the merchants were the leading political groups, and the division of power between them was satisfactory to both.

I
Structural Changes
1791-1815

CHAPTER 1

Representative Government and the Rise of the Bourgeoisie, 1792-1802

However excellent in itself the new Constitution may be,... I conceive the foundation of it must rest upon a due proportion being maintained between the Aristocracy and the lower Orders of the People, without which it will become a dangerous Weapon in the hands of the latter. Several Causes at present unite in daily lessening the Power and Influence of the aristocratical Body in Lower Canada.—Milnes to Portland (November 1, 1800), Kennedy, DCC, 1918, 238.

On December 26, 1791, the new constitution came into force. Banquets were held and toasts were drunk to liberty, fraternity, and the king, with the bourgeoisie conspicuously prominent in the celebrations marking the introduction of representative government. Such was the rejoicing that some even had the fleeting impression of being witness to a small-scale French Revolution promising, besides political, civil, and religious liberty, the abolition of "feudalism."[1] Reality came back into focus as the euphoria faded. The constitution, while it recognized the old social régime, left it to the Lower Canadians themselves to decide the fate of the seigneurial régime, the Coutume de Paris, and church privileges, including tithing. In 1792 the vast majority of the population undoubtedly wished the survival of the old social régime. The constitution, though no politico-social revolution, nevertheless meant a major political change in favour of the merchant bourgeoisie. The reform not only gave recognition to their predominant role in the economy, but in the circumstances facilitated their rapid rise to social and political leadership. That, at least, was how the merchant class interpreted the immediate improvement in their standing, and their optimism helped mitigate their disappointment over the colony's division into two provinces.

The business community's ambitions, indeed, acquire a certain clarity in the light of the situation taking shape in 1792. For the next ten years the traditional major sectors of the economy, furs and wheat, benefited from the economic growth stimulated by a general upward movement in prices. The prosperity, if not of boom proportions, in turn stimulated population growth and diversification of occupations, and economic and population growth together brought about numerical increase and diversification in the business community. The rise of the liberal professions which began in this period was one of the consequences. Meanwhile, the aristocracy and old-guard seigneurs continued to lose ground, with increasing rapidity after 1791, and by the beginning of the nineteenth century this once-powerful class was already thoroughly decadent. Papineau, on the death of L.-J. Duchesnay in 1825, wrote: "He lived on seven or eight hundred louis per year, saving nothing, and half of this revenue came from positions which died with him. Here we see yet another of those old families fated to pass into obscurity, for it is left with negligible fortune and no influence or education."[2] By the middle of the century the class had all but disappeared. In the meantime, powerless to resist the winds of change, the aristocracy was obliged to come to terms with the long-despised merchant bourgeoisie.

Inevitably, social change affected the operation of the political system. With the decline of the aristocracy and the concomitant rise of the merchant and professional classes, the system's democratic elements gained strength, altering the constitutional balance of powers established in 1791. The weakening of the counterweight provided by the aristocracy was a phenomenon whose importance can hardly be overstressed.

I Economic Growth

In this decade, Canada was riding the same tide of prosperity enjoyed by Great Britain and the United States. As general as it was, not all segments of the society benefited equally, for the incomes of certain social groups failed to keep pace with the overall increase in prices, but the climate of optimism for the future pervaded all classes. Upward price movements began in England and the United States between 1785 and 1789, gathering momentum after the outbreak of the revolutionary wars, and were reflected in Canada. Between 1789 and 1801, the price of beaver rose by 52 per cent, with other furs following suit,[3] and agricultural prices rose between 24 and 68 per cent depending on the product. In the decade 1791 to 1801, the price of wheat in England rose 41 per cent. These conditions appear to have been the largest factor in Lower Canada's increased import and export volumes. In general, the balance of trade between 1785 and 1800 was favourable to the colony, a fact to be noted. Even forestry and fishing, while they remained secondary, shared in the general prosperity. It was the dominant sectors of furs and wheat, those best integrated into the imperial market, which responded most vigorously to the expansionary thrust.

The fur trade would have been in trouble by this time, had the 1783 treaty provisions on frontiers and western posts been applied, and would perhaps have already dropped to secondary status. It was pressure from the Indians and from merchants whose influence was strong in London that postponed settlement of the border question. In any event, the British refused to hand over the western posts, claiming that the Americans had not fulfilled their obligations; indeed, it is questionable whether the latter were yet ready to occupy the territories ceded to them under the treaty.[4] But the Americans became more aggressive as the competitive strength of their fur trade improved. In order to put pressure on England, they resolved to bring an end to Indian opposition by force. After some initial reverses, in 1793-94 the American general Anthony Wayne defeated the western tribes in battle, effectively breaking their resistance.

Meanwhile, negotiations between London and Washington dragged on. The English diplomats, espousing the position of the Canadian merchants and the Indians, sought to have the west recognized as a neutral zone where the Indians could continue to hunt undisturbed. The Americans rejected the proposal. Eventually the two sides settled on a solution which for the time being safeguarded the interests of the Montreal merchants. Jay's Treaty, signed in 1794, confirmed the decisions of 1783 and set 1796 for final cession of the western posts, but guaranteed freedom of movement back and forth across the border for Canadian fur traders. In 1803 the North West Company moved its centre of operations from Grand Portage to Kaministiquia. The decline of the fur trade economy thus began about 1800 with the effective cession of the southwestern region to the Americans.

A series of delays won through pressure from the Montreal traders, the rearguard action conducted by British negotiators, and perhaps weakness on the part of American fur traders had meant a twenty-year reprieve for the beaver-trade empire. The stability of the transcontinental economic space thus obtained, together with growth in demand, brought a minor boom in production between 1783 and 1802. Undoubtedly the French revolutionary wars dampened demand in

Europe at times, but the American market was expanding and fur exporters took advantage of it. In this decade, as compared to the averages for the preceding ten-year period, shipments of beaver, mink, marten, raccoon, and skunk rose by 2, 21, 30, 39, and 162 per cent respectively, exclusive of sales to the United States. Innis asserts that, in the same period, exports of bear and muskrat pelts (to all destinations) doubled and quintupled respectively,[5] an observation which underlines the importance of American outlets. The growth in exports to the American market was temporary, however, and its price was a situation of dependence. The day eventually came when American merchants began to show hostility in the competition for their home market, and then the Canadian merchants were to experience heavy losses. The lucrative Canadian fur trade was in danger.

While expanded production and price increases were fattening the merchants' coffers, clouds were gathering in the form of cost factors. Prices of articles used for barter were rising steadily, and broadening reaches of territory to be covered in fur-gathering meant greater costs in pay and transport.[6] Vigorous competition would have pushed the costs much higher still. The North West Company, however, succeeded in eliminating its competitors in the interior by absorbing them. Its reorganizations of 1787, 1792, and 1795 did much to assure its monopoly and keep profits on the rise. And the Nor'westers who had staked their future in that territory reaped the fruits of their intuition and labours. Men like Simon McTavish and Joseph Frobisher rose from modest beginnings to be the richest and most powerful of the fur traders. The weakness of the competition at the time certainly facilitated the building of this vast monopoly. The Hudson's Bay Company, while it improved its position, was not yet a serious threat; it controlled 14 per cent of the trade in 1795,[7] 26 per cent in 1800. Nor were the Americans yet ready to compete seriously in the region. It was only with the turn of the century that competition once more became part of the scene, and then it sent profits into almost continuous decline. The formation of the XY Company, known also as the New North West Company, renewed competition internally at a time when external competition too was on the rise.

The fur trade, the oldest of the colony's economic activities, thus gave its best performance in this decade, both in volume and profitability. However, there were mounting signs of the forthcoming decline; increasing scarcity of beaver in certain locations, reduction of territory with the cession of the Great Lakes posts, and, in the last years of the century, a vigorous renewal of competition. Furthermore, the fur trade had already lost its commanding position in the colony. The proportion of the population engaged directly or indirectly in the trade diminished with the increase in population. There being an abundance of available land, it was agriculture which was absorbing the demographic surpluses. Farmers and their sons could even work seasonally in the fur trade, and indeed formed an integral part of its manpower. During this decade, trade in agricultural products tended to equal or even surpass the trade in furs.

After the 1780-84 recession, agricultural production reached unprecedented heights. At the turn of the century the harvest in wheat, the backbone of Lower-Canadian agriculture, may well have exceeded four million bushels. Only in the poor crop years of 1789 and 1795 was the rise in production interrupted, as reflected in the export volume in each following year; in 1796 only 24,866 *minots* passed through the port of Quebec, compared to the current yearly average of 405,660 *minots*. Sales abroad kept up with production; for the three years 1793-95, wheat exports amounted to 1,473,813 *minots*, and for 1801-3, 2,253,043 *minots*. The increase cannot be attributed to production in Upper Canada; though that province supplied the fur trading posts and still had some left for export, it was never responsible for more than 10 per cent of total wheat and flour sales in the last decade of the century, since it was still in the early stages of its agricultural development. Nor was American wheat of more than secondary importance in Canadian exports in this period. The increased export volumes, then, came essentially from Lower Canadian producers.

In Great Britain in this decade, there were fewer bumper crops than average or poor, with the result that the mother country was obliged to import huge quantities of wheat from continental Europe, the United States, and Canada.[8] In the circumstances, the Corn Laws, whose purpose was to protect the British producer from foreign competition, did not block massive importation. The price of wheat, which rose to 128 shillings per quarter (eight bushels) in 1800, made the legislation inoperable. The mother country may have afforded its colonies no protection whatever against foreign competition, but hard times for its home subjects were spelling joy for Lower Canadians.

With demand so strong from Great Britain, the West Indies, and the fishing industry, the *habitants* were spurred to clear and cultivate more of their land. The grain merchants, particularly if they were seigneurs, built new and better-equipped flour mills. Their agents scoured the countryside to buy grain surpluses from seigneurs, curés, and peasants, and to preach the benefits of greater production. In 1801-2 the harvest was so abundant there were not enough ships to carry it all away. Was an agricultural revolution under way? The abrupt reversal after the turn of the century suggests otherwise.

This unprecedented demand for wheat on the imperial market at the close of the eighteenth century came at a time of burgeoning population in Lower Canada. The marriage rate rose from 8.2 per 1,000 in the period 1782-92, to 8.6 in the succeeding decade; the death rate for the same periods dropped from 26.8 to 24.9, and the birth rate rose from 50.6 to 50.9, signifying interaction between economic conditions and demographic context. From analysis of curés' reports on the tithe, we obtain an insight into the principal variants on the rural scene. It is clear that the greatest increases in grain production occurred in new parishes and those where population growth was most marked. These were the ones which, besides their natural growth, received the spillover from already overcrowded seigneuries. Here new land was cleared and brought under cultivation. In 21 parishes in the Montreal region, the wheat harvest rose from 197,054 *minots* in 1784 to 424,644 *minots* in 1802. Similarly in the Quebec region, 16 parishes produced 106,340 *minots* in 1784 and 229,320 *minots* in 1798. In both cases the increase was 115 per cent.

In other groups of parishes, in contrast, production increased far less strongly or even declined, suggesting near or complete demographic saturation. In 16 such parishes in the district of Montreal, wheat production increased only 23 per cent from 1784 to 1800, from 260,074 *minots* to 315,062. In the district of Quebec we see the first signs of tension between demographic increase and the growth of agricultural production. These were the long-established parishes around Quebec City, from which population was migrating to less crowded parishes where land was still abundant. As early as 1784, the bishop of Quebec had perceived an agricultural malaise in many parishes in the district, which almost certainly failed to follow the general trend between 1784 and 1798. In 17 of these parishes, wheat production declined from 150,280 *minots* in 1784 to 137,774 *minots* 14 years later, a decline of 8 per cent. The situation prevailing at these locations announced not only a buildup of demographic tension, but also the beginning of the wheat decline in Lower Canada.[9]

The higher production volumes do not necessarily mean that agricultural practices had changed. The peasantry in fact remained attached to the same habits of thought and action that had prevailed during the French Régime. Absence of crop rotation, failure to make use of natural fertilizers, shallow cultivation, chronic shortages of pastureland, meagre herds of livestock—these were still the typical agricultural features. There did exist an agricultural élite, enriched by a few Scottish immigrants who had brought a knowledge of improved techniques developed in Britain, but it was too small to influence the peasant masses. The average farmer continued to use methods which eventually drained the soil of its fertility; the subdivision of farms, a consequence of the laws of succession, contributed to the process. What increased the agricultural yield in this period was the growing population's cultivation of new, rich land, of which there was still an abundance in many seigneuries. For the seigneurs, for whom higher agricultural prices, increasing settlement, and higher rates for seigneurial dues spelled increased revenues, it was good business to concede whatever land was asked for. But the circumstances, while encouraging higher production, tended to strengthen faith in long-established agricultural custom.

The circumstances also led to land speculation, a North American phenomenon by no means peculiar to Canada;[10] in the United States in this period it was stimulated by demographic pressures in certain areas. In Lower Canada we see the attraction of landed property manifested in farmers' sons' abandonment of their parishes for richer lands and wider spaces, in merchants' investment in seigneuries, and before long in the land quarrels between merchants, American speculators, and the political élite.

Seigneurial land was not as yet seriously affected by speculation, for, while its extent was virtually frozen, there was still no real shortage of farmland within seigneurial limits. And then, generally speaking, it was not in the seigneurs' interests to limit settlement. The seigneurial system's transfer taxes, the *lods et ventes* and the *droit de retrait*, whose purpose was to encourage stability of land tenure, placed a damper on speculation by the *censitaires*, the seigneurial "tenants." A capitalist could, however, speculate by acquiring an entire fief and then using his rights as seigneur to circumvent the *us et coutumes*, the proper established practice, in other words, to thwart the purpose of the system. Once seigneurial farmland became scarce, many seigneurs turned out to be speculators. When the trade in lumber became lucrative, seigneurs used their powers to corner vast areas of forestland. It was no accident that in these ten years British merchants acquired as much seigneurial land as they had in the previous twenty. A number of them were certainly speculating on a grand scale, and purchase of a seigneury brought social prestige and promise of growing revenues along with prospects of capital gain. After the turn of the century the speculator-seigneur was no longer the exception. Land speculation was therefore not, as has been asserted,[11] confined to the Eastern Townships.

The townships, with their ten million acres of land, were a speculator's paradise after 1791. The decision to grant land under English tenure outside seigneurial limits was taken at a time when land shortages were far from either French or English minds. British immigrants, except the very poorest, could readily settle on the seigneuries, and their dislike of "feudalism" was offset by the fact that the seigneuries were closer to the markets. Pressure for the establishment of the townships had come from disbanded soldiers and from American immigrants anxious to settle near the American border, not yet from the humbler population.

The political leaders, on the other hand, had high hopes for this vast virgin territory. They saw it as a region to be settled by British immigrants, where a landed aristocracy would emerge to give weight to the aristocratic side of the constitutional balance, an increasingly urgent preoccupation in these years. The introduction of English land tenure implied also that English civil law should apply in the area. The revolutionary wars and strained relations with the United States were to bear heavily on land policy, for the governors, profoundly disturbed by French revolutionary propaganda and spasmodic peasant agitation, were convinced that the French Canadians were ready and anxious to return to French domination. Governor Prescott wrote to Fawcett on September 5, 1798:

> I am happy to acquaint you that in these parts of His Majesty's Dominions we enjoy perfect tranquillity, more the consequence of fear than regard for the British Constitution. I have every reason to believe that the Canadians are more attached at present to France, than they were even before the Revolution, which change has no doubt been effected by secret Emissaries, who notwithstanding every vigilance on my part, have found means to introduce their Poison among them. The inlets of this Province being so numerous and distantly separated, that with the small force I have it is impossible to watch them all, as effectually as I could wish.[12]

Fearing infiltration of revolutionary ideas into peasant minds, he concluded that it would be dangerous to have French Canadians colonize the Eastern Townships, particularly near the American border. The French-Canadian peasantry, in truth, was not even interested in such a remote region. In any event, Prescott envisioned keeping the area for British immigrants and former Americans of proven loyalty. The attention paid to American immigrants was the greater for the fact they were seen as the principal source of manpower for a major colonization programme, and also as having the virtue of being already convinced of the superiority of British institutions. Distrust of Americans in general was offset by hope that there were enough of them still loyal to Britain to provide massive immigration to Lower Canada. Still, the task of sifting immigrants on the basis of loyalty was a formidable one.

But the reliability of the settlers was not the only problem with the

Eastern Townships. The governors were instructed to foil the avaricious machinations of speculators, of whom there were many—Americans, local merchants, and even civil servants. Very soon, beginning with Dorchester, they locked horns with members of the executive council who had close relationships with the merchant bourgeoisie. When Governor Prescott arrived in 1796 there was total confusion in the administration of land grants; some 1,400 requests for grants had been received and 150 survey permits had been issued for as many townships, but the grant mechanism had been suspended by a recent decision in London. A quarrel developed between Prescott and the lands committee of the executive council over reactivation and clarification of the land policy. Later, he wrote as follows to Portland:

> I had not been many weeks in this government before I discovered in part, the schemes and designs that had been laid by some of the members of the council connected with other persons of Property and Influence for the purpose of monopolizing immense quantities of the Waste Lands; but it was some time before I had any suspicion (and still longer before I could really believe) that they had it in view to extend their schemes so far as to comprehend within their Grasp, the townships that had been actually settled on and rendered valuable at the labour and expenses of the former Applicants....[13]

What worried Prescott most was that the assembly might become involved, for its membership at the time was largely sympathetic to business and landed interests. "If the speculators succeed in bringing this question before the members of the Assembly," he wrote, "they will have no difficulty achieving their ends with the House composed as it is at present...."[14] The conflict and uncertainty continued until he was recalled in 1799 and was replaced as administrator by Sir Robert Shore Milnes. From 1799 to 1807, massive tracts of land were granted around the seigneuries.

For the purpose of colonization at the time, the system of "leaders and associates" inherited from the American colonies seemed best suited to local conditions and the implementation of royal intentions.[15] Under this system, all or part of a township would be acquired by a group of colonists associated under a leader, who would assume the costs of the concession. Each individual would receive 1,200 acres but would keep only 200, conveying 1,000 acres to the leader in consideration of his expenditures past and future. Lists of associates were provided, often containing fictitious names. It was a system of speculation, but it would also create a class of large landowners, the basis of a landed aristocracy; the township leaders, together with the seigneurs, would uphold monarchist and aristocratic traditions and, as the reigning political philosophy required, provide the counterbalance to popular elements. Providing the township leaders were sufficiently wealthy and energetic, the system did have the advantage of giving immediate leadership in a region under development. Philemon Wright of Hull was one such leader who did much to advance the economic development of his region, and he was not unique. But the story of disappointing immigration, absence of government roads policy, the incompetence of many township leaders, and the prevalence of speculation is told in the large proportion of failures compared to successes. A number of townships were granted to ex-servicemen and militiamen, but on the whole these operations did not do much to place more land in the hands of farmers who needed it, nor was that really their purpose. Among the township leaders, the most numerous were fur and wheat merchants, then civil servants, seigneurs, and professionals, particularly surveyors. The new large landowners were almost all English-speaking, and a number were Americans. The near-absence of French Canadians among them reflects the socio-economic disparities between the ethnic groups, perhaps a lack of interest, and certainly discrimination.[16] Concern over ethnic aspects of the land question arose only in the succeeding decade.

It was the traditional economic sectors, then, which were responsible for economic growth in this period, as seen in the expansion of the fur and grain trades and the activity in land concession. The general rise in prices had less effect on fisheries, forestry, and the Forges du Saint-Maurice. The period's novelty was a modest beginning in shipbuilding. Settlement and colonization were proceeding apace in Upper Canada, to be sure, increasing Montreal's sphere of influence. This development heralded rather than launched a socio-economic revolution. A growing population and a vigorous economy were bringing social transformations whose importance must not be underestimated. In the onrush of change certain stars grew bright while others waned; particularly apparent was the rise of the middle classes, in contrast to the deepening problems of the old seigneurial families.

II Social Diversification

The middle classes were the primary beneficiaries of the period's economic achievements. Within their ranks, the merchant bourgeoisie gained in number, diversity, and power. Increased profits provided them with funds for larger investment in most sectors of the economy. Thus, a fur merchant might diversify his operations to include grain, landholdings, fishing, lumber, or shipbuilding; or an exporter might begin importing. With the major commercial enterprises concentrated in the hands of the North West merchants, their prestige and influence was strong throughout the society, not only in the cities but in the country districts as well, and a number of them developed distinctly aristocratic leanings.

In their shadow there developed a class of lesser commercial lights with similar interests, values, and aspirations. At the bottom of the commercial ladder, growing with the economy and the size and number of villages, was a mass of small urban and rural businessmen, general storekeepers, butchers and bakers, publicans and innkeepers, peddlars, and *coureurs des côtes.* In 1792 there were 432 such small businessmen recorded.[17] The *coureurs des côtes,* the middlemen between local producers and landowners and the dealers in agricultural produce, seem to have been losing ground numerically. In the rural parishes, the number of general storekeepers was increasing rapidly. Many of these began in the ranks of the army of itinerant peddlars who roamed the highways and byways, and were accused by local merchants of exciting acquisitiveness in the people with their worthless wares, and of cornering so much of the money in circulation that the local merchants were forced into ruinous credit selling.

The rapid growth of the merchant class was both rural and urban. Reports of the curé of the parish of Quebec, however, show that from 1792 to 1805 French-Canadian merchants increased only 20 per cent in number, whereas the corresponding English-speaking group quadrupled in size (see Table 4). This despite the fact that the statistics underestimate the English-speaking Protestant population. The total French-Canadian population growth recorded is similarly only in the order of 20 per cent, which suggests migration toward the country districts, accentuating the increasingly rural character of the French-Canadian society. Strong growth in the number of craftsmen and labourers reflects increasing demand for their services and also a certain volume of British immigration, which in this period was still relatively small.[18]

The commercial class, then, was growing in number, wealth, and power, and was increasingly English at all levels of the economy, particularly among the wealthiest and most powerful. Though most apparent in the cities, English domination reached even into the rural seigneuries. The widening of economic disparities between the ethnic groups was beginning to look irreversible. Not until a social élite had recognized this reality and taken it to heart as the product of an injustice did there emerge a powerful ideology based on ethnic primacy. During this final decade of the century, however, what resentment existed was harboured in private. The French-Canadian middle class was not yet disposed to express it collectively.

The rise of the liberal professions is significant in this perspective. Many of the class possessed a social awareness which was to have profound effects socially, ideologically, and politically. With the decline of the old seigneurial families, moreover, there was room at the top for new leadership. While not yet ready to assume it, a body of lawyers, notaries, doctors, and surveyors developed quietly in the shadow of the merchants and the traditional élite, namely the clergy and the seigneurs.

The conditions which so favoured the middle classes also hastened the decline of the aristocracy. Yet the constitution of 1791 had given that class a significant role, and assured its place on appointed governing bodies. In 1792 it was even respectably present in the assembly, having won its share of the popular vote. By 1800, however, Lieutenant-Governor Milnes was writing: "Hence by degrees the Canadian Gentry have nearly become extinct ....Very few of the Seigneurs, as I have already hinted, have sufficient interest to insure their own election or the election of any one to whom they give their Support in the House of Assembly."[19] The government, however kindly disposed, could reverse neither the popular disaffection nor the social and economic depreciation it reflected. Indeed, the old aristocracy kept hoping for an opportunity to demonstrate their traditional military importance, but that did not come until 1812; by then it was too late. The cause of their decline was in part sheer improvidence. Clinging obstinately to a style of life befitting their station, many simply would not tailor their expenses to their incomes. The second cause was the practice of subdividing a fief among a seigneur's heirs upon his death, leading to smaller and smaller individual landholdings and revenues, and often a corresponding loss of prestige. The resultant insecurity led the old families to redouble their efforts to obtain sinecure appointments and pensions and arrange marriages with rich merchant families, all of which merely put off the final evil day. A great number of seigneuries thus passed into the hands of the English and the more financially astute French Canadians. By 1800, 55 per cent of the seigneurs were not members of the old families. But neither the intrusion of the middle classes into seigneurial ranks nor state favours could give the aristocracy any real new lease on life. With the growing tendency of the new seigneurs to regard their acquisitions as investments rather than a source of social prestige, the seigneurial régime came to be regarded as an obstacle to progress. And the old aristocratic families, overwhelmed by the rise of the middle classes, went from economic decay to social and political extinction.

In contrast, the financial lot of the clergy was improving toward the end of the century, thanks to prudent management of their fiefs, the institutionalized generosity of the faithful, and a range of lucrative sources of revenue. While seigneurial dues paid in cash were fixed, thus losing value in time of inflating prices, the rates could be increased in contracts with new *censitaires*. With dues paid partly in kind, a growing population, and increasing land values, the revenues of the ecclesiastic seigneuries were on the rise. For the parishes and their curés, revenues were following the upward trend of prices. The tithe, which provided the parish curé's personal revenue, was one-twenty-sixth of the harvest and thus reflected production volume and population growth (see Table 5). The revenues of the parish *Fabriques*, with a broader range of sources, reflected conditions in a more complex manner. Fees for baptisms, marriages, and burials reflected events affecting the population; parish coffers were enriched, for instance, by an epidemic which increased the mortality rate. The sale of pews by auction benefited the church while fanning social rivalries. Sunday and holy day collections did their part as well, though it was *la quête de l'Enfant Jésus ou des biens de la terre* which appealed most directly to the generosity of the parish faithful, calling for donations mostly in farm produce which was subsequently sold on the local market. The records of this *quête* reveal much of the nature of the local economy; wheat and pork were for many years the predominant items donated (see Table 6). On the whole, the fluctuations in the revenues of the *Fabriques* are a rather loose indication of the prosperity of parishioners and the state of the economy.

The Catholic Church of Lower Canada, then, possessed a healthy economic base. The only financial disappointment in this period was the disposition of the Jesuit Estates with the death of Père Casot, the last Jesuit in the province. The secular clergy had counted on taking possession of these extensive seigneuries, proposing to use the revenues for education, but in 1800 it was the government itself which took possession of them. The decision did not really harm the church's existing financial state, for it left its other properties intact, as well as its traditional privileges. It also left the church in control of education and hospitals, and with the easy defeat of a proposal to establish a lay university, its monopoly in these two domains had seemed assured. The passage, in 1801, of the act creating the Royal Institution for the Advancement of Learning, which brought the state into primary education, therefore took the clergy rudely by surprise. Still, there was ample room for confidence, for the church's social role was firmly established. True, there was a germ of religious disaffection and anti-clericalism in certain élite circles, where a few individuals were as eager for the abolition of seigneurial dues and tithing as for political freedom, but as yet there was no risk of it spreading to the masses. The virulence of certain reformist pronouncements was no indication of broad-based support; there was in fact no movement afoot in the society liable to endanger the existing order in any real sense.

What the clergy of Lower Canada really feared was an external danger, namely the spread of revolution from France. In their eyes, absolute monarchy and the divine right of kings were central and basic; society was a hierarchy beginning with the king and descending first to the élite, which is to say, the clergy, the aristocracy, and the political authorities, and thence to the people. Social relationships were governed by the dual principle of authority and obedience. The events in France were therefore seen as a total, world-wide cataclysm which threatened the very roots of those traditional values so carefully nurtured in order to bring man to God and salvation. As the Revolution unfolded, with the declaration of the rights of man, the abolition of church privileges, and the liquidation of the French nobility and monarchy, the Lower Canadian clergy watched with dismay and increasingly open hostility. Then there came religious persecution and the confiscation of church properties, which were considered sacred and essential to the continuance of the divine mission, and with this their worst fears were confirmed. As far as they were concerned the liberal revolution was not confined to France but threatened everywhere, even in Lower Canada; its beginning was already manifest in the United States. They became hypersensitive to anything on the local scene which might symbolize the revolutionary message. When émigré priests arrived from France to settle in Canada they were therefore warmly welcomed, for their coming promised not only to alleviate the shortage of priests but also to provide reinforcement for the struggle against liberal ideas. In 1790, commenting on a plan to import English Catholic priests, Monseigneur Hubert declared, "There may be reason to fear that these gentlemen, accustomed as they are to reasoning freely on all political matters, may make some disadvantageous impressions on the minds of a people to whom we have always preached strict obedience to the orders of the king or his representatives, and total submission to any properly established system of laws, without question or discussion."[20] Clearly, the Bishop of Quebec's ideological preoccupations outweighed any cultural worries he might have. Only when the bishops realized the extreme difficulty of importing priests from France did they turn to local training through a system of classical colleges.

At the root of the clergy's distrust of representative government was their fear of French revolutionary ideas, which they considered to have been spawned by the philosophy of the Enlightenment. "Judge of it," wrote Bishop Plessis, "by those among our fellow citizens who have had the misfortune to fall into the trap of those monstrous principles preached by Diderot, Voltaire, Mercier, Rousseau, Volney, Raynal, D'Alembert, and other deists of the century."[21] The contagion of liberal ideas, he declared, was not only carried by infamous books and French emissaries, it was institutionalized in the parliamentary system. With extension of suffrage to the lower classes, freedom of debate, and possibility of popular representation by the newer classes, the clerics saw risk of social instability and even disintegration. Though such consequences were not visible in the last decade of the century, in the political strife which materialized after 1800 the clergy were convinced they were witnessing the realization of their predictions: parliamentarianism was indeed proving to be the vehicle of revolutionary thought and inclinations. In the midst of the crisis of 1810, Monseigneur Plessis declared, "It is a grave sin, a mortal sin, I will not say to revolt (which I believe to be far from the thoughts of all who now hear me), but even to oppose the commendable views of this government and defy its orders."[22] The clergy were still an Old Régime élite; for them, be the body called States General, States Provincial, or House of Assembly, it was merely a consultative institution and such it must remain.

Things being as they were, the clergy saw Great Britain as the staunch defender of throne and altar, and their praise for her role in the world and for membership in the British Empire knew no bounds, especially after 1793. Plessis declared from the pulpit in 1799:

> She [Great Britain] is the bulwark on which all your hopes repose. If she should triumph her glory will be your salvation and assure you peace. But if she be overpowered, then will your tranquillity and your governments be at an end. In the midst of your cities the deadly tree of liberty will be planted and the rights of man will be proclaimed.... Your laws will be made a mockery and a plaything for the arrogant foes of the human race; you will share in all the pitiable woes of the fate befallen France; you will be free, but with a freedom of oppression, which will make the dregs of the citizenry your masters and cast into the dust the estimable leaders who now possess your affection and confidence.[23]

From a state of affairs which demonstrated the mother country's inestimable service in preserving the old social régime, it was natural for the notion to emerge that the conquest had been a stroke of providence.

The Catholic clergy were not alone in their reaction to revolutionary currents. Their Anglican counterparts were just as volubly opposed, and the aristocracy, too. In the middle classes of Lower Canada there was at first cautious sympathy for the French revolutionaries, provided they establish political liberty through a constitution similar to Great Britain's. This was the attitude of the English-speaking in general, once they had seen the rights of man proclaimed and Catholic church privileges abolished. In the ranks of French-Canadian merchants and professionals, among whom there were powerful champions of the old social régime, the reactions were more complex, and only a small minority were even cautiously sympathetic. But the day the French Revolution undertook to liquidate monarchical institutions, the middle classes turned hostile almost to a man, for this was a violation of their conception of liberty as reposing on a balance of the three principles of government embodied in the British constitution, namely monarchy, aristocracy, and democracy. In their eyes, democracy as incorporated in a republican system tended to anarchy, which in the end would only lead back to despotism.

Against a background of war between England and France and tensions between Canada and the United States, the leading classes of Lower Canada drew together in ideological and emotional unanimity, becoming extraordinarily sensitive to anything liable to jeopardize peace and order in the society. In the climate of alarm, exacerbated by the activities of French agitators and resistance to certain measures among the lower classes, the political leaders were wholeheartedly supported by the social leaders, both English- and French-speaking. The clergy, the magistrature, the captains of militia, the legislative assembly, and "loyal associations" of prominent urban and rural figures were mobilized to ward off what was perceived as a major threat.

It is true that agents of revolutionary France were at work in the United States, propagating the idea of a reconquest of Canada. Genet, and later Adet, sent emissaries into the country districts of Lower Canada, not only distributing pamphlets but spreading rumours of every description. In particular, in the autumn of 1793, there was word of a planned attack on Canada by a French fleet. The rumours, much more than the printed propaganda which reached only a few first hand, spread quickly, became inflated, and sowed confusion among the people. In one form or another the invasion idea was kept alive by the propagandists in the hope of provoking a popular uprising. In 1797 the day seemed really at hand, for the long-expected French fleet was reported to be nearing Quebec. It was known, in fact, that Ira Allen of Vermont[24] was at work in Paris between 1796 and 1800, preparing an expedition to seize Lower Canada. A climate of anxiety and suspicion reigned in all strata of the society as well as in official circles, heightened by the presence of the French emissaries who always seemed to be one jump ahead of the authorities. At last one of them, David McLane, an American, was arrested, tried for high treason, and sent to the gallows in 1797, which appeared to justify the authorities' claim that the popular unrest was tied to revolutionary propaganda spread among the ignorant peasants and labouring classes. On this point, Attorney General Jonathan Sewell wrote in 1797:

> The Cause and Origin of so many Offences against Government is found in the numerous French Emissaries with which this Province has lately been infested and the steps which they have taken to execute Disturbances are in every respect similar to those which they adopted in 1794, particularly in one respect. On that occasion, the Militia Act was made the pretext [;] in the present instance the Road Act has been used to draw the Canadians from the Duty of their Allegiance.[25]

In truth, the political and social leaders exaggerated both the extent and significance of the outbreaks of unrest. Each episode was spontaneous, localized, and short-lived. It all began early in 1794 with a dispute between the seigneur of Berthier and a number of his *censitaires* over the building of a bridge. About the same time, the governor laid before the assembly a new militia bill conceived in the light of the ominous relationships with France and the United States. The bill was passed and in May the governor called out 2,000 militiamen, which provoked widespread resistance around Quebec and in Montreal. At Charlesbourg near Quebec, 300 armed peasants threatened violence over the arrest of objectors. The disobedience subsided but flared anew two years later when the assembly passed an act obliging the people to build and maintain public roads bordering their properties, through a *corvée* system similar to that used to build the Quebec-Montreal highway during the French Régime. Once again the centres of resistance were Montreal and the region around Quebec; the agitation continued for part of the autumn of 1796 and erupted again in January and March of 1797.[26]

Undeniably the war, the multiplicity of rumours, and the propaganda from revolutionary agents helped to create a climate of instability. Recognition of this, however, is not the same as stating categorically that the populace, out of attachment to France and hostility to the institutions of the Old Régime, was on the brink of revolt. For the lower classes, the issue of military service was a sensitive one at a time when fears of deportation were still very much alive. There was fear among militiamen, too, of being forced to serve outside the country, though they declared themselves ready to resist invasion. Interestingly enough, popular opposition manifested itself against the assembly as well as the government. Hostility to the introduction of the *corvée* for public purposes, when it was still a practice in many seigneuries, seems to be related to the old fear of state-imposed taxes. The *habitant*, to whom it was a traditional point of pride to be exempt from state taxation, saw himself in effect being taxed under the legislation, and at a time when seigneurial "taxation" was also increasing. From a letter written in 1797 to John Neilson by Louis Labadie, a schoolmaster in Verchères, we see that the revolutionary propaganda had indeed at least superficially reached the lower classes.

> I have with great difficulty brought a number of persons to see the rectitude of our present government, and have so filled them with horror for the beggarly... and abominable French, their laws and liberty, that they are in agreement with me. It is a very sad thing for this Province, that ignorance is so great in parts of our country districts, that from time to time there appear small uprisings, over the Road Act, or over taxes which they say they must pay. And I tell them, I would find you too fortunate if our House did not do this. It must come for the good of all.[27]

The discontent at this time found no sympathy with the élite and had no real depth or durability. Discontent of a more lasting nature was to develop in the next decade; perhaps this was a foretaste.

This periodic unrest could be read as a response to an underlying economic malaise. The eruptions of the autumn of 1796 and the following winter came on the heels of a province-wide crop failure; legislation which imposed burdens on the people was bound to be doubly unpopular at such a time. And yet expansion in agriculture and the fur trade suggests a general improvement in the standard of living among the peasants and workers. Country people, travellers observed, were taking advantage of it to buy more imported goods, even changing their habits of dress to use more woollens and other textiles from England. The rise in import volumes supports this view. Though the society was increasingly rural, there was also progressive diversification of occupation in the country districts: more villages, more small merchants, more carpenters, millwrights, cobblers, cartwrights, blacksmiths, and masons. It could be that the Militia Act aroused greater anxiety over a potential loss of farm labour than over possible deportation. However, the improved rural standard of living was not felt equally everywhere. The conflict between the seigneur of Berthier and his *censitaires* speaks volumes for the attitude of many seigneurs; increased seigneurial dues more than likely swallowed up all or most of any increment in peasant profits. In 1794 many parishes were already in a state of crisis. In Charlesbourg, for instance, the population dropped from 1,998 in 1784 to 1,854 in 1790 and to 1,417 in 1825, despite 1,354 births and only 735 deaths between 1794 and 1821, indicating demographic pressures and emigration. The tithe, that yardstick of agricultural production, followed a similar curve. It is around Quebec that this is most noticeable, and where signs of the strife to come in the nineteenth century can best be read.

III The Bourgeoisie Comes to Power

The constitution of 1791, in providing for a legislative assembly, laid the groundwork for the development of political parties. Parties are not created artificially; they emerge from a concurrence of existing forces and needs in a society. There is a necessary relationship between social structure, the tensions within it, and political structure. If in 1791 ethnic origin had been the basis of the dominant ideology, political parties would have emerged naturally and promptly, the members of the assembly polarizing consistently according to their ethnic origin. The middle-class coalition which had fought for and won a parliamentary system would have disintegrated.

The situation indeed appeared to be evolving in that direction from the very first meeting of the new assembly, when there was heated debate over the election of a speaker. The English members nominated William Grant, stressing not only his long experience in public affairs and grasp of local conditions, but also his mastery of both languages (bilingualism at the time was an English prerogative). The French put forward Jean-Antoine Panet, lauding his qualities as a respected jurist and member of a family of lawyers, and minimizing the importance of bilingualism; they were the majority and Panet was elected. Similarly, regarding the official language of the assembly, the English held that their language should have supremacy over French; the debate ended in agreement that for official texts the two languages would be equal.[28] This ethnic alignment of the members did not last, however; Lieutenant-Governor Alured Clark wrote to London:

> The Canadian members having judged that they had shown their importance, by proving to the people that they were acting in concert and could have their way on any matter debated, and having

observed that the English members in general conducted themselves with composure, moderation and reason befitting public
service, before prorogation there vanished almost completely the
unfortunate distinctions which had at first arisen.[29]

The question of Crown lands might have stimulated an ethnic polarization, or else a political movement backed by land speculators
which, the governor feared, would be supported by the merchant-
dominated assembly. Neither came about. The assembly at the time
was more preoccupied with military service and other measures designed to combat the influence of the French emissaries than by nationalism or the land question. The popular unrest, too, could have
been used by a budding nationalist movement, or could have given rise
to one. Governor Prescott, who doubted the loyalty of all French Canadians, conveyed such fears to Portland in 1796, reporting that he
had decided "not to call the Legislature together so early as usual, great
hopes being entertained by the promoters of disorder and sedition that
the Assembly may be brought to serve their purposes."[30] In fact, none
of the governors had any difficulty obtaining whatever legislation they
considered necessary for the security of the state. There was no division among the political élite on that point.

Quarrels between certain seigneurs and their *censitaires*, too, could
have been channelled for political ends, particularly where the seigneurs in question were English. In 1794, referring to the case of David
Alexander Grant and the *habitants* of Longueuil, Governor Dorchester
wrote: "This matter is likely to cause much unrest and may lead to
aristocratic and democratic distinctions being made; any such would
weaken the Province and be detrimental to the King's Government;
seditious papers spread through the countryside seem to give hint of
an inclination of this kind among the people."[31] But far from seeking
to mobilize the masses around either nationalism or democracy, the
politicians of the assembly passed the Road Act, imposing *corvées* for
public works on the country people.

The assembly's attitude on these various problems, then, betrays no
tendency among the politicians to divide along anything like party
lines. Indeed, while they were not a homogeneous group, there seems
to have been among them a remarkable community of interest and
thinking, and even of values up to a point. On the French emissaries
and unrest in the populace, they stood firmly together. The circumstances were such that no nationalist or liberal movement could have
arisen directly from the lower classes; the flarings of unrest were
insufficiently sustained to bring forth leadership or ideology, and there
was no real class-consciousness underlying them. If it had been other-

wise the elections of 1796 and 1800 would have radically changed the composition of the assembly (see Table 7).

Though the two elections did bring many new faces to the assembly, the newcomers were socially not very different from their predecessors. Furthermore, the professionals, who made the most inroads—largely at the expense of the merchants—were not yet standing apart from the merchants. It was a combination of internal and external factors that prevented political parties from emerging in this decade. The French revolutionary wars, uneasy relations with the United States, and the activities of the French agents gave rise to fears of an external threat which, the more for being mightily exaggerated, called for concerted efforts to pour oil on troubled social waters. Popular unrest is always seen as a threat to the social order. Whereas a context of social and ideological conflict could have found certain élite elements seeking to make political capital out of both the unrest and concurrent external events, the élite of Lower Canada closed ranks at this time. In this sense the political stability, not to say torpor, was due to local conditions.

The absence of political contention in this period can be attributed to the fact that the middle classes were resting on their laurels. They had got what they wanted in the representative government they had been clamouring for since 1765, namely a share in political power and economic policy-making. They were now well ensconced, both socially and politically. Prosperity in the fur and wheat trades had brought them wealth and prestige. Despite their impatience with an all-too-durable social structure, they were even showing signs of erecting their own aristocracy. They had begun to feel the need of a banking system, but were not inclined to fight for one. The revolution in transportation had yet to affect them; the province was still producing enough wheat for the export market and most of the producing parishes were within easy reach of the St Lawrence or its tributaries; surpluses in Upper Canada were not yet large enough to pose a transportation problem. When the Road Act of 1796 imposed an extension of a seigneurial tradition, the *corvée*, only the peasants objected. The bourgeoisie, though dominated by the English, did not seem to find the seigneurial régime and the Coutume de Paris really so incompatible with the existing economic structure. The opponents of these institutions seem to have been more intellectually than practically motivated. In fact, the half-heartedness of attempts at reform indicated that there was only superficial hostility to and even considerable support in the middle classes for the old social régime. In any event, the achievement of representative government and subsequent developments seem to have cooled their reformist ardour.

For French Canadians, whose outlook was so strongly influenced by absolutist traditions, the introduction of a parliamentary system required a readjustment in thinking. For opponents of the reform, such as the aristocrats, it was particularly difficult. Even those who had been involved in the reform movement before 1791 needed a period of apprenticeship in handling the constitutional and procedural subtleties of the system. Joseph Papineau, father of Louis-Joseph, was a member of the first assembly. "How difficult it was for him," wrote the son, "to undertake this English and parliamentary education, out of devotion to his country, alone and without guidance, and burdened with the traditions of French absolutism."[32] Papineau also reported that William Grant lent books on parliamentary theory and practice to a number of assembly members. For those most keenly aware of the demands of the system, this was also a period of new acquaintance with English writers like John Locke and William Blackstone, and with French admirers of the English constitution, especially Montesquieu and Voltaire. The constitution reflected more the ideas of eighteenth-century philosophers than the political thinking of Bossuet. New concepts and procedures called for new attitudes, which were necessarily slow in developing, for the teachers of future leaders, namely the clergy, with their abhorrence of liberalism and the French Revolution, were more firmly attached than ever to absolute monarchy and its attendant values. The challenge for Louis-Joseph Papineau was hardly less than the one his father had faced.

If the need to adapt was urgently felt by assembly members anxious to participate fully in public life, the ordinary people, both urban and rural, made the transition from subject to citizen and elector with relative ease. One suspects that at the grassroots level the electoral system was seen simply as another outlet for local self-expression. The creation of electoral ridings institutionalized inter-parish and interseigneurial rivalries, which appear to have waxed strong in the first elections, even where there were broader issues at stake (see Table 8). In any event, neither the people nor their political leaders were yet ready to channel popular discontent through to the elected assembly.

The aristocrats were in a different situation. Their presence in the appointive organs of government was a reflection not so much of their political significance as of the ideology of the governors. Though names like de St-Ours, de Belestre, de Longueuil, de Léry, de Boucherville, de la Naudière, and Duchesnay lent grace to the executive and legislative councils, the governors, who were not fools, seem to have been aware that the aristocracy was an increasingly unstable class. The political decline of the class is most apparent in the elected assembly. To win his election in 1792, De Lavaltrie declared to his *censi-*

taires, "Mes chers enfants, for you I will give up my lods et ventes, my droit de retrait, my days of corvée and my rents, and I will give you a deed passed before a notary whenever you want."[33] He was elected, along with nine other aristocrats, probably without having to keep his promise. After the next election in 1796, only de la Naudière and Taschereau were left, and in 1800 only one more. True, in 1805 eleven of the class were elected, but this was the swan song. The aristocrats' declining political fortunes do not imply disenchantment with the seigneurial system, or that the seigneurs as a group were being set aside, since the aristocracy and the seigneurial group were no longer one and the same.

Despite their decadence, the aristocrats clung to their pretentions. Realizing they were losing their position of leadership, they were staunch supporters of the guardians of the established order, those who were most likely to serve and protect their interests. Though they had opposed the introduction of representative government, which in a sense made their *censitaires* their equals, once it was in place they not only ran for election and voted but attempted to use the institution to defend their privileges. In any event, their decline was upsetting the tripartite balance of powers that was considered so essential; some other group would have to move into their place to restore it. The social revolution was thus to have a profound effect on the political system.

The balance of powers was in fact, in this final decade of the century, a precarious one, and the unanimity in the middle classes proved in the longer term to be just as fragile. There were assembly members, representatives of the liberal professions, who began to find appeals to ethnic distinctions electorally expedient. Clearly the new élite could not remain indifferent to the French Canadians' disadvantages in commercial activities. In certain of the English merchants there were already signs, too, of hostility toward attitudes which seemed unsympathetic to their interests and aspirations. The new century brought changes which were to destroy the existing equilibrium.

CHAPTER 2

The Birth of French-Canadian Nationalism, 1802-1812 (Part One)

Indeed it seems to be a favourite object with them to be considered as a separate Nation; La Nation Canadienne is their constant expression....
—Craig to Liverpool (May 1, 1810), Kennedy, DCC, 1918, 260.

The political and social climate in Lower Canada changed radically soon after 1800. Distrust and antagonism became the order of the day. Differences took on a distinctly ethnic flavour. Among members of the assembly, earlier alignments had been predominantly a reflection of differences in social status, but now ethnic origin was increasingly the determinant. Governor Prevost, who had inherited the quarrels of the preceding decade, wrote thus to London in 1814: "The divisions in the House of Assembly have become national in character; on one side the English minority, with whom the official class is allied, on the other the Canadian majority backed by the mass of the people. The heat engendered by this party strife passes from the House of Assembly to its constituents."[1]

When political parties formed in this decade, then, they did so more in response to ethnic than to social realities. The merchants' party, the minority in the assembly, was composed mostly of English merchants, though some were French Canadians, members of the old seigneurial families and professionals with connections in business and government circles. In October, 1809, it had twenty-two members in the assembly, of whom nine were French Canadians.[2] After the election the following month, its representation fell to sixteen, four of them French Canadians.[3] The Canadian party, whose strength was in the professionals and lesser French-Canadian merchants, had twenty-eight members (one English) in the first instance and thirty-four (two

English) in the second. The ethnic division was therefore not total. At all levels of the society there were individuals who held to other imperatives; particularly among the clergy and the old seigneurial families, social standing was still the major consideration. The tendency which was to become more pronounced in later years was nevertheless already unmistakable.

After 1800 change came rapidly in the social structure. Economic upheavals created deep-running instability, leading to a breakdown in relationships among the governing classes. External danger was no longer enough to assure cohesion among the élites. Ideologies and values suffered the consequences of the climate of change, and the old social equilibrium began to lose its appeal. New ways of thinking emerged, but the old were not about to fade and die.

As the separate camps forming in the society moved further apart, quarrels arose at every level. Real issues were inflated by emotional involvement and further exacerbated by the personalities of the political leaders; unquestionably the autocratic Craig and the combative Bédard, to name only two, did much to heighten political and social tensions. All was not due, however, to "tyranny" on the one hand and "demagogy" on the other. The epithets of the day by no means explain a situation which arose from a broad range of interrelated factors.

I The Economic Background

The economic crisis developing after 1802 and strong inflation in 1808 affected all levels of the society. None completely escaped the effects of the decline in the fur trade and the fall-off in wheat production. Then, as wheat production improved again and general price increases accelerated, the lumber trade took a sharp upswing, not only signalling a recovery but changing the pattern of economic development, which proved to be another source of tension. "It is an undeniable fact," wrote a contemporary, "that trade in these provinces has grown as rapidly in two years as it has ever done anywhere in the United States in a similar period, in proportion to the population."[4] The new prominence of lumber, as much as the dislocations in furs and wheat, inevitably created uncertainty and fear in the most traditional sectors of the society. Land speculation was another feature of the changing scene.

A comparison of average annual prices of agricultural products for the decade preceding and that following the turn of the century shows increases ranging between 25 and 69 per cent, depending on the commodity. At Quebec the price of wheat rose from 5.15 to 11.5 *livres tournois* per *minot*, flour from 11 to 28 *livres* per barrel (five *minots* of wheat yield a barrel of flour), while hay, one of the best indicators of structural tensions in agriculture, fluctuated between 30 and 90 *livres* per bale. The rise was not steady from year to year, but was strongest after 1808, due to the international military situation toward the end of the period (see Table 9).

One of the most significant changes of the period was the beginning of the decline of the fur trade, the dominant commercial activity since the seventeenth century, particularly up to 1790. Exports of wheat and other agricultural produce had been rising constantly, and by the end of the eighteenth century were already equalling fur exports in value. From then until 1822, the fur trade was beset with problems and fluctuating conditions. For the people of the St Lawrence Valley the effects were far-reaching, for the fur trade had been more than just another economic activity; its transcontinental ramifications and its dependence on export, particularly to England, provided links with the west and with the mother country; it had been not only a major source of income in the colony and a stimulant to importation, but, wholly or partially for everyone, a way of life.

However, for all the prestige and "superior style" of the merchant adventurers,[5] after 1780 the west progressively lost importance in the eyes of a growing proportion of the population. As agriculture grew more profitable, more of the demographic surpluses gravitated to that sector and less to the fur trade, which was in no position to absorb them in any event. By the beginning of the nineteenth century large segments of the society—specifically the liberal professions, most of the seigneurs, the local merchants, and a large proportion of the rural masses—had ceased to have any contact with the western trade. After 1806, furs were unmistakably secondary in exports. In 1810, lumber (if ship sales are included) accounted for 74.5 per cent of the total value of exports, agricultural products 14.7 per cent, and furs only 9.2 per cent. In the space of a few years, lumber had supplanted furs as the principal staple trade, and the spread continued to widen.

The decline of furs was clearly no mere fluctuation but a sign of a major structural change tied to a new set of economic conditions. Coinciding with a weakening in the European and United States markets, the supply of beaver began to diminish as territorial expansion toward the west reached its limits. Costs increased with the great distances to be covered and erratic movements in the prices of articles used in the trade; and, with the prices received for furs dropping sharply at the same time,[6] profit margins shrank. The upward pressure of costs was compounded at this time by a renewal of competition;

after the formation of the XY Company in 1800, the Indians demanded more for their furs, and so did the merchants' employees for their services. To avert the looming disaster, the North West and XY Companies resolved to merge. The old North West Company, however, having been obliged by the agreement to absorb its rival's employees, found itself saddled with manpower which was quite disproportionate to its needs. Harold Innis describes the company's difficulties thus:

> The decline in furs throughout the Northwest, the growing effectiveness of the Hudson's Bay Company's competition with its reorganized personnel policy and its initial geographic advantage and the inability of the North West Company to adapt its expanding organization to permanent conditions and its consequent demand for new territory led to increased hostility between the two companies. The disappearance of beaver and the increasing cost of transportation, of provisions and supplies were of vital importance....[7]

The most serious competition, then, came from outside. The English Hudson's Bay Company, with its greater efficiency and major advantage of lower transportation costs, steadily gained the upper hand over its Canadian rival. The North West Company, whose strength had lain in energetic territorial expansion, failed to adapt once there was no more new territory left. The Americans, too, were entering the fray in force. The Louisiana Purchase in 1803, Lewis and Clark's expedition up the Missouri River in 1804, and the foundation of the American Fur Company in 1808 and the Pacific Fur Company in 1810 were important steps in their offensive, with Jacob Astor's manoeuvres perhaps the most perilous for the Montreal merchants' monopoly. The decline in profits continued, despite multifarious efforts to reduce expenses. Eventually the North West Company yielded and was absorbed by the Hudson's Bay Company.

And so after the turn of the century the call of the west was heard by a steadily shrinking minority of Lower Canadians. Even supplementary sources of income were sought elsewhere than in the fur trade, and attention tended naturally to turn to the lowlands of the St Lawrence Valley. Lower Canada therefore became, in the eyes of the population, not only a political space but an economic space as well.

But a phenomenon not unlike the decline of the fur trade was under way in the agricultural sector, too. The shrinkage in grain exports by an estimated 40 per cent from the level of the preceding decade (discounting American grain content) was more than a mere temporary downturn due either to aberrant export market conditions or the effects of weather or epidemics on production (see Tables 11 and 12). In it we see the beginning of structural change in an agricultural scene whose essential characteristics had been established during the French Régime. The poor harvest of 1804-5 was the first in a long series of crises punctuating a progressive decline in the cultivation of wheat on the farmlands of Lower Canada. It was not specifically tied to conditions in the export market; indeed, the Napoleonic wars and tension with the United States should have brought Canada a greater role in the mother country's food supply, and there was strong demand as well from the West Indies and the fishing industry. Broadly speaking, wheat price movements during this decade must reflect the failure of local production to meet the strong demand; it is most unlikely that the major drop in wheat export volumes was due to a sudden upsurge in urban consumption at Quebec, and less still at Montreal. The lumber industry began to be significant enough to affect local wheat consumption only in 1806; earlier lumber exports were mostly of American origin. After the poor harvest of 1804-5 there was an improvement, to be sure; flour and wheat exports rose from 22,000 barrels in 1805 to 79,000 in 1808, only to fall back to 18,000 in 1811, but this level was a far cry from the figures of 132,000 and 230,000 in 1801 and 1802. Clearly, there were serious tensions in production which led to the higher prices. The agricultural price index calculated by Professors Wallot and Paquet increased between July, 1807, and July, 1811, from 155.8 to 224.7 for Montreal and from 187.2 to 297.0 for Quebec. The inflation was exacerbated by the activities of speculators, who, while not responsible for the short supply, were not slow to play on it (see Tables 11 and 12).

Pressure from external demand began to be felt by the agricultural system after 1802. In that year local urban demand was incontestably weak. Despite strong demand from the imperial market, rural prices on the whole were weak because wheat production had been so abundant in most parishes; prices were stronger in those parishes where production was falling off, which is to say, where the soil was nearing exhaustion from long cultivation. In subsequent years average crop yields slackened despite generally strong demand, with the result that prices rose rapidly in rural areas, particularly in the major wheat-producing parishes. With pressures felt increasingly in local production, the spread between urban and rural prices tended to disappear, the rural often touching even slightly higher levels than the urban (see Table 9). After the poor harvest of 1804-5 there were others less disastrous, but the situation never returned to a healthy state. The yields of farmers producing surpluses grew smaller, many were producing short crops (see Table 10), and some even gave up growing wheat.

The excess of demand over supply became more or less chronic, pushing prices and the cost of living constantly higher. Seigneurs, curés, merchants, not to mention speculators, fared considerably better than the average urban consumer or rural family man.

In this period Upper Canada was not yet a serious competitor in the wheat market, since its agriculture was still in transition from the pioneer stage; transportation costs were high so that in order to export profitably Upper-Canadian producers were obliged to mill their wheat into flour (see Table 86). The fur-trading posts were still their principal market. But languishing production in Lower Canada was to prove a stimulant to the upper province. More immediately, the decline awakened new interest on the part of the Montreal merchants in Upper Canada's development and its potential as a market for imports, in improvements in the waterway of the St Lawrence, and in construction of flour mills up-river.

With wheat production flagging in Lower Canada, marriage and birth rates dropped slightly but the growth in the French-Canadian population was still very vigorous. Immigration from the United States, while not massive, was beginning to have sufficient proportions to alarm the French-Canadian élite; wheat, wrote a contemporary in 1807, "cannot provide sufficient employment for the new generation, which is large."[8] The seigneuries as a whole were not yet really overpopulated, but there were steadily increasing signs of overcrowding in a growing number of them, particularly those favoured with rich soil and advantageous location. A situation combining fixed seigneurial limits, backward agricultural techniques, and demographic pressures generated new resentment on the part of the French Canadians toward the immigrants.

In short, the conditions which had brought high agricultural yields and overall production, namely the possibility of expansion to new and richer land, were disappearing; not only was the supply of undeveloped seigneurial land running out, but the seigneurs, for a variety of reasons, were distributing what there was of it to the *habitants* with less liberality. In the circumstances the absence of innovation in farming techniques becomes highly significant. The margin of shortfall between wheat production and population growth in any event was widening constantly. Behind unsuccessful attempts to stimulate the growing of hemp, from which a new staple trade might emerge, we see an awareness of approaching agricultural crisis. Increased potato production, modest though it was, furthermore suggests a search for a subsistence-level solution.

Thus there began a long process of disintegration in the traditional agriculture centred on wheat as both a subsistence and an export commodity. The notion of subsistence as the prime agricultural objective by no means disappeared. On the contrary, with the relationship between the farmer and the imperial market breaking down, agriculture tended increasingly to turn inward. In the minds of the French-Canadian lower classes and élite as well, economic space came to be identified with Lower Canada, more specifically the territory within seigneurial limits.

Though the expansion in lumber provided the new staple trade so urgently sought, it did not immediately enlarge the economic space, for though the industry was dependent on the imperial market, the resources of Lower Canada long remained its major source of supply. The lower province therefore came to be regarded by the majority of its people not only as a political unit or even a cultural space, but as an economic reality as well. This development provided a framework for French-Canadian nationalism, helped to awaken opposition to the colonial system, and motivated resistance to the union of the Canadas.

In the eighteenth century, England had already taken some steps to stimulate colonial forestry operations. Before 1774 there were certain tariffs intended to encourage the production of barrel staves. In 1795, parliament imposed a preferential tariff of 10 shillings per load on Baltic timber, which was quite inadequate in view of rising prices and transportation costs; the immense forests of the English colonies remained practically untouched. With the advent of the nineteenth century, however, the circumstances changed radically. The breach of the Peace of Amiens led England to realize the inadequacy of her sources of supply, particularly for her shipyards on which her navy depended. With depletion of her own forests and burgeoning domestic consumption, she had become entirely dependent on importation, and now Napoleon's continental blockade was threatening to cut off her established sources. In 1805 the preferential tariff was raised to 25 shillings, and then timber dealers began to invest large sums in New Brunswick and Lower Canada. The result is revealed in English import statistics. Expressed as a percentage of imports from the Baltic, lumber from the North American colonies was only 1.2 per cent in the period 1793-1802, but 7 per cent in 1803-7, and 169 per cent in 1808-12. The progression is explained in part by re-adjustments of the tariff to compensate for rising transportation costs. Thus in 1809-10 it was raised to 34s.8p. per load. With inflation and hazardous conditions on the high seas, however, this too was soon inadequate, and after 1810 there was a serious recession in lumber. In 1814 a further tariff increase to 65s. per load opened the way to vigorous post-war expansion in lumber for Lower Canada (see Table 19).

The new industry was relatively independent of the declining fur and wheat trades. Lumber camps provided an important market for Lower-Canadian agricultural products, but they were not dependent on them, for there were other sources of supply nearby. It was demand from the British and West Indian markets that conditioned the industry's growth. Its impact on the colonial economy[9] was vital in the circumstances of the day (see Tables 18 and 20).

The traffic in the port of Quebec was revolutionized by the large numbers of ships arriving to take on cargoes of lumber. The high percentage arriving in ballast, furthermore, was later to be an inducement to massive transportation of British immigrants. British shipowners were not the only beneficiaries; in the region of Quebec the lumber trade was soon the principal source of commercial profit, both strengthening the position of local businessmen and attracting investment from England. In 1810, the English timber dealer Idle sent William Price to take charge of his branch in Quebec. With the experience he gained in that capacity, Price built a prodigious empire in the forest industry; by 1850 he owned some fifty sawmills.[10]

Lumber thus became Lower Canada's principal commercial activity, until 1825 almost the only dynamic element in the economic structure. Since part of the wealth it generated found its way into the hands of the population in general, it was also a major stimulant to local consumption.

Squared timber was not universally beneficial, since it came largely from a single region, the Ottawa Valley, and required little processing. Nevertheless, cutting and transportation to Quebec required the mobilization of large numbers of workmen, mostly lumberjacks, log drivers, and stevedores, who were recruited in both the cities and country districts. The lumber camps created a need for leather and pork and other agricultural products, and thus for further transportation.

Shipbuilding at Quebec took an upturn, doubling in tonnage in the first decade of the century. Local demand for squared timber, planks, and deals was therefore swelled, and there was employment for a growing contingent of shipwrights and labourers from the cities and nearby country districts.

While squared timber was the major product it was not the only significant one, as some have maintained. Processed lumber was also produced, and the market for it, locally, and in Great Britain and the West Indies, was considerable. Sawmills were built where supply was plentiful and easily accessible, many in the Ottawa Valley but more around Quebec, and it was there that the biggest sawmills in the province were located. Soon there was a sawmill in every parish that could claim a favourable location. This subsidiary industry came to play an important economic and social role. There was also an export and local market for staves, which could be produced as a supplementary source of income by any *habitant* with timber on his land. Potash was also in demand, and was a major contributor to the prosperity of the industry; in 1810, more than 30,000 barrels were exported. In this period there were still considerable quantities of forest products imported from the United States, but these diminished as the industry became established in Lower Canada.

In 1810, 661 ships and 6,600 sailors were plying the Atlantic at the service of the industry. While the lion's share of the wealth it generated remained in the hands of the English, both old-country and colonial, everyone benefited.

Its revenues were largely responsible for the importation of exotic commodities (tea, coffee, sugar, and molasses), foodstuffs (beef, pork, butter, cheese, tallow, and lard), spirits, leather, and wool and other textiles into both Upper and Lower Canada. It was around 1810 that tea began to be a common item of consumption among the lower classes. During the period 1808 to 1850, the fortunes of the lumber industry were increasingly reflected in import fluctuations.

In the period 1802-12, however, sudden acceleration in the pace of change, inflation, and speculation created a climate of instability in the society, and rumblings of unrest began to be heard. The French-Canadian middle classes began to interpret the economic supremacy of the English-speaking as a product of discrimination. Ethnic distinction acquired a new and significant dimension. Conflict in the society now had a distinctly ethnic flavour.

II A Society in Ferment

With economic change, the status of the social classes, too, began to undergo change and re-examination, and ideologies evolved. The old social structure was in jeopardy. Its traditional foundations remained, in particular the seigneurial régime and the Coutume de Paris, and also a broad base of traditional mentality, but certain strata of the society no longer recognized its validity. Besides the merchant bourgeoisie, whose innovative influence had long been felt, there were now new groups with new views on the organization of society and its underlying values. Battle lines were drawn between the traditional and the new élites, each with its conception of society in terms of its own beliefs and interests. The credo of the Old Régime, espoused more doggedly than ever by the clergy, still had adherents at all social levels besides the derelict old seigneurial families. Among the clergy, the merchant bourgeoisie, and the French-Canadian middle classes a

struggle began, sometimes under cover, sometimes in the open, sometimes in partial or temporary alliance, with control of the society as the
goal. And while the struggle was social in its dimensions and objectives, its ethnic overtones were strong. For the liberal professions,
whose popular support was already considerable, it translated frankly
into a battle over precedence of the ethnic over the social, or so they
maintained.[11] Developments indeed began to unfold as though henceforth there were two hermetic social structures without interaction of
any kind, one English- and the other French-speaking, each seeking to
impose its primacy by political means. In fact, there were many levels
of interaction—economic and social as well as political. But the nationalist ideology proclaiming the precedence of ethnic values over all
others was now held by a class which was in a position to sow it in
other levels of society.

The merchant bourgeoisie was overwhelmingly dominated by the
English-speaking, the proprietors of most of the business ventures of
any consequence, and most strikingly in the new sectors of lumber and
shipbuilding. The English also owned almost all the conceded land in
the Eastern Townships and about a third of all seigneurial land which, at
the turn of the century, they shared in roughly equal thirds with the
French-Canadian clergy and laity. Between 1802 and 1812 they acquired some sixty townships and twenty seigneuries. Nor were they
absent in retail trade, which the French Canadians were anxious to have
to themselves. They were indisputably the economic leaders. Among
the directors of the Board of Trade founded in 1809 to serve the business community, not a single name appears which could be read as
French-Canadian.[12] While it is true that the system of patronage favoured the English-speaking and often far from justifiably, the socio-
economic disparities between the ethnic groups can by no means be laid
solely to benefits conferred by patronage; the economic inferiority of
the French Canadians cannot be interpreted first and foremost in terms
of discrimination. What is important is that the French-Canadian professional bourgeoisie now saw it in those terms. Having become keenly
aware of the disparities, they concluded that their cause lay in the unde-
served political privileges enjoyed by the English-speaking.

The English bourgeoisie itself was undergoing a change in numbers
and composition.[13] The old-style merchant-adventurers were fading
away and being replaced by new men who were far less tolerant in
their attitudes to the old social régime. Undoubtedly the decline of
the fur trade, the rise of the lumber trade and shipbuilding, and the
settlement of Upper Canada had much to do with their impatience,
but economic instability and their own tribulations must have contributed, too. The newcomers from the British Isles and the United

States had left countries where a certain progress had already been achieved, where above all there was no "feudalism." They were very different from the immigrants of the eighteenth century. In their modern world, banking institutions, roads and other communications, and the reform or abolition of the seigneurial régime and the Coutume de Paris were necessities that were long overdue. They had a different conception, too, of the role of the state in economic development and institutional reform. Their judgment of French-Canadian society was harsh, for they saw its aspirations as obstructing progress and institutional reform.

The new merchant bourgeoisie of the nineteenth century, then, became demanding and aggressive, like the old generation which had fought for representative government. Structural upheaval in the economy and the violence of its fluctuations were a source of insecurity. The only dynamic economic sector after 1806, the lumber trade, was disquietingly dependent on the military situation and imperial legislation, and the merchant class were fearful that Great Britain would revert to its traditional colonial policies with the return of peace. They had economic power but they did not have sufficient political power to assure adoption of the policies which they considered essential. Their proposals for reform and the development of Upper Canada, they felt, were dependent on the whims of the French-Canadian majority in the assembly. With the entrenchment of fundamental disagreements between themselves and the French-Canadian professionals, they saw their economic and political power threatened.

The threat was related to economic conditions, but more acutely to new social and political factors. The clergy, though they did not share the English merchants' economic and social values, were not the only or even the principal adversaries; long experience (since the beginning of the French Régime) had taught them to be content with the lesser of evils. With the old seigneurial families, too, the relationship was a mixture of agreement and disagreement. But between the English merchants and the French-Canadian professionals there developed the most profound and undisguised antagonism, for the latter were challenging the leadership of the former, on both social and ethnic grounds. The merchants, the French-Canadian professionals maintained, were dominated by their desire to "create a mercantile aristocracy, the most abominable, the most pernicious of all orders, equally prejudicial to the authority of the Crown, to the interests of landowners and to the liberties of the people."[14] The English bourgeoisie was shocked by the criticism, whose tenor was one of justification for the rise of a new social power group. They were even more shocked to perceive the French-Canadian professionals using the parliamentary system and lower-class support to constitute a formation of such awesome political power that they began to fear the collapse of their own power. Their programme of economic and institutional renewal was imperilled. The belligerence of their response, as exemplified in articles published by the *Quebec Mercury*, reflected the insecurity of the English minority. The paper's attacks on the Frenchness of the province, jibes at the military degeneracy of French Canadians, and taunts about their indifference to progress were calculated to play on the prejudices of the English-speaking and unleashed bitter reactions from the French-speaking.

For most businessmen, it is true, ethnic distinctions came second to their economic interests, but the same could not be said for all segments of the English minority composed of merchants, professionals, and civil servants. The professionals of British origin enjoyed a richer clientèle and lived closer to the business community than their French-speaking counterparts, but were resentful of their competition both professionally and in the jostling for administrative posts. The civil servants were alarmed by the rise of the French-Canadian professionals in the assembly and their aspirations to power and patronage. The notion of ministerial responsibility dangled by Bédard and his admirers was particularly distasteful to them because it challenged their hold on administrative appointments. In the previous decade, seeing the possibility of greater French-Canadian participation in administration, a small coterie of functionaries had decided that the civil service should be the private preserve of the English, and seemed bent on assuring that it should remain so. It is true that the number of French Canadians equipped to fill administrative posts was still small, but there were influential figures who played far too loudly on that chord. In any event, it looked as though French Canadians were being systematically blocked from the higher echelons of the civil service at a time when they had become most eager to accede to them. These jealousies were soon aggravated by the intrusion of partisan politics as a criterion for the distribution of patronage. Milnes observed in 1802, "The mixture of Canadians and English in this colony gives rise to jealousies which can only be avoided by the established hospitality and impartiality of the Governor towards both...."[15] The railing and talk of assimilation and "unfrenchifying" in the *Quebec Mercury* look suspiciously like the work of the so-called "Château Clique," the little band of which Herman Ryland was an extreme example.[16]

It is apparent that the English minority had begun to see the precariousness of their position in a colony where they were overwhelmingly outnumbered. But the solidarity among them was not without cracks. If there was or appeared to be unanimity in the pursuit of their economic and social goals and the preservation of their political power, they were divided when it came to religion. Most were Protestant but many were not Anglican, though an Anglican bishopric had been created for Quebec in 1793 and the Church of England was ostensibly the established church.

To Bishop Jacob Mountain's exasperation, the "dissident" Protestants remained aloof, and it was the Catholic Church, by virtue of its greater power, prestige, and financial resources, which, *de facto*, played the role of established church. "Compared to the respectable Establishments, the substantial Revenues, and the intensive power and privileges of the Church of Rome, the Church of England sinks into a merely tolerated Sect," complained Mountain to Milnes in 1803. Effective and dignified organization of the Church of England, he maintained, "would go near to unite the whole body of Dissenters within its pale. Upon such a *union* I need make no comment; of its religious benefits (great as they must be) I say nothing. Its political advantages, in times like these, would be incalculable." But the government, he suspected, was preparing to recognize, not only in practice but in right, two established churches. "To authorize the Establishment of two Bishops of the same Diocese, of different religious persuasions, would be a solecism in Ecclesiastical Polity, which I believe never took place in the Christian world; to attempt the *union of different Churches* within the *State* would be, I hardly conceive, an experiment in the science of Government not less dangerous than novel."[17]

He called on the British government to proclaim the supremacy in right and in fact of the Church of England, hoping, by rallying the Protestant dissidents to the Anglican banner, to strengthen the unity of the minority. He demanded that the status of the Catholic Church be redefined in terms of a strict definition of English juridical traditions. The king's representatives, who feared the power of the Catholic clergy and were looking for ways to undermine it, turned an attentive ear. The ideas made headway during Milnes' tenure, and received wholehearted endorsement from Craig, who was strongly influenced by Ryland and Mountain. Yet to the authorities in London in those troubled years, the Catholic Church still looked like the province's staunchest defender of the established order, and the Anglican bishop was to be disappointed. He was also disappointed by the English minority, who were not disposed to support a church so transparently hungry for privileges. In the following decade the authority and aspirations of the Church of England were to be contested not only by French-Canadian Catholics but also by the "dissenting" Protestants, in different ways seeking a division of privileges or their removal altogether.

The socio-economic malaise felt by the English minority was aggravated by the wars with France and by strained relations with the United States. Loyalty became a preoccupation of major proportions, and a political issue. The governors, in their anxiety to combat the external peril and restore harmony in the society, sought support in those social sectors considered dependable. On occasion, singular lack of judgment was displayed, the most glaring being Governor Sir James Craig's over the loyalty of the French Canadians.

The French-Canadian majority, too, was uneasy, far from confident in the future, and for reasons aplenty. The traditional social equilibrium was undergoing a major change in the substitution of a new élite for an old. This internal development, along with fresh currents of thought blowing from the French Revolution, was preparing the way for a new alignment of forces. Throughout the eighteenth century, despite the rise of the bourgeoisie, the clergy and the lay seigneurs, particularly the old seigneurial families, the "gentry" or aristocracy, had maintained their position as leaders of the society; both groups held and diffused the same values. By the end of the eighteenth century they were sharing their leadership with the bourgeoisie, more or less in harmony. Soon after the turn of the century, however, the old equilibrium was no more. With the accelerated decline of the old families the authority of the gentry melted away, leaving a vacuum. The seigneurial régime survived, because many purchasers of seigneuries, particularly the French Canadians, came to its defence against more modern notions of land tenure. But the aristocracy was no longer a force to be reckoned with. In 1807 Bishop Plessis wrote sorrowfully, "The Canadians who enjoy a certain esteem in the Province most often owe their place only to protection paid for dearly, and often at the price of flattery or shameful dissimulation of their principles, for fear of offending or displeasing those who rule over them. The [earthly] hopes of the century concern them more than the interests of God; they fawn upon the powerful without reflecting that the powerful profit by it to hold them in humiliating servitude...."[18]

The clergy was then obliged to reconsider its alliances. Bishop Plessis, who was the principal architect of clerical strategy, examined the possibilities. Of the liberal professions, who seemed less conscious of the old hierarchies and less respectful of traditional values than he considered proper, he wrote: "After them [the gentry] come the advocates and notaries and members of the House of Assembly. The firmness of our principles regarding lending at interest places us in opposition to the first of these; with the consequence that there are very few advocates who frequent the sacraments and many denounce the clergy as holding to a doctrine injurious to commerce and the public interest...." The prelate's distrust of the rising class in fact went further than disapproval of lending at interest; the aspirations of the class as such were suspect. Haunted by the spectre of revolution since 1789, the clergy had the impression that an entire segment of the society had espoused liberal ideas and was using them to upset the social order and undermine religious values. As for the rest of the French-Canadian laity—élite or lower-class, rural or urban—though he regarded them as "true Christians," Plessis saw little hope of effective support from them; they were too timid and ignorant. In short, he wrote, "the clergy of Canada have nothing to hope for from the lay Catholics, in their interests in general or in the interests of religion."[19] Like the merchants and the civil servants, the ecclesiastics were feeling the effects of the insecurity and hostility reigning in the province and elsewhere.

Seeing the intrusion of liberal ideas in Lower Canada, the clergy reacted as though the French Revolution itself were at the colony's gates. In Monseigneur Plessis's sermons, that "frightful tempest," that "horrible fracas,"[20] that despotic, bloody, parricidal, and sacrilegious revolution symbolized evil in all its forms:

... France as we once knew her [was] beloved of her children, fearsome to her enemies, devoted to her religion.... But since God in His mercy has placed us under another Empire, O Heaven! What disastrous changes that unfortunate realm has undergone! The enemy of salvation, jealous apparently to see the rule of God so firmly established, came under shadow of night, I mean with the sinister stratagems of a deceitful philosophy, and covered the length and breadth of that rich and fertile land with the dangerous seed of heresy, impious works, incendiary books. The seed has germinated; impiety and licentiousness have taken root; hearts and minds have fallen prey to the beguiling attractions of a religion without dogma, a morality without precept. The seductive expressions of liberty, philanthropy, fraternity, equality, and tolerance have been eagerly seized and repeated by every mouth. The sovereign authority of the Prince has been called tyranny; religion, fanaticism; its consecrated practices, superstition; its ministers, imposters; God Himself, an illusion! When once those barriers are down, what will become of Man, my brothers? Left alone with his depraved reason, is there any misdoing of which he is incapable?[21]

Despite his Concordat of 1801 with the pope, Napoleon was still the child of the Revolution in the bishop's mind, for he had given sanction to the works of misguided men mesmerized by liberal thinking.

> Thus the ravages of impiety are the first lesson brought to us by the past twenty-six years. The depravity of ambition is the second.... Sacrilegious ambition, which with one and the same hand we have seen re-establish the Jews against the order of Heaven, exile the bishops of Italy, disperse the members of the Sacred College, strip the Sovereign Pontiff of his estates, furtively remove him from his See, and drag him into captivity which for five years deprived him of all communication with the Catholic Church outside....[22]

Together with the horror inspired by revolutionary France, needless to say, went an equally extreme idealization of the France of the Old Régime. But contemporary England was also idealized. Plessis was convinced, or perhaps convinced himself, that the French constitution of 1792, "as illegal and bizarre in its form as montrous in its principles,"[23] had nothing in common with the English constitution, though that was what it was modelled after. What was essential for him was that England, by opposing revolutionary France, appeared in Canada and in the eyes of the world as the defender of the old politico-religious conceptions, especially monarchy by divine right, the privileges of state-allied churches, and aristocratic heritage. He was less interested in the reality of England than in the forces of evil England opposed, namely republicanism, the source of all ills. "Of all the sophistries indulged in this last while, to entice and mislead nations and dispose them to revolt," he declared, "this is perhaps the most vicious, as also the most false and most absurd, I mean the system of sovereignty of the people."[24] His attitude to representative government in Lower Canada and his interventions in the quarrels between the government and the new political élite begin to be understandable.

It was in the light of the philosophy of Bossuet that Monseigneur Plessis persisted in seeing the parliamentary institutions of Lower Canada. That was the teaching at the Seminary of Quebec. Though the clergy could hardly pronounce themselves openly in favour of abolition of the legislative assembly, lest they offend believers in British institutions, the approved line implied a negation of the principles underlying the parliamentary system; clerical criticism of the assembly betrayed distinct apathy for it. Plessis, it must be remembered, was a man of the Old Régime, who thought in terms of orders, namely the clergy, the aristocracy, and the third estate, with a monarch chosen by God presiding over all. The kings of France had only summoned the estates general occasionally; the kings of England permitted the third estate to elect representatives periodically, but their function was solely to express an opinion to the sovereign. The legislative assembly therefore had no share in sovereignty. Where Canadian politicians had erred, in his thinking, was in having transformed the assembly into an instrument of social and "national" assertion, and worse, a vehicle for revolutionary ideas and the tool of a revolutionary class.

The constitution of 1791, as used by the French-Canadian professionals, he therefore saw at the root of Lower Canada's political and social disharmony. Before the constitution, he wrote, "the faithful were more docile and still sheltered from the frightful advance, upon their minds, of the principles of liberty and democracy propagated by our new constitution and by the noxious example of the French Revolution...."[25] Those whom God had placed in authority were to be obeyed without question or discussion: "[Your] religion demands that you recognize that it is God who disposes crowns, who presides over empires, joins them and divides them as He chooses and places at their head those whom He chooses to place there."[26] Little wonder that he condemned the behaviour of French-Canadian politicians, that he considered French Canadians incapable of putting the new constitution to the service of the society.[27] Little wonder, too, that the curé of Laprairie, sharing his ideology, branded the Canadian party as revolutionary.[28]

In the bishop's mind, the insubordination reigning in the province contained an element of the naturally alluring influence of "evil" on humans and "the weakness of man given over to his inclinations," but its principal cause was the influence exercised over the people by the new political élite.

The support afforded to Governor Craig by the Catholic bishop and clergy, then, was prompted above all by their fear of seeing the old social edifice collapse. In 1809 Plessis wrote, "*Le Canadien* has risen from its ashes, through a new and ample subscription. You cannot imagine the ravages caused by this contemptible paper. It is going to destroy all principles of subordination and set the Province afire."[29] Evidently, he felt there was a movement of revolutionary character afoot in Lower Canada, which called for a reinforcement of the relationship between the Catholic Church and the state. "It is clear," he wrote, "that the spirit of democracy has wrought havoc among us; I am in despair of it and all the more that this spirit has come to light at a time when the interest of religion calls for a conduct quite contrary."[30] In the circumstances of the day—war with France, tension with the United States, internal conflict—the Catholic Church, argued the bishop, was the only one capable of playing the role of state church.

Plessis was not blind to the determination of the king's representatives, who were strongly influenced by Mountain, Ryland, and Sewell, to bring the Catholic Church to heel. In 1807 he noted the formation of a "cabal" whose aim was to "destroy the authority of the Catholic Bishop in Canada, seize control of public education, and appoint curés; these, unless I am mistaken, are the three objectives of our adversaries. . . ." The ultimate objective, he felt, was to dress his church in Anglican garb; "calculations by which my Church would soon be made an Anglican church . . . ."[31] But he had confidence in the good faith and good sense of the authorities in London. His church was not in a state of servitude, he considered; it obtained its status and dignity from its union with the state. Bishop Mountain's plans, whether or not they were supported in official circles in Lower Canada, seem to have had no effect on Bishop Plessis' policies, unless it was to strengthen his resolve to demonstrate their worth to the established authority. Not even in the moments of greatest tension did he feel it necessary to seek assistance from the liberal professions, who would immediately have brought the religious question into the political arena and appealed to the people. The struggle between the two bishops in fact involved only themselves.

In the crisis of 1810, Plessis read the governor's proclamation from the pulpit and went on to deliver a violent political sermon. He called on his curés to do likewise and furthermore to campaign openly in the election in favour of candidates supported by the government. This was a time, it should be noted, when any sign of defection would have boded ill for the outcome of discussions between church and state regarding their relationships. The fervour of church intervention in the elections, which went far beyond anything the governor could have wished, and the clergy's redoubled vigilance over their flocks were part of the campaign to demonstrate unswerving loyalty to the government in place and outdo the Anglican Church into the bargain. When the election was over, one of the curés wrote to his bishop, "Unfortunately the neighbouring parishes, in greater number, brought my people to their way of thinking and they unanimously elected the two Messrs Bédard, whom I would better have seen set aside. I have not let pass the opportunity to tell my people since the election that they must not expect to be complimented on their choice."[32]

Plessis was pained by the legal uncertainties of his church's position and by his own formal designation only as "Superintendent of the Roman Churches," but, spurred by his rivalry with the Anglican bishop, he continued to argue that close collaboration between church and state was the only effective way of governing a people and protecting the interests of all: "the Catholic religion is, of all the world's religions, the most apt to create faithful subjects because it is the only one which renders them so through principles of conscience...."[33] On the strength of this conviction he had no hesitation in asking the government to increase his salary, urging the mutual benefits of his presence on the legislative and executive councils.[34]

In 1819 he expounded his political philosophy to Lord Bathurst: "I persist in believing, Milord, that in fostering the Catholic religion in H.M. Provinces in North America your Lordship is working effectively for the support of the government of H.M. and that our altars protect the throne as the Throne protects them. If there are few persons truly convinced of this reciprocal benefit, it is because it is given to few persons to perceive things on as grand a scale as your Lordship perceives them...."[35]

But a closer relationship between church and state must not undermine church independence. Plessis's vision of a state-allied church was in the best Gallican tradition, and he rejected Sewell's identification of Gallicanism with Anglicanism. Particularly offensive was the proposed nomination of curés by the governor, for it would weaken the bishop's authority over the parish clergy, interfere with the clergy's freedom in religious matters, and discredit them politically, making the church, in short, a mere creature of the state. A Catholic Church that was strong, influential, and faithful to its traditions, free in its movements yet dependent on the state, he maintained, would be an incomparable instrument of social and political stability and an obstacle to the rise of troublesome elements in the society.

When the electorate rejected most of the candidates opposed to the Canadian party in the 1810 elections, Craig and Plessis suffered a defeat. And the curé of Laprairie wrote thus to his bishop: "But, Monseigneur, after the commotion the clergy had made, we must expect only unyielding hatred from the revolutionary party.... We hope that your prestige will bring us the protection of the Government and His Excellency the Governor General."[36] Plessis, however, won his case with the government in London.

There is no question that by their thinking and attitudes, and by the manner in which they sought to establish their position in society, the "revolutionary party," the new French-Canadian political élite, gave credibility to the fears they aroused. To accusations of disloyalty, however, they reacted with indignation:

Is it not astonishing that in the critical circumstances in which we find ourselves at present, on the eve of war and so to speak in plain view of the enemy, is it not astonishing, I say, that there have been raised unconscionably the most ill-founded fears and the most insulting suspicions regarding the loyalty of Canadians; that, despite the many and recent evidences of their loyalty, their unequivocal declarations of constant and unshakable devotion to the British Constitution are doubted; that these fears are laid to those worthy Canadians whose past service and the confidence of the people have placed at the head of our militia groups.[37]

The new prominence of this group was a product of a number of factors. Around 1790, professions had been ill-defined. Joseph Papineau, for example, was both notary and surveyor. Physicians were still few and far between; healers with magic and other obscure powers abounded. Many parish curés served as notaries and all of them dabbled in more or less medical practices. But with economic development and occupational diversification the society's needs changed and the liberal professions emerged within the middle classes, alongside and at first overshadowed by the merchants. The exercise of multiple professions was soon to be forbidden.

The French-Canadian professionals, even those born and raised in the cities, even the sons of craftsmen, professionals, or merchants, were deeply imbued with the values of their overwhelmingly rural society; with perplexing facility, peasant atavism seems to have suffused the entire class. Nevertheless, they were not impervious to the enticing if rather frightening values of the English merchant bourgeoisie, or to those of aristocratic tradition. They were, perhaps, torn between different value systems and attracted by a multiplicity of allegiances.[38]

They had all been educated at the Seminary of Quebec or the Seminary of Montreal, or later at the classical colleges created on the pattern of the seminaries. All these institutions, the principal stepping stones to social betterment, existed primarily for the training of future priests, a major preoccupation for the church, and all sought to instill the principles of authority and obedience. The regulations of the College of Sainte-Anne-de-la-Pocatière, for instance, reveal clearly that the pupils were to be isolated from the world in order to remove them from its influence, and that their moral and intellectual life was to be controlled and religion implanted as the dominant force in their existence.[39]

The programme of studies was faithful to the ancient scholastic tradition, and was based heavily on Latin. For entry at the lowest level at the Quebec Seminary in 1790, a pupil had to "be able to read in French and Latin and also to write...."[40] The first six years were spent doing French and Latin translations and memorizing them along with the Gospels. The introduction of a textbook written in French by

Charles Rollin, a severely Jansenist French educator of the early eighteenth century, was an innovation signalling the decline of Latin, but hardly a revolution, for Rollin's conception of teaching was one of authority, with eyes turned toward a glorious past. "The personalities of the pupils were never involved; their participation was entirely passive, their effort entirely directed toward imitation; in their minds, their hearts, their spirits, there were to be only those traditional values the master would place there...."[41] The philosophy was in the scholastic tradition of syllogistic rigour. The French masters studied, however, were acquainted with Cartesianism and even John Locke.[42] Even the philosophers of the eighteenth century were touched upon, usually for additional support of certain points in traditional philosophy. The Encyclopaedists, generally made the villains directly or indirectly in this system of teaching, were in fact more present in the minds of both masters and pupils than the content of their textbooks would indicate. With the intrusion of theocratic and ultramontane influences, Gallicanism declined, though not for the Sulpicians of Montreal. Geography was introduced at the Quebec Seminary in 1790, history after 1800, and also mathematics and physics as disciplines distinct from philosophy, which is to say, theology. Yet such innovations by no means meant a change toward progressive or more liberal leanings.[43] In fact, reactionary tendencies gained strength.

In 1804, the year in which Papineau completed his studies, more than half the graduates of the Seminary of Quebec were destined for the priesthood; most of the others joined the liberal professions and one only entered the world of commerce. The classical colleges served for social advancement; a smaller proportion of graduates became priests and others returned to the land, entered the liberal professions or commerce, or became school teachers.[44] The clergy emerging from the classical colleges were certainly closer to the people than were their predecessors of the eighteenth century, in that they resembled the professionals, but their mentality was still very much of the Old Régime, predisposed toward established order and against novelty.

The seminary or classical college experience left a profound mark, even on those who turned to the liberal professions. With few exceptions, individuals would begin to question and re-evaluate only on confronting the world, having left those austere halls and the straight, sure path trodden by all within. Many never did even then. The influences encountered by a young professional serving a clerkship in law, medicine, or surveying often clashed harshly with the ideas advanced by their classical masters. Future lawyers and notaries found themselves probing the writings of the theorists of natural law; the more enquiring discovered philosophers whose thinking was far more alive than the decadent scholastic theses they were accustomed to. In a country with representative government, it was more normal to read Montesquieu and John Locke and even Voltaire than Bossuet. One can easily imagine such readings giving birth to doubts and new convictions, too, without going so far as to attribute the widespread religious disaffection of the period, as does Canon Lionel Groulx, to "keeping company with bad books."

The young professional of the early nineteenth century displayed far more impatience than his predecessors. Leadership by the existing élite, the clergy, the aristocracy, the seigneurs, and the merchants was a fact he would no longer accept without question. He readily lent his support to a movement which looked to be on the way to placing his own class among and perhaps at the forefront of the leaders. Toussaint Pothier later wrote that the professionals built their strength on the ruins of the old families. They certainly outstripped the aristocracy in being closer to the people and more alive to their feelings if not to their interests. Though many may have aspired to supplant the aristocracy only in power, they nevertheless harboured a class-consciousness.

Their relationship with the clergy was more subtle, for the clergy's power was real. They were more anti-clerical than anti-religious. The professional, urban or rural, was irritated by socio-political thinking which opposed the aspirations of his class. Politics for him was the road to social betterment, and therein lay the deepest source of conflict with the clergy, who were not permitted to run for election and saw their ideological leadership threatened by political activity.

The English merchant bourgeoisie and the bureaucracy, the one having economic control and the other political, were clearly the principal obstacles to realization of the French-Canadian professionals' ambitions. Class-consciousness therefore emerged not so much in opposition to the clergy and the aristocracy as in ethnic identification. The inferior economic position of the French Canadians, seen as the fruit of English usurpation of political power, lent justification to the professionals' aspirations as a leading social class and nationalist élite capable of contesting the economic and political power of the English.

In the context, the fur trade, the target of bitter attacks, was seen not only as "an obstacle to the progress of agriculture,"[45] but the major source of corruption for the voyageurs, Indians, and merchants involved in it. The principal victims of the English-speaking merchants' "thirst for gold" were Indians and the rural French Canadians: "a new, necessarily agricultural people must not be led to habits and moral conduct tending to destroy the very roots of all social order.... For if landed property is the basis of civilization, even an ancient people soon becomes vagrant and uncivilized if, losing through commerce or other-

wise its moral thinking, and despising the laws of good order, it aban-
dons the tilling of fields to roam the forests." [46] Condemnation of the
fur trade led to condemnation of commerce in general, which is to say,
capitalism; "... all these circumstances, brought together and examined, prove incontestably that Canada can never achieve a great measure of prosperity through commerce, and that its natural leaning is to
agriculture, which, of all conditions, is the least precarious; ... it can
readily be concluded that commerce in no way profits Canada as certain would have it believed, that only a small number of individuals
make fortunes from it, and that most of the inhabitants, particularly in
the cities, have only an illusory appearance of wealth." [47]

Singled out for particularly harsh reproach were the English merchants of the North West Company, to whom the professionals attributed the French Canadians' loss of standing in the fur trade: "This
body, as you have observed, has made itself famous gathering all to
itself, but less through an immense capital than through its credit and
machinations. It has too assiduously sought to stifle emulation, to
smother the rivalry which is its source, to crush all those who have
dared to aspire to the same career." [48]

The English dominated the newer economic activities, too, and
were just as vigorous as the French in establishing themselves in the
liberal professions. A menace to the very survival of the entire
French-Canadian society loomed in the image of an arrogant English
bourgeoisie which thought of the development of the country in
terms of capitalist economic expansion, revolutionized transportation, massive immigration, and institutional reforms. Capitalism, for
the French-Canadian professional class, symbolized a society dominated by a small group of wealthy individuals, who were English,
and nourished by a rural and urban proletariat, which was French.
Therefore a capitalist and English plot was afoot which, since the
clergy and the aristocracy were impervious to the idea of "nation,"
justified the role of the French-Canadian professionals as the national
élite and defenders of those traditional institutions in which were
enshrined the principal attributes of French-Canadian society.

Yet the professionals' nationalism by opposition to the English
bourgeoisie by no means dampened their loyalty to Great Britain.
Their admiration for British institutions remained steadfast, and they
saw no contradiction between their nationalism and membership in
the British Empire.

> ... cannot a Canadian be, and is he not in reality, English, in his
> love of English liberty, in his attachment to the English govern-
> ment, and his aversion for French principles? Does loyalty consist

in identity of language? If it does not, and if loyalty can be found only in identity of principles, why should Canada be disenfranchised? In what essential point are Canadian subjects different to English subjects? If there is such a difference, why did the Americans, whose language, religion and ways were those of the English, withdraw from their allegiance and call the French to their aid?[49]

England, far from being an enemy, was regarded as the protector against the English minority's plots, the French Revolution, Napoleonic despotism, and American democracy. The French-Canadian professionals, too, were haunted by the external peril. The *Chesapeake* incident in 1807 prompted *Le Canadien*, which had a penchant for versification, to address the Americans as "Yankees, Austrogoths, Vandals ... Cannibals, ..." and to assure the English:

Yes, proud English, never doubt,
Side by side we will win out,
For you will find our arms are stout ....[50]

The American peril was not only hypothetical and military; it was concrete and living next door in the American immigrant already settled in Lower Canada. His image was almost as repugnant as the English merchant's; he was greedy for money and the baser pleasures, a born speculator, obsessed with liberty and domination and turbulent in the extreme, to the point where "the ties of blood are of absolutely no account for him." The American, whether invader or immigrant, was a formidable enemy bent on reducing the French Canadians to "the sorry condition of slaves."[51]

Behind the stereotyped images conceived by the new French-Canadian élite we see the seriousness of their anxieties. The American speculator was the worst kind of capitalist, the natural ally of the local merchant bourgeoisie; the professionals saw him dangling the lure of riches before the eyes of a credulous peasantry to get his hands on the richest land, when in the seigneuries there was already precious little to go around. What would become of the simple country folk? "For as soon as these families have multiplied on land constricted and impoverished by too frequent cultivation, they flock to the cities where they lead a life of even greater hardship and privation than the first."[52] As the professional class saw it, the vocation of the French-Canadian nation was agricultural, and its guarantee of survival was possession of the land; the land of Lower Canada, the "national" territory, was not limited to the seigneuries but extended to those areas not yet granted. From this perspective, American immigration was an unmitigated evil, worse in its effects than an armed invasion. "The great wrong for the country is to have given entry to a certain class of half-civilized Americans. For what kind of people are the settlers of the townships adjoining the United States? They are people for the most part without morals, vagabonds, who will not suffer any kind of social subordination."[53]

If these stereotypes were concocted by the professionals and not the French-Canadian merchant class, who had greater cause for resentment, having been displaced from leadership in the commercial sector, it was perhaps because the professionals were intellectually better equipped for conceptualizing. Certainly their collective ambition and vulnerability stimulated their inventiveness and capacity for rationalization. According to them, indeed, it was their intellectual superiority which justified their accession to power. The ideology they evolved, moreover, was not simply a reflection of their own class interests but was conceived to evoke response in all ranks of society—merchants, seigneurs, aristocrats, clergy, and most of all the lower classes. Deep-seated frustration found an outlet in the new nationalism. The first chord it struck was in the lesser French-Canadian bourgeoisie, particularly those never involved in the fur trade, the small urban and rural merchants, shopkeepers, and innkeepers. Next were the seigneurial landholders, who could hardly remain unmoved by the emphasis on the importance of the seigneurial régime and the Coutume de Paris to the survival of the nation. And since the message included the Catholic Church among the nation's valuable institutions, even the clergy and some of the aristocracy were susceptible in due course. With general economic instability and with scarcity of land, real or artificial, becoming acute, anxiety and discontent in the rural populace, too, was ripe for channelling against the state, the English bourgeoisie, and American immigrants. Nationalism, though conceived to promote the interests of a single class, thus became the ideology of the entire French-Canadian society. By diverting attention, particularly among the lower classes, to the English as the source of all ills, the self-appointed analysts of those ills obscured the real root of the French-Canadian problem, namely the old social régime. Idealization of institutions and the traditional state of things spawned resistance to any real adaptation to the imperatives of the day.

Yet this nationalism—conservationist ideology, to use Marcel Rioux's expression—was not a purely static intellectual conception. New ideological developments followed the emergence of a nationalist party along with the formulation of political strategy which dictated, in particular, an alliance between nationalism and political liberalism.

CHAPTER 3

The Birth of French-Canadian
Nationalism, 1802-1812 (Part Two)

III   The Political Crisis

Politically, the salient feature of the first decade of the nineteenth century was a crisis beginning in 1805 and involving all social classes. It was no passing superficial episode destined to disappear with the circumstances which were its immediate cause; it was the beginning of a half-century of turbulence. While historians are divided on its origins and nature, most consider it purely political and place the blame on the shortcomings of the constitution of 1791, namely the absence of responsible government and the inadequacy of the assembly's control over finances. Others perceive an ethnic confrontation at a time when, as A.R.M. Lower puts it, the French Canadians were discovering themselves.[1] A number discern it as a stage in the struggle for survival, or the subjugation of French Canadians to the pan-Canadian nation. Creighton, for his part, sees in it a sudden aggravation of the conflict between agriculture and commerce. The reality appears to be rather more complex. It was certainly political in the sense that it involved social and nationalist groups and conflicting interests and ideologies, but the problem it reflected was not a purely constitutional one. It cannot even be divorced from the external military situation which weighed so heavily on the social climate in those troubled times.

In the first few years of the century, before the period of bitter antagonism between the assembly and the councils, the political malaise simmered rather than boiled. The adoption of the education bill creating the Royal Institution for the Advancement of Learning in 1801 would have been unthinkable a few years later. Monseigneur Plessis remarked to Governor Craig, "You say our Church never sleeps, but you will allow that we were asleep, and very profoundly too, when we suffered that Act to pass."[2] Yet as early as 1800 Milnes was expressing anxiety in his dispatches to London. Five years later there was unveiled hostility between the government and the majority in the assembly.

Milnes was not a reformist. He perceived society in terms of orders, the upper and lower classes, and the constitution in terms of equilibrium among the three branches of government, the executive, the aristocracy, and the people's representatives. The power of the latter, in his view, had been unduly advanced by the constitution of 1791, to the detriment of the executive and the aristocracy. He attributed the cause to the decline of the aristocracy, the ascension of the Catholic Church to a status equivalent to that of a state within a state, and the "disembodying" of the militia after the conquest, by reason of which its officers had ceased to play their proper military and social role. Nevertheless, he observed, at least the clergy were well disposed toward the government, and the people were loyal to the crown and not yet contaminated by liberal thinking. His objective was to prevent a deterioration of attitudes by correcting the constitutional imbalance.

In response to Milnes' concern for bolstering the power of the existing aristocracy, the government in London was sceptical: "as the Canadian Gentlemen can derive no influence from their Landed possessions, it must necessarily be left to the particular exertions, ability and ambition of the Individual Seigneurs to emerge from their present state of insignificance."[3] Nevertheless, Milnes still hoped, by granting townships to respectable men, to build up the kind of landed aristocracy he considered so important: "thereby an inter-mixture of English and Canadians will take place and ultimately an aristocracy of both may be formed."[4] No such happy eventuality came to pass, of course.

The revival of the militia, besides serving for the defence of the province, was likewise intended to aid the re-establishment of social and political equilibrium. Under the French Régime, Milnes explained to London, the militia bodies created by royal authority had helped to maintain strong monarchical sentiment in the people, and the Captains of Militia had performed many besides military functions, thus providing a counterweight to the clergy and the seigneurs. In 1800, he reported, there were 292 Captains of Militia "chosen from among the most respectable of the Canadian Habitants," and a general staff of sixteen, "in general chosen from among the Seigneurs."[5] A revival of the system, making the Captains officers of the Crown, "would effectually tend to keep alive among the great Body of the People the Spirit of Zeal and Loyalty for monarchical Government which I believe to be natural to the Canadians, but which for the want of an intermediate Class to whom they can look up, and from having no immediate Connexion with the Executive Power is in danger of becoming extinct."[6]

In the Catholic Church, despite its tendency to excessive independence, Milnes saw a powerful force to be brought to heel but not destroyed. In this he was closer to Sewell's thinking than to Ryland's and Mountain's. He envisioned two state churches, in short; but the condition was the Catholic Church's submission to the authority of the state, particularly over appointments, which was not to the Catholic bishop's liking since, as the latter saw it, it meant relinquishing control over internal discipline.[7] In London Milnes' suggestions were favourably received, though Portland, agreeing in principle to an increase in the bishop's salary, advised Milnes to be cautious over the question of church-state relations. Negotiations between Milnes and Bishop Denaut began only in 1805, when the latter agreed to petition the king for clarification of the status of the Catholic Church. The petition remained unanswered while the British government pondered the legalities of the matter. Under Thomas Dunn, who was Administrator between Milnes' departure and Craig's arrival, Plessis was allowed to succeed Denaut as titular bishop. Craig, however, redoubled the previous efforts to undermine the power of the church. For all that, at the height of the crisis Plessis declared, "After God, the Catholic Church finds protection for its ministers only in the government."[8]

Milnes' plan for restoring the constitutional balance included curbing the power of the popular elements in the assembly, using the clergy and officers of militia to influence the people's choice of representatives. Though in his dispatches he spoke of situations tending to encourage dangerous democratic thinking, he made no reference to political parties which might exploit it, or to the existence of any nationalist movement. His criticism of the assembly was in fact only for its chaotic mode of operation. "From this and other Causes the Business of the House of Assembly is transacted with so little System or regularity that the oldest Members are some times unable to form a judgment of what is likely to be the result of their deliberations on the most common Subjects."[9] The sources of his concern appear to have been rather broadly social.

Between 1792 and 1810 there was considerable turnover in the membership of the assembly; thirty-two new faces in 1796, twenty-seven in 1800, thirty-seven in 1809, and fourteen in 1810. This is not necessarily an indicator of political instability and disruption. Members were unpaid and during sessions those from outside the City of Quebec were obliged to neglect their businesses and clientèle. Many could simply not afford to serve for more than one term. Until the turn of the century more than 50 per cent were merchants, but that proportion dropped to 37 per cent in 1800 and 31 per cent in 1810, with more small merchants and fewer engaged in the fur trade (see Table 7). The proportion of professionals rose; 18 per cent in 1792, 29 per cent in 1800, and 35 per cent by 1810 (see Table 7). In that year, Craig wrote, "the House has never been as it is now, filled up with Avocats, and Notaries, shop-keepers, and with the Common Habitants, as they are called, that is the most ignorant of the Labouring farmers...."[10] Just as significant is the governor's observation that the French-Canadian majority was now acting in unison within a party which was violently anti-English and bent on disseminating "democratic principles." One elected candidate, he remarked, had even declared that he would refuse to sit if an English candidate were elected as his colleague in his riding. In 1810 J. Viger wrote of the Cuthbert Brothers, who were English-speaking seigneurs: "These persons enjoy a great influence, and when we have succeeded only in putting one of these Messrs Cuthbert out, it will still be that much gained, say our papas in political matters."[11]

The basic lines of the English and Canadian parties were laid down between 1804 and 1810. Besides the ethnic identity the names imply, there was an element of social distinction in their composition. R. Christie writes:

> The commercial interests at Quebec and Montreal formed the base of the Tory official party.... It was from this party that the Executive Council had been chosen. It predominated in the Legislative Council.... On their part the French Canadians just as naturally also became a political party.... This element—notaries and advocates—formed into a political party which was distinctly French in character and determined to resist all encroachments which might be attempted against the privileges and liberties of the people they represented....[12]

In reality the two parties drew their support from a less compartmentalized social spectrum than Christie suggests. The core of the English party was the merchant bourgeoisie, particularly the English, but it also had the support of the bureaucrats, some of them French Canadians, and the old seigneurial families. The aristocracy, however, French or English, sided with the other camp under certain circumstances. And the clergy, though they did not participate directly in party politics, were generally not sympathetic to the Canadian party. With the emergence of the parties there appeared two newspapers, the *Quebec Mercury* on November 9, 1804, and *Le Canadien* on November 22, 1806.

While the Canadian party's leaders were mostly French-Canadian professionals, many of the organizers and rank-and-file were small rural and urban merchants and shopkeepers. But it also attracted some influential English-speaking members, notably John Neilson and James and Andrew Stuart who were to play a prominent role among the nationalists. When Neilson first ran for election under the party banner, Bédard wrote to him thus: "We can pay you no greater compliment than to consider you as the Canadian party candidate, not exactly because Canadians are better than others but because that demonstrates the high regard they have for you, a regard they can express no more strongly due to that excellent sentiment they have, that there is nothing better than to be Canadian...."[13] A number of French-Canadian professionals, however, those who had more or less close connections with the administration or the business community, opposed the Canadian party; such men were termed traitors or *chouaguens*. An English party candidate in 1809, J.-M. Mondelet, for one, paid the price of what was considered national disloyalty. He wrote to J. Voyer:

> You have heard no doubt; one Joseph Bédard declared during the poll and in public that I should not be elected because I was a creature of the government, capable of sacrificing the electors, their wives and children for a place; that these traitors to their country must not be nominated; that I was serving the interests of the ministry at the expense of the electors; others that I had proposed to have a tax levied, of ten *piastres* per head.... Would it have taken more to make me lose an otherwise most certain election?[14]

The jails issue of 1805 helps to clarify the decade's political transformation. The disagreement was not over the necessity of building new jails to replace the dilapidated old ones, but over the manner of paying for them. The merchants were incensed by the proposal to increase customs duties for the purpose and demanded a land tax instead, which enraged the defenders of agricultural and landed interests, both French and English.[15] After a month of uproar, the legislative council of aristocrats and English merchants passed the law as first proposed by the assembly. Milnes gave his assent to it, seeing the dispute merely as conflict between agricultural and commercial interests. The mixed nature of the support for the winning side makes it difficult to discern a nationalist current at work here. Yet J.-P. Wallot writes, "the jails dispute became the symbol of the struggle for supremacy in Lower Canada between the two racial groups living there."[16] While it is true that there was no French-Canadian support for the merchants' position, the interest groups were in fact three in number, the English merchants and their allies, the landed aristocracy, and the French-Canadian professionals and their allies. The clash, however, was between the economic conceptions of two opposing groups, the one claiming to be protecting the interests of farmers and landholders and the other, in the name of commercial interests, seeking a more flexible distribution of the tax burden, with the aristocracy naturally on the side of the first. It was the ensuing event which turned the affair into an ethnic dispute.

The English merchants, who were particularly sensitive to the effects of the current economic crisis, refused to accept their defeat. They petitioned the legislative council, the lieutenant-governor, and the authorities in London in an attempt to have the bill disallowed, but failed at all levels. In March, 1805, they held a banquet at which many toasts were drunk, some of them disparaging the French-Canadian members of the assembly who had been responsible for increasing the tax on imports—all of which was reported in the *Montreal Gazette*. Shortly after the opening of the next session of the assembly, a committee of the House concluded that the banquet chairman and the editor of the *Gazette* had violated the privileges of the assembly, and ordered their arrest. The editor of the *Quebec Mercury* published an article which spoke of "Napoleonic despotism" and dangerous consequences arising from the violation of the liberty of the press perpetrated by French-Canadian members of the assembly: "it is certain that nothing could be more gratifying to our arch-enemy and the French nation, than a prohibition on our presses."[17] He even insinuated that the spirit of tyranny was a very French atavism. He, too, was ordered arrested by the majority in the House.

The dispute was more a symptom than a cause of the nationalist feeling which now boiled to the surface. The *Quebec Mercury* launched a campaign which brought into the open the disagreements between the ethnic groups in economic and social matters. The English paper's invective led a group of French-Canadian members of the assembly to found their own paper, *Le Canadien*, to defend the interests of the "nation." The two papers were intimately linked with the respective political parties; the opinions they expressed were not simply those of individuals but to a great degree reflected the ideologies of the parties. The quarrel unquestionably served to crystallize modes of thinking and behaviour. And for the Canadian party, the hyper-sensitivity of the peasantry to land taxation, particularly at a time of recession, was an electoral manna.

Repercussions from the jails incident were felt long after. The Canadian party, called the popular party by H.T. Manning,[18] girded for a struggle in which one of its objectives was to prevent English-speaking candidates from being elected; only those who shared the Canadian point of view, or appeared to, were spared the ostracism.[19] The election campaigns of 1809 and 1810 show the rapidity of this development. The Canadian party soon had an organization of considerable strength in both the cities and country districts. Regional and local leaders obeyed predetermined guidelines. In all ridings, careful consideration was given to the choice of candidates. At this level there was agreement between party and local leaders. In the rural districts the party generally had little trouble establishing its hold; in the cities and towns there was more opposition, due to the influence of English-speaking merchants, government pressure, and the fluidity of popular opinion among the urban lower classes.

As the political crisis intensified, and with increasing success at the polls, the Canadian party presented an image of solidarity, which was not, however, easily achieved. The party's organization became increasingly complex, perhaps in the attempt to resolve its internal problems. The leaders recognized that nationalism and the party's political objectives would have to be impressed in the minds of the lower classes, a purpose which would be aided by the establishment of elementary schools in all parishes. The rural people enjoyed the rough and tumble of politics, and brought to it all kinds of extraneous local and family rivalries and ambitions. In such a context, could a member be other than a spokesman for local against outside interests? Appeals to ethnic prejudice and the local fear of taxes were prodigiously effective at election time and easier than political education. Rivalry between rurals and city-dwellers was lively, too, and popular prejudice against "ladder-jumpers" was easily aroused. But basically the cohesion of the rural vote behind the Canadian party reflected an awareness in the country folk of concrete problems emerging, and these were translatable into nationalist terms.

The traditional rivalry between Quebec and Montreal was another complication. Its source was not only local prejudice but also the specific conditions in which the two cities developed. In this period the party leaders were from Quebec, the principal cradle of French-Canadian socio-economic problems; competition for leadership came from upstart Montreal. In 1814 Bédard was to write, "The people of Montreal have never been much in accord with those of Quebec in political thinking and there is not nearly as much zeal and public spirit in Montreal as in Quebec, and none at all in Trois-Rivières."[20] Interestingly enough, Papineau had the same reproach for his colleagues of Quebec, when after 1815 the centre of socio-economic malaise had moved to Montreal, and helped him accede to the party leadership.

From 1808 to 1810, in any event, the Montrealers were the moderates of the party. Joseph Papineau referred contemptuously to "so-called reformers" behaving like "housebreakers."[21] Marguerite Viger wrote to her husband, editor of *Le Canadien*, "you must be on your guard against advice that will be offered you, particularly by certain hot-headed gentlemen;... [D.B. Viger] counsels you to listen to everything in order to understand people, but not to let yourself be carried away, and to pay particular heed to undoing, by your moderation, the prejudices to which *Le Canadien* has given birth."[22] After 1815 the roles were reversed; Quebec became the site of moderation, due largely to the benefits of the lumber industry, and Montreal became the centre of malaise and political activism. The rivalry between the two cities in any event became a permanent source of intra-party discord, division, and challenge of leadership.

The party owed its cohesion to its role as the instrument of strategy for the liberal professions, a class aspiring to power for itself, but on behalf of the "nation." Its political strength was in the group as a whole rather than brilliant and vigorous leadership.

Pierre Bédard was not that kind of leader. He was born in Charlesbourg in 1762, the son of a farmer, and studied at the Seminary of Quebec.[23] Three of his brothers entered the priesthood and a fourth, like Pierre, became an advocate, which led him, too, into politics. Bédard's marriage to the daughter of a respectable surgeon, François Lajus, and niece of Monseigneur Hubert, was not a success. After retiring from politics he described his wife as domineering, extravagant, untidy, and snobbish, and his home as a hell-hole:

> Before she was married she read only devotional books and the lives of saints; after she was married, for a time she read novels as well as the lives of saints, and then she stopped reading anything but novels. She is totally ignorant of anything to do with housekeeping or anything useful, or in a word anything which cannot be learned from reading novels or the idle conversations of what are called lovely and witty harebrained ladies who read nothing but novels.[24]

His contemporaries were not impressed by his physical presence. He was, writes F.-J. Audet, "small, wizened, rather ugly of countenance and sickly of appearance."[25] He was keenly aware of his physical and other deficiencies; a man tortured by a pronounced inferiority complex yet a man of talent. He confided in Neilson in 1814:

> My insignificant appearance, which is both cause and effect of the first trait, is a second. I have not the talent to impress anyone and I

am incapable of inspiring either fear or respect or any of that sentiment felt by men who bestow their esteem, and which keeps them
at a distance one from another.... I was omitted on distribution of
that gift of Providence. I am in no way great or amusing; I have
none of that kind of atmosphere about me. As soon as people see
me close they lose that feeling of reserve with which they are accustomed to approach one another. They take possession of the space
around me; they trespass; the discomfort I have so often felt causes
me to shrink, make myself as small as I can in order to occupy as
little room as possible; but the smaller I make myself, the more I
shrink, the more they encroach and the time comes when I am so
small and beset that I must regain possession of my ground.... I am
a man in a state of war with other men, a man incapable of exercising the least authority, a man incapable of playing the husband, of
being the master, in short a man incapable of playing the man's role
with other men. Experiencing these difficulties magnifies the
trouble. I am more and more timid. That is how I am in my natural
state.[26]

This cruelly lucid self-portrait, though undoubtedly provoked by his
disappointments in politics and marriage and by unfulfilment after his
retirement from public life, seems to come close to the real cause of
his personal problems. He speaks of his timidity in terms that ring
true. "I am extraordinarily shy. The approach of a person whom I do
not know, even a child, dismays and confounds me. It has always been
an agony for me to be obliged to speak in public and it is something I
have never been able to do with composure."[27] Introverted, inhibited,
awkward, Bédard was certainly not an easy man to meet for the first
time, so strong was his self-image as an outsider, a social misfit, "to the
point of feeling removed from the abode of the living." In his own
recognition, he constantly had his foot in his mouth: "I have said more
stupid things in my lifetime out of fear of saying them, and have been
more upset by the fear of upsetting, than from any other cause."[28]
With his rumpled appearance, his awkward manner, and his ineptitude in handling his own affairs, he was probably considered an eccen-
tric by those who came in contact with him. He certainly took a
certain pleasure in his own gloom.

How, one wonders, could such a man have achieved sufficient stat-
ure in public life to have acceded to the leadership of a political party.
No doubt alcohol helped him overcome his social inadequacies, but
this hardly explains his political effectiveness. Behind his inferiority
complex there seems to have been a grain of superiority.

It is only on certain occasions, when I am uplifted by some accident or taken unawares, that I find myself like others; then I feel that nothing is pressing me and nothing resisting me; I feel that nothing can do so and I act freely and without fear; then I speak without anxiety, without that great deference toward others. I lose that feeling of shyness and the merit of others diminishes, becomes as nothing for me, and what is curious is that mine appears to grow in their eyes in proportion to the shrinking of theirs.... This is how I see myself, from within. I do not know how I am seen from without. It seems to me that I am never so good as when I am considered bad and never so bad as when I am considered good.[29]

For a time politics seem to have afforded him glimpses of respect from others, and fulfilment. After his retirement from politics he became a judge, and thereafter lived unhappily in Trois-Rivières, brooding bitterly over his failures but cherishing the recollection of his moments of glory.

As for many professionals, his life was not an easy one. He came of a large and impoverished family and turned to advocacy without great conviction. Perhaps the first French-Canadian professional politician, he was elected to the assembly two years after his admission to the practice of law and was re-elected repeatedly from 1796 until his retirement after the 1810 crisis. In 1798 he requested the grant of a township but was refused. In 1803 he had lost his employment and was in search of another in order to support his family, since he could not earn sufficient from the practice of law and wrote too badly, he said, to become a secretary. A year later he was trying to consolidate his debts and was in a state of deep depression: "they affect my illness to be a nervous illness, which is a polite way of saying I am odd."[30] Three years later, through Neilson, he requested a militia appointment. J.-F. Perreault's response was not kind: the government engaged only men of prestige, capability, and talent; besides, Bédard should change his political behaviour.[31] In this distribution of political patronage, political persuasion seems to have been a criterion as early as 1807. All of which no doubt helped embitter him and make him a reformist.

Bédard had pronounced intellectual tastes. He read voraciously and had a keen interest in geometry. Outside the political milieu, however, he had the feeling of being in a vacuum. In 1813 he wrote to Neilson, "I am writing you because I do not know what to do with myself, weary of always doing the same thing without diversion. At times I am sick of all books. There are many different things, much variety of all kinds in books, but all these varieties as inexhaustible as they may seem are all the same in that it is books which provide them; always books for work, books for recreation, books for relief from books, I cannot get away from them; the mind becomes blunted, loses its curiosity and in the end becomes useless."[32]

His political thinking reflected both the realities of his society and the period's intellectual currents; his conceptions were governed first by the necessities of politics. Intellectually, he was unquestionably the leader among his confrères of the professional class. Not that he was more cultivated than other bright lights of his party: F.-X. Blanchet, who had studied in the United States, D.-B. Viger, Joseph Papineau, the Stuart brothers, and John Neilson. He seemed at the time to be bolder and more systematic than they, and in a way more attentive to class aspirations and social problems. This was the quality which made him the predominant figure in the edification of a new ideology. For all his defects, the mark he left was a considerable one, as recognized even by his adversaries; wrote J.-M. Mondelet, "That is how they always end, such great men as the patriot in question, with no friends left."[33]

Bédard was never a republican or a democrat. Like Montesquieu, he believed that democracy would not work in a large country; too much liberty would lead to anarchy and ultimately dictatorship. For France, that hotbed of revolutionary ideas, he harboured a deep distrust: "If Hospice [his son] goes to France, he will forget what he knows of the English language and bring back behaviour and ideas which are not very suitable here."[34] His nationalism and anti-republicanism made him virulently anti-American. Craig was mistaken when he branded the leaders of the Canadian party as pro-French democrats.

The British constitution was greatly admired by Bédard, for in his view it was founded on a balanced conception of liberty. "The advantage we have is great," he wrote, "that is [the opportunity of] learning what liberty is...."[35] The constitution as applied in England was a masterpiece whose "stimuli" could bring fulfilment to the French-Canadian society. But for the constitution as applied in Canada his judgment was harsh. "I recall," he wrote to Neilson, "a book you lent me in 1810 recalling all the difficulties a colony had encountered in order to be heard."[36] He observed, with Montesquieu, that colonies dependent on free governments invariably suffered from the predominance of local aristocracies: "It is always the aristocratic or the rich of a colony who preserve the correspondence to the citizens of the mother country."[37] In Lower Canada it was the English who controlled communications with London and, by manipulating certain of the French-Canadian élite, dominated half the government.[38] "How is it conceivable," he asked, "that one of the parties be in possession of one of the branches of the legislature and the other party be in possession of the other branch? Does it not seem that things have been arranged expressly to cause a division in the Legislature itself? Is not the whole like a machine composed of weighted parts pulling in opposite directions?"[39] Bédard reasoned that the British constitution worked because of the supremacy of the legislative assembly, not a balance of powers, and concluded that the constitutional machinery in Lower Canada had broken down under the pernicious influence of English and aristocratic pressure groups, with the collusion of administrative figures and sometimes even the governors.

> The divisions of the House of Assembly become national, the English on one side forming the minority, with which the government is allied, and the Canadians on the other forming the majority, to which is attached the mass of the people; the heat of these national divisions passes from the House of Assembly to the people. The whole country is thus divided in two, the English government party on one side and the mass of the people on the other.[40]

The idea that his own group might be depicted as a minority which was using nationalism and liberalism for its own special ends was something Bédard simply refused to see. He and those about him spoke in the name of the nation, claiming to represent it in every sense. His adversaries were no more than spokesmen for a social and ethnic minority; French Canadians who espoused their cause were devotees, traitors, *chouaguens*. Yet professional men and the lesser merchants would clearly have been the first to benefit from the changes his party was advocating.

Central in the reforms envisaged by the Canadian party was the concept of ministerial responsibility. Notwithstanding Aileen Dunham's contention that the concept emerged in England and not until 1832,[41] the leaders of the Canadian party were propounding it as early as 1807.[42] It was perhaps Bédard himself who wrote in *Le Canadien*:

> As if there could be administration without ministry, or that there could be no ministers were they not such men as Pitt or Fox. It is even a maxim of our ministry that there is no ministry here, and that it is the governor who directs everything. This maxim, which suggests that the king's representative is responsible for all the counsel of ministers, is as unjust as it is unconstitutional, in that it exposes the king's representative to loss of the people's confidence through the errors of his ministers.[43]

There was more than legal responsibility in this notion. In 1809

Bédard was more explicit: "It was clear that this concept of a ministry was not a vain one as some of the members have claimed, but essential to the very existence of our constitution."[44] The idea that the governor held all power and was responsible only to London infuriated Bédard. There were indeed ministers, he claimed, but they chose to remain in the shadows, for it was not in their interest to have their status clarified if they wished to continue to speak for the minority and remain without responsibility.

> Not only at the time of the land tax has the ministry been in the minority; it has found itself there so often since the beginning of our constitution that the position has become habitual to it, and it considers it a natural one. Thus one cannot tell which is the opposition; some regard the majority in the House of Assembly as the party in opposition and others give the ministry that function, and that is perhaps one of the reasons preventing them from taking the title openly.[45]

The conclusion is clear: those who refused to recognize the existence of a ministry did so because they did not wish to find themselves obliged to resign. And the governor had necessarily to compromise himself by supporting the minority of whom his ministers were members.

Bédard's solution and its ramifications were much in advance of their time. To begin with, there would have to be acceptance of the fact that the king's representative could not err, and must observe strict neutrality in his relationship with political parties. This would imply that he must choose his advisers, which is to say the members of his ministry, or at least a large proportion of them, from among the "principal members of the majority in the House of Assembly."[46] He did not ask that the principle be applied to the limit, in other words that the minority be excluded from representation in the ministry, but only "that a number of council posts or other positions of honour and profit be accorded to those having the greatest influence over the majority in the House of Assembly, that they depend entirely on their [incumbents'] success at maintaining themselves in [the House], and that it be assured and recognized that there would be no other way of obtaining them."[47] Thus, though not fully developed, the theory of ministerial responsibility took form in Bédard's mind; in effect it meant substitution of the primacy of the legislative assembly for the theory of the balance of powers.

The Canadian party's adversaries quickly grasped the disastrous consequences this would have for them. If the governor were obliged to choose most of his advisers from the majority party, the distribution of royal favours would be mostly in the hands of the leaders of the Canadian party. And with an entourage and advisers of that ilk, the governor's voice in London would no longer be that of the English minority but of the French-speaking majority. Judge Monk accused the Canadian party of hatching revolutionary plots, Governor Craig foresaw his vital prerogatives slipping from his hands, and the placemen and the merchants began to fear for their future. Indeed, acceptance of the principle would imply a concentration of power in the hands of a French-Canadian middle class dedicated to the preservation of traditional heritage and opposed to capitalism and English-speaking immigration. And Bédard was preaching elimination of ethnic distinction!

Implementation of a reform deriving from a theory which had not yet even been formally defined in England was unthinkable in the circumstances; it would have necessitated a complete overhaul of the colonial régime in a manner incompatible with both colonial tradition as founded on mercantilism and the notion of political dependency. Furthermore, the matter was raised at a time of growing economic dependence since the mother country was increasing her tariff protection for the North American colonies. And then there were the pressures of the Napoleonic wars and the weakness of the advocates of free trade and colonial autonomy in England, neither likely to aid a development signifying a radical change in the power structure.

Ministerial responsibility was not the only issue in the struggle for power and control of patronage. In these turbulent years the Canadian party, impressed by the rapid rise of state revenues, began to demand recognition of the assembly's rights in financial matters. Milnes had cautioned London against any concession in this domain as early as 1800, being convinced that the control of subsidies by the assembly would risk further stimulating the democratic elements of a political system already far too heavily weighted in their favour. Governor Craig, who felt he was exercising authority in a perpetual state of crisis, was positively horrified when the leaders of the Canadian party presented a carefully worded statement of their claims regarding control of the public purse. Constitutional theory, he realized, not only involved abstract principles but tended to have real consequences capable of upsetting the status quo. His heated reactions were indicative of the reigning atmosphere of hostility, in which both sides were blind to compromise.

At any other time the quarrel over the exclusion of judges from the assembly would perhaps have been resolved with relative ease. But when the judge in question was De Bonne, a staunch adversary of the

Canadian party and a personal enemy for a number of its members, when the English party was so clearly in the minority and likely to remain so, when the political climate was so fired with animosity, solution appeared impossible.[48] Hardened attitudes emerged in demagogy, as shown in the Hart affair.

In 1807, the merchant Ezekiel Hart, a Jew, was elected to the assembly under the English party banner. In England neither Jews nor Catholics could sit in the House of Commons, but the constitution of 1791 contained no clause disqualifying Jews or indeed anyone on religious grounds. Hart's election, however, raised a storm which raged for some years. The majority in the assembly, which professed to liberalism, thought nothing of invoking British tradition to expel him from the House, which they succeeded in doing twice, despite the wishes of his electors. Racism and religious prejudice enflamed the debate. The Canadian party, while on firm legal ground in its stand, seemed to ignore the dangerous implications for the rights of Catholics in Lower Canada. Surprisingly enough, it was Governor Craig who upheld the only constitutional interpretation which could guarantee the political rights of Jews, and consequently of Catholics. What had happened to the Protestant plot against Catholics?

The constitutional conceptions and behaviour of the Canadian party are best understood when viewed in the light of a struggle of one minority against another in the quest for political and social power, the French-Canadian middle class against the English merchants and administrators. Liberalism, for Bédard and his associates, justified the objectives and strategy of the French-Canadian middle class; nationalism, reflecting the economic and social conservatism of the political élite of that class, appealed to the lower classes. The economic renewal and institutional reform sought by the English-speaking merchants were to be resisted. Political partisanship therefore polarized the vital interests of the various social groups.

In his preoccupation with political balance of power and the peril of strong democratic tendencies, Milnes had paid little attention to the ethnic question and did not understand the new element in the 1805 political crisis. Craig, whose background was military, brought a different view to bear. According to H.T. Manning, his "bias against the French race was obviously connected with the times in which he lived and with the part he himself had played in world affairs."[49] Chapais, however, feels that on his arrival Craig did in fact distinguish between the French and the French Canadians, but that his attitude changed subsequently. Documents which have since become available support this view. It appears incontestable that Craig's authoritarian nature, revealing the military disciplinarian with little understanding of civilian life, was the cause of the behaviour which earned him his reputation as a dictator.

While Craig's character explains much, it was the circumstances attending his governorship which brought out its extremes. Napoleon's continental blockade was bearing fruit and seriously upsetting the British economy. Hostility toward France and the French was widespread in Lower Canada, even among French Canadians; Craig arrived shortly after the Chesapeake incident and had not witnessed the demonstrations of loyalty on the part of the French Canadians on that occasion. Danger was perceived very close to home, at the American border, and military security was thus the new governor's first preoccupation. Finding political disharmony in the territory under his jurisdiction, and interpreting political opposition as a threat to the security of the state, he committed the error of identifying the French Canadians and their aspirations with the French and their revolution. The military situation being what it was, with his highly developed sense of order and authority he determined that the power of the executive must be strengthened and social stability and political harmony imposed, by force if necessary.

The attitude adopted by the new governor, it must be said, was conditioned partly by pressure from the local English-speaking minority. The English party, representing above all the interests of the merchants, was increasingly frustrated in the assembly. The crisis of 1805 had made it clear that through solidarity the French Canadians were capable in certain circumstances of dominating not only the assembly but also the legislative council. After the 1810 election, the English merchants, having even less influence in those bodies than before and afraid of becoming a permanent minority, lent an attentive ear to Ryland and Sewell. Together with the English-speaking administrators who feared the rise of French Canadians in their domain, they turned to the governor, calling on him for protection of the English-speaking minority.

Craig did not take sides immediately. From October, 1807, until June of the following year he withheld his judgment and merely observed. Then, recounts Chapais, the tone of his dispatches changed almost abruptly to one of hostility toward the leaders of the Canadian party.[50] At that point he became thoroughly involved in the disputes between the parties, disdaining any pretense at diplomacy. With characteristic bluntness, he labelled the majority as a set of unprincipled advocates and notaries and illiterate peasants, incapable of understanding the parliamentary system, dominated by ambition and greed for positions, and bent on seizing power with the intention of establishing a democratic régime, more specifically a French-Canadian republic; in short, a band of nationalists whose sole objective was to drive the English from their ruling position. Craig was convinced by now that all French Canadians ardently looked forward to victory for Napoleon and were even prepared to support an American invasion of Lower Canada; what he had on his hands, as he saw it, was an authentically revolutionary movement with control over the most independent legislative assembly in the world and a fearsomely effective organization throughout the territory.

In Craig's eyes the state of affairs was therefore alarming in the extreme. The power of the executive being feeble and his own influence minimal, what was to be done? He was prepared to negotiate with the clergy, whom basically he mistrusted, but had no intention of temporizing with the Canadian party. His plan was to weaken it and eventually destroy it. In June, 1808, he had a number of leaders of the Canadian party dismissed as militia officers. In 1809, on the pretext of irregularities in the House, he prorogued the assembly amid much fracas. Disappointingly, the subsequent election returned the Canadian party in even greater strength. On February 26, 1810, on similar pretext, he dissolved the House. In March, determined to break all resistance, he seized the press of *Le Canadien* and jailed its printer and then its principal editors, including Bédard. With the governor evoking the bogeyman of disloyalty, all segments of the society were caught up in the crisis, including the clergy who took sides with the government, partly from conviction and partly under government pressure. The results of the next election, however, were a resounding and humiliating defeat for the king's representative and the Catholic clergy.

Yet Craig had succeeded in one sense. By putting Bédard behind bars he had provoked a leadership crisis in the Canadian party which was not really resolved until 1827. For the remainder of his tenure there was relative calm. Bédard, obstinately and for tactical reasons, remained in jail long enough to lose his grip on his party. After his release he accepted a judgeship in Trois-Rivières, an appointment which he later described as recompense for his wrongful imprisonment: "recognition on the part of the government of its injustice toward me."[51] But his life thereafter was one of melancholy and banishment. "I am uncomfortable, divided between conflicting duties and interests; I may have a place, but I do not feel free to give of myself for the good of the country; for twopence I would give up my place and become again what I was. In poverty, it is true, destitute, but happier; but I have creditors, I have a family, I am in sad straits."[52] His political career was at an end.

Bédard's political downfall was not, it seems, due to Craig alone. If his leadership had been uncontested his imprisonment might have made a martyr of him, strengthened his prestige as leader, and given new impetus to the nationalist movement. But the Papineaus, father and son, the leaders of the party's Montreal branch, were waiting in the wings and seem to have made haste to turn the situation to their own advantage; they certainly were not anxious to see him made a hero. Bédard came to regard them with personal enmity. In the wake of a heated argument between him and Papineau senior while he was in jail, Papineau junior pronounced a panegyric in the assembly which Bédard considered a devious piece of treachery. "He praised my conduct in an exaggerated and unreasonable manner. That occasioned a long retort against me on the part of Mr Bowen in which I was denounced as fully as I had been praised excessively by Mr Papineau."[53]

Though Craig had been unable to obtain a change in the composition of the assembly, he was not yet beaten. He could still strengthen the legislative and executive councils through appointments of his own choosing. Ryland proposed adding "eight or ten members to the Legislative Council, three or four of whom might be Canadians of the most respectable character and families, and the remainder Englishmen of the best stamp and abilities."[54] Craig, after reflection, suggested the addition of four, two of them French-Canadian aristocrats. He also sent Ryland to England with proposals for some radical constitutional amendments: extension of the electoral roll and stiffer qualifications for assembly members would keep certain of the extremist elements out of the assembly; the creation of ridings in the townships would assure a better balance of ethnic representation; most important, the two Canadas should be unified. A redefinition of the status of the Catholic clergy was also recommended.

Ryland's mission was a failure. The British government, preoccupied by military matters at home, was unwilling to envisage any major change. Besides, Craig and Ryland were less than favourably regarded in London, Craig for his heavy-handed tactics, Ryland for his narrow views. It was felt that while the two were expressing anxieties which might be real for certain social strata in Lower Canada, they were representing at best the opinions of a minority within a minority, perhaps only personal opinions.

French-Canadian nationalism was not created by Craig, though his part in its development was important. It was an ideology which was born of the interests and aspirations of a social class, and which, when offered for the consideration of the French-Canadian society as a whole, found growing response.

CHAPTER 4

Lower Canada
and the War of 1812

It has become commonplace to regard the War of 1812 as a kind of tragi-comedy in which the leading actors found themselves embroiled in spite of themselves, so to speak. In fact neither the English nor the Americans nor the North American colonists appear to have really wanted it, at least not the majority in each case. But the circumstances of the Anglo-French war and the multifarious complications arising out of it eventually pushed the Americans into declaring war on England, thereby aligning themselves with Napoleon. The war in Europe having acquired such major economic dimensions and the United States being so heavily involved in international commerce, American neutrality had become a fiction in any event. "The pressure from both sides was so intolerable that she sought an escape by accommodation with either, which of course meant the abandonment of neutrality."[1] The conflicts which led to an invasion of the Canadas were far more complex than the usual legal explanation reveals. Though basically the situation for all the British North American colonies was one and the same, there were certain currents of popular opinion peculiar to Lower Canada.

I Origins of the War

The final phase of the Anglo-French war began in November, 1806, with Napoleon's Berlin Decree, which was directed against England's export trade. Napoleon's previous attempts to use direct or indirect economic weapons had been only partially successful. Now, however, his Grande Armée having swept through North Germany, the Emperor controlled Italy, Switzerland, Spain, Holland, and the entire German coastline along the North Sea and as far as Danzig on the Baltic.[2] The capture of Hamburg, one of the largest distribution centres for British exports, was a major coup in the economic war. By the autumn of 1806 Napoleon had all he needed to apply his continental blockade with full force.

He was well aware of Europe's importance to the British economy; it absorbed 50 per cent of Great Britain's exports and provided no less than a third of her timber, grain, and other essentials. By denying Europe to British trade he hoped to provoke a food-supply and industrial crisis in Britain leading to massive unemployment and social unrest, and thus his enemy would soon be brought to her knees. His chances of success were good,[3] but only if the blockade were applied long enough to have cumulative effect.

The brutal impact of the blockade on the British economy bears out the validity of the postulates underlying the Berlin and Milan Decrees. Particularly during the early months of 1808 and from June, 1810, until the Russian campaign, Britain lived a period of real economic crisis. But Napoleon's meddling in Spanish affairs and his attack on Russia facilitated a proliferation of contraband networks. Another error on the emperor's part was underestimating the importance of the United States, to which Britain exported 26 per cent of its manufactured goods. Without American co-operation the blockade could not be fully effective; "the closure of continental Europe alone," writes F. Crouzet, "even if Napoleon succeeded in imposing it, could inflict certainly serious but not crippling difficulties on these industries. The situation would become catastrophic only if there were a conjunction between the continental blockade and discontinuance of Anglo-American trade relations."[4] Yet Napoleon, regarding the Americans as pawns of British trade, imposed restrictions which at first caused more resentment in the American public than did Britain's Orders-in-Council. Not until August, 1810, did he decide to seek an alliance with the United States. When the Berlin and Milan Decrees were lifted for the Americans their policy toward Britain, and American public opinion, began to harden.

The Orders-in-Council of November and December, 1807, were Britain's reply to the blockade. Their purpose was to force openings for British and colonial products in continental Europe, and to screen neutral trade with that area by requiring all neutral ships to call at British ports, obtain permits, and pay duties. The Americans were placed in an impossible position, since the Milan Decrees then dictated that ships subjected to British inspection should be confiscated, which effectively denied their access to ports under French control. As A.L. Burt writes, "Theoretically, the two belligerents were equally oppressive; but practically, legally and psychologically they were not. Britain's control of the seas, being greater than Napoleon's control of the land, gave her greater power of enforcement. Much more important was the legal difference. Her seizures were made at sea and therefore, according to her own admission, were a violation of neutral rights under international law, her justification being that it was a necessary reprisal against Napoleon."[5]

Britain's rigidity toward the United States, the most important of the neutrals, had other sources. The revolutionary and Napoleonic wars had brought unprecedented growth to American foreign trade and American shipping. The conviction of certain influential English business interests that this growth had been achieved at Britain's expense carried considerable weight with the politicians. Burt continues, "As British people believed that Americans were abusing their neutral rights to the vital injury of Britain, so were Americans convinced that Britain was abusing her temporary belligerent rights to serve her permanent economic interests and that in so doing she was furtively dealing a dangerous blow at their country, ... to monopolize the commerce of the world."[6] Furthermore, in response to inducements offered by American shipowners, British sailors were deserting British ships in disturbingly large numbers; consequently, English political leaders believed that only extreme firmness would avert war with the United States.

The British government, encouraged by the economy's resilience in the face of the continental blockade and unwilling to admit that the country was in fact in a state of economic crisis, for a time resisted pressure to lift the Orders-in-Council from American ships. The pressure came first from a small group of English merchants whose primary trade was with North America. Soon this group was being supported by both industrialists and the working classes, who were beginning to feel the pinch acutely. The cause was carried into the political arena by such influential parliamentary figures as Henry Brougham, Alexander Baring, and Samuel Whitbread, and eventually the government capitulated, but not until June 23, 1812, five days after President Madison had declared war on Britain and too late to avert armed conflict.[7]

With France and Britain both violating American rights and national honour, the long-standing American irritation with Britain's dictatorial attitudes in her command of the seas had turned to frustration, and the declaration of war was the result. Yet the United States had indeed prospered as the Anglo-French wars progressed. Her exports had quintupled and her merchant navy had grown from 350,000 tons in 1790 to 1,089,000 tons in 1808. British ships, which had carried 50 per cent of American exports to Britain in 1790, were transporting only 5 per cent in 1800. After 1793, American ships were also carrying surplus produce from the French West Indies and, to some extent, the British West Indies. The period was also one of remarkable growth in American agriculture, notably cotton.[8] There were still regional divisions, particularly between the North and South, but the national economy was certainly export-oriented, the more so because of the nature of the growth, and the ties were largely with Great Britain. The United States therefore had far more community of interest with Britain than with France. "The plain truth," observes Burt, "is that the mass of the people, even outside New England, were not convinced that their vital interests were in any grave danger. . . . The feebleness of the popular response may also be traced to the unformed character of the nation."[9] At the beginning of the continental blockade there was no élite or popular American pressure group with an interest in fomenting bad blood with Britain. American political leaders were therefore on delicate ground as interpreters of popular opinion over infringements of the national sovereignty.

The Non-Importation Act of April, 1806, was the first measure of reprisal against British harassment of American merchantmen. Twice, application of the Act was suspended because of temporary improvements in diplomatic relations. The anger provoked in the American public by the *Chesapeake* incident in June, 1807, brought the country to the very brink of war, but having no really deep base it subsided gradually. When France and Britain applied new economic sanctions affecting American trade, President Jefferson obtained passage of the Embargo Act forbidding shipments to both.[10] The Non-Importation Act was at the time also preventing importation from Britain, but its effect was tempered by a further law passed on February 27, 1808, which shortened the list of prohibited imports. The American blockade did not really take effect until the end of 1808, and by then the continental blockade was weakening. Anglo-American trade was nevertheless adversely affected by rumours of war throughout 1808; movements from Britain to the United States dropped by 50 per cent, and from the United States to Britain by 72 per cent. "It therefore appears," writes Crouzet, "that Jefferson's policy was far more effective than Napoleon's, and more damaging to the British economy."[11]

But now the American economy was suffering acutely, and the embargo was disobeyed increasingly as the continental blockade faded. A new and tighter embargo was passed on January 9, 1809, but hostility to it in New England was so great that it was largely ineffectual. Its successor was the Non-Intercourse Act forbidding trade with France and Britain but exempting other countries, which facilitated systematic violation. Never had there been so many American ships sailing for the Iberian Peninsula or the Azores. By mid-1810 it was clear that the Non-Intercourse Act had failed as a weapon of economic warfare. The Macon Act of May 1, 1810, was in a sense an American capitulation to Britain. Having been informed that France would lift her Decrees from American ships if they respected the continental blockade against Britain, President Madison ordered the re-enforcement of the Non-Intercourse Act, effective February 2, 1811, if in the meantime Britain had not rescinded her Orders-in-Council. By 1811, Britain was suffering a severe depression due to the interruption of her trade with Europe and a drop of £6 million in her exports to the United States.

Yet once again it was the American economy which was suffering the most. The New Englanders blamed the American government or France for the economic tribulations and remained firm in the conviction that war with Britain would not serve the national interest. But their attitude was not shared throughout the United States. In the west, a crisis in agriculture had begun in 1808 and worsened steadily,[12] and in the south the boom in cotton was ending, with prices deteriorating from 1808 on. In these areas, war with Britain, it was thought, would both safeguard national independence and solve the economic problem for which the former mother country was considered responsible; Britain was the villain and there was no conflict between national interest and national pride. "South Carolina," observes M. Latimer, "had developed a decided urge for war. Excited by considerations of her primary livelihood, the export trade in cotton, South Carolina became one of the major protagonists of the conflict."[13] Taylor notes, "Western agriculture suffered ... a severe economic depression in the years just before the war, and this depression was an important factor in determining the support which the frontier gave first to the Non-Intercourse Acts and finally war."[14] A group known as the War Hawks exerted considerable influence, though it never succeeded in converting New England or convincing the mass of the American people as a whole. Writes B. Perkins, "The war came, not because of the President, but despite him. The war came not for any single reason, but from the interplay of many. The nation did not want war, and surely it did not embark gleefully on a great crusade ... neither side sought the war of 1812, and in the short run it was tragically unnecessary."[15] The conquest of Canada, it can be seen, was never a vital or primary objective for the Americans; it was only through Canada, however, that they could strike a telling blow at Great Britain.[16]

II The War and Public Opinion

Lower Canadians, though they had been at peace since the American Revolution, were constantly haunted by the spectre of external peril. The revolutionary wars had been distant but their echoes had been felt, with the activities of French emissaries and adroitly spread rumours of invasion giving the impression, rightly or wrongly, that war was imminent. Recurrent tensions with the United States and the *Chesapeake* affair and other such incidents further fostered a war mentality. In one of his pastoral letters Bishop Plessis declared, "... from the unprecedented ardour manifested immediately in all parts of the Province, one would say you had long been prepared and trained to take up arms."[17] But despite the confidence inspired by the mother country's armed might, it is clear that there were never even covert designs of conquest, only a broad-based determination to defend the country. W. Berczy wrote, "... though the party spirit is considerable here, there is great unanimity when it comes to defending the country, and unless I am much mistaken in such case each man will do his duty with ardour."[18] The solidarity among social, religious, and ethnic groups in the face of the American enemy contrasts sharply with the attitudes at the time of the American Revolution, when the Lower-Canadian peasants were determinedly neutral. For the lower classes and even the élite, or at least many of them, the imperatives were not the same as in 1775.

The clergy expressed themselves more militantly than ever in this time of peril, their exhortations reflecting their age-old reasoning on the nature of political power and their own relationship to it. "The sacred religion which we preach to the people," declared Plessis, "... is necessarily the enemy of independence and all injudicious reflection upon the conduct of persons whom God has established to govern you."[19] Said the Abbé Lartigue, "Be obedient to all those who govern you, even when they are unjust toward you, for that is the will of God." The church, particularly at such times, must support the state; "For it is not the moment to tell your pastors that they must bring you the Gospel without meddling in political matters.... Since when have the duties of subjects toward their sovereigns ceased to be religious dogma?"[20] Thus, whatever the government might do, in time of crisis the church had only one choice, and that was to place its prestige and authority at the service of the state.

Support for the state at this time, it must be said, was entirely compatible with the church's anathema for anything emanating from revolutionary France, and of course the corollary, its own dependence on England and the Crown for protection: "... Great Britain, shining

with a thousand rays of glory amidst all the shattered thrones... ,"
intoned Vicar-General Roux.[21] And Plessis: "... a government to
which oppressed peoples, dethroned sovereigns, untold victims of the
ambition and perfidy of an insatiable conqueror, come in search of
asylum and the means of recovering their liberty, or defending what
little is left to them."[22] England's protection of monarchies, state-
allied churches, and the traditional élite acquired even greater merit
in ecclesiastic eyes as the war with the United States brought French-
Canadian Catholics into the thick of the universal struggle pitting the
forces of good against the forces of evil; for American democracy and
American attitudes were simply further manifestations of the impiety
sown by the philosophers of the Enlightenment. "Let [the people]
sense that our religion will be endangered by the presence of these
enemies who are now threatening us, and who are without principles
or morals," declared Roux.[23] "The Lord will not permit a nation so
gallant and so Catholic to fall prey to these arrogant unbelievers," said
Lartigue from the pulpit.[24]

The war was painted by the clergy as a punishment sent from
Heaven upon a guilty people, and an American invasion as a threat to
all the Church had won since 1760 from a beneficent conqueror.
"What nation has ever had so much right to gratitude from another
people as the English Nation has from you? For more than fifty years
you have been under its rule; what benefits have you not received?
Your holy religion is sanctioned, your pastors are respected, your ancient laws have been preserved, your land, your possessions, your persons are assured and protected, your trade, your industry encouraged;
these are a small part of the wealth you owe to the protective government which has conquered you."[25] Such pronouncements, while
sincere, were not without ulterior motive. Plessis in particular was
mindful of Mountain's and Ryland's schemes, and the situation at
hand provided an opportunity for the church to demonstrate its value
to the state.

When Plessis addressed French Canadians he was addressing the
Catholic faithful and Catholic subjects. At no time did he appeal to
French-Canadian nationalism, even in the face of American invasion.
Abbé Lartigue, in appealing for loyalty, addressed the Canadian na-
tion, a Catholic nation, and this was an innovation.

... my compatriots, these gallant Canadians, [must not] degrade
their national character, be guilty of ingratitude toward the mother
country, and disregard the most sacred duties of religion.... I will
say it again, to fail in loyalty and courage at this critical time would
be to sully our national honour with an irradicable stain. What

nation were ever more valiant, more fit for the dangers of combat, more devoted to its Prince than the Canadian nation.... What dishonour it would be to the Canadian name... if we were to show less eagerness, less good intent, than our British fellow subjects in the defence of our home and the glory of our king.[26]

In these words of the future Bishop of Montreal we see the germ of a nationalism destined to be embraced with fervour by the ecclesiastics of Lower Canada and by those lay Catholics who, often despite liberal pretensions, came to associate their religion with their ethnic identity.[27]

As for the old aristocratic families, while it was fashionable among them to display a certain anti-clericalism, they in fact shared the clergy's traditional politico-religious ideology and its implications. Besides, in reviving their military significance, the war gave a fillip to their faded glory. The de Salaberry family, for instance, whose noble lineage went back at least to the sixteenth century, had been a shining example of distinguished service, naval, military, seigneurial, and administrative. All of them married aristocratic ladies. Charles-Michel, the "hero" of Châteauguay, had begun his career in the West Indies, was a brigade major in Ireland in 1808 and a lieutenant-colonel in 1812. Six years later he was appointed to the legislative council. He died in 1829.[28] Devoted to the service of the king, albeit by self-interest as well as conviction, strongly attached to their seigneurial lands and traditions, these old families were of a class which, though it dabbled in the fur and grain trades and absorbed many successful merchants through marriage and otherwise, stoutly maintained its traditional values. In 1812 these fervent monarchists identified with the British régime and regarded the American invasion as a menace both political and social. Together with the clergy, their concern was more for the preservation of monarchical institutions, the social hierarchy, and their own system of values than for the defence of the Canadian nation. Abbé Lartigue, who had studied law, was alone among these two classes to think in nationalist terms.

The attitude of the liberal professions and French-Canadian merchants can really be gauged only in the light of their nationalist ideology. Though there was a certain liberalism in their thinking in that they believed in such things as freedom of the press and education of the masses, they were hardly Rousseau disciples. On balance they were probably closer to Burke than to Fox. In any event, they roundly denounced "Allen's bible and Paine's Age of Reason."[29] Their thinking was too fragmented and too involved with the prevailing circumstances to lend itself to easy assessment, but at least they were clearly anti-republican. "The French Revolution, whose repercussions have undermined or completely overturned almost all of the political, civil, and religious institutions of Europe, and whose shock waves have been felt in the furthermost corners of the world, has taught the human race a terrifying lesson," wrote D.-B. Viger.[30] One wonders even what depth there was to this class's conception of freedom, for it went hand in hand with a highly developed sense of authority. "Canadians in general," continued Viger, "particularly those who are perspicacious, are bound to the government by the principles of their moral and religious education which has made their obedience and submission a bounden duty."[31] It was also Viger who wrote in *Le Canadien* in 1809, "The British constitution is perhaps the only one in which the rights and interests of the various component branches of society are so carefully nurtured, so wisely counterbalanced and interrelated as a whole, that they provide clarity to and support for one another through the very opposition resulting from the simultaneous exercise of the powers bestowed."[32] British liberty thus conceived is significant in its contrast to the American democratic liberty and Napoleonic despotism so abhorrent to the French-Canadian middle classes. Napoleon, as Philippe Aubert de Gaspé observed, was widely judged to be tyrannical and even "anti-Christ,"[33] and democratic liberty the symbol of irreligion, unbridled freedom, and abolition of social distinctions; ". . . when liberty and equality mean only confusion of all ranks and all distinctions. . . . I think I would be happier in Russia than there among men where I would be obliged to fraternize with every ruffian and every black, white or yellow good-for-nothing I might meet."[34]

French Canadians, as the middle classes conceived, were so dependent on the protective might of the British Empire in the face of American invasion that they were even more closely bound to the mother country than were the "old subjects," the British immigrants. "An old subject . . . has less aversion for the people and government of the United States, and all considered, the result is that a Canadian is much more strongly bound to the interests of the mother country where the preservation of this country is concerned. The Canadians, being incapable of protecting themselves, have no other recourse but the protection of the mother country. With this country lost, they would have no homeland to turn to; an Englishman would still have his homeland."[35] An American invasion would have the same effect as massive American immigration; the French Canadians would not only be numerically submerged by the newcomers but would lose the political influence they had acquired and thus their power to preserve their traditions. "They have hopes of their population's always being the largest in the country and, with the constitution the mother country has granted them, of having the means of preserving their religion and all that is dear to them."[36] The fact that the English of Lower Canada were favourably disposed to American immigration made the Americans even more dangerous: "... the English party is opposed to the Canadian party on precisely that point relating to [the Canadian nation's] life and existence as a people."[37]

The élite of the French-Canadian middle classes, claiming to represent "an emerging people,"[38] therefore rallied round the new governor to meet the external peril—not only to give the lie to those who had cast doubt on French-Canadian loyalty and military competence but also to show Britain that the French Canadians were the strongest possible bulwark against American influence, suggesting even that the English element was the unreliable one: "Those of the English party are opposed to [the Canadian's] interests in that having much greater affinities with the Americans through their customs, their religion, their language, they encourage American population as a device for ridding themselves of the Canadians.... A colony peopled with Americans appears to them a more English colony."[39] The claim that the British régime's survival depended largely on a middle class closely identified with the French-Canadian nation was merely an adaptation of the strategy already laid out.

The war, far from dampening the struggle for leadership between classes, simply provided a context in which class rivalries continued with different modes of expression. In their effort to demonstrate their inimitable social usefulness, the aristocracy, the clergy, and the French-Canadian middle classes vied in loyalty. The loyal fervour discovered by the laymen among the élite, it must be said, was not unrelated to the distribution of militia posts by the new governor.

French-Canadian middle-class insinuations notwithstanding, the élite of British origin also were determined in their loyalty and their hostility to France and to American democracy. On that score Bishops Plessis and Mountain were not far apart. Mountain, while not a believer in monarchy by divine right, was unswervingly devoted to monarchical and aristocratic institutions and the unity of church and state. He respected the popular element in the constitutional balance but leaned in preference to the monarchy and aristocracy (hereditary or acquired). British liberty for him was the fruit of an equilibrium giving precedence to those most respectful of the rule of law.[40] While he did not identify liberty and licence as did his Catholic counterpart, he was keenly aware of the dangers of democracy as expressed by local demagogues, American immigrants, and Methodist ministers. American democratic liberty could only lead to chronic anarchy and despotism; France was the supreme example of the dire consequences to be expected from liberty based on equality.[41] So great did he consider the superiority of English political and social institutions that the society he envisioned for the Canadas would have to be English in every sense.

The senior civil servants shared these attitudes, but in a rather more pragmatic way, at least as far as American immigration was concerned. To this group the American immigrant was an economic asset, energetic and enterprising whether merchant or farmer, especially in view of the disappointingly meagre immigration from Britain over the previous twenty years. To those who feared infiltration of the democratic poison or the deplorable habits spawned by abuse of liberty, they would retort that the newcomers, once established in Lower Canada, would come to realize the superiority of British institutions and their underlying values, particularly the British sense of moderation. The Canadian party leaders were convinced that the favour with which the civil servants looked upon American immigration was due to their desire to see the French Canadians eventually outnumbered. It seems more likely that in the minds of the bureaucrats economic considerations outweighed the cultural, the more so the closer their ties with the business milieu. With the outbreak of war, however, that pragmatism disappeared, to be replaced by distrust and outright anti-Americanism.

The merchants for their part were sharply aware of the importance of defending the British Empire and its traditions. For a number of reasons, some ideological and others tied to their waning political influence, they were anti-democratic. Their dominant motivation, however, was economic. The merchants of Lower Canada had always been dogged by American competition, yet they welcomed American immigration, channelled American timber and wheat to Britain, and traded on the financial markets of New York. Ideology, in short, had never stood in the way of trade and monetary exchange. Even during the war there was lively movement in contraband between the two countries. But for all that, the English-speaking merchants regarded the Americans as rivals whom they had hopes of supplanting at least in the important West Indies market. In fisheries and timber the Americans clearly had the upper hand. The scene of the most bitter competition was the fur trade; there the war seemed to offer the merchants of Lower Canada a golden opportunity to take the upper hand, for they attributed their troubles not to an irreversible decline in the trade but to the treaties of 1783 and 1794 ceding the Great Lakes posts to the Americans. In 1812 the Nor'Westers had visions of repossessing the posts and territories they had lost, thus restoring the kingdom of the fur trade to its former glory.[42] For the merchants of all sectors, loyalty was tied to the identity of their interests with those of the empire.

Thus the élite classes of Lower Canada, English- and French-speaking, whether in agreement on internal questions or not, were unanimous in their refusal to envisage annexation to the United States. Not one among them appears to have found anything to be gained by collaborating with the invaders.

Such unity was bound to have an influence on the lower classes, yet this seems not to be the whole reason for the rural and urban lower-class loyalty which contrasts so sharply with the attitude of neutrality in 1775. The circumstances in 1812 were different. There was no longer any fear of deportation, and the economic situation, instead of holding the *habitant* to his land, encouraged farmers' sons to depart and take part in the conflict. The people's attachment for the monarchy and their traditional politico-social beliefs were thereby reinforced. It seems, however, that a large factor in their readiness to leap to the defence of their country was the nationalist sentiment whipped up by the French-Canadian middle classes, the latter preaching neither rejection of monarchical institutions nor hatred of the mother country but focusing attention on the misdeeds of merchants, functionaries, French-Canadian "traitors," and American immigrants. The *habitant* was by now feeling the pinch of seigneurial land shortages and had become very sensitive to anything which threatened to further complicate his existence; fear of immigrants had become ingrained. With dislocations arising in rural districts and external peril looming, nationalist feeling was brought to the surface by the propaganda directed at the people by the élite. Declared Judge Panet in 1812, "Canadians who are so fortunate to live under the British government, without taxes on land or wealth, protected in the free practice of your religion.... What may you hope for if the Americans seize the country? That will be the case if you refuse to defend it.... Do you know these Americans, or rather, have you not known them since the time they [first] came through our countryside doing business with you, business which was never to your advantage...?"[43] In resisting the invaders, the people felt they were defending their interests and protecting their cultural heritage.

III The Development of the War

When Sir George Prevost arrived in Quebec in September, 1811, to take up his post as governor and commander-in-chief, the situation was not as critical as he might have believed. His predecessor's dispatches had given the impression that war was inevitable and that the *habitants*, goaded by a revolutionary minority, were awaiting the propitious moment to reveal their disloyalty. Ryland had taken pains to inform him that peace had been maintained only through Craig's firmness in suppressing the "demagogues."[44] But the new governor also knew the anxiety aroused in England by his predecessor's behaviour. He intended to make his own assessment of the situation.

Prevost was a soldier, the son of a Swiss-born British army officer, and had served with distinction against the French in the West Indies. In 1805 he was made a major-general and a baronet. But he was more than a soldier, for as governor of St Lucia and lieutenant-governor of Nova Scotia he had experienced the problems of civil administration. He was therefore not unduly perturbed by the caprices of popular assemblies. His natural preference, moreover, was for diplomacy rather than coercion. If he harboured a certain prejudice against his predecessor, as Ryland suggested, it was hardly surprising.[45] His mission was to prepare the English colonies to repel a possible American invasion, and in its accomplishment he was not content with merely attending to the material problems. Two months after his arrival he wrote to Ryland, "In the short time I have been in this province, I have visited it in a way to enable me *to form a correct judgment* of the genius and disposition of the Canadians. Travelling without pomp, I had frequent opportunities of seeing the inhabitant in his true character. I found the country in the hands of the priests, and at Quebec that *prelatical pride* was not confined to the Catholic Bishop."[46] In those two months he had grasped the true tendencies of public opinion, and to a large degree the nature of the various groups' ambitions; this led him to abandon Craig's strategies, much to the annoyance of his predecessor's advisers. Once convinced of the Canadians' loyalty, he set about seeking support from the population at large, realizing that he was risking the displeasure of certain of the élite whose support from that quarter was minimal, yet attempting to satisfy the English-speaking minority to the extent possible. In so doing he was not following a bias in favour of the French element; he was responding to a lucid evaluation of the military situation in all its aspects.

The balance of powers was his guiding principle, a kind of idealistic projection of social and ethnic equilibrium in political terms. Though he did not envisage ministerial responsibility as a solution to political problems, he nevertheless felt that the executive councillors must be men of influence in the community and not simply civil servants raised to that distinction.[47] The governor, as representative of the crown and empire, must necessarily remain the real executive head. Decisions were to be his; the members of his council were to be his advisers, not his masters.[48]

Prevost's determination not to be the pawn of any clique is revealed in his dismissal of Ryland as secretary to the governor, his efforts to change the composition of the executive council, and his spurning of Bishop Mountain, whom he considered better suited to political intrigue than theology. His role, as he conceived it, was that of arbiter between the various political and social interests. His proposal for appointments to the legislative council he explained thus: "... to enable me to form in that branch of the Legislature a counterpoise to the House of Assembly, thereby transferring to the Legislative Council the political altercations which have hitherto been carried on by the Governor, in person, and which, in some degree, might have been spared him by a well composed Upper House, possessed of the consideration of the country, from a majority of its members being independent of the Government."[49] In his mind the legislative council, in order to provide the desired counterpoise, should represent those social and ethnic groups ill-represented in the assembly; it should, however, include more French Canadians, chosen for their firmness and moderation. He was aware that the system, since it depended on permanent councillors and transitory governors, could lead to the governor's being dominated by his councillors. His hope was to make the governor independent of political factions; if this were to be, the legislative council would have to assume its full responsibilities vis-à-vis the assembly. This application of the constitution, of course, would only work if everyone played strictly by the rules and with willingness to compromise.

Prevost might conceive his role as colonial governor as he wished and do much to change the composition of the two councils the better to achieve his objectives, but he realized he would have to live with the legislative assembly as elected by the people. Indeed, he entertained no thought of trying to influence the people's electoral decisions. Ethnic identification and nationalism, he discerned, had much to do with political allegiance; furthermore, the English party had not only lost its formerly considerable influence, but was by now a distinctly minor force in the assembly. "I plainly saw," he wrote, "that I could not rely upon the strength of the English party in the House for effecting those measures I might wish to carry through it." This decline he attributed to discredit in the eyes of the electors brought by the party's cosy alliance with Craig and his senior civil servants. Yet such clear rejection of the party, which after all represented the colony's commercial interests, he felt, would have been inconceivable had the security of the state not been such a major preoccupation.

In other circumstances his attitude to the English party might have been more amenable. As it was, he wrote, "I was sensible that by

conciliating the Canadian representatives I could alone hope to succeed in the accomplishment of any object I have in view." While he
was impressed by the Canadian party's strength in the assembly, more
significantly he perceived that its leaders were neither revolutionaries
nor of a mind to truckle with the Americans: "This may be true with
regard to some few members of the House, altho I very much doubt it,
but as respects the majority I conceive is unfounded, and that their
loyalty and attachment are sufficiently strong to be proof against any
such attempts to seduce them." In short, it was their loyalty, representativeness, and majority position in the House which led the governor
to seek the support of the party's leaders for legislation he considered
necessary for the defence of the colony. It was certainly not admiration
for them; indeed, as he noted with some disdain:

> ... these leaders are chiefly lawyers, men who as it appears to me are
> seeking an opportunity to distinguish themselves, as Champions of
> the Public for the purpose of gaining popularity and who are en-
> deavouring to make themselves of consequence in the eyes of the
> Government in the hope of obtaining employment from it ... [;]
> some of them held offices conferred on them by myself and all of
> them I have reason to think was it necessary to purchase their ser-
> vices would be willing to barter them ....[50]

On the strength of these observations, Prevost made liberal use of
government patronage, that coveted source of prestige, profit, and authority. For Bédard, the discredited leader of the Canadian party, he
obtained a judgeship; Taschereau, Blanchet, Borgia, and Bédard, who
had been stripped of their militia appointments by Craig, recovered
them; Louis Bourdages, one of the most rambunctious of the party's
leaders, was promoted to colonel, while Panet and Debartzch were
appointed to the legislative council;[51] the ambitious Louis-Joseph
Papineau was elevated to the modest rank of captain, being still a little
young. Not all French Canadians were so sure the patronage was such
a blessing; "the grave of Canadian industriousness," one observer
called it. "Besides, what bowing and scraping, what fawning it takes to
keep a little place that earns you barely enough to live on; without
considering how you must bend to comply with the thinking of those
who employ you."[52] James Stuart, Craig's foe and now the Canadians'
friend, posed a special problem, for he was aspiring to succeed
Bédard. The governor would have had to offer him too much, and so
he tried to isolate and thus neutralize him. But the war effort was not
sufficiently all-absorbing to prevent the pursuit of other struggles, and
Stuart seized the opportunity to rekindle old quarrels which had lain

dormant since 1810.[53] The English party meanwhile was awaiting a propitious moment to launch a counterattack. All of which goes to show that the calm brought about by Prevost was a fragile one.

The French-Canadian middle classes in fact had deeper motivation for loyalty than mere desire for immediate and, realistically speaking, rather paltry gain. Prevost recognized their political and social power; if he erred, it was in underestimating it, having concluded that it was the clergy who were the real leaders of the French-Canadian society. Impressed by the power and prestige of the church, and judging that it would provide not only reliable support in time of war but a counter-balance to the middle classes in peacetime, he went out of his way to win over the ecclesiastical hierarchy, and through them the curés and their parishioners. He met with Monseigneur Plessis and even suggested that Plessis prepare a memorial on the *desiderata* of his church.[54] Subsequently he obtained an annual allowance of a thousand *livres* for the bishop, and undertook measures to give the church a closer relationship to the state.

Once reassured on the complexion of public opinion in Lower Canada, Prevost turned his attention to the defence against invasion. With only 5,600 regular soldiers in the Canadas and 4,220 in Nova Scotia,[55] he was well aware how vastly his forces were outnumbered. Since Britain was in no position to divert either reinforcements or substantial sums of money from her war effort against Napoleon, it was urgent that the governor provide for rapid relocation of his troops according to need as well as for the mobilization of local militia groups, and to find ways of financing the operations from the economic resources of the colony itself.

Great Britain had been in the grip of a severe economic crisis since 1808. Bank discount policies and the state's swollen financial needs had been exerting great inflationary pressure and the pound sterling had depreciated drastically, exacerbated in 1812 by the need to export funds for the maintenance of British troops abroad and provide aid to allies. Currency was in short supply, moreover (partly because of illicit trading in currency and precious metals),[56] and the risks of transporting it by sea were great despite Britain's maritime supremacy. Even the most endangered colonies were therefore obliged to work out their own systems of financing their defence.

But the colonies, too, were suffering from inflation and the repercussions of the British financial crisis. Since 1806 the growth of the timber trade and greatly increased imports had swelled the state's coffers, true enough, but not sufficiently to cover the cost of defence. Then in 1811 government revenues began to shrink, for exports declined and imports inevitably followed suit. Exports of beaver, for instance, had fallen off 43 per cent. Despite domestic demand for planks and boards and the stimulating effect of the war on shipbuilding, the lumber industry was experiencing a recession; as previously noted, high costs for transportation and maritime insurance eventually forced Great Britain to re-adjust its protective tariff in 1814 to 65s. per load. But it was in the agricultural sector where the most alarming situation was developing. In August, 1812, Bishop Plessis, on government instigation, sent a circular letter to all curés requesting them to ask all parishioners not called for military service to assist in seeding the fields.[57] But shortage of labour only partly explains the succession of poor harvests in most areas of Lower Canada, beginning in 1812. In April, 1814, Monseigneur Panet, Plessis's coadjutor, mentioned "the poor harvests we have suffered for some years" as one of the woes sent upon the people for their "drunkenness, unchastity, hatred, deception and bad faith."[58] By December, 1815, the situation was so serious that the bishop requested reports on the state of harvests from all curés. These reports show that thirteen parishes had small surpluses, forty had enough for subsistence and seeding, twenty-four would have difficulty providing both, and twenty-seven were seriously in want.[59] During the war agricultural production shortages of one kind or another brought high prices and speculation, and poverty for a great number of people.

The resultant fall-off in exports, and consequently in ordinary imports, meant that there was precious little to spend on defence. Yet the militiamen had to be paid, equipped, and fed, the regulars supplied, and fortifications and warships built, all to a great extent with imported goods, causing a rise of 88 per cent in total import volumes during the war. Interestingly enough, lively contraband trade with the United States meant that local production shortfalls were largely compensated for from enemy sources in New England.

In the circumstances it would have been exceedingly difficult to finance the colony's war effort without "army bills," paper money issued by the government of Lower Canada and guaranteed by the British government. These, Prevost decided, were preferable to bills issued by a bank under imperial guarantee. He obtained the approval of the assembly without difficulty, even from those members opposed to the establishment of banks. A first issue of 250,000 *livres* was followed a year later by a second of the same size. In 1814 there were 951,510 *livres* of the bills in circulation, and by the end of 1815, 1,205,683 *livres*. The paper money experiment, conducted with caution, for once did not lead to bankruptcy and indeed was such a success that the assembly proposed continuance of the system. Between 1815 and 1817 the bills were redeemed in an orderly fashion and without difficulty.

In the absence of any vigorous increase in production the army bills were in fact a boon, particularly to the merchant classes: importers and those with shipping interests most of all. The effect for other social categories is difficult to gauge. Peasants with surpluses of wheat, oats, and hay made handsome profits, but in this period of inflation farmers in less happy circumstances and urban workingmen were undoubtedly in hardship; for this class the militiamen's pay helped greatly to make ends meet.

For Prevost, to whom fell the defence of all the North American colonies, strategy was not easy. London recommended a defensive posture. The governor outlined the position as he saw it in his memorandum of May, 1812. Stressing the vulnerability of Nova Scotia and New Brunswick, he set aside thoughts of trying to defend them systematically. He proposed to concentrate on protecting the Canadas, which seemed to him to be the most likely targets for American attack, particularly Upper Canada. Not that he underestimated the strategic importance of Lower Canada; Montreal, he considered, was particularly vulnerable and "would become the first object of attack," while Quebec, "the only permanent fortress in Canada," with its naturally strong position would be the key to the entire system of defence. As for manpower, he would depend mainly on the regular troops; the militia was to play a secondary role despite the unlikelihood of obtaining regular reinforcements. In Upper Canada, where General Brock was in command, Prevost estimated 11,000 militiamen, "of whom it might be prudent to arm no more than 4,000," and in Lower Canada 60,000, "ill-armed and without discipline," who would have to be trained in order to be useful.[60]

As early as April, 1812, Prevost requested the legislature to authorize raising a force of 2,000 militiamen between the ages of eighteen and twenty-five, whose pay was to be equal to that of the British regulars. The governor also invited Michel de Salaberry to recruit a corps of *Voltigeurs*. These volunteers were promised an additional sum of four *livres* plus fifty *arpents* of land at the end of their service.

Though war had yet to be declared the recruiting went smoothly, even, as noted by certain observers, with enthusiastic response.[61] That the enthusiasm cooled subsequently at some localities is hardly surprising, for material conditions were often deplorable due to inadequate organization. There was much resentment over the quality of food, lodging, and equipment and also the high-handedness and sometimes incompetence of officers. Nevertheless, there was only one incident of resistance worth noting, at Lachine in late June when a group of conscripts rioted, claiming that compulsory service had not yet been sanctioned by law. J.-P. Wallot, having spoken of "these conquerors and grave-diggers of New France," admits to finding no evidence in the details of the "Lachine riot" to validate "the hypothesis of an inclination to rebellion against the king or the British government."[62] Indeed, the most striking thing about the entire exercise is the fervent solidarity manifested against the invaders by the lower classes. Chief Justice Sewell, in early July, 1812, noted "universally a sincere and loyal desire to assist in every way for the defence of the country exceeding any expectation, and I am informed that the same inclination is manifested in the country parishes."[63] At the same date quite a different climate reigned in Upper Canada. After war was declared there was even greater cohesion among the social classes, and French Canadians fought not only in Lower Canada but in Upper Canada as well.

Defending Canada might have been well nigh impossible. "Had the Americans followed a sound line of operations," writes C.P. Stacey, "they would have concentrated against Montreal, using the excellent communications available by Lake Champlain and the Richelieu River. The capture of Montreal would have severed the essential line of communication—that by the St Lawrence—on which the defence of Upper Canada entirely depended, and the whole of that province would have fallen into their hands at an early date."[64] The geographical distance separating the populations of the two colonies might have worsened the situation. But the Americans were far from united over the war, and the states bordering Lower Canada were flatly opposed to it. Divided popular opinion, lack of skilled strategists, indifferent military leadership, and a small and poorly trained army all worked to neutralize their numerical advantage. A month before the declaration of war the American army numbered less than 12,000. For these and other reasons the Maritimes were never attacked, and Lower Canada suffered only one serious invasion. The principal theatre of military operations was Upper Canada.

The year 1812 was relatively uneventful for the forces of Lower Canada. On October 23 a detachment of *Voltigeurs* in an advance post at St Régis was taken unawares by a force of American militiamen, who retired with twenty prisoners and a quantity of equipment and supplies. A month later, Cornwall and Glengarry militiamen carried out a successful raid on an American post on the Salmon River. The single large-scale encounter was at Lacolle on November 20, when Major-General Dearborn, having at last resolved to launch the conquest of Lower Canada, advanced with 6,000 men and clashed with de Salaberry's *Voltigeurs* and 300 Indian allies, who were well entrenched and turned back the enemy without difficulty. Dearborn retired to Plattsburg and spent the winter there.

1813, too, was quiet, until August. Early that month President Madison received a plan of invasion from his secretary for war and approved it. A force led by Wilkinson was to seize Kingston and continue down the St Lawrence to Montreal. Meanwhile, Hampton was to lead a second force from Plattsburg against Montreal.[65] On September 20 Hampton crossed the border with 4,000 men, only to retreat again for reasons unknown since there was only a force of a few hundred under de Salaberry to oppose him. Governor Prevost hastened to Montreal on September 25 to prepare the city's defence. To the 3,000 militiamen already in service he added a further 5,000. On October 16 Hampton was ordered to lead his forces down the Châteauguay River. Five days later he again crossed the border, with 4,200 men, mostly badly trained and unruly recruits according to Purdy.[66] A contingent of 1,400 militiamen from the state of New York had refused to follow. De Salaberry was waiting with 1,600 men, including a contingent commanded by Lieutenant-Colonel G. Macdonald. An apparently brief engagement took place on the afternoon of October 26; few of the troops on either side had even encountered the enemy before the Americans decided to withdraw. With this reversal the campaign against Montreal faltered, and it ended with Wilkinson's defeat at Chrysler's Farm near Cornwall on November 11.

Until the month of September, the year 1814, too, was uneventful for Lower Canada. Having received major reinforcements from Britain, Prevost decided to take the offensive, moving to attack Plattsburg on two fronts, by land and also by water, to destroy the American fleet that controlled Lake Champlain. A force of 10,351 British regulars invaded the United States on September 1, and on September 6 laid siege to Plattsburg.[67] Before the troops moved to take the city, however, the British fleet was routed by the Americans. Prevost ordered a retreat. The defeat loosed a flood of recriminations against the governor, both from officers participating in the expedition and from political opponents.[68] Prevost was recalled to England in 1815 and died before his conduct of the campaign was judged. The historian Hitsman sums it up thus: "The Plattsburg fiasco was the result of leaving a defensively minded general in charge of operations once the tide had turned."[69] The same might be said of the American generals, Dearborn and Hampton.

The consequences of the war were various and difficult to delineate. It certainly stimulated commerce between Upper and Lower Canada, renewed interest in canalling to improve St Lawrence navigation, and paved the way psychologically for the establishment of banks. It did nothing to stop the decline of the fur trade and wheat production in Lower Canada. It served the Catholic Church admirably; by 1815 the

Anglican bishop had lost all hope of obtaining supremacy for
church. It also stimulated French-Canadian nationalism. In local l
the Battle of Châteauguay became a great French-Canadian victo.,
and the turning point in the war, and de Salaberry became a hero, for
all his anti-nationalist convictions. The historian Chapais writes of the
event with a lyricism matching that of de Salaberry's contemporaries:

> Through the leader's tactics and the soldiers' fearlessness, it rightly
> marks a glorious day for our race. It was primarily a French Cana-
> dian victory. It is ours and no one can take it from us.... Château-
> guay was our reply to Craig's, Ryland's, and Sewell's imputations.
> Châteauguay was our revenge. Châteauguay was the assertion of
> our undeniable loyalty and ardent patriotism. Châteauguay was an
> heroic illustration of our national spirit.... Salaberry and his gallant
> men gave to English arms a thing of no small glory, a French
> victory.[70]

The poets of the day would have been hard put to do better.

II
Crisis, 1815-1840

CHAPTER 5

The Rural Economic Crisis

The golden age of the fur trade—merchant adventurers, *coureurs des bois*, and close economic ties between Indians and whites and between the east and the far west—was virtually a thing of the past by the beginning of the nineteenth century. With the Napoleonic wars as a stimulus, lumber emerged as a new staple trade. Without it the collapse of the fur economy would have been disastrous.

In the early years of the new century, wheat production tended increasingly to fall behind a burgeoning population growth, to a point where, by 1830, Lower Canada had become a major importer of wheat. The decline, of course, progressed more rapidly in some regions than others, and some producers were slower than others to read the writing on the wall and abandon the old, wasteful agricultural methods. But not a single rural parish was spared, and by 1840 the entire farming population was more or less seriously affected.

A major shift in production structures occurred as wheat production failed even to fulfil subsistence requirements and farmers turned to other crops, notably oats and potatoes, and discovered a new interest in livestock. But the basic problem remained, namely the inadequacy of farming methods resulting in disappointing yields and quality. A proportion of farmers found outlets locally for their produce, but it became increasingly difficult to be competitive in the urban marketplace. With growing rural dependence on imported wheat, self-sufficiency became impossible. The agricultural crisis became a social one, whose effects spilled from the rural districts into the cities.

Despite the convergent ill winds of falling agricultural production and a general decline in prices, certain sectors of the economy were making progress. Trade in Upper-Canadian and American produce to fill the vacuum in both the Lower-Canadian and imperial markets stimulated growth for the transportation sector and for the city of Montreal. The new trade patterns and the lumber economy necessitated the appearance of banks. With the end of the continental blockade Great Britain continued to protect her colonies with preferential tariffs, and the lumber trade, far from returning to its previous marginal state as feared by Quebec City merchants, continued to flourish.

Forestry became the dominant economic activity in the Ottawa Valley and many townships, and while local contractors and the middle classes of Quebec profited most from it, it also provided a supplementary source of income for much of the population in the rural parishes, especially in the Quebec district.

Thus the economy of Lower Canada changed, but remained profoundly affected by the crisis in agriculture, the sector whose fortunes weighed most heavily on the lives of the greatest number of individuals and especially on the future of the French-speaking population.

I The Agricultural Crisis

It has been contended by Professors J.-P. Wallot and G. Paquet that there was no agricultural crisis in Lower Canada until after 1815, that the fall-off in wheat exports in the first decade of the century was due to instability of demand on the export market, that the decline in sales to Great Britain was more than offset by increased sales in a domestic market revolutionized by the lumber trade, and that the *habitant*, with admirable perspicacity, diversified his production in response to market movements, and prospered withall.[1] In proof of this last point, they cite statistics on revenues of a number of parishes, but without allowing for factors relating to their increase, as though the wealth of curés and ecclesiastical institutions guaranteed that of the peasant. We know, however, that the population of Lower Canada was doubling every twenty-six years, and that parish coffers were enriched by such fecundity, just as they were by epidemics which increased the number of deaths. Since payments were often made in kind, moreover, parish revenues were considerably affected by prevailing prices. In 1792, for instance, the Quête de l'Enfant-Jésus brought from the *habitants* of Varennes contributions of 100 *minots* of wheat which, sold at 3 *livres* per *minot*, yielded 300 *livres* for the parish; in 1814, the wheat contribution was only 75 *minots*, but since the market price was then 18 *livres* per *minot*, the benefit to the parish was 1,350 *livres*. An increase in parish revenue therefore does not necessarily reflect an increase in production. The evidence in fact is contrary to the contentions of Professors Wallot and Paquet, revealing in particular a progressive decline in wheat exports of Lower-Canadian origin between 1803 and 1842, traceable by subtracting American and Upper-Canadian wheat from total exports at the port of Quebec (see Tables 11, 12, 21, 85, and 86). Owing to incomplete information on imports for 1802-12, the drop in local exports for the period (31 per cent) is unquestionably minimal; the real decrease likely surpassed 40 per cent, perhaps considerably. Wallot and Paquet's price index increase from 111.3 in 1792 to 291.0 in 1812 tells us nothing of the change in wheat production levels or peasant standard of living, whereas movement in the production curve is in fact the most significant indicator of the crisis and its origins. Lower-Canadian exports eventually ceased altogether; the trend was to import on an increasing scale for domestic consumption. And this in a period, 1800 to 1840, when the market situation should have stimulated Lower-Canadian production. From 1816 to 1839, 13,187,865 *minots* of wheat were imported for domestic consumption and re-export (see Tables 11 and 12).

Wheat from Upper Canada accounted for only 7 per cent of the total exported at Quebec in 1801-2, but by 1806-7 the proportion had risen to 23 per cent. Upper-Canadian and American wheat was therefore competing effectively with the Lower-Canadian product despite high transportation costs.[2] Immediately after the War of 1812 the Lower-Canadian content in wheat exports was only 28 per cent of the total, and declined thereafter almost constantly. After 1832 Lower Canada was a regular customer for Upper-Canadian and American wheat (see Tables 21 and 86).

There was a decline, too, in quality. A report of 1823 notes, "Wheat from the district of Montreal cannot produce sufficiently good flour (not white enough) to compete with American flour on the West Indies market."[3] In the period 1821-24, with demand in the British market weak and quality a competitive factor, only 9 per cent of wheat exports through the St Lawrence was of Lower-Canadian origin. The inferior quality of Lower-Canadian flour was due to a poor product of poor agricultural techniques, not poor milling; there were inadequate seigneurial mills, true enough, but improved milling facilities had been installed by many seigneurs and merchants. In 1806, the agent for the seigneury of Laprairie wrote to the commissioners of the Jesuit Estates requesting mill improvements, pointing to "General Burton's and Mr McTavish's mills" as "masterpieces."[4]

The picture of changing agricultural structures obtainable from the various indicators shows the decline in wheat production beginning around 1802 overall, and earlier in certain regions[5] (see Table 13).The principal variables at work were three, soil fertility, stability of landholdings, and population growth. Providing the soil was fertile and landholdings stable, in all cases peak yields were attained toward the end of the first major phase of settlement in a given region, with stagnation or decline thereafter. In the oldest parishes where, even in the eighteenth century, settlement was rapid, cultivation intense, and subdivision under way, the decline in production began between 1790 and 1802. In certain parishes the progress of urbanization was an important factor in patterns of change. Such was the case with the parish of Montreal, where the English-speaking led the way in commercializing agriculture; there the wheat decline was reflected in a shift toward oats and particularly potatoes (see Table 14).

Thus a transformation occurred between 1800 and 1840 which saw wheat fall from between 60 and 70 per cent of all agricultural production (the level which had prevailed since the seventeenth century) to 21 per cent in 1831 (a good crop year) and to 4.4 per cent in 1844. Production per farm family in good crop years from 1760 to 1802 had averaged between 100 and 200 *minots*, but was only 56.5 *minots* in 1831 and 12 *minots* in 1844. In 1831 the average per family was less than 50 *minots* in 37.9 per cent of the parishes and less than 100 *minots* in 76 per cent; in 1844 the average was less than 50 *minots* in 98 per cent of the parishes. Attempts were made to increase the production of other grains such as barley, rye, and buckwheat from which flour might be made, either alone or with some wheat content. They succeeded only marginally, the reason of course being the same as for the decline in wheat production (see Tables 6, 15, 16, and 52).

By 1833, though he was consuming less bread, the *habitant* was dependent for his very subsistence on grain produced by his competitors in Upper Canada, and he was to remain so. The roles were now reversed. Over the long term the wheat crisis, along with the lumber trade, was to strengthen the economic ties between the Canadas. Isolation in self-sufficiency was now impossible in any event. Wheat was no longer the mainstay of the *habitant's* diet and his source of supplementary income but a commodity to be bought if he could afford it.

A change in production structures was inevitable, but the *habitant*, alas, was slow to change his habits until forced to do so (see Table 17). W. H. Parker's conclusion that the decline of wheat began after 1830 with a blight of wheat flies and that oats became a major replacement crop[6] does not appear to be born out by the records. Tithe reports between 1805 and 1831 and parish inventories of 1827 and 1831 show that in most seigneuries the proportion of oats to total harvest remained about the same as during the French Régime. It is true, however, that the proportion of oats rose to 33 per cent by 1844, but there is no indication that oatmeal acquired importance in the French-Canadian diet. Most of the oat mills were probably built to serve the English population (see Table 51).

The principal replacement crop was in fact potatoes, a rich source of nourishment. Modest quantities had earlier been grown for feeding pigs, but during the difficult years from 1813 to 1816 the *habitant*, having insufficient bread, discovered a liking for this food and it soon came to have a place of honour on his table. In 1819 a contemporary observed, "Potatoes were introduced in Canada only after the Conquest of 1760; and all now grow them in abundance. The quantity sown every year has increased fourfold since 1816, because they were almost the only recourse in that year of shortage."[7] Parish inventories of 1827 and 1831 show potatoes accounting for 47 and 46 per cent of total harvests. It seems, however, that the French Canadians did not grow them for sale. In the cities, lumber camps, and even rural areas there was a fairly strong local market, but the biggest producers were English-speaking, and it was they who supplied that market. For the French Canadians potatoes were a subsistence crop, but, grown by traditional methods, they proved after 1830 to be subject to adverse conditions and also costly in soil fertility (see Table 51).

With the dwindling supply of wheat and less money in rural hands, the rural diet contained not only less bread but less imported sugar, about the same amount of peas, more maple sugar and above all, along with potatoes, more pork. In 1784, a hog count of over four per household was registered in 41 per cent of seigneurial parishes; in 1831 the proportion was 75 per cent, but fell to 11 per cent during the following decade. Demand was strong and prices on the whole fairly good; some of the rural folk were undoubtedly raising hogs to increase or maintain their incomes, but the majority were more concerned with subsistence than sales. The hog-raiser with pork surpluses, moreover, had difficulty competing with foreign producers in the urban market and by and large was obliged to sell his product in the rural districts. With the new emphasis on hog-raising, the *habitant* once again paid the price of poor farming methods and found himself in most difficult straits in the post-1830 depression. Between 1831 and 1842, the average number of hogs per farm in the Montreal district dropped from 4.7 to 3.3 (see Table 51).

The decline in rural incomes after 1815 also forced the *habitant* to turn to his own devices to clothe himself. In 1819 it was observed, "Flax is grown in great quantity at present in this district [Quebec] and a rough linen is made from it for domestic use. The farmer now finds himself more obliged to pay attention to this article and [also] to increase the number of his sheep in order to have enough to clothe himself while the products of the land are at such low price on the markets of Great Britain."[8] And in 1821, in the midst of a market crisis, "Unless the habitants of the district of Montreal begin more generally to make their own cloth with which to dress, they will soon be unable to protect themselves from the rigours of the seasons."[9] Sheep-raising in this period increased considerably in comparison with that of the eighteenth century. Parish inventories show an average of more than four sheep per farm in 87 per cent of the parishes in 1831 and the same in 1844 (68 per cent in 1784). In regions of sheep-raising on a larger scale, however, the size of flocks diminished after 1832, the proportion of parishes with an average of over 16 sheep per farm falling from 10 per cent to 2 per cent by 1844. Here again, the produce of the seigneuries was uncompetitive in the marketplace. Only the English-speaking attempted textile manufacturing on a commercial scale.

Similar observations can be made regarding cattle-raising for milk, butter, cheese, leather, and meat. Deficiencies in local production kept prices from following the general decline after 1815, and after 1820 there was an increase in the size of cattle herds; in 1831, 16 per cent of the parishes registered average herds of more than 10 "*bêtes à cornes*" per farm, but the proportion was only 8 per cent in 1844 (3 per cent in 1784). Since English-speaking farmers were the most active in this domain, they were the most severely affected by the post-1830 depression (see Table 51).

As the scarcity of new, fertile land became acute, the inadequacy of farming methods began to have disastrous consequences. European practice forbade the sowing of wheat two years in a row in the same field because it would impoverish the soil and produce poor-quality grain, but the *habitant* ignored the rule, often in contravention of the terms of his concession. When the soil began to show unmistakable signs of exhaustion, or when the needs of a growing family required, or when export market demand encouraged it, he would turn to newly cleared land. When subdivided, the land would lose its fertility all the more quickly. During the second half of the eighteenth century, the average wheat yield per *arpent* had been between six and twelve *minots*, but by 1831 it was only about three *minots* and even less in the following decade. Agricultural societies, noting the effectiveness of experiments in the British Isles, campaigned with little success for crop rotation and for fertilization with manure, which was ordinarily thrown into rivers or dumped in some far corner of the farm. They also tried to stop the *habitant* from denuding his land of trees, which not only destroyed his reserves of wood but contributed to the impoverishment of the soil. Even before 1820, the agent for the seigneury of Laprairie was writing that "none of the concessions of the seigneury of Laprairie has any wood left either for firewood or fences."[10]

Resistance to change pervaded all aspects of farmwork. Ploughing and harrowing were shallow, as they had always been, for farm implements were essentially the same as had always been used; there were often more thistles in a field than wheat. The agricultural societies organized exhibitions of the latest equipment used in Great Britain; some progress was noted but more often the lack of it, for while some farmers did begin to modernize their equipment, most clung to their old implements and customs. A change to horses as draft animals in place of oxen was progressing, but slowly. The proportion of parishes with an average of less than two horses per farm in 1831 and 1844 was 46 per cent and 53 per cent respectively (76 per cent in 1784).

Stock-raising suffered from the chronic underproduction of forage. There is no doubt that hay shortages became more pronounced after the beginning of the nineteenth century; though hay prices fluctuated widely they presented more resistance to the general downtrend than any others. The quality of products from undernourished animals cannot be high. In the eighteenth century common pasturelands served well enough, but particularly after 1815 more and more of the commonlands were parcelled out to the *habitants* and put to the plough. With increased activity in livestock, moreover, the "Canadian breeds" were imperilled by importation of animals and haphazard breeding; deterioration was frequently noted by contemporary observers. The agricultural societies campaigned for production of new types of feed, seeding of grazing grounds, and selective breeding. The results were disappointing on the whole; quality did not improve along with quantity. Lower-Canadian beef, pork, lard, butter, and cheese, together with homespun wool and linen, found meagre acceptance on either the imperial market or the urban domestic market. The volume of agricultural produce from the United States and Upper Canada, some of which was re-exported, indicates that the cities and lumber camps were essentially supplied from outside sources (see Table 18).

When depression set in after 1830, the size of herds and the volume of imports both declined. The large livestock producers of the Montreal region, most of them in the townships and a lesser number in the seigneuries, demanded protection against foreign competition in the hope of assuring themselves a hold on the urban market, but the imposition of prohibitive tariffs was opposed by grain exporters and lumber contractors who feared price increases prejudicial to their businesses. Moderate tariffs were adopted, however, which accounts for the decline in imports and also certain changes in the nature of American imports (uncured skins and whole animals in place of leather, for instance).

The *habitant* was no more inclined to give up growing wheat than to improve his farming methods. A contemporary observed in 1821, "The price of wheat naturally affects the price of labour and of all agricultural production; perhaps in this country more than any other, for here wheat forms by far the greatest part of the habitant's food."[11] Declining production, vanishing surpluses, and the reluctance or refusal of the *habitant* to change his ways brought progressive constriction to what was already a chronically poverty-stricken rural existence. Most of the scant surpluses a farmer might possess passed into the hands of seigneurs, merchants, and clergy. This had been the case even in the eighteenth century; the inequities of the division of wealth deriving from the land had been noted as early as 1789, a year of crop failure in a period of generally increasing production:

> The unfortunate peasant is always enveloped in hardship. Nothing can pluck him from indigence. The export of wheat enriches the State, but does not bring plenty to the countryside; those who draw off its substance spread it in the cities, and in the country hardship remains. But, say those men who see things only from afar, with all the fields being tilled and the harvest increasing in price, the peasant at work must be growing rich. To that there is only one way to reply. Is it he who works the land who reaps? Has it not been shown that most of the land belongs to seigneurs, or to rich individuals who spend its revenue in the cities? When this is agreed, the conclusion is that the countryside is inhabited only by poor labourers, who reap no wheat at all or only what is necessary to feed their families, and who in consequence do not profit by the increase in price of a product which they consume; on the contrary, if they do not have enough of that product, they must buy it more dearly, and being paid no more for their days of work they grow still more impoverished. There will be found in the country no more than ten farmers in a condition to await those happy turns of trade which will enrich them. Pressed to repay the money they owe, they hasten to sell their wheat to the grasping merchant, who exports it or locks it away in storehouses which cannot be opened unless he be given a golden key, and the wretched man who has none expires at the door.[12]

In the eighteenth century, as estimated by several contemporaries, the *habitant* had consumed 3 pounds of bread a day, representing an annual per capita consumption of 13 *minots* of wheat. Gauldrée-Boileau, French consul in Quebec from 1858 to 1863, estimated the Gauthier family's wheat harvest of 165 *minots* to be divided as follows: food for the family of nine, 118 *minots*; seed, 25 *minots*; tithes, 6 *minots*; surplus, 16 *minots*.[13] Another observer estimated 40 *minots* to be the minimum necessary for a colonist, his wife, and three children,[14] the equivalent of 72 *minots* for a family of nine. In poor crop years a family either ate poorly in order to keep enough for seeding or ate reasonably well and had nothing left, and then would have to buy seed. On a farm in the seigneury of Murray Bay over the period 1838 to 1849, the wheat yield varied between 8.4 and 2.2 *minots* per *minot* sown; the amount sown, 8 to 40 *minots*, was thus 11 to 45 per cent of the amount harvested.[15] Surveys made in the poor crop years of 1813, 1816, 1826, and 1833 show a high rate of indebtedness; in 1833 most of the debts contracted in 1826 had yet to be repaid.

Besides food and seed, there were fixed obligations in bad years as in good, such as the *cens et rentes* paid to the seigneurs. The fee at seigneurial mills was about 1/13 of the wheat brought for milling. In the seigneury of Laprairie in 1806, the *rente* brought a total of 646 *minots*, and milling fees 2,400 *minots*. Revenue for 1815 from *lods et ventes*, payable by sellers of land at the rate of 1/12 of the price of sale, amounted to 9,171 French *livres*.[16] There is no doubt that the small producer's obligations to the seigneur weighed more and more heavily as production declined and prices eroded. The church also extracted its share. The tithe, the basis of the curés' personal incomes, took 1/26 of all grain harvested; reports of 46 parishes in the Montreal region for the years 1834, 1835, and 1836 show that 16 curés collected between 1,000 and 3,000 *minots* and 18 others between 500 and 1,000 *minots*.[17] Parishioners also made personal gifts to their curés. Then there were pew rentals, Sunday and holy-day collections and the Quête de l'Enfant-Jésus (a subscription to which each gave according to his means), masses to be paid for, fees for baptisms, marriages and burials, and special contributions for church construction and repair. Like the seigneurs, the curés, both personally and as administrators of the *Fabriques*, had considerable quantities of agricultural produce for disposal in one way or another. The seigneurs and the curés in any event seem to have reaped considerably more than the farmers from the export and urban grain trade after the turn of the century.

The *habitant* had necessarily to sell some of his produce to meet his cash payments to the seigneur and the curé, and to obtain imported commodities he would need for his own consumption. The transactions were rarely to his advantage. Dealers, through agents known as *coureurs des côtes*, bought heavily in good crop years at low prices and sold dearly in bad years. Between the export market and the increasingly important domestic market such speculation became very complex, the new local merchants acting as middlemen. The average *habitant* was invariably vulnerable. In the eighteenth century his lot had been bearable since he often had surpluses to sell and he and his sons could earn extra money in the fur trade, but from 1800 on, with declining production, more frequent crop failures, and a waning fur trade, his condition worsened progressively, and after 1830 he was in sore straits indeed. A wheat harvest of 56 *minots* per family (an average of 6.4 persons) in the relatively good crop year of 1831 clearly reveals the depth of the crisis.

In the circumstances, the lumber trade began to play a major role in rural life, particularly in the townships, and in the district of Quebec where in 1831 nearly half the sawmills were located. Seigneurial land near Montreal, however, was already stripped of much of its timber and by this period it was here that the agricultural crisis was most cruelly felt.

II Forest Industry Development

As overall prices tumbled in Europe and North America, the forest industries enjoyed unprecedented growth. An economic structure based on healthy agriculture and the fur trade yielded to one of ailing agriculture and the lumber trade. By reason of dependence on external factors, in particular protective tariffs, the growth in lumber was not seriously affected by agricultural deficiencies, though the two sectors were to some extent interdependent (see Table 19).

In response to demand from Great Britain and the West Indies and aided by dwindling resources in the United States, exports of Lower-Canadian forest products rose vigorously. Production for local use increased at the same time. With a few short-lived downturns, demand remained firm throughout this period, growing steadily for squared timber used in shipbuilding and railway development, for deals and for barrel staves, and more modestly and spasmodically for other categories such as squared oak, for which local supply was running low or becoming inaccessible. Exports of potash and pearl ash fluctuated with demand and particularly with local conditions; since there was little wood left on the farms in the seigneuries after the first decade of the century, exports of these products were dependent on availability of wood from new land-clearing and, increasingly, imports; after 1815 the Lower-Canadian share of export volume fell rapidly from 50 per cent to 30 per cent.

Without the mother country's protective tariffs, established in time of war to assure supplies and not to stimulate long-term development, there would have been no such growth in the industry, for Europe, the United States, and even New Brunswick had the advantage of more favourable location. Rising transportation costs rendered the early tariffs ineffectual and they were raised modestly a number of times and eventually more decisively in 1814 to 65s. per load. Colonial suppliers were thus provided with an effective differential, and were further favoured by the beginning of a long-term price decline. While there was no guarantee that the tariffs would remain after the return of peace, the post-war depression brought Great Britain to realize the importance of her colonies as outlets for her products and surplus population, and she found it expedient to maintain the system as a matter of policy. Besides, it became apparent that without the lumber industry the Lower-Canadian economy would become more and more anaemic, which would jeopardize the upper colony's development and perhaps even cause the Canadas to look to the United States for salvation. Despite the post-war deflation, the 1814 tariff was maintained until 1821, when, in response to pressure from English merchants, the rate on Baltic timber was dropped from 65s. to 55s. per load and a duty of 10s. per load was imposed on wood from the colonies. This new tariff structure remained until after 1840. The colonial lumber industry was still protected well enough, for the Americans ceased to be a threat to it after 1830, and henceforth competition came only from northern Europe. Growing opposition to the mercantilist policy both in Britain and Canada, however, was a source of anxiety for Lower-Canadian businessmen.

The boom in lumber brought a surge of activity to the ports of Lower Canada. In 1812, 362 ships were cleared through the port of Quebec; in 1823, 609 ships manned by 6,330 men; in 1825, 796 ships with 8,973 crewmen; in 1834, 1,213 ships with 13,341 crewmen. There were besides large numbers of schooners doing a coastal trade, steamships plying the St Lawrence between Quebec and Montreal, and a miscellany of vessels moving between the same cities and ports in Upper Canada and the United States. After the lumber trade, the principal stimulus behind all this activity was agricultural produce from outside Lower Canada.

Since the Navigation Acts had created a kind of monopoly for British shipping in the transport of colonial produce and since, in any event, Quebec and Montreal businessmen had insufficient capital to finance the many ships needed for the trans-Atlantic trade, most of the ships built at Quebec were sold to British and West Indies shipping interests; the local shipowners concentrated on tonnage for local traffic. The result was that profits from the lumber trade fell largely into the hands of British shipowners.

Since the transport of lumber meant far more export bulk than import, incoming ships arrived mostly in ballast, a situation which kept costs higher than on other routes and led ships' masters outbound from Britain to offer bargain rates to immigrants, who upon arrival would seek employment in lumbering, often in the hope of earning enough money to buy farms. In this sense the lumber trade stimulated immigration to Lower Canada. In 1832, though 50,000 immigrants disembarked at Quebec, 470 ships out of a total of 1,008 still arrived in ballast.[18]

The boom in lumber attracted considerable capital, some in investment by British interests and some brought by wealthy immigrants. Lumber profits aided the growth of the industry and also led to a certain diversification even in the country districts. With the new investment activity, banks soon became necessary. Imports, too, were stimulated, from the West Indies, Britain, and even China by way of Britain, but most markedly in agricultural produce from Upper Canada and the United States. For wool and other textiles statistics are unfortunately lacking (see Table 20).

Since import arrivals at Quebec and Montreal were destined for both Lower and Upper Canada, the influence of the lumber trade on consumption is difficult to evaluate. Upper Canada's rapid settlement alone could account for a large share of the sharp rise in purchases of foreign goods. Per capita consumption of wine and coffee, in demand by the upper classes, remained unchanged. Molasses, which was bought by all classes, remained stationary or perhaps declined. The use of imported sugar increased markedly despite a sharp rise in maple sugar production in Lower Canada. Imports of spirits dropped after 1818 but this was offset after 1825 by an increase in local distilling, an activity well advanced even earlier in Upper Canada. The most spectacular rise was in the consumption of tea, to which the poor classes had taken great liking.

Despite criticism that the lumber trade left little profit in the colony and gave employment to few, the mass of the people, both urban and rural, unquestionably benefited from it. Shipbuilding employed many skilled and unskilled workmen in and around Quebec; the production of squared timber, though concentrated in the Ottawa Valley, employed a large number of loggers and raftsmen, and in time there appeared a class of dockers who took over the loading and unloading of ships which had previously been done by sailors. Subsidiary to the trade in squared timber, the mainstay of the industry, other activities developed: the production of deals for both the local and imperial markets progressed steadily throughout the period. There were 727 sawmills by 1831 and 911 by 1844; in 1831, 248 of them were in the district of Quebec and some of them were very large; elsewhere most were of modest size. Farmers produced staves, hoops, and barrel ends for the local and export market. Production of potash and pearl ash brought benefit to farmers who had woodlots or who were clearing land, as well as to contractors. In 1831 there were 489 potash installations, 462 of them in the district of Montreal.

Lumber was Lower Canada's salvation in the precarious context presented by the crisis in agriculture, for it became the mainstay of a large segment of the commercial class and a major prop to the standard of living of an appreciable proportion of the lower classes. In the colony's relationship to the mother country it assumed the place once held by the fur trade, but that relationship was now one of even greater dependence by virtue of the protection provided by the system of preferential tariffs. As long as the British Empire was virtually the sole market, Upper-Canadian lumber could not compete with Lower-Canadian; only around 1846 when the American market began to open did the industry begin to play a major role in Upper Canada's economy.

III Western Resources and the Revolution in Transport

The faltering agricultural situation in Lower Canada stimulated Upper Canada's agricultural development and this, together with access to surpluses from neighbouring American states, gave impetus to movements between the west and the ports of Lower Canada, all of which was to have important economic and social consequences. With the commanding location of the port of Montreal, that city's merchants soon obtained control of the movement of agricultural produce and eventually of other sectors, notably import trade. Quebec began to lose its predominance in this period.

In the period of happier circumstances for Lower-Canadian agriculture, markets for local produce had opened shortly after 1760, first in the West Indies and southern Europe and then in Great Britain. The Corn Laws, however, worked against colonial exports except in poor crop years in Britain. In 1773, for instance, wheat imports were prohibited unless the price reached 48s. per quarter (eight bushels), which was rare in peacetime, and in 1791 the threshold was raised to 52s., giving further protection to British farmers. Fortunately for the colonies, inflation after 1790 rendered the threshold price meaningless, but it was not until 1815 that the British government began to revise its policy and make concessions to the colonies, setting a threshold of 80s. per quarter for foreign wheat and 67s. for colonial wheat. When prices fell after the Revolutionary and Napoleonic wars, however, the colonies no longer had an advantage. In 1821 an observer wrote:

> In the existing law concerning wheat the British Imperial Parliament has made a distinction between the English colonies and foreign countries ... but with the decrease which has occurred in prices and which appears to be permanent, this distinction no longer serves any purpose; so that we are in fact as much excluded as foreigners without sharing in the advantages they have, since they are not subject as we are to the trade restrictions imposed by the statutes of Great Britain.[19]

Pressure exerted by English merchants with interests in colonial trade brought the threshold price for colonial wheat down to 59s. per quarter in 1822. With prevailing prices continuing to decline, a further adjustment was made in 1825.

Grain merchants in the Canadas, having both to strengthen their position in the imperial market and ensure sufficient supply to meet the demand, called for continued effective protection by Great Britain and at the same time unrestricted admission of American produce which they could re-export. Increased production in the upper colony, in view of the decrease in Lower Canada's production, did not seem to them to be adequate to assure the supply. In their competition with New York, their eye was not only on their place in the imperial market but also on a greater presence in the West Indies and a greater share of the fish trade.

Despite fluctuations in demand from Great Britain, the circumstances were ripe for an increase in trade between Upper Canada, certain American states, and the ports of Lower Canada. Wheat and other agricultural imports gave the English-speaking merchants of Montreal a firm hold on goods bound for Upper Canada, though the latter also imported, legally and illegally, from the United States. Major stimulus for this trade came only after 1825, with increasing demand from Great Britain and crop failures in Lower Canada (see Tables 12 and 21). In 1828-29, Lower Canada's wheat deficit was more than 400,000 *minots*. British imports between 1823 and 1827 averaged 277,800 quarters annually, but in the next five years rose to 1,375,800 quarters. After 1832, while British demand declined, Lower Canada was importing large quantities of wheat for local consumption, the volumes mounting sharply between 1838 and 1842 when demand was again strong in Europe. The growing British, West Indian, and local demands and the application of the British preferential tariffs to re-exported produce all played a role in the steady rise of agricultural imports.

Over the long term, the trend destroyed the forces dividing the economic territory and allowing Lower Canada to remain economically independent. The decline of the fur trade with its continental ramifications and the retreat of Lower-Canadian agriculture into a self-dependent shell had spawned isolationist attitudes in which the political border between Lower and Upper Canada was seen to be economic and cultural as well. Upper Canada having developed as an economic colony of Lower Canada and of Montreal, there were isolationist tendencies at work there, too. Montreal's hold over Upper Canada's economy and the Lower-Canadian legislative assembly's control over its revenues aroused impatience and resentment; a strong desire for autonomy for the upper colony is visible in antagonism to the 1822 union proposal, quarrels over the division of customs duties, demands for Montreal to be annexed to Upper Canada, and bitterly divided attitudes over the union of 1840. Unity of the commercial empire of the St Lawrence was far from being a readily acceptable fact for most Upper Canadians. Nevertheless, the growth of the lumber industry and of interprovincial trade was pointing to greater economic unity, and a step beyond, political unity. And while the Lower-Canadian farmer might look upon his Upper-Canadian counterpart as a competitor, he was nonetheless becoming increasingly dependent on him; anything that might bring down the price of bread, even canalling the St Lawrence, came to appear justifiable. Other factors countering isolationist tendencies were the establishment of banks, the revolution in transport, and new conceptions in the realm of public finance.

As early as 1792 certain Montreal merchants connected with the fur trade had proposed a bank to resolve the problem of currency shortages and the diversity of coin in circulation, but nothing had materialized. After the beginning of the nineteenth century, new economic structures emerging made the need even more pressing. In 1808 John Richardson made a new proposal but encountered adamant opposition from the French-Canadian members of the assembly. The failure aroused bitter resentment in business circles, for at that time there were problems not only of currency but of financing new ventures. The success of the army bills during the War of 1812 did much to change the minds of many influential figures, for the war-time prosperity was widely attributed to the bills and the post-war depression to their disappearance. It was French-Canadian assembly members in fact who proposed that they be made permanent. Thereupon the English-speaking merchants made yet another proposal, and the following year, 1817, the Bank of Montreal was founded with a capital of £250,000; some years later a branch was opened in Quebec. The Quebec Bank and the Bank of Canada, in Quebec and Montreal respectively, were established in 1818, and then the City Bank of Montreal in 1833 and the Banque du Peuple in 1835, the latter founded by members of the French-Canadian élite with a capital of £80,000.[20] In 1831 the Bank of Canada was absorbed by the Bank of Montreal.[21] With the appearance of savings banks in the two cities the system was completed.

The pacesetter was the Bank of Montreal. Though its charter was modelled on that of the first American bank, it followed the traditionally cautious British banking practices and all the other banks followed suit, which accounts for their successful resistance to a series of financial crises. Lower Canadians did their business with a small number of strong banks rather than a large number of smaller and weaker ones (see Table 22).

Not surprisingly, there was much criticism of the banking system, particularly of the Bank of Montreal which was accused of trying to establish a monopoly for itself. Though a certain amount of the criticism came from the Bank of Montreal's competitors, some had obvious political undertones. After 1830 the *parti patriote*, seeing the system as a major source of power for the English-speaking, waged a bitter campaign against the banks, using arguments borrowed from the Jacksonian Democrats, but differently and in a different context. Anachronistically, the founders of the Banque du Peuple were not only rivals of the Bank of Montreal and certain of its directors but members of a political party whose leaders were opposed to banks. But criticism notwithstanding, the banks continued to gain strength, serving an economic territory which reached considerably beyond the borders of Lower Canada; though the financial crisis of 1837 forced them to suspend their operations for a time, the survival of the system was assured.

As the agricultural focus shifted westward, financed by the banks, major changes in transportation were in store. With the steady fall-off in wheat production in Lower Canada and declining prices and profits after 1815, the construction of the Erie Canal by the Americans and its completion in 1825 increased the threat of foreign competition, and the merchants' anxiety over the high cost of transport became acute; the need for a system of canals and deeper river channels along the St Lawrence and its tributaries became imperative.[22]

John Molson's St Lawrence steamboat service, begun in 1809, was the prelude to a transformation of great importance. Until 1840 the number of steamboats operating between Quebec and Montreal increased steadily.[23] In this period merchants were also attempting to establish a steamboat link with the Maritimes; in 1825 they declared, "these colonies are less acquainted with each other than with the most distant lands."[24]

Pressure for inland navigational improvements had been exerted since the middle of the first decade of the century. The problems were not really serious between Quebec and Montreal, but above Montreal, the port of trans-shipment on the St Lawrence route, there were the redoubtable Lachine Rapids, and even if that obstacle were overcome the shallowness of Lac St-Pierre would still impose stringent limits on the size of vessels navigating that section of the river. With the Lachine Canal finally completed, in 1826 the Montreal merchants proposed that a channel be dredged through Lac St-Pierre,[25] but though the plan was described as "inexpensive" the Quebec merchants, fearing loss of business to Montreal, were unenthusiastic. Applicants for incorporation of a proposed St Lawrence Company in 1835 cited in their preamble "difficulties in trade communication between the two Provinces and the resultant uncertainty, delays and loss of time and money ... which greatly diminish trade and retard the progress of the Provinces and prevent them from deriving the full benefits of the preference accorded their products by the policies of the Mother Country and also prevent their products from competing with those of foreign countries."[26]

Controversy over canal construction inevitably became political. Once the problems had been espoused as articles of faith by opposing factions, solutions were bound to be no more than partial.

In 1815 the legislature of Lower Canada appointed three commissioners to study the Lachine Canal project and voted £25,000 for its realization, but the plan was set aside. In 1819 a private company was formed by a group of Montreal merchants to revive it, but two years later ran short of funds and ceased work. With even such a modest enterprise foundering for lack of funds, it was becoming apparent that there was insufficient private capital in the Canadas to finance a major canal system. In 1821 the government of Lower Canada took over the project itself, the assembly having revoked the company's charter and voted funds to reimburse the shareholders for their expenditures and for completion of the work, more than £100,000 all told. The canal, 8½ miles long, 20 feet wide and 5 feet deep, was opened for traffic in 1824; though only a small part of a larger system most urgently needed, it was a major stimulus to the development of Upper Canada and of Montreal.

A second government project, the Chambly Canal, was begun in 1830 but not completed until after the rebellions of 1837 and 1838. While a private company was building a railway between Laprairie and St-Jean,[27] the canal construction suffered one delay after another, due to cholera epidemics in 1832 and 1834, torrential rains in 1833 and 1835,[28] and spiralling prices in 1836. In view of the extraordinary predominance of imports over exports at the port of St-Jean, it is apparent that the assembly's preference for this project over further improvements to the St Lawrence route was politically rather than economically motivated.

While the business community and the nationalists squabbled over St Lawrence canals, the British government, with an eye more on military security than economic considerations, undertook to build a navigable waterway between Montreal and the Great Lakes by which Upper Canada might be supplied without risk in time of war, at a cost of over £1 million. The major phase of the project was the Rideau Canal linking Kingston and the present city of Ottawa through the Rideau Lakes, a distance of 133 miles. The work, supervised by Colonel By, a British military engineer, was begun in 1826 and finally completed in 1834. There remained a hazardous series of rapids on the Ottawa River; these were bypassed by small canals which only partly facilitated navigation.

With the completion of the Erie Canal in 1825 the Americans had a considerable margin of commercial advantage. The money spent on the Rideau-Ottawa route did nothing to help the Montreal and Upper-Canadian merchants regain the competitive ground they had lost, as they might have done had the British government spent it instead on the St Lawrence route. The economic health of British North America was poorly served by such blind preoccupation with military security a decade and more after the end of the War of 1812.

A programme of massive investment in canals along the St Lawrence route would inevitably weigh heavily on the public purse. Rationally, the two colonies needed to pool their resources in pursuit of a common goal. Money might then have been raised in the imperial market.[29] As it was, however, Upper Canada took that initiative by itself and thereby jeopardized its financial stability. Once again the rational course was defeated by political rivalry. In Lower Canada the necessary change of attitudes was not forthcoming, either toward re-division between the colonies of import duty revenues, the major source of public funds, or toward diversification of revenue sources and borrowing. The legislative assembly continued to oppose the principle of land taxes and the very idea of borrowing money. Only a small proportion of the colony's budget was voted for public works and canalling. Between 1823 and 1827 only 12 per cent of expenditures was allocated to canals, and between 1828 and 1832 only 10 per cent, whereas 15 per cent might have been adequate. The assembly of Lower Canada, notwithstanding its complaints of government disregard for its wishes, clearly had a predominating influence over the use of public funds[30] (see Table 23).

The context of changing economic structures no doubt created firm solidarity between certain interest groups, but it also brought forth or accentuated sources of conflict. The under-representation of French Canadians in major business activity became even more pronounced in this period. In the lumber and grain trades and in shipbuilding the English-speaking were overwhelmingly dominant. In 1830 French Canadians held 19 per cent of Quebec Bank and only 2.9 per cent of Bank of Montreal shares, and in 1837, 2 per cent of Bank of Montreal and 4 per cent of City Bank shares. Even in the small Banque du Peuple their ownership was 62 per cent, not virtually total as might be expected. In transport, too, their ownership was small, an average 2 per cent in the nine largest transport companies.[31] Only in seigneurial landholdings (about 55 per cent) and in small urban and rural trade were they satisfactorily represented, and even there they had strong competition from English-speaking merchants. The real reasons for such a degree of ethnic socio-economic disparity are less important than the fact of it, and particularly the attitudes which emerged as a result of it.

The chronic discontent in the farming population due to steadily deteriorating conditions could as easily have erupted in popular resentment against the government, the seigneurs, and the clergy as in a nationalist movement opposed to the English state, bureaucracy, and bourgeoisie. Adoption of new agricultural methods would undoubtedly have been the best response to the farmers' problems, but fear, the dominant reaction, helped to channel the discontent toward a quest for easier solutions. The economic situation, whatever analysis might be made of it, served in any event to unite the French-Canadian lower and middle classes in a single nationalist movement.

CHAPTER 6

Demographic Pressures

Economic change and its concomitant problems had created anxieties and exacerbated tensions in the society. No segment, whatever its rank in the social hierarchy, could remain unaffected by the cloud of uncertainty and growing discontent hanging over Lower Canada. The frustrations of the poor and of the French Canadians in general, with their paltry share of economic power, were bound to erupt in one form or another. Louis-Joseph Papineau wrote thus of the English-speaking élite:

> They alone have the necessary breeding and fortune to receive. Not a single Canadian family can do so.... The country's resources are gobbled up by the newcomers. And though I have had the pleasure of meeting among them some educated and estimable men, who take pleasure in seeing me, the thought that my compatriots are unjustly excluded from sharing the same advantages saddens me in the midst of them.[1]

The economically powerful English were also dogged by worry, for their future depended not only on overcoming obstacles to economic development but also on political conditions in Britain as well as in the Canadas. But the crisis in Lower Canada had many aspects, not only economic. One of them, particularly for the lower classes, was demographic.

The demographic crisis had been brewing since the beginning of the century; it became a reality between 1805 and 1815 and persisted until at least the beginning of the twentieth century. The crux of it was the failure of economic growth to keep pace with population growth. Wheat production fell far behind the needs of the population and new economic activities were inadequate to fill the gap, for they

could not absorb enough of the surplus population. The forest industries provided seasonal or part-time work to many, but stable, full-
time employment to few. To a point this was the case in shipbuilding
as well, though more employed in that sector were able to earn a living
from it. Most of the people continued to live and work on the land.
There, the demographic pressures were tied to three vital factors, the
rate of population growth, the quality of farming methods, and the
quantity of available seigneurial land. The location and fertility of the
land also played a part. Seigneurial policy over land concession was at
least as important as the government's land policy. The political quarrels which arose over the seigneurial régime versus the township
system had repercussions at all levels of the society.

Overpopulation in the seigneuries, competition for possession of
new land, and massive immigration were the basic dimensions of the
crisis. It brought social and political strife and rapidly became a major
factor in the nationalist fermentation of the period.

I The Population Explosion

The demographic factor which was new was the nature and volume of
immigration; between 1815 and 1840 nearly 400,000 immigrants arrived at the ports of Lower Canada. Most were bound for Upper Canada and United States, but those who remained in Lower Canada to
settle in the cities, seigneuries, and townships added to the already
severe demographic pressures.

There was no significant change in the natural population growth
rate. In the period 1800-1839 the birth rate dropped very slightly
from that of 1790-1800, from 52.5 to 51 per 1,000, and the marriage
rate from 8.7 to 8.5, revealing neither a change in attitude toward
marriage nor a trend toward birth control[2] but perhaps reflecting emigration to the United States. The death rate, instead of increasing,
declined slightly from 27 to 25.8 per 1,000, a consequence perhaps of
the establishment of a medical profession or of the role of potatoes in
the *habitant's* diet. Despite short-term fluctuations, influenced vari-
ously by good and bad harvests, epidemics, economic factors, the War
of 1812, and the rebellions of 1837 and 1838, the long-term population growth in any event remained unchanged at 25.4 per 1,000. From
1815 to 1840 the French-Canadian population increase was almost
250,000, but from 1831 to 1844 the proportion of children under
fourteen dropped from 49 to 45 per cent (see Table 24), a consequence perhaps of emigration to the United States.

Over the short term, the recorded death rates reflected the occur-

rence of epidemics more than economic conditions or military operations. Generally speaking, epidemics were less frequent and less severe
in the nineteenth century than in the eighteenth. Between 1760 and
1800 the death rate exceeded 30 per 1,000 as many as nine times, but
between 1800 and 1840 only five times, most strikingly in 1832 and
1834, years of crippling cholera epidemics; in 1832 the rate climbed
to 45.7 per 1,000, and the statistics are incomplete at that.

Without any doubt the 1832 epidemic was brought to Lower Canada by immigrants, who numbered 52,000 in that year. It began in
Quebec and quickly spread to Montreal, where it claimed 230 victims
in the first few days and 947 between June 10 and 27. A contemporary
wrote, "Montreal is in straits difficult to depict; business has ceased....
When friends meet, they bid each other adieu as though they will
never see each other again. Day and night, wagons are seen carrying
bodies to the cemetery; sorrow and terror reign on every face, and the
continual spectacle of death and the tears and sobbing of those who
have lost relatives or friends are enough to sadden the hearts of the
most callous."[3] The epidemic was centred first in the cities, where, it is
said, infants and the aged were less affected than adults in the prime of
life. The wealthy were less affected than the lower classes whose standards of hygiene were often deficient, yet Joseph Papineau wrote to his
daughter, "The sickness has carried off many respectable citizens as
you will see from the Newspapers."[4] In a letter to his son Benjamin he
declared, "fear causes more harm than the sickness itself."[5]

From Quebec, where at least 785 immigrants succumbed to cholera, and from Montreal, the epidemic spread to the country districts,
particularly those parishes along the path taken by the immigrants. But
the rural folk, too, moved from place to place and city notables took
refuge in the country. "The city is almost deserted [for] all those who
can are fleeing to the country," wrote Joseph Papineau.[6] Louis-Joseph
Papineau sent his family to Verchères and D.-B. Viger went to
"Ecores." In Berthier there were 200 deaths. In St-Eustache there were
600 cases of cholera and 61 deaths; at Rigaud and Vaudreuil, 680 fell
ill and 96 died, and at Chambly there were reported to be 600 cases of
cholera and 30 deaths. The dead were often carted to cemeteries and
buried without the usual formalities. The physicians of Quebec reported to a committee of inquiry:

The exact amount of the mortality that is occasioned among the
inhabitants of this city cannot be clearly ascertained, for many who
are known to have fallen victims to the cholera have been openly
interred in the old cemeteries, and there is no doubt that multitudes
have obtained some coveted indulgence, without attracting public

observation; but although the total number of deaths cannot be precisely determined, it is known to exceed considerably three thousands. It is in evidence before the committee that in one lodging house thirty-three cases have occurred, in another eleven and so on.[7]

Despite the efforts of physicians, hastily organized medical clinics, and the imposition of a quarantine, the epidemic ran its course and broke out anew in 1834.

In the heat of the moment, political passions were relegated to the background. Violence over an election in Montreal West abated at least temporarily. Wrote Joseph Papineau, "... in the city attention is paid only to the cholera. Politics have fallen victim to it."[8] It was a postponement, no more; and the epidemic itself was to have a profound effect on socio-political convictions. Once the danger had passed the fear remained and took on an ideological colour. The younger Papineau wrote to his wife, "We cannot look back on the past year filled with anxiety, bereavement, death and misfortune without a profound feeling of grief. What irreparable losses, those of so many of our fellow citizens, such dear friends and relatives who have been taken from us! What moments of anguish and dread of the dangers risked by those dear to us in the midst of this frightful contagion."[9] As early as August, 1832, Charles-Séraphin Rodier expressed the reaction of the nationalists in a speech at l'Assomption, which the Montreal *Gazette* reported in translation (verbatim as printed):

When I see my country in mourning and my native land nothing but a vast cemetery, I ask what has been the cause of these disasters? and the voice of my father, my brother and my beloved mother, the voices of thousands of my fellow citizens respond from their tombs. It is emigration. It was not enough to send among us avaricious egotics without any spirit of liberty than that which can be bestowed by a simple education of the counter, to enrich themselves at the expense of the Canadians, then endeavour to enslave them, they must rid themselves of their beggars and cast them by thousands on our shores; they must send miserable beings, who after having partaken of the bread of our children, will subject them to the horrors following upon hunger and misery, they must do still more, they must send us in their train pestilence and death.[10]

A month earlier, L. Winter (a French Canadian despite his name) bitterly linked the epidemic to the holders of economic power: "I believe that the Scottish rabble has been spared by the cholera only because the devil, seeing himself so certain of having them, gives them rein to bring perdition on the rest. They are such friends to him, that I believe they will be people of [privileged] place under his government; woe betide us if we go that way!"[11] The emotions unleased by the nightmare must be seen in relation to the economic conditions of the time, the overpopulation of the seigneuries, and the impact of massive English immigration in both urban and rural districts.

Immigration was massive after 1815, and the immigrants were wretchedly poor for the most part, fleeing economic depression and misery in the British Isles, and lured by visions of greener fields and by bargain fares offered by captains of lumber ships which, without them, would have to make the westward voyage in ballast. Most were English and Scottish until 1832, and then Irish, but the greater number of the latter enshipped for New York (see Table 25).

Most of them disembarked at Quebec. Between 1819 and 1825 roughly a third chose to remain in Lower Canada and the rest moved on to Upper Canada and the United States in more or less equal numbers. Thenceforth the proportion remaining in Lower Canada diminished: 23 per cent between 1825 and 1830, 14 per cent in 1831, 10 per cent in 1834, 8 per cent in 1835, and 4 per cent in 1836; half of those arriving in this period went to Upper Canada and the rest to the United States. Entrepreneurs did brisk business moving them out, but neither that nor the richer land available further west accounts for the immigrants' increasing disinclination to remain in Lower Canada. Nor should their distaste for seigneurial land-tenure be overestimated. Judging from the facts and from remarks by contemporaries, most were capable of overcoming that initial reaction. This was noted by the agent of the seigneur of Beauport: "... the emigrants no longer have any repugnance for seigneurial tenure, for they perceive that they can become possessors of farms without purchase."[12] The immigrants, with or without money for land purchase, appear indeed to have had a preference for land in the seigneuries, for it was more valuable and closer to the markets. As many as 225 obtained concessions from the seigneurs of Gaudarville and Fossambault,[13] and an undetermined number from the seigneur of Portneuf. These and other examples belie the view that the seigneurial régime was the "shield of the French-Canadian nation." More important factors seem to have been the growing shortage of land in the seigneuries, the seigneurs' reluctance to concede land, the distance and poor communications involved in settling in the townships, and last but not least the political climate and nationalism.

According to the best-informed contemporary observers, an immigrant settling on a farm, in order to have something to live on while awaiting his first harvest, would need the equivalent of six months' to a year's subsistence for himself and his family; W.B. Felton, for example, estimated the minimum necessary for six months for a family of three at 18 *minots* of wheat, 270 pounds of pork, 100 *minots* of potatoes, and a cow, or else a sum of £21.[14] The merchant Isaac Man of Ristigouche observed that "a man setting himself up must have the means to provide himself and his family for at least a year after coming to his farm.... I have always considered twenty to twenty-five *louis* as the least sum a man must have when leaving Quebec to settle on a farm."[15] An immigrant might manage without some initial capital, according to Felton, only if the farm he acquired was close to market; "when he is favourably situated in the neighbourhood of an establishment and has a market for his work, the necessity of capital disappears; but his comfort will be greater and his progress hastened by possession of capital." Since, according to evaluations after 1830, the wealth of an immigrant averaged only £9 to £10, it is clear that a very large number were completely destitute. Before 1820 there appeared a sorely needed charitable organization, the Society for the Relief of Emigrants in Distress.

The immigrant without capital would have to find what employment he could in the city of Quebec, for even if he intended to move on to Upper Canada he would at least have to earn his steamboat fare. Lieutenant Skeene, who proposed the creation of an agency to advise immigrants on employment prospects and ways and means of acquiring farms, noted that "several of those who have had a few weeks of employment at the King's Shipyards have been able to go upriver."[16] From November, 1821, to November, 1822, 700 immigrants worked in the shipyards, where a system of monthly turnovers was established; their pay was 2s. 6d. per day. Immigrants would in fact accept whatever work and pay was offered. Many worked on farms or clearing land, often in the townships. Felton noted, "The usual wages given in the townships to good men experienced in country work or logging, are from twelve to fourteen *piastres* [dollars] per month, with food, washing and mending, during the six months of summer; these men rarely contract for a year, being principally young men looking to establish themselves.... Europeans who contract for a year are usually given seven to ten *piastres* per month, with food, and they are lodged and their clothes washed and mended; after the first year, many of these men earn as much as the labourers of the Country."[17]

The combined effect of massive immigration and the vigorous natural growth of the French-Canadian population caused a multiplicity of problems. These would no doubt have arisen in any event, but with lagging economic growth, a scarcity of easily available land, and widespread social discontent, excessive demographic pressure could only exacerbate existing tensions and conflicts. It certainly did much to stimulate French-Canadian nationalism—perhaps more than any other factor.

II Overpopulation and Crisis for the Seigneurial Régime

Throughout the eighteenth century settlement in the seigneuries had proceeded without major constrictions. Good land had been plentiful and it was to the seigneurs' advantage to concede whatever was requested. Seigneurial dues had increased, true enough, but agricultural production had outpaced population growth in response to export market demand. By 1820 the picture had changed drastically to one of crisis. John Neilson, called to testify before a committee of inquiry into the causes of the crisis, declared:

> ... from 1793, but particularly from about 1800, to the close of the late war in Europe, the progress of the settlements in the seigneuries was very great; where the lands were good, and were obtained at little expense, and on something approaching to the old terms, they were readily taken up, settled upon, and the roads laid out and made at the common expense, according to law. The distant journeys, delays and expenses and difficulties in obtaining Procès-verbaux, both before and after homologation, were a general subject of complaint; the high prices of agricultural produce, occasioned by the war in Europe, enabled however the settlers to bear all, and overcome all obstacles in making the roads. Since the close of the war, the progress of the settlements has been yearly diminishing; the decline in the prices of agricultural produce, the obstacle of unusually high rents and new and onerous conditions of the grant, and absolute refusal to concede on the part of many of the seigneurs, with the expenses and difficulties of laying out roads as before mentioned, are more than they can bear.[18]

Though Neilson plausibly identified the causes of the crisis, he appears to have situated its beginning a decade late. He also estimated the French-Canadian population to be 600,000 in 1823 and to be doubling every twenty years.[19] This appears to be an exaggeration of French-Canadian fecundity. The census taken by parish priests in 1822, which is admittedly incomplete, shows a population of 360,000, and it was more likely doubling every twenty-five or twenty-eight years.

Settlement progressed at different rates in different parishes depending on the various factors previously mentioned, but there were invariably signs of saturation after the first phase of settlement in each region. On the Île d'Orléans, for example, the signs were already apparent in the seventeenth century. The island was fertile but small. There was a constant drain of the younger elements of the population; if there had not been, there would have been severe overpopulation and extreme land subdivision even early in the eighteenth century, and a crisis of catastrophic proportions. Its people, however, were careful to preserve a balanced distribution of land. In 1831, 41 per cent of heads of families were not property owners (see Table 26). Many parishes around Quebec were soon in a similar situation, population pressures becoming evident before the end of the eighteenth century. Their surplus population migrated and hastened the development of localities where there was surplus land.[20]

Late in the eighteenth century settlement was very rapid in all three major districts, Quebec, Trois-Rivières, and Montreal; in the first two decades after 1800, growing signs of stagnation sowed anxiety. Around 1808 Pierre Bédard was already denouncing the incursions of American immigrants (see Table 27).

To aid understanding of the demographic ferment, we have calculated natural population growth in fifty-three Quebec and Trois-Rivières district parishes from curés' reports on births, marriages, and burials. Comparing these figures with the censuses of 1790 and 1822 enables an estimation of migration, that is, arrivals and departures. With corrections in compensation for missing birth and burial records, the total population in the fifty-three parishes in 1822 can be estimated at 120,727 (instead of 113,899 as calculated from the records), an increase of 128 per cent in thirty-two years over a base of 52,942 in 1790. It is apparent that most of these parishes were not absorbing their natural growth; there was a net emigration from 62 per cent of them. Some 20,000 individuals or more appear to have left for less populated parishes; the estimated increase in those among the fifty-three which received immigration was 8,343 (5,747 from the records). The counties of Beauce, Dorchester, and to some extent Lotbinière were popular destinations.

After 1800 a population growth below the general average is apparent in an increasing number of these same parishes, and there was a decrease in thirty-one parishes between 1822 and 1825 and in twenty-four between 1825 and 1831. From 1831 to 1844 the tendency accelerated. During this entire period new parishes were created in which growth was rapid at first and then slowed, often to the point of stagnation. The major consequences of overpopulation were farm subdivision, the emergence of a rural proletariat, and migration (see Table 3).

Thus there was considerable movement, first from parish to parish within a district, toward the Beauce and downriver toward Rimouski in the Quebec district, for instance, and later between districts. John Neilson reported of the *habitants* of the Quebec region, "they proceed to different parts of the country settled by Canadians; chiefly to the district of Montreal."[21] Abbé Jérôme Demers was more specific, noting that they migrated north of Montreal and to the Richelieu Valley, to Châteauguay, Blairfindie, Ste-Marie-Monnoir, St-Constant, St-Jacques, St-Roch, St-Esprit, and St-Benoît.

> I presume that these emigrations would be much less frequent in the District of Quebec, if the farmers had greater facility than they have to settle on unconceded lands in the old seigneuries or on Crown lands.... [The] causes are, in some localities, the severity of the climate and the poor quality of the soil for agriculture; in some others, the extraordinary expenditures they must make to dig deep ditches in order to drain sometimes considerable areas of land; in almost all, the shortage of roads for access to places where communities might be established. To these various causes perhaps might be added the excessive *rentes* which certain seigneurs, it is said, would like to establish on the lands they concede.[22]

The cause of overpopulation, then, was first a shortage of fertile, easily accessible land, and later of seigneurial land of any kind. Quarrels between seigneurs and *censitaires* over division of common lands, where the soil was rich, was a further symptom of the development.

One of the gravest consequences was subdivision of farms, which was part of the legal tradition and was carried to excess. About 30 per cent of farms were of fifty *arpents* or less according to the 1831 nominative census which shows only consolidated landholdings and therefore does not tell the whole story of the state of subdivision. The *terrier*, a register of landholders, gives a more accurate picture. The parish of Laprairie is a good example (see Table 28). In 1822 the surveyor Joseph Bouchette noted "that in many parts of this province [the farms are] subdivided to a point where they no longer suffice for a farmer and his family."[23] In the same year John Neilson said, "almost all the original grants are cut up into narrow strips of land, some not much broader than an ordinary highway, and perhaps a mile in length; on the fronts of many of the original grants the houses and out houses are now so close to each other, that they form, as it were, a street for several miles."[24] This is seen, too, in the 1822 parish census: in three large parishes, Rivière-Ouelle, St-Philippe, and Bécancour (one in each of the three major districts), the proportion of farms with a frontage of less than two *arpents* was 64 per cent, 54 per cent, and 72 per cent respectively. The testimony (reported in English) of Pierre Trépanier, a *censitaire* at Batiscan, is eloquent: "Much misery is thereby occasioned.... The parish is thereby impoverished. The people are very often unable to meet their engagements, live with less comfort and are often ruined. The father [has] very often found it difficult to open [sic] and support himself and his children upon the whole of his land, upon its being divided, wood [is] become more scarce, the soil is usually worn out, and charged with the support of two families instead of one."[25] Few farms of less than fifty *arpents* could effectively produce wheat. Such fragmentation of arable land made wheat production virtually impossible, rapidly sapped the soil of its fertility, and led to crippling indebtedness.

Besides fragmentation of farms, overpopulation produced a kind of proletariat of young men unable to find land on which to establish their own farms. This class of rural labourers often represented over 20 per cent of heads of families, in certain localities as much as 40 per cent. The censuses do not adequately reflect this proletariat, since individuals are not identified apart from the families they were living with. In 1821, James Cuthbert, seigneur of Berthier, reported, "The population in the old seigneuries is very dense, and in my division of militia in 1804, there were from nine hundreds to one thousand militiamen, and in 1820, twenty-four hundreds men above sixteen years of age.... If I had held ungranted seigneurial lands of good quality, I could have conceded two or three hundreds farms in one year."[26] In the Jesuit seigneuries in the Trois-Rivières district, over 300 young men awaited land grants which never materialized. Such population surpluses were to be found everywhere by 1820, and worsened subsequently. The young were much attached to their families and their home parishes and were loath to leave. "At Lotbinière," recounted the farmer Joseph Lemay *dit* Poudrier, "in view of the lack of concessions, there are a great many mature men and young men who need farms and who in the hope of having one have stayed in the parish."[27] Only when they had given up hope would they decide to leave, for other parishes or the townships or other districts or, in last resort, for the United States. With the population crisis began a continuous stream of emigration to the United States. Economic conditions after 1800 hampered the opening of new parishes in the further reaches of the seigneuries. Generally, the soil there was not particularly rich and deteriorated rapidly under cultivation. Settlers, for whom the first few years were arduous to say the least, found the building of roads and churches a heavy burden, but in new localities, in the seigneuries and townships alike, such investment in time and money, particularly for roads, was essential.

In the first decade of the century the venerable institution of the seigneurial régime itself entered a period of crisis. Many seigneurs began to have a new attitude to land concession. With the development of the lumber industry, uncleared land, which is to say, standing timber, increased in value, which, with inflation and the increasing scarcity of farmland, led to speculation. Roderick Mackenzie, seigneur of Terrebonne, remarked in 1821, "No augmentations to seigniories having been made since 1759, and of course not expected to be made hereafter, may be a principal cause for the delays observed in the Settlement of some Seigniorial lands. Proprietors expecting no increase as formerly wait favourable opportunities to make the most of what they have."[28]

Early in the century a number of seigneurs were already limiting their concessions or even ceasing them altogether. De Lanaudière, owner of several seigneuries, gave as his reason that "the land would become more valuable in process of time and that he preferred to sell them 5s. per acre, and preserve to himself a nominal rent."[29] Robert Jones, agent for the Widow Barrow, reported that there had been no land conceded in the widow's seigneuries between 1800 and 1806. After that date concessions were few and far between. The surveyor Olivier Arcand, referring to the seigneuries of the Sieur Joly de Lotbinière in 1834, stated, "For twenty years there has been a constant refusal to concede lands."[30] In fact, though de Lotbinière drastically reduced the number of concessions he granted he did not cease them, for in 1833 the *censitaires* of Lotbinière parish complained that since the death of the seigneur and the appointment of Joseph Papineau as administrator of the estate no concessions had been made and that 200 or 300 individuals were vainly awaiting a change of attitude.[31] The agent of the Jesuit Estates in the Trois-Rivières district would grant no land after 1815. Habitants of the seigneury of Beauharnois petitioned the legislative assembly, declaring that for thirty years, since 1803, they had been unable to obtain title to farms on which they were settled as "squatters."[32]

The notion that land was a commodity to be bought and sold like any other, and that proprietorship was individual and absolute, had crept in by the back door, so to speak. It was quite contrary to the precepts of the seigneurial system, in which the key was free concession for the purpose of development. The *coutume* forbade a seigneur to sell land which had never been conceded. Many seigneurs, however, resorted to a system of indirect sale in order to sidestep the *coutume*, and bribery had become widespread. Certain seigneurs demanded between eight and forty *livres* for a farm, and if a *censitaire* were unable to pay the sum in cash he would be obliged to sign a note for the debt, which did not relieve him of seigneurial dues. Another common practice was to allow "squatting"; the owner of a fief, on regaining possession of the land in question, could then consider it developed and could sell it. A third method of indirect sale was to use intermediaries; "The practice is to grant to one individual in his own name some eight, ten or more lots, which he sells separately to as many individuals, and some of them have been sold as high as six dollars an acre."[33] Once released in this way, land was subject to the law of supply and demand. Adversaries of the seigneurial régime were thus able to point to the seigneurs as the most unprincipled of land speculators. The seigneurs, indeed, through the combination of an artfully applied policy of limiting concessions and indirect sales, became capitalists in attitude and in fact, without having to free the peasantry of seigneurial and feudal servitudes. Such practices did much to undermine the seigneurial system. Lower Canada was in its own way reliving the experience of European countries.

Land the seigneurs were inclined to grant in this period was poor or mediocre or difficult of access; *censitaires* often complained of this. "They find the rates too dear," recounted the notary Chèvrefils, "besides those lands are very difficult to drain, and considerable expense would be necessary for letting the water flow; and there is no road of access thereto."[34] With population pressure and declining prices, the seigneurs sought to increase their revenues through indirect sales and increased *cens et rentes.* In the second half of the eighteenth century the rates had increased along with land values and prices as well as growing agricultural production. With the turn of the century they tended to stabilize, but, it was observed, "the seigniories in which the rents have not been raised are almost all settled." To the extent that dues were payable in money, however, even where they remained unchanged, they became a heavy burden for the farmer, particularly with the decline in wheat production.

In many seigneuries there were successions of rate increases, some of them substantial. For 60 or 90 *arpents* in the Widow Barrow's seigneuries, for instance, 4s. 10d. until 1780, then 6s. 2d. plus 2 *minots* of wheat, and after 1820, 12s. 1d. plus 4 *minots* of wheat; for 60 *arpents* in Beauharnois, 5s. plus one *minot* of wheat between 1757 and 1760, then a slight increase, and then 7s. plus 3 *minots* of wheat between 1802 and 1821, and 25s. plus 5 *minots* of wheat between 1821 and 1833. Notary Joseph Badeaux remarked of Toussaint Pothier's seigneury, "the rate of rents is so exhorbitant that very few persons venture to take any land there,"[35] and of the seigneury of Nicolet, "some lands remain for which the seigneur exacts high rents."[36] A farmer who was agent for the seigneur of Batiscan declared, "There is moreover a large number of young men who would have taken some, and who have been disgusted by the high rate of rent required."[37] Farmers protested what they considered ruinous rates of 9 *sols* per *arpent* exacted by G. Christie (one *sol* equalled about one English penny):

> ... in my opinion [said Luc Fortin de Noyan], these exhorbitant rates of rent exacted in these seigneuries are the total ruin of the poor folk who settle on these vast lands and greatly retard the progress of agriculture, for it is almost impossible for a poor family man who must open up a new farm and provide for his family's needs, to be able to pay all these *cens et rentes*; and after three or four years he is obliged to abandon or sell his farm, often at low price, and the unfortunate man finds himself on the road with his family.[38]

From the beginning of the century, moreover, many seigneurs would strip their land of saleable timber before conceding it, and virtually all began to keep rights to all the standing oak and pine on land they conceded. Many also kept a sharp eye on their seigneurial rights, reactivating those which had been allowed to lapse and even insisting on certain rights which they had never had in their original deeds. Hunting and fishing rights, which were of little economic value in most localities, were retained firmly where hunting and fishing were important. In contracts, the *corvée* was retained much more frequently than in earlier days. Though many seigneurs did not fulfil their responsibility for building and maintaining a common mill, they would not permit anyone else to build one within their fiefs. They kept the most favourable locations for flour and sawmills for themselves and in order to recover sites they wanted for this and other purposes would use the *droit de retrait*. And the *lods et ventes*, the seigneurial tax on land sales, remained an essential element. At Lauzon, Beauharnois, Lotbinière, and elsewhere the terms of contracts were applied with jealous rigour.

The seigneurial régime began to have a thoroughly unkindly mien. Not all seigneurs were insensitive and avaricious, but the situation as described was sufficiently general to allow the conclusion that the institution had become oppressive. Contemporaries were divided between admiration and contempt for it. James Cuthbert, seigneur of Berthier, saw two virtues in it; it placed land at the disposal of the peasant classes without cost and it provided a bulwark against republicanism. To him it was the foundation of a well-ordered social hierarchy, whereas the system of free and common socage tended to establish legal equality in the society; the solution to the land shortage and the danger of republicanism would be to convert the townships to seigneuries. Roderick Mackenzie, seigneur of Terrebonne, was in agreement, stressing the lack of expense in acquiring seigneurial land. He himself, however, while recognizing the demand for land in his seigneury, admitted without giving reasons that he could not grant the concessions requested. The seigneur de Lotbinière, called before a committee of the legislative assembly, denied having refused concession or having asked for bribes. His increases in *cens et rentes* he justified by property value increases. He insisted on his right to standing timber on unconceded land and claimed that in reserving timber on concessions he was encouraging his *censitaires* to concentrate on developing their farms. His seigneurial rights, he said, were the law of the country, and contracts were entered into voluntarily. His testimony shows two conflicting conceptions of landed property, the one limited and tending to inhibit the mobility of ownership, the other individual and absolute, either of which the seigneurs might invoke according to the circumstances.

Another group of seigneurs was bent on seeing the system abolished, for they considered it an obstacle to mobility of ownership and economic progress. One of these was Edward Ellice. In 1833 he openly declared his belief in absolute ownership and his hostility to the permanent servitude imposed on seigneurs. His position was clear: the seigneur could do what he wished with his seigneury. He could increase seigneurial dues, cut the timber, claim any reserves he wished, and drive out squatters when and if he wished. His preference was for free and common socage and he was developing his seigneury on capitalist principles. From 1822 to 1839 his revenues multiplied through property rents and other initiatives, and so did his profits.[39] The seigneury of Beauharnois was only one of his numerous businesses. He would not re-invest his profits in the seigneuries of Lower Canada but in the United States or England. In his eyes a seigneury did not lend itself to innovation and the seigneurial régime was an obstacle to investment.

The Seminary of Quebec was a different case. It had been given a number of seigneuries by the king of France to enable it to pursue its purpose of education and the training of priests. Abbé J. Demers, in his testimony before the committee, stressed the economic and social stability inherent in the seigneurial régime in comparison with capitalist proprietorship and its inevitable creation of great landed wealth on the one hand and an agricultural and urban proletariat on the other. For him the seigneurial structure was a major support of religious and moral life and values and, implicitly, of the social, religious, and economic role of the clergy, and he therefore proposed its extension to the entire province.

> I am fully persuaded the Feudal System, confined within proper limits with regard to seigneurial and permanent rents, is the most advantageous mode of inducing His Majesty's Canadian subjects to become proprietors of the unconceded lands in the Province.... These new proprietors are indeed charged with a permanent rent, but if the original grantees of the Crown enter fully into the true spirit of the Feudal System, all they can impose, is very moderate seigneurial and permanent rents, and such as the new grantees will always be able easily to pay. If the government adopted the Feudal System in granting the Crown lands, their grants might regulate the rates of the seigneurial rents for every square acre of ground.[40]

Admitting the *rentes* in the Seminary's seigneuries to have varied from time to time and in certain cases, Abbé Demers considered them nevertheless to be modest, which may be taken with some scepticism. The revenues procured, however, were far from those of Ellice's seigneury. After the turn of the century they appear to have grown less rapidly than the population in the seigneuries concerned (see Table 29).

When Abbé Demers related rate increases to the price of wheat and market conditions as well as local land fertility and proximity to markets, he was acknowledging the significance of economic and geographic factors in the evolution of the seigneurial régime. Louis-Joseph Papineau identified another aspect in 1835 when he wrote:

> There was [in New France] an immense production of this kind of produce and very few consumers. The produce was certain to be of little value.... There were 12,000,000 *arpents* of conceded land and a population of only 60,000 souls. It was this circumstance more than any other which made the rates for concessions so uniform and so modest. When a few seigneurs would become so grasping as to try to raise their *rentes* more than their neighbours, their farms would remain vacant.[41]

It was not in the interest of either Demers or Papineau, of course, to find arguments for the abolition of the system. Papineau was after all a seigneur and as such not immune to a certain pride of aristocracy, but his preference for the régime was more complex than that. In any event he came to idealize the system and to see in it a "national" institution closely tied to French civil law. While he admitted abuses on the part of certain seigneurs, he considered the assembly capable of correcting those abuses through legislation and arbitration of conflicts between seigneurs and *censitaires*; the representatives of the nation would assume the role formerly played by the intendant in the days of New France. His ideal seigneury was that of the French Régime, when owners of fiefs conceded land on request and when seigneurial dues were fixed at modest levels. His ideal seigneur was less an agent of colonization than a father figure whose duty it was to assure equality in the conditions for his *censitaires*. His ideal society was one of small property holders under sentence of equality.

This combination of benevolent paternalism and utopian democracy, in whose relationships he refused to see anything feudal, led to an unfortunately unrealistic attitude on his part. The circumstances under which the seigneurial system had worked in the French Régime were long gone; land shortages were now an inescapable fact. He himself admitted as much: "Nine tenths of these seigneuries are [already] improved and occupied, and the tenth that is not is the sterile portion."[42] Not even in his isolated seigneury of La Petite Nation could he himself conform to his image of the ideal seigneur. This was the nineteenth century and the practices of an age when rural life was totally untouched by capitalism were no longer possible. The legislative assembly's efforts to play the role of Old Régime intendant went awry because they were in contradiction with developments in the economy and in the society. Papineau's dream, albeit espoused by the *parti patriote*, was simply inconsistent with reality. Inequality was inherent in the seigneurial régime, and the stability which was its feature did nothing to prevent a proliferation of unequal destinies for those living under it; disparities between one farmer and another were immense, and the number of individuals for whom property ownership was out of reach was growing constantly. The image of the ideal seigneury as an instrument of national survival had only one purpose, and that was to prevent the rural lower classes from questioning an institution which served the interests of the French-Canadian middle classes and, in particular, of the leaders of the *parti patriote*, that company of starry-eyed lovers of landed property, many of whom were seigneurs.

In England the idea of converting the townships to seigneuries was not well received. The British parliament passed laws for conversion in the other direction, but without giving much incentive for the conversion. The interest groups in Lower Canada rallied, the landed aristocracy and the French-Canadian middle classes to the old, outmoded conception of property and the English-speaking commercial classes to the capitalist conception.

III The Struggle for Possession of the Townships

By 1820, with immigration swelling to major proportions, the land question had become thoroughly political. Surplus population and im-migrants alike urgently needed somewhere to settle. Even in the first decade of the century Pierre Bédard had made the problem one of the issues of nationalism. At that time the government had already granted many townships to the commercial élite and prominent figures in government. The leaders and associates system had contributed to the concentration of township land in English-speaking hands, and in rela-tively few at that. But the failure of the system was not really due either to the absence of egalitarian virtues in it or to the fact that the leaders were not farmers. It might have been effective if more of the leaders had been wealthy, enterprising, and enthusiastic, the townships more advantageously located, and the flow of immigrants greater at the time.

Many township landowners had done nothing to attract settlers to their land, and simply logged it, if their wood could be floated to market, or made potash. Timber became important enough to aid de-velopment in many of the townships only after 1820. Many propri-etors, whether resident in the country or not, simply awaited a change in the circumstances, either to develop their land for agricultural pur-poses or in the hope of making speculative profits. The huge land grants made early in the century certainly complicated the formulation of policy for colonization, but that was not the greatest source of problems. The notary Jacques Voyer, who had obtained township land, declared it to be only "a source of expense and worry"; when asked why the townships were so slow to develop, he mentioned, as had others, the failure to provide roads prior to the granting of land:

> Not having laid out, before granting any of these lands, three high-ways or roads leading from the cities of Quebec [and] Montreal [and] from William Henry [Sorel] to the Line ... I sincerely believe that this lack of important roads, from which, at very little cost, roads could have been made for communicating in the townships on either side of them, has contributed much to retarding the estab-lishment of these lands.[43]

After 1815, both the Canadian-born and immigrants wishing to obtain township land had to approach the township leaders or government representatives. The government in theory was already distributing "waste" lands free of charge, but applicants were often frustrated by lack of information, red tape, delays of every description, and onerous fees for services. The fees, in the neighbourhood of 30s. to obtain a 200 acre lot, were more than most farmers or immigrants could raise, not to mention the price of buying an existing farm. In 1826 W.B.

Felton, as crown commissioner of lands, was placed in charge of implementing new legislation intended to put an end to speculation. Under the new system, land was to be auctioned to the highest bidder. The minimum an individual could acquire was 200 acres and the maximum 1,200, and the price was to be paid in four annual instalments. There were special provisions for the poor, including purchase on credit with annual land rental of 5 per cent of the purchase price, which was payable in 20 years.[44] The land problem remained insoluble, however, until 1840, and the government was under constant attack. The foundation in 1831 of the British-American Land Company (with a capital of £300,000) to handle the sale of crown lands renewed hostility toward a government which was perpetually suspected of favouring speculators and seeking to confine French Canadians to the seigneuries.[45]

The possession of large tracts of land by individuals outside the colony was an obstacle to colonization, partly because the owners paid little attention to their land but also because road-building traditions did not allow for piecemeal settlement. The existence of large Anglican clergy reserves also hampered settlement and was a source of much discontent among non-Anglican Protestants; French-Canadian politicians long remained silent on the subject for fear of drawing attention to the vast properties in the hands of Catholic ecclesiastics. In 1823 the assembly passed a series of resolutions calling for the abolition of crown and clergy reserves, but by the time of the rebellions of 1837 and 1838 the question was still unsettled.

Despite the obstacles, colonization did progress in the townships; their population, from an original nucleus of former Americans, rose from 20,000 in 1814 to 38,000 in 1825, 54,500 in 1831, and 82,295 in 1844. Around 1820 most of the settlers were of British origin, and in English-speaking circles the townships were widely regarded as a kind of fiefdom for British immigrants and a focal point for everything British. Settlement, though fairly dense in certain localities, was thin and scattered for the most part, creating an air of isolation. A French-Canadian element appeared little by little, at first close to seigneurial limits.[46] The merchant and large landowner Alexander Rae attributed the slowness of this development "principally to their religous, social and local customs; to their more or less strong prejudices against free and common soccage, and the difference in the religion, language and customs of those who inhabit the townships."[47] Yet by 1831, 20 per cent of the population were French Canadians and in 1844 almost 30 per cent, still largely concentrated near the seigneuries.

As the War of 1812 ended there were rumblings of discontent in the townships and they intensified year by year, mostly directed against the legislative assembly for its failure to provide roads. The key to the region's development, the settlers perceived, was access to market for their produce, and most of the townships were indeed condemned to lead a closed economic existence for lack of it, particularly for heavy loads. Felton declared, "Another cause operating greatly against the prosperity of the Country, is the lack of general communications with the markets of the Capital and other places. In the population's present state, the major routes of communication, if they are made, must be made at public expense, and there must be a judicious amendment of the present roads laws [to assure] road upkeep without oppression."[48] The old laws for road construction and upkeep were suited to settlement along the St Lawrence and its tributaries; the *corvée* system had been used to build the highway between Quebec and Montreal during the French Régime and the assembly had revived it late in the eighteenth century, but in the nineteenth century, with much wider-flung settlement, it was no longer practicable for either regional or local roads. The laws obliging inhabitants to maintain the roads bordering their properties were also in need of revision.

In short, a rational colonization policy would have to incorporate a roads policy, for the realization of which the public purse and the taxation system would have to pay. On this, as on other matters, the inhabitants of the townships met with opposition from the majority in the assembly. Not until 1829, when canalling the St Lawrence tributaries was also an issue, did the assembly allocate any significant sums to the building of roads. By 1831 there were sixty-two road projects under way in the townships and seigneuries.[49] These were the responsibility of commissioners answerable to the assembly; there were many accusations of patronage. Unfortunately such investments ceased after a short while, and since the laws on road upkeep remained unchanged the new roads were soon virtually impassable.

The settlers of the townships had long been demanding a new electoral map which would give them representation in the assembly. The reform was not completed until 1831. In 1826 the assembly created the judicial district of St-François, which incorporated a large part of the Eastern Townships, but it refused to allow the application of English civil law. The majority party's strategy included replacing free and common socage by the seigneurial system and establishing French civil law in the townships, thus making the townships the ideal outlet for surplus population from the seigneuries, whereas the imperial government seemed to assume that English law applied in the townships. The townships' inhabitants were quite aware of the strategy: "The French Canadian House of Assembly has not been desirous that Emigrants from Britain or of British origin should have inducement to seek an asylum or become settlers in Lower Canada. If such indeed is its object, it has failed of partial success...."[50] The assembly's campaign, by holding up reforms and agreeing only to piecemeal changes, was certainly effective in preventing large numbers of immigrants from flocking to the townships, but equally it blocked access to them by French Canadians. A roads policy actively pursued for purposes of colonization and not for political advantage would probably not have been detrimental to French Canadians in the long run. Nor would the establishment of land registry offices, another bone of contention and a source of great anxiety for the notarial profession. Moreover, a radically improved road system would undoubtedly have forced the seigneurs to scale down their pretensions.

With inadequate roads and consequently onerous transportation costs, economic development in the townships was erratic and slow. Where forest industries were feasible and particularly where access to markets was good, it progressed satisfactorily. In the agricultural sector, potatoes, a subsistence crop in the seigneuries and the more inaccessible townships, became commercially important; wheat, however, was grown for subsistence, for its production was marginal. A second important commercial activity was cattle-raising, stimulated by urban demand for meat, leather, and dairy products, but there was stiff competition from the United States and Upper Canada, and the producers clamoured for tariff protection. The same producers raised sheep for wool from which flannel was made. Commercial-scale maple sugar production also began in the townships. The agricultural élite of the townships were more involved in commercial farming than were those of the seigneuries. Charles Kilborn of Stanstead had 200 animals, three houses, two barns, a flour mill, a sawmill, and a fulling mill, yet he declared, "There are other persons in this township whose farms are more advanced, who have more animals and whose buildings are worth more than mine."[51] With 400 acres, 100 of them cleared, he was not an average farmer nor was he among the large landowners. Philemon Wright, founder and leader of the township of Hull, gave the following statistics for his farms for 1820: 3,025 acres under cultivation, 164 labourers, 806 animals and harvests of 9,285 *minots* of grain, 26,000 *minots* of potatoes and 1,230 tons of hay.[52] For the 1842 census he declared 7,427 *arpents* of land, 1,492 under cultivation; 400 *minots* of wheat, 800 of oats, 150 of peas, 150 of corn, 2,500 of potatoes; 72 cattle, 28 horses, 154 sheep, and 92 hogs. The same year, D.-B. Papineau, owner of the Plaisance fief, and, incidentally, administrator of La Petite Nation seigneury for his brother, listed 1,229 *arpents* of land, 320 under cultivation, 8 *minots* of wheat, 45 of barley, 100 of oats, 34 of peas, 45 of corn, 20 of potatoes; 36 cattle, 7 horses,

57 sheep, and 12 hogs. Though most of the agricultural élite in both the townships and the seigneuries were English-speaking, a respectable number, too, were French-speaking. In 1831 the merchant J.-B. Dumouchelle of St-Benoît harvested nearly 3,000 *minots* of grain and 1,000 of potatoes and kept 350 animals on a farm of 3,000 *arpents*, 2,000 under cultivation; and he was not alone in that category.

Yet the lot of most small farmers in the townships was poverty and isolation, and problems were not unlike those in the seigneuries. Even commercial-scale agriculture suffered in the post-1830 depression. There was no overpopulation but ownership of land was a goal beyond the reach of many. This was perhaps a larger factor in the success of the *parti patriote* in the townships after 1830 than the democratic leanings of settlers of American origin.

Land shortages and demographic pressures combined, in any event, were rapidly leading to an explosive situation. Between 1790 and 1820, more than 20,000 individuals left fifty-three parishes in the Quebec and Trois-Rivières districts in search of land elsewhere, and a significant proportion converged on the district of Montreal. The mobility of the population did not prevent increasing subdivision of farms and steady growth in the size of the rural proletariat. Even in the Montreal district, between twenty and thirty parishes were unable to absorb their natural growth and the outflow of population was very appreciable. In the parish of St-Laurent near Montreal, the population grew from 879 in 1784 to 2,489 in 1831, whereas agricultural production as shown by tithe reports fell drastically from 1802 onward (see Table 30). In the Parish of Ste-Geneviève the population growth was only 22 per cent in the thirty-two years from 1790 to 1822, and in many other localities was well below 40 per cent. In the region of St-Eustache, to which there was a considerable influx for a time after 1790, a point of stagnation was reached by 1822; thereafter, despite much subdivision, there was an excess which drifted away (see Tables 31 and 32). Here, too, farm production declined after 1808, between 20 and 30 per cent in the case of wheat, most drastically between 1831 and 1842 (see Table 33). Added to population pressure and poor farming methods, the wheat-fly epidemic worsened the crisis, for the region was heavily dependent on wheat (see Table 34). The seigneury of Argenteuil, whose inhabitants were English-speaking and whose economic structure was more diversified, fared well by comparison.

In time the Montreal region came to be the principal centre of rural anxiety and discontent, particularly in the seigneuries. The region's heavy dependence on wheat and its unsuitability for conversion to a lumber economy made it the more vulnerable. Initiatives like the Laprairie railway, the Chambly Canal, and trade with the United States by way of the Richelieu River did little to cushion the impact of the agricultural crisis and population pressures. Growing financial demands from the church and the seigneurs burdened the belaboured rural folk even further, and the seigneurs were increasingly parsimonious over land concession. Traditional values, particularly the role of the family, were sorely tried. Whereas the discontent might have given rise to a reform movement directed against the seigneurial régime, tithing, and the legislature, the French-Canadian élite chose to idealize the old institutions in the eyes of the people, seeking to polarize the discontent against the English capitalists, the English government, and the English immigrants. The immigrants were an easy target for French-Canadian resentment; in the rural districts they were competitors in the search for land and in the cities rivals for clientèle and jobs.

It would be misleading to assume religious or ethnic homogeneity in either the rural or the urban lower classes. Two-thirds of the Anglicans and Presbyterians and 90 per cent of the Catholics lived outside the cities. In 1831 there were English, Scottish, and Irish minorities in many seigneuries; the socio-economic disparities between the ethnic groups were noticeable even there. In the cities, however, the scene was one of great diversity and mobility. In 1831, 27 per cent of the population of Quebec and Montreal was Protestant. In 1844 the Irish in Montreal, Catholic in the majority, numbered 9,595. After 1822 the number of French Canadians in the two major cities remained more or less unchanged while the population of British origin increased so rapidly that a number of French Canadians predicted the rapid demise of the French culture in the cities. As early as 1831 the majority in Montreal were English-speaking. Everywhere the socio-economic disparities between groups were striking. Cheap labour was largely Irish, though the Irish were present at all levels. The economically powerful were overwhelmingly English-speaking, particularly of English, Scottish, and American origin. The French Canadians had their professional, religious, and commercial élite, but most were small merchants, craftsmen, and labourers. Political awareness and class consciousness were strong in the urban upper and middle classes but ill-defined in the lower classes, where attitudes were highly subject to immediate circumstances.

CHAPTER 7

The Geography of Social and Ethnic Tensions

Agricultural crisis, rural overpopulation, increasingly burdensome seig-neurial dues, increasingly apparent socio-economic disparities between the ethnic groups, particularly in the cities with the arrival of swarms of English-speaking immigrants—these were the principal sources of the progressive social instability of the years 1815-40, and of the popular discontent which was general throughout Lower Canada but more in-tense in some areas than others.

Early in this period the Quebec region, the first to suffer the various manifestations of crisis, had been relieved of much of its surplus popula-tion; the city was enjoying the benefits of the lumber and shipbuilding industries and the surrounding countryside was less dependent than previously on agriculture. Lumbering, fishing, navigation, and the con-struction of small vessels provided seasonal employment for much of the rural population and helped keep popular discontent within tolera-ble bounds. In the townships of all three districts, economic develop-ment proceeded unevenly, often depending on the existence or adequacy of roads, and agriculture was largely centred on potatoes and stock-raising; potential overdependence on the agricultural sector in certain areas was counterbalanced to some degree by lumbering and even small manufacturing. In the Ottawa Valley, particularly around Hull, lumber was without doubt the sector which dominated the re-gion's development and social hierarchy. In the seigneuries of the Mont-real district, agriculture was still the only significant economic activity, and the traditional dependence on wheat was its principal feature. There, too, the demographic pressures were at their worst. This region was now the hot-bed of general popular discontent.

The atmosphere was ripe for a proliferation of quarrels among the leading classes. Class-consciousness deepened along with class antago-nism involving interests, aspirations, and values, and year by year there was more bitterness, hidden or overt. The clergy, despite their cherished relationship to the state, pursued their objectives with their own peculiar strategy. Clerical ideology acquired a new orientation, which, with the new social equilibria, brought forth a revised vision of the ideal society. In this development, Monseigneur Lartigue, the first Roman Catholic Bishop of Montreal, seems to have been the guiding light. Overshadowing all else on the social scene, however, was a deepening cleavage in the middle classes. The wealthy bourgeoisie, in great majority English-speaking, was dominant and continuing to gain in economic and social power, but with a growing feeling that what had been won was jeopardized by both institutional impediments and lack of policies likely to stimulate economic development; for all their wealth and prestige, political power seemed to be slipping further and further from their reach. The interests and values of this group were shared by most English-speaking merchants and professionals and also by a fair number of their French-speaking counterparts. But the disaffection separating these groups from the larger number of French-Canadian professionals and small merchants widened during this period to an impassable gulf. The majority of the French-Canadian middle class were proclaiming more loudly and distinctly than ever that their interests and aspirations, not to say ambitions, were quite different from those of either the clergy or the English-speaking. In short, the situation was rapidly leading to a three-way struggle for ascendancy.

I Merchant Classes and Cultural Identity

The conflicts of interests and values which had begun to appear late in the eighteenth century had nothing to do with industrialization versus the colonial system. Industrialization, such as it was, had been achieved within the colonial structure. Shipbuilding, the forest industries, and the businesses attached thereto were directly or indirectly dependent on the imperial market. Even the brewers and distillers serving the local market had common interests with the grain merchants, and they, too, were oriented toward the British market. What split the middle classes of Lower Canada was the ethnic factor and its place in the socio-economic structure. The professionals and merchants of French-Canadian origin would simply not become agents of capitalism.

Between 1815 and 1830, the numerical strength of the urban merchant class grew spectacularly, much faster than the overall urban population or the total population of the colony. This expansion is attributable to the growth of the lumber and shipbuilding industries, trade with Upper Canada and the United States, massive immigration, and also natural population increase. In the city of Quebec, the number of merchants of all categories rose from 370 in 1805 to 961 in 1831; in Montreal, there were 648 in 1819 and 1,203 in 1831. In the following ten years the merchant class growth was slower, 19 per cent (urban and rural combined) compared to rural population growth of 37 per cent and urban growth (Quebec and Montreal) of 25 per cent. Local agricultural troubles and the overall crisis, particularly in the second half of the decade, seem to have weighed heavily in this.

In Quebec City, lumber merchants, shipbuilders, and importers dominated the bourgeoisie. They were influential with the banks and maintained contacts with the insurance companies. Associated on the Quebec Board of Trade,[1] they kept a close watch on all developments in the imperial markets, both Great Britain and the West Indies. British interests had agencies in Quebec, but local merchants cultivated direct contacts with British houses involved in North American trade. Well-developed imperial market connections were essential for both shipbuilders and lumber merchants; Britain's navigation laws gave advantage to British shipowners in the transport of colonial produce, and the British had long specialized in heavy cargoes such as squared timber, deals, and staves. The local entrepreneurs certainly lacked the capital to assemble their own merchant fleet; perhaps they lacked the initiative too. In shipbuilding, lumber export, and import of exotic and manufactured goods there was strong competition from northern Europe, the Maritimes, and the United States, which is not to say that the Quebec merchants had no economic connections with their rivals.

For the Quebec bourgeoisie, progress was vitally tied to the survival of the colonial régime, more specifically to differential tariffs on timber and to the navigation laws. Neither stationary fisheries on the fringes of the great international fishing grounds nor the ailing local agriculture offering any real promise, it was to forest industries and shipbuilding that this class looked for advancement. Since the British market was the vital one for them, reducing transportation costs was their greatest concern, and their sense of security was anything but strong.

In England the free-trade movement was loudly denouncing the disadvantages of mercantilism and protective tariffs. The reduction in 1821 of the tariff on Baltic timber from 65s. to 55s. per load and the imposition of 10s. per load on colonial timber was no great blow, since prices and transportation costs eased after 1815. Yet the move raised fears in the local merchants that their adversaries, French-Canadian politicians among them, were bent on total abolition of protective tariffs.

The bourgeoisie of Quebec, it must be said, firmly believed their interests and the interests of Lower Canada as a whole to be one and the same. They were active in the region surrounding the city, as seigneurs, timber reserve and sawmill owners, suppliers of imported goods to rural areas, and buyers of agricultural surpluses. Similarly with the bourgeoisie of Montreal. The interests of the urban merchants extended into the townships and up the Ottawa Valley, particularly in those areas where timber was abundant and accessible. And despite differences and rivalries between the merchants of Quebec and Montreal, there was nevertheless considerable solidarity within the class; there was much coming and going between the two cities and Quebec was still the major port.

British immigration and the economic developments taking shape after 1806 swelled and diversified the commercial ranks, mostly to the advantage of the English-speaking. While 28 per cent of Quebec's population had been English-speaking in 1795, in 1831 the proportion was 45 per cent. As socio-economic disparities widened, Quebec looked increasingly like an English-speaking city; even in the lesser commercial activities the English-speaking were strong competitors and the French Canadians felt threatened (see Table 35). Between 1831 and 1842, however, with the movement of immigrants toward the west and of ambitious businessmen to Montreal, the pressure from the English-speaking in Quebec seems to have lessened. By 1842, though the proportion of English-speaking merchants of all classes was still 53 per cent, the English-speaking proportion of the city's population had dropped to 40 per cent. This decrease is the most striking development of the decade in the city of Quebec.

In the rural areas around Quebec City, particularly where non-agricultural activities were important, the English presence in commerce was also notable. In 1831, out of 18,900 heads of families, 421 were businessmen.[2] In 100 rural parishes, 7 per cent of the population but 21 per cent of the businessmen were English-speaking (see Table 37). In Rimouski in 1842, 5 per cent of the population but half the businessmen were English-speaking.[3] The English not only settled in the most active of the rural centres of the Quebec district but dominated trade and manufacturing there. Throughout the region, moreover, local French-Canadian merchants were dependent on English shipbuilders, timber and grain merchants, bankers, and importers in the city. The situation, hardly surprisingly, produced growing ethnic friction.

In the district of Trois-Rivières, which included both sides of the St Lawrence, the conditions were the same. The population was small, 3,972 in 1831, 15 per cent of British origin, but 34 per cent of the businessmen were English-speaking and among them were the economically predominant, particularly the Hart and Bell families (see Table 38).

After 1830, Quebec remained the political capital but yielded its role as the major commercial centre to Montreal, due mostly to rapid growth in trade with Upper Canada after the completion of the Lachine Canal. The important merchants of the city were principally engaged in trade, downriver in agricultural produce from the more populous rural centres of the district, and from Upper Canada and the United States, and upriver in English and West Indian imports moving toward Upper Canada. Wheat was the most important trade commodity, largely bound for the imperial markets, but increasing quantities remained in Lower Canada. The Americans had natural competitive advantages in wheat export, however, and the Montreal merchants, like their Quebec counterparts, were vitally dependent on the colonial system and its protective tariffs. They were also keenly aware of the importance to them of free entry of American agricultural produce for export via the St Lawrence. For them, far more than for the Quebec merchants, a St Lawrence canal system was an urgent necessity, the only possible way of reducing transportation costs and preventing Upper Canada's economy from turning toward the United States. Montreal's strategic position on the St Lawrence trade route was the reason for the importance of its financial institutions. The city was indeed the commercial centre of both the Canadas, and it was here that the ethnic socio-economic disparities were most visible (see Table 36).

For all the economic problems of the decade 1830-40, Montreal continued to exert a strong attraction for the masses of immigrants arriving after 1815. While in Quebec English-speaking domination diminished from 1831 on, in Montreal it was on the rise; in 1831, 54 per cent of heads of families were English-speaking, and ten years later, 61 per cent. In major enterprises French Canadians were making some progress, but cases like that of Joseph Masson, who began as a minor salesman, rose to partnership with Colin Robertson (of fur trade fame) and became one of the leading merchants of Lower Canada, were rare. Most of the major economic initiatives bypassed the French Canadians, whose vision of economic space encompassed only Lower Canada, and who, even within those limits, were encountering strong English-speaking competition.

In 1831 in the rural area about Montreal, there were 812 merchants out of a total of 34,445 heads of families in the seigneuries and townships combined. Between 1831 and 1842, the number of businessmen rose from 195 to 199 in 22 seigneurial parishes and from 63 to 104 in 6 townships, indicating commercial as well as agricultural stagnation in the seigneuries; perhaps also an inclination among the English-speaking to seek their chances elsewhere. But wherever they were, they were active in commercial and manufacturing initiatives, and as in the other rural districts the socio-economic disparities between English and French were unmistakable.

In the townships, the dominance of inhabitants of British origin was almost total. In Stanbridge Township, for example, there was not a single French Canadian among the 13 local merchants. In Hull Township, where forestry was the principal economic stimulant, 11 per cent of heads of families were businessmen; 26 merchants, 10 innkeepers, 3 bakers, one butcher, one storekeeper, one agent, one brewer, 3 salesmen, one bookkeeper and one printer, all of them English. A little to the east, Louis-Joseph Papineau's seigneury of La Petite Nation was much less active, but the only 2 merchants were English-speaking. Some seigneuries had been settled mostly by British immigrants. At St-Armand in 1831, the 20 merchants and 4 innkeepers were all English-speaking; by 1842 there was some diversification, with 17 merchants, 6 innkeepers, 2 grocers, one distiller, one manufacturer, one butcher and one baker, and only the butcher and one of the innkeepers were French-Canadian. In Argenteuil in 1831, 20 per cent of the population and 16 per cent of the businessmen were French Canadians; in 1842, French Canadians comprised 27 per cent of the population but only 3 per cent of the businessmen (see Table 39). In the seigneuries where the majority of the population was French-Canadian, the proportion of English-speaking businessmen was still very large. In the parishes of St-Eustache, St-Benoît and Ste-Scholastique, though in 1842 only 4 per cent of the population was English-speaking, the proportion of English-speaking businessmen was 32 per cent, which, however, was a decrease from 68 per cent in 1831 (see Table 40). The proportions in Soulanges and Vaudreuil were roughly similar (see Table 41).

The strength of the English-speaking in rural areas seems to relate to their attraction to the larger business undertakings and to those of a relatively innovative nature in the local context. Thus brewers, distillers, paper manufacturers, in short, the majority of those engaged in manufacturing in general were English-speaking. After 1831 the construction of the Chambly Canal attracted a great many individuals of British origin to Chambly parish; in 1842, 36 per cent of its population and 73 per cent of its businessmen were English-speaking (see Table 42). The parishes in and bordering on the seigneury of Laprairie had enviable connections with Montreal and also with the means of communication with the United States, due in particular to the railway built after 1831, in which year the area's population was 8 per cent

English-speaking and the business community 32 per cent English (see Table 43).

In both urban and rural areas, then, the English-speaking business community was engaged in an unlimited range of activities whose scope was an economic space encompassing both the Canadas. The crux of its preoccupations was American competition in the imperial markets, which is to say, Britain and the West Indies; competition from the Maritimes in fishery, shipbuilding, and forestry also weighed to a varying but significant degree. This group's interests were bound to the economic development of the two Canadas and thus to the colonial structure and its preferential tariffs on wheat and timber. The tendency was to look upon the seigneurial régime as a major obstacle to economic progress.

In contrast, the French-Canadian merchant class, that is, a mass of average and small businessmen, carried on and developed their activities within an economic space whose limits were the boundaries of Lower Canada. General storekeepers, butchers, bakers, innkeepers, and the like, whether urban or rural, shared the interests and values of the rural milieu. Their lot was in large measure conditioned by the fortunes of the agricultural sector, which was by now in a chronic state of crisis. They valued land in all its guises, but above all seigneurial land; for them, accession to the dignity of seigneur was a treasured upward step in the social hierarchy. In other words, aristocratic aspirations ruled much of their thinking. Many of them, indeed, were by no means resigned to mediocrity, and they boasted a dynamic and enterprising élite. Some speculated on land and agricultural produce and some acquired an interest in banking. Modest initiatives in banking in a number of parishes in the Montreal region demonstrate that many had obtained an understanding of the sources of growth and power. The Banque du Peuple and an import company were founded in Montreal and there were attempts to penetrate the transportation sector and steamboat operation. But at every turn the English-speaking were there, too, and more and more seemed to be blocking the advance of the French Canadians.

The blockage, moreover, came to be regarded by the French Canadians as systematic, part of a deliberate plan to exclude them from important new ventures. They were increasingly led to attribute the consistent superiority of Lower Canadians of British origin to the control exerted by the latter over the distribution of patronage, and the political system which determined that distribution.

The English-speaking business community, for its part, considered most French-Canadian businessmen too obtuse to grasp the imperatives of an economy which must encompass and develop within a broad North American and imperial context, and too short-sighted to accept the institutional changes on which economic and social progress depended, namely the introduction of land registry offices, civil law reform, and abolition of the seigneurial régime.

The schism of misunderstanding between the two groups, which really never was a matter of ethnic difference, continued to deepen, reaching its lowest point in 1837. The two factions of the merchant bourgeoisie behaved toward each other like totally antagonistic social classes.

II Social Change and the Roman Catholic Clergy

Since the beginning of the nineteenth century, the Catholic clergy had been severely rocked by economic and social change. The threat of a disastrous redefinition of church-state relationships had been averted when, external peril assisting, the British authorities had been persuaded of the socially stabilizing influence of the Catholic Church. But there were graver fears raised by the behaviour of the French-Canadian middle classes; their introduction of French revolutionary philosophies and their determined drive for power led the clergy to intervene vigorously on Craig's side in his struggle with the upstarts. Then came the War of 1812 and American invasion, restoring a measure of solidarity between the clerics and the middle classes for a time, and strengthening the church's relationship with the British authorities into the bargain.

The future thus having taken a more promising turn, Bishop Plessis then set about winning support from all three other interest groups—the state, the English-speaking merchant class, and the French-Canadian middle class—hoping to regain clerical control of primary education and to bring to his immense diocese his own conception of order and dignity.

The law of 1801 establishing the Royal Institution for the Advancement of Learning had caught the Catholic clergy and the French-Canadian assembly members off-guard, and had given control of primary and secondary education to the state, to Protestants in other words. Plessis protested vigorously if belatedly. The basic iniquity of the new system, he perceived, was that it infringed the Catholic Church's exclusive right over education and would turn little Catholics into little Protestants, which, it cannot be denied, was precisely what certain of its proponents intended. He urged his curés to resist the establishment of royal primary schools and to found church-controlled parish schools. In 1809 he wrote to Vicar-General Roux, "If this worthy curé and others in as fortunate condition had taken pains to establish schools, the government schools would not have come about. Some have heard me and profited by it. *Most have shown inconceivable indifference thereupon.*"[4] The system he envisaged, however, would need support from figures capable of influencing the legislative process. Such support was not easily won, for many laymen considered patriotic and liberal education more important than Catholic education. Nevertheless, after ten years of effort, and largely because the Canadian party wanted to avoid a head-on confrontation with the clergy, Plessis had his way, and in 1824 the assembly passed the Parish Schools Act giving control of teaching to the curés and the local parish wardens.

The Royal Institution's schools did not disappear for all that. By 1818 there were already thirty-five of them, seventeen in French-Canadian communities.[5] The authorities hoped to mollify the clergy by inviting Plessis to become a member of the board of the institution, but he refused. Lord Dalhousie, then governor, thereupon suggested a radical reform incorporating a second royal institution to be controlled by the clergy and lay Catholics, this second body to parallel the existing one controlled by Protestants. Since the church would thus have the control it sought as well as financial assistance for its schools, Plessis accepted the proposal, but it was rejected by London.

Since disagreements over church-state relationships had seemingly ceased around 1815, the subdivision of the huge Roman Catholic diocese of Quebec, which had under its wing all of Britain's North American colonies, might have been expected to go relatively smoothly. The establishment of apostolic vicarates and bishoprics at Halifax, Charlottetown, Kingston, and in the northwest had met with no real opposition either in London or in Rome. The creation of the Catholic diocese of Montreal and the appointment of Abbé Jean-Jacques Lartigue as its bishop, however, launched a series of interrelated conflicts which were not resolved until 1836. The clergy divided and quarrelled so bitterly over the question that the whole society became involved.[6] In the thick of it were the Sulpicians.

The Gentlemen of the Order of St Sulpice were the seigneurs of the Island of Montreal and the owners of several other fiefs as well. The appointment of curés in Montreal was the prerogative of the Sulpicians, who always made their appointments from members of their order, and in the surrounding rural district the superior of the order, as grand vicar to the bishop of Quebec, had considerable influence. Unlike the Jesuits, the Sulpicians had not only survived the conquest but had preserved their distinctive character. A number of French Canadians who had attended their college had joined their ranks, Lartigue among them, but in 1820 the majority of the members of the order and the individuals in authority were of French origin and tended to look down their noses at the French-Canadian members. The Canadian-born Abbé Lartigue's appointment as Bishop of Montreal they regarded as part of a plot to destroy the order's distinctive character and its religious authority in the district, even to dispossess it of its extensive properties. They suggested that Lartigue establish his residence in some rural parish, which would have limited his influence; when they discovered that neither Plessis nor Lartigue himself would back down, they applied pressure in every conceivable quarter in Canada, France, and England in order to thwart the suspected plot. Central to their argument was their championship of Gallican traditions which were in opposition to the growing ultramontanism of the French-Canadian episcopate and clergy. In the words of a partisan of the Sulpicians, the French-Canadian clergy were seeking "to establish the doctrine of the infallibility of the pope, his independence of the canons, his sovereign authority both spiritual and temporal throughout the world. Happily the church of France has never accepted this doctrine."[7]

But the Sulpicians were menaced by another group, too, namely the English-speaking Montreal merchants, who were demanding that the Island of Montreal be restored to the crown with, naturally, abolition of all seigneurial rights.[8] Here again the Sulpicians' Gallican conceptions of close church-state relationships appeared to them a valuable weapon in their hands, a kind of avowal of their loyalty and dependability as a bulwark against the rising tide of French-Canadian nationalism, both lay and clerical.

Plessis's death in 1825 came at a moment of acute partisanship and dissention at all levels in the ranks of the clergy of Lower Canada. The governor was convinced that there was a coalition between the French-Canadian clerics and the Canadian party for the purpose of achieving supremacy for Catholic interests. But the co-ordination was less real than it appeared. Between the clergy and certain segments of the French-Canadian middle classes there was in fact a considerable degree of antagonism. If the wealthy English bourgeoisie was inclined to take sides, it was because it suited their interests in the immediate circumstances. As for the aristocracy, their support one way or the other was no longer significant. Dalhousie noted "the impoverished state to which all the Old Canadian Families are reduced. Their landed properties have vanished by subdivision into children's portions and the want of means of education, pride, and of industry, all equally unfit the rising generation for any pursuit that might re-establish the fallen fortunes of their families."[9] In the eyes of the lower classes, the clerical bickering only served to tarnish the image of the clergy in general.

The scene was thus well set for Lartigue's rise to prominence as the architect of a new clerical strategy. Plessis's anodyne successors, Monseigneurs Bernard-Claude Panet and Joseph Signay, brought no new direction to episcopal attitudes; they supported both the creation of the Montreal diocese and Lartigue's claim to his bishopric.

Monseigneur Lartigue was a man of a very different stamp. Son of a farmer and cousin of Louis-Joseph Papineau, he had studied law before joining the Order of St-Sulpice. He was a worrier. He considered the clergy and the Catholic religion to be endangered from every quarter, and he trusted neither the government nor the English-speaking Protestants nor the French-Canadian middle classes. Doctrinaire and authoritarian, he sought to project a church image which was not one of passive participation in events as they occurred, but one of aggressive instigation. It was he, as a young priest, who had first painted the French-Canadian society as a Catholic and French nation. While most of his clerical colleagues deplored nationalism for its association with French revolutionary liberalism, he seized on religion and nationality as essential co-ordinates. His thinking had developed through contact with the philosophers of the French theocratic and ultramontanist school, de Maistre, de Bonald, and Lammenais, and perhaps to some extent with certain of the French social writers.[10] His new ideology, embracing rather than rejecting nationalism, was thus strongly tainted with ultramontanism. He held to a divine right of kings which must be absolute in its exercise. He also believed in the union of church and state; but contrary to the Gallicans, for whom the church was *in* the state, he believed, though he was careful not to say it too loudly, that the church was *above* the state. It followed that for him the clergy was the leading class *par excellence*, and thus the chosen élite of the nation; the lay élite and heads of state alike were first and foremost the servants of the church. With Lartigue a movement was therefore born which, if pursued, would inevitably have a clericalizing influence on the society. In his strategy, control of education was the keystone.

Lartigue's militancy and authoritarianism, not to mention his lack of deference toward the government, led his superiors, the bishops of Quebec, to urge him a number of times to behave with more discretion, particularly when he began to talk of founding a militant newspaper. Undaunted, Lartigue forged ahead with his own plans of action in order to combat the Protestant and liberal perils he found lurking at every turn.

Secondary education was not one of Lartigue's larger preoccupations, for there was already established a classical college system owned and controlled by the clergy, and the training of future priests as handled by the various existing institutions seemed to him to be adequate. Primary education was another matter. Lartigue remained unshakably convinced that the Royal Institution was the result of an ongoing Protestant plot against the Catholics. In 1826 Governor Dalhousie suggested to Bishop Panet the formation of two committees within the Royal Institution, one Catholic and one Protestant. Lartigue rose in opposition. "Please God preserve us from it,"[11] he wrote; it could only be another Protestant machination, for as far as he was concerned the Parish Schools Act was perfectly adequate. As discussions continued between the government and the church hierarchy in Quebec, Lartigue redoubled his opposition. In 1827 he wrote to D.-B. Viger:

> We [have] enough with our four large colleges, perhaps adding another in the county of Cornwallis (Kamouraska), and with our parish primary schools, to give our compatriots a high level of common education, and particularly a Catholic and Canadian one. I believe that these two committees, of which the Protestant will always have the influence, will confound each other in the end or fight with each other, and from this will result grave ills for our country.[12]

Further goading him was the fact that liberal thinkers had their own notions on education. While Plessis was still alive, Lartigue had written to him thus:

> Your Quebec philosophers are resolved it seems to destroy the principle of the education act passed last year, introducing in the House of Assembly the biblical system, thrown hastily together under the name Lancaster. The prothonotary [Court registrar] Perreault who is so enamoured of it does not realize that Borgia and Co. intend to use it to ruin the influence of the clergy, who for their part have not put enough effort into setting up schools in the countryside as provided for by the last bill. This impious new plan must be aborted.[13]

In vain, Lartigue deplored the curés' penchant for building manorial presbyteries and over-enthusiasm for adorning their churches, which meant less money and attention devoted to schools. The indifference toward the latter on the part of the lower classes unfortunately matched that of their spiritual advisers. Since only thirty-five such schools were established between 1825 and 1829, the Parish Schools Act can only be considered to have failed in its purpose.

Lartigue could always count on French-Canadian middle-class support when the interests of the "nation" were at stake. One of these occasions was the quarrel with the French-born Sulpicians over the diocese of Montreal. If the superior of the Sulpicians could deal directly with the English government over the seigneurial status of the Island of Montreal, the clergy was surely justified in appealing to the nationalist leaders with power to arouse the population. But in 1826 the relationship between the clergy and the middle classes became less cozy again. Lartigue began to suspect that the *patriote* movement's ideology was as inimical as the Protestants' to the Catholic Church and clergy. In its liberal thinking and even more in its democratic and republican leanings, the movement's principal goal, it seemed to him, was the establishment of an egalitarian, lay, and even atheistic society. Deliberately or otherwise, it would whittle away the power and influence of the church and perhaps even relieve it of its possessions.

The Assembly Schools Act passed in 1829 was an abomination to Bishop Lartigue, for it gave control, supervision, and partial financing of the school system to the legislative assembly, in other words, to laymen more interested in producing loyal patriots than devout Christians. In a given community, the school would be controlled by trustees elected by the local property owners.

These schools proliferated astonishingly; there were 981 by 1830 and 1,530 by 1836, when the legislative council refused to agree to the law's renewal. In opposing them, Lartigue felt he was doing battle not only with the Protestants but also with impious Catholics. Over 90 per cent of the rural people were incapable even of signing their names, yet Lartigue remarked, "it would be better for them to have no literary education at all than to risk a bad moral education."[14] He was still to suffer some serious setbacks. The parish councils bill of 1831 (which was finally set aside) proposed giving representatives of local property owners a part in the management of *Fabriques*. Then came a proposal for a lay French university, and in 1836, the last straw, a bill for the establishment of normal schools. Lartigue wrote to the Bishop of Quebec: "What the act of 1829 has done to debase our primary schools and remove them from the hands of the clergy and place them in those of lay persons, the new normal schools will do with respect to the training and education of our schoolmasters throughout the province."[15]

The disarray caused by the non-renewal of the Assembly Schools Act in 1836 suited Lartigue nicely; he urged the curés to gather the schools to the bosom of the church, but, he warned them, it should be done without giving the impression that the clergy was "snatching the education of the people as if by right."[16] He even considered bringing priests, nuns, and brothers from France, the better to ensure that the schools would be fully staffed and controlled by the church.

In this period, despite the colony's economic problems, there is no doubt that the church enjoyed considerable power and financial comfort, too. Nevertheless, the clergy felt constantly insecure. Internal quarrels and enduring misunderstandings between the episcopate and the rural clergy[17] sapped clerical energies at a time of intense competition between the English-speaking business community and the French-Canadian middle classes. New imperatives dictated an easing of the church's formerly close relationship with the government. No longer would the clergy envisage sharing power with any lay élite group. What alarmed them most was the rise of the ambitious, power-hungry French-Canadian middle classes with their semi-democratic ideology. Bishop Lartigue's dream of making the clergy the true leaders of the French-Canadian society received some rude blows over the short term; in the long run, however, with his successor, Monseigneur Bourget, the dream came very close to reality.

III The Liberal Professions as a National Elite

The emergence and growth of the liberal professions in the 1790's, a manifestation of the rise of the middle classes soon after the conquest, was by no means a purely French-Canadian phenomenon; it was a natural result of the diversification of occupations, and many of the new professionals were English-speaking. Most significant is the rapidity of the group's growth, far outstripping the total population growth, and impelled by new attitudes emerging in the last decade of the eighteenth century (see Table 44).

By 1825 there was talk of there being too many notaries, advocates, and physicians. Economic conditions could not afford a living to so many. Competition and rivalry within each discipline were intense. Far more than in merchant circles, opinions were formed along ethnic lines. Clearly, the growth in numbers of English-speaking professionals was not unrelated to their better contacts in trade, manufacturing, and financial circles, and even with large landowners. After 1815 their ranks were also swelled by immigration (see Table 45).

The majority of physicians were English-speaking, for the French-Canadian apprenticeship system did not provide normal access to the profession and most aspiring physicians were obliged to study outside the country, in the United States or better still in Scotland. McGill University established its Faculty of Medicine in 1829. Between 1824 and 1835, 218 individuals were admitted to the practice of medicine, and 144 of them were English-speaking, fully 20 per cent immigrants.[18] Even in the country districts the local physician was more often than not English-speaking. The numbers and proportion of French Canadians in the profession increased most markedly after 1825. Most of these went abroad for their training, some even to France.

French Canadians destined for other professions invariably worked their way through the apprenticeship system after graduating from a classical college or seminary. These institutions, whose prime purpose was the training of priests, therefore played an important role in the recruitment of French-speaking professionals. The notarial profession, the most typically French-Canadian, demonstrates how dependent were the majority of French-speaking professionals on the seigneurial system and the Coutume de Paris inherited from the Old Régime. This dependency helps to explain the vigorous opposition to the establishment of land registry offices, particularly from notaries who foresaw their function being pre-empted by civil servants. A fact worthy of note: around 1838 only 64 per cent of the total number of professionals were French Canadians, meaning under-representation on the basis of population, which in 1844 was 75 per cent French-Canadian. This was an inevitable source of friction. Considered geographically, the imbalance is even more striking. Even in the country districts, where the English-speaking population was 7 per cent, 17 per cent of the professionals (and 21 per cent of the businessmen) were English. In the district of Quebec, urban and rural combined, the proportion of English-speaking professionals was 34.7 per cent, and in the Trois-Rivières district 30 per cent.

It was in Montreal where the proportions were the most unfavourable to the French Canadians. In the district as a whole, if the available data is to be believed, the proportion of English-speaking professionals rose from 42 per cent in 1831 to 57 per cent in 1842 (English-speaking businessmen, 49 and 66 per cent respectively). Alexis de Tocqueville noted that in Kamouraska, "the population is only French, and yet when one comes across an inn or a shop, its sign is in English."[19]

As the social context and atmosphere deteriorated after 1815, the French-Canadian professional class, with their keen sense of cultural identity and their educational and intellectual advantage over their merchant compatriots, built themselves a reputation as interpreters of situations and conceivers of ideologies. They had a ready-made following in the French-Canadian merchants whose activities were confined to Lower Canada and particularly those with no government contacts. The two groups, suffering from English-speaking competition, turned their orientation more strongly than ever toward land ownership and the rural milieu (see Tables 46 and 47).

When de Tocqueville visited Lower Canada in 1831 he was particularly struck by the revolutionary potential inherent in these reactions to English-speaking power and control. "In the cities," he wrote, "the English make display of great wealth. Among Canadians there are but fortunes of limited extent; hence, jealousies and petty irritations.... The English have all the external trade in their hands and are the leaders in all the internal trade. Hence Jealousy once more.... Every day the English gather to themselves lands which the Canadians consider reserved for their race."[20] His conclusion was succinct: "They [the English] are indeed the leading class in Canada. I doubt that it will long be thus."[21] In any event there now seemed to be much more community of interest and ambition uniting the French-Canadian professional and merchant classes in opposition to the English-speaking bourgeoisie. Class-consciousness and cultural identity worked one upon the other and gave impetus to their quest for power. Whatever stood in the way of their social advancement and promotion to the rank of leading class was perceived collectively as a threat, an obstacle to the realization of the group's objectives.

The French-Canadian middle classes, by virtue of their conception of proprietorship and its stability under the seigneurial system, regarded the system as a form of protection against the machinations of the English-speaking bourgeoisie, whose goal, they were convinced, was to destroy the fundamental ties between the French-Canadian nation and the land. On the British government's plan to liquidate seigneurial rights on the Island of Montreal (with the consent of the Sulpicians), Papineau declared:

> But it is the importance which he [Stanley] would give to British proprietorship, having recognized [the proprietorship] of land to be principally in the hands of the native-born population, which is ridiculous.... Compared to the value of capital used for the purchase of land, worked by the proprietors themselves and not by another class of capitalists who in Europe take it on lease, the value of capital on loan or converted into securities and manufactured goods is almost nil. The class in possession of the land is in possession of the fortune of the people.[22]

The seigneurial system, according to this thinking, far from suppressing middle class advancement, on the contrary contributed to it and to the stability of the class.

So blinded were the French-Canadian professionals and merchants by their fear of the English-speaking bourgeoisie that they underestimated the power of the Catholic clergy. There was certainly considerable religious indifference among these groups, but anti-clericalism was far more widespread for a variety of reasons, largely the clergy's disapproval of the rise of their class and hostility toward their supposedly liberal nationalism. They were frequently at odds with the curés in the city and in the country, these social upstarts bent on re-creating the society to suit their own objectives, and on hoisting themselves to the top of the social totem pole. The hostility was at first kept more or less in check, but after 1829 became increasingly undisguised as the laymen conceived and launched a series of measures to strengthen the role of leading lay individuals in local affairs. The competition for power between clergy and laity was now in the open. Over the amendment to the Parish Schools Act, Théophile Bruneau warned Papineau: "What I feared on the question of the notables has occurred; the clergy are irritated and are stooping to the [same] excess of abuse for which they would reproach certain members of the House; it is a deplorable thing for them and for the House, [and] they have many more partisans than I imagined."23 Papineau's reactions to the matter, written to J. Viger, illustrate the kind of jousting that went on:

> It matters little who are the men of the hour, but rather what are the principles which will prevail. Let each raise his loudest voice, the one for monarchy and the *fabriques*, the other for liberalism and a republic; 50 years from now the reasonable side will win out; for, in an age when miracles and trickery have ceased, reason must eventually win out. There are no more blindly accepted prescriptions or compulsory professions of faith, and everything [now] ends in debate. Sceptres, mitres, parchments are playthings become objects of derision. Make your choice, compose waggish couplets or lament over ruins; each side has its lyricism....24

Papineau's optimism for the long term was not shared by all. At almost the same moment A.-N. Morin was writing to Ludger Duvernay that "these days the republic [plan] is going badly.... And then the clergy will be marauding the republic at the next elections; they have already threatened to."25 A pamphlet attacking the entire Old Régime, social and political, written by Félicitée de Lamennais and entitled *Paroles d'un Croyant*, was printed and distributed by the élite laity. The clergy condemned it immediately. Wrote Charles-Ovide Perreault to E.-R. Fabre: "The Bishops have written to the various curés prohibiting the circulation of *Paroles d'un Croyant*.... But if the Bishops intend to prohibit the circulation of political principles and meddle unfittingly in our political beliefs, dictate to us what we must believe concerning principles of government, they will come a cropper."26

There was a minority among the middle classes who regarded the clergy as the principal enemy, for whom the destruction of clerical power was a priority, achievable only through the abolition of the seigneurial régime and tithing, the separation of church and state, and total control of education by the latter. For many of the lay élite, however, religious conservatism, acknowledged or instinctive, was still strong, and the clergy's social role still an important one. The English bourgeoisie on the whole loomed much larger as the principal opponents in most middle-class minds. This element perceived the church as indispensable to the French-Canadian nation's survival, so serious was the threat presented by the English-speaking Protestants.

Thus the majority's conception of the clergy's role as diffusers of the nation's essential values kept clerical status and privileges from becoming a major issue. The clergy's attitude over the 1822 union proposal and the dispute over the creation of the diocese of Montreal furthermore gave the appearance of community of interest between the clergy and the middle classes. The spread of nationalism among the clergy tended to mask the depth of the differences between the two groups and the myth of a "national" clergy for a time gained strength in lay quarters. After 1830 the differences resurfaced, but still in 1831 Charles Mondelet wrote as follows to de Tocqueville:

Perhaps there could be detected in them a hidden propensity for governing or directing; but it is a thing of small account. In general, our clergy is eminently national.... Every time it has been necessary to oppose the English, the clergy have been in the forefront and in our ranks. They have remained liked and respected by all. Far from opposing ideas of liberty, they have themselves preached them. All the measures we have taken in favour of public instruction, almost by force and despite England, have found support in the clergy.... What gives us to believe that our priests' political character is peculiar to Canada is that priests arriving from time to time from France demonstrate on the contrary an acquiescence and spirit of docility toward the government which we [ourselves] cannot conceive.[27]

The true liberals entertained no illusions regarding the apparent solidarity with the clerics, and the clergy's behaviour provoked increasing disenchantment among the rest. Anti-clericalism spread, but the "national" clergy myth survived, an ambivalence exemplified in Papineau, who wrote in 1835:

As for the bigotry of the priests, who perceive in the declaration of the sovereignty of the people the overthrow of Catholicism, it is lunacy for them to reason so ill in the midst of a Catholic people dominated by a Protestant government. Passive obedience would be the ruin of their form of worship.... They are [either] two-faced or inconsistent when they do not see that for the English government it is a maxim which it will never abandon, that it must denational-ize us in order to anglicize us, and that to achieve that end, it will attack our form of worship with as much ardour as our laws, our customs, and the language of the country... and that since it is its will to beset us in our nationality, it will do so in all that is part of it.[28]

The French-Canadian middle classes, seeing developments in purely ethnic terms, seem not to have understood the clergy's new objectives as instigated by Bishop Lartigue. More than ever, the English bour-geoisie appeared to be the principal obstacle in their quest for power. With continued English domination of the economy and of patronage, the economic disparities between the ethnic groups seemed to be con-stantly widening. More enterprising spirit on the part of French Cana-dians might overcome the disparities, claimed some. "May their efforts and perseverance restore commerce to the hands of the Canadians,"[29] declared the Société St-Jean-Baptiste to a distinguished gathering. But the predominant feeling was that the colonial civil service, en-couraged by the British government and the English-speaking mer-chants and professionals, was practising systematic discrimination, the goal being not merely to keep the French Canadians down but to destroy the French-Canadian nation.

It was a political problem to which there could only be a political solution, namely political power in the hands of the French-Canadian middle classes. The banks, the St Lawrence canal system, the protec-tive tariffs on lumber and wheat, the saga of the Forges du Saint-Maurice, the land registry offices, the attacks on the seigneurial régime and the Coutume de Paris, the massive immigration, and con-tinued attempts to unify the Canadas, all reinforced the conviction, rightly or wrongly, that the French-Canadian nation was in mortal peril. The identification of the middle classes with the nation and their proclamation of a state of emergency fired with increasing intensity their desire for power and their determination to mobilize the masses behind them. Staking all on politics, their own and the society's destinies, they used the all-encompassing cultural peril to channel lower-class discontent toward achievement of political transformation without social revolution. E.-E. Rodier, writing in 1834, seems to have grasped the anachronistic character of the aspirations of a certain number of his class:

I began this year in circumstances of poverty and I shall be very happy if I do not finish it in the tattered rags of destitution.... In short I have been much luckier than many ambitious patriots richer than I, but who have emerged like me from obscurity, who have constantly on their lips [the words] people, patriotism, liberty, equality, and who will not deign to sit at table with an honest merchant-tailor or a worthy merchant-grocer, and who to pursue their path to celebrity lend to the cause of their country what they have received through usury, who lend to their friends for the sole pleasure of having it known, who posture as critics in order to be taken for some Socrates, who in covetous mediocrity assume the dignity of a great man of whom they are not even a pale image, and call it "aristocracy," who combine ignorance with envy and find their consolation in bootlicking from certain incense-bearing sycophants....[30]

IV Popular Discontent and the Choice of Nationalism

As the power struggle intensified among the élite groups, so did popular discontent. After 1815 it reached the cities, largely due to massive immigration from the British Isles; survival and prosperity for the French-Canadian urban working class began to look even more uncertain than for their rural counterparts. Having talked with a number of farmers near Quebec, de Tocqueville wrote:

They already feel strongly that the English race is expanding about them in an alarming fashion; that it is wrong that they should confine themselves within a compass instead of spreading freely throughout the country. Their jealousy is sharply whetted by daily arrivals of newcomers from Europe. They feel that in the end they will be absorbed. It is apparent that anything said on the subject stirs their passions, but they do not clearly see the remedy. The Canadians are too timid to learn anything of the world, they are not shrewd enough [you will say]. You are quite right, of course, but what of it? Their replies are as I say.[31]

With heavy immigration and economic change, the working-class proportion of the urban population increased; in Quebec from 62 per cent of heads of families in 1805 to 68 per cent in 1842, and in Montreal from 62 to 67 per cent in the same period; shipbuilding in Quebec would account for the difference in 1842. Most of the growth was in unskilled labour, from 12 to 15 per cent in Quebec between 1805 and

1842 and from 18 to 26 per cent in Montreal between 1831 and 1842 alone. Skilled labour remained relatively stable and in Montreal even declined slightly. The colony's economic tribulations weighed heavily on this complex urban working class. The general decline in prices between 1815 and 1835 provided some relief, but the domestic price of bread, always subject to the state of export demand and local and import supply, increased substantially between 1822 and 1830. Poor showings in livestock production affected tanners and other skilled categories, and the recession in shipbuilding between 1825 and 1834 brought hardship to many, both skilled and unskilled and both urban and rural. Even competition between the government and the assembly for control of the public purse had repercussions on the lot of the workers. In 1833, Etienne Parent wrote to Duvernay: "You cannot imagine the distress felt by people in business here after the rejection of the subsidy bill by the Council. It has removed from our circulation some forty thousand *louis*, and if this shortage is to be compounded by another rejection, it is most important that it not be due to the slightest fault of the House."[32]

Immigrant labour, of course, was in competition with the native-born, of which there was already an oversupply, and in particular came to provide the nucleus of cheap unskilled manpower. The cities therefore offered slim pickings for the surplus rural population. "The emigrants [both] slothful and employment-seeking," wrote a contemporary in *La Minerve* in 1834, "can only be regarded by the natural-born as intruders, rejects from their own country."[33] Two months later there was further comment in the same newspaper. "We do not want them because this yearly flow of mendicant population does considerable injustice to the proletarians already established in this country."[34] The resentment against the immigrants was now distinctly ethnic.

In the city of Quebec the English-speaking proportion of the working class swelled spectacularly, from 19 per cent in 1805 to 40 per cent in 1831, then diminished to 34 per cent in 1842 as Montreal became the more attractive destination for immigrants. Montreal's English-speaking working class, already 50 per cent in 1831, grew to 56 per cent in 1842, with the unskilled category swelling from 50 to 63 per cent. While the French Canadians remained strong in the woodworking trades, tanning, masonry, and carting, the English-speaking tended to dominate in cobbling, tailoring, cabinetmaking, and generally in the newer skills. Unskilled labour was increasingly Irish, particularly in Montreal (see Tables 48 and 49).

With economic conditions as poor as they were, if there emerged no working-class social movement it was no doubt due to the immigrant population's mobility and even more to sharp ethnic and religious divisions within the class. There was antagonism even among the Irish, Scottish, and English groups. The Irish Catholic priests and leaders exhorted all Catholics to unite against the Protestant menace, not without effect; but to the French-Canadian working class an immigrant was an immigrant and as such was a competitor for too few jobs or customers. More than evocations of rich versus poor or Protestant versus Catholic, suggestions that a conspiracy was afoot to drive the French Canadians from the cities struck a responsive chord: "traps laid to deprive a people of their happiness and turn them into hewers of wood and drawers of water for foreigners come among us."[35]

Even among the middle classes, efforts at building class solidarity finally foundered, mainly over questions of ethnicity and differences of interest between the ethnic groups as such. Ethnic confrontations were particularly bitter in Montreal.

In rural Lower Canada, too, the scene was one of economic and social instability. Rural communities had long since ceased to be simple pastoral collectivities led by curés and seigneurs, for professionals, merchants, skilled tradesmen, and labourers had become permanent fixtures (see Table 50). The farming population nevertheless continued to dominate numerically. In 1831 this category was still largely dependent on wheat for subsistence and income (see Table 52). While the proportion of surplus producers was still as high as 50 per cent in certain areas, overall it was only around 20 per cent, and declined drastically thereafter. In the fertile counties of Lislet and Kamouraska below Quebec, the wheat harvest dropped from 350,000 *minots* in 1831 to 15,000 in 1844. In 25 seigneurial parishes in the Montreal district, the average production per farm fell from 97.4 *minots* in 1831 to 19.0 in 1842. By the latter date the proportion of producers harvesting 50 *minots* or less was 91 per cent (47 per cent in 1831), and only 1.4 per cent were producing more than 100 *minots* (27 per cent in 1831). A partial solution was found in other crops, principally oats and potatoes (see Tables 51 and 52). In the Quebec district the shift brought an increase of 94 per cent in oat harvests and 27 per cent in potatoes between 1831 and 1842, but in the previously mentioned 25 Montreal district parishes the oat harvest increased only 28 per cent and potatoes declined by 7 per cent.

The French-Canadian farmers were the most severely affected by the wheat crisis, and particularly those of the Montreal district. English-speaking farmers paid little attention to wheat and concentrated on potatoes and, to a lesser extent, oats. The large producers near the cities were English-speaking. In the parish of Montreal, 41 per cent of the English-speaking producers harvested over 1,000 bushels of potatoes in 1831, against only 8 per cent of the French-speaking producers. A similar situation prevailed around Quebec. In oats, the English-speaking producers again harvested higher averages than the French-speaking, who were still trying to produce wheat as well.[36] The English-speaking agricultural élite were to be found in both the seigneuries and the townships. Their French-speaking counterparts were more exceptional and were located in certain parishes in the Quebec and Montreal districts where the soil was fertile and landholdings stable; for the most part they were large wheat producers.

Most strikingly, however, English-speaking producers of all categories fared better than the French-speaking, which is not to say that all English-speaking farmers were prosperous; many located in townships where roads were poor or non-existent could eke out only a subsistence-level existence. English-speaking stock-raisers were severely affected by depressed market conditions for meat and by American competition between 1831 and 1842, having responded to favourable conditions between 1820 and 1830 by greatly increasing the size of their herds. In 1831, 33 per cent of English-speaking cattle-raisers owned 16 head and over, compared to only 6 per cent of the French-speaking. The difference was less marked in hog-raising, 54 per cent of English-speaking and 34 per cent of French-speaking producers owning 6 hogs and over (see Tables 51 and 53).

It is apparent that the French Canadians increased their activity in livestock primarily in response to subsistence needs, though there were some large producers among them. In 1831, Jean Huot of Châteauguay owned 163 cattle; J.-B. Dumouchel of St-Benoît, 134 head of cattle, 144 sheep, and 61 hogs; J.-D. Lacroix, seigneur, had 1,250 sheep; Mathieu de Lachenaie had 150 cattle and 350 sheep.

The recession in stock-raising after 1830 affected hog-raisers most of all. The proportion of English-speaking producers owning 6 hogs and over dropped from 54 per cent in 1831 to 16 per cent in 1842, compared to 34 and 14 per cent respectively for the French-speaking. Cattle-raisers suffered too, but less severely.

With the agricultural crisis spreading and deepening after 1830, the Montreal region proved to be particularly vulnerable, especially in the seigneuries and more especially still for the French Canadians, due to the region's heavy dependence on agriculture and its resistance to a shift away from wheat. In the Quebec region the rural economy was more diversified, with fishing, navigation, and lumber providing a degree of compensation for the decline in the agricultural sector. The situation in the Trois-Rivières region was much the same. In the townships, forestry and small business initiatives played a compensatory role (see Table 54).

Where there were secondary economic activities, there tended to be more merchants and professionals and also more tradesmen and, to some extent, unskilled labourers. Where there was little or no activity other than agriculture, however, the unskilled labourer category was more in evidence. The effect of a shift from a purely agricultural economy to a more balanced one is exemplified in the parish of Lavaltrie (St-Paul in the Montreal district), where the seigneur, Barthélemy Joliette, decided in 1825 to invest in forestry and related industries.[37] The effect on occupational structure was not immediate, but between 1831 and 1842 the proportion of tradesmen rose from 5 per cent of heads of families to 14 per cent, and there were 55 fewer labourers and 63 fewer farmers. The *village de l'industrie,* as the small "manufacturing" centre was called, eased rather than solved the economic and demographic problems of the parish; the recession in lumber dealt a harsh blow to the population. In 1834 Curé Manseau wrote, "I am beginning to know my village. Two thirds are labourers, penniless carters, and tradesmen with little work. Still practically incapable of paying [even the price of] burial for their children."[38] Such secondary activities were either non-existent or insignificant in a great many of the Montreal district seigneuries. It was here that the rural proletariat was most numerous and the fragmentation of farms the most extreme (see Table 54).

Thus many factors pointed to social and political upheaval: overpopulation and fragmentation of landholdings in the seigneuries, both contributing to progressive soil exhaustion and lower and lower standards of living for the French-Canadian farming population; immigrant competition for jobs in the cities; the steadily growing presence of the English-speaking in the cities, townships, and even in the seigneuries; the landless proletariat swelling between 1831 and 1842 from 28 to 38 per cent of the rural population in the Montreal district and from 27 to 28 per cent in the Quebec region. In such a context the French-Canadian society could no longer cling to its traditional identity as a people closely related to the land and land ownership, nor to its belief in the equality of conditions within a class, even in the rural population (see Tables 55 and 56).

Had there existed a genuine class-consciousness in the rural lower classes, there might have arisen a mass movement, on the one hand against the state for the deficiency of its land policy, and on the other against the institutions of the seigneurial régime and tithing. Wrote Alexis de Tocqueville in 1831:

We have perceived in our conversations with the people of this country a deep hatred and jealousy of the seigneurs.... We have perceived also that the peasant conceives ill the clergy's right to levy tithes, and looks with resentment upon the wealth that this tax places in the hands of a few ecclesiastics. If religion ever loses its hold on Canada, that is the breach by which the enemy will enter.[39]

The French-Canadian middle classes as a whole had no desire to channel popular discontent in that direction. A truly liberal and democratic ideology, and the mobilization of the masses behind it, would not serve the new French-Canadian élite's real aspirations and interests. The nationalism this class had been nurturing since the beginning of the century, on the other hand, laid responsibility for all the ills suffered by the rural folk at one door, labelled ENGLISH—government, capitalist, and immigrant. De Tocqueville observed:

> In short this population seems to us capable of being led though not yet capable of leading itself. We have arrived at the moment of crisis.... A man of genius who understood, felt and were capable of exploiting the national passions of the people would here have an admirable role to play. He would quickly become the most powerful man in the colony. But I do not yet see him anywhere.[40]

The rural folk were bound to respond to an ideology founded on the spectre of their own material and cultural extinction. The English were there in flesh and blood, always with some kind of advantage, merchants, professionals, seigneurs, tradesmen, or farmers, not to mention the immigrants, land-hungry in the townships and seigneuries, job-hungry in the cities.

Particularly in Montreal and the surrounding region, the economic, demographic, and social crisis kept deepening, with the wealthy English bourgeoisie, the French-Canadian middle classes, and the Catholic clergy vying for social leadership and power. The English bourgeoisie felt increasingly frustrated in the political arena by the aggressiveness of a nationalist movement backed solidly by the majority of the population. The French-Canadian middle classes, now confident of support from the masses, strong in the conviction that the drive for national regeneration resided in them, and determined to rally all elements capable of lending strength to their movement, concentrated their energies against the English bourgeoisie. What they failed to perceive was that the progressive conversion of the Catholic clergy to nationalism and ultramontanism was itself a weapon designed to combat liberal-tainted nationalism, establish the clergy's social leadership, and make the French-Canadian middle classes the servants of the church. In short, the leaders of the French-Canadian middle-class élite failed to realize that the clergy's own campaign for power was as political as their own.

CHAPTER 8

The Paralysis of the Political System, 1815-1828
(Part One)

The Canadian Party and Revenue Control

There were many facets to the political crisis gathering over the years 1815-37. Without doubt it arose largely from the economic problems and demographic tensions underlying the instability at all social levels and the deep and widespread discontent in the lower classes. Antagonism among the leading classes was exacerbated by growing tensions emerging from the socio-economic structure, and turned into a power struggle that could have sparked a social uprising by the masses. Intergroup conflicts and alliances were influenced by religious persuasion and certain religious situations, but the ethnic factor, already strong in 1815, became the most powerful polarizing force in the society, with religion perceived as an agent of "national" cohesion.

With this perspective, we find political conflict involving groups and classes rather than individuals motivated by abstract principles. The political parties with their ideologies and theories became the tools of socio-ethnic groups, each of which, lusting for power or fearful of losing it, identified the whole society's interests and aspirations with its own. Ideologies reflected the ambitions of certain groups but served also to attract others, particularly the masses; ideological ambiguities, even contradictions, were rationalized in order to win over otherwise incompatible elements. The *patriotes*, as the followers of the Canadian party came to be called after 1826, attracted sympathizers at home and abroad with their confusion of nationalism, liberalism, and democracy. H.S. Chapman, for example, an English immigrant radical of what R.S. Neal calls "the middling class,"[1] saw no real difference between the *patriote* movement and the radical movement in England.

The paper he founded, the *Daily Advertiser*, for the eighteen months of its existence, proclaimed that "the impetus to conflict in Lower Canada derived from the clash of the rival political principles of aristocracy and democracy, as embraced by opposing classes, and not from racial differences and aspirations as was maintained by the English ascendancy in Canada."[2] Liberals, democrats, and Catholics, whether English, Irish, or American, saw situations analogous to those in their own countries. All chose to ignore the nationalist dimension of the *patriote* movement, partly due to their own ideological blind spots and partly to the more or less deliberate confusion of principles in *patriote* ideology.

Lord Durham, an aristocrat of radical leanings, when he first arrived in Lower Canada, observed facts which apparently validated the thesis of a conflict between aristocratic and democratic principles. "I looked on it," he wrote, "as a dispute analogous to those with which history and experience have made us so familiar in Europe,—a dispute between a people demanding an extension of popular privileges, on the one hand, and an executive, on the other, defending the powers which it conceives necessary to the maintenance of order." But he continued, "One by one the ancient English leaders of the Assembly have fallen off from the majority, and attached themselves to the party which supported the British Government against it. Every election from the townships added to the English minority. On the other hand, year after year, in spite of the various influences which a government can exercise ... the number of French Canadians, on whom the government could rely, has been narrowed...." On *patriote* ideology he observed, "being a majority, they have invoked the principle of popular control and democracy, and appealed with no little effect to the sympathy of liberal politicians in every quarter of the world.... But when we look to the objects of each party, the analogy to our own politics seems to be lost, if not actually reversed; the French appear to have used their democratic arms for conservative purposes, rather than those of liberal and enlightened movement; and the sympathies of the friends of reform are naturally enlisted on the side of sound amelioration which the English minority in vain attempted to introduce into the antiquated laws of the Province." What he saw was a progression of ethnic polarization and of conservative nationalism in the guise of democratic ideals. "I expected to find a contest between a government and a people: I found two nations warring in the bosom of a single state: I found a struggle, not of principles, but of races."[3]

Alexis de Tocqueville had also been struck by the nationalist fermentation in 1831: "*Le Canadien* has as epigraph: *our religion, our language, and our laws*. It is difficult to be more frank. The content corresponds with the title. Anything which can enflame popular passions great and small against the English is raised in this paper. I have seen an article in which it was said that Canada would never be happy until it had an administration of Canadian birth, principles, thinking, prejudices even.... The Catholics in Canada and the United States are invariably supporters of the democratic party. Does it follow that Catholicism is the bearer of democratic principles? No. But those Catholics are poor and almost all of a country where the aristocracy is Protestant."[4]

In the spring of 1837, the French Ambassador to the United States declared, "But this population is French, and the word alone gives the key to the present situation. That feeling of nationality which so powerfully stirs simple, guileless men, is awakening, still hazy and confused for the Canadians, to the call of a few ambitious men."[5]

In order to understand the conflicts which led in 1837 to a total breakdown of the political system and a situation ripe for rebellion, we must examine the relationships between the political movements and socio-ethnic structures. We must also delineate the respective expectations of the élite groups and the masses. As always, the voice of the silent majority, even when heard distinctly, speaks in riddles.

In response to currents of popular opinion among the élite and in the masses, the *patriote* movement became progressively more radical—in ideology, in the ranks of the Canadian party, and at the grassroots, the electorate. Papineau's rise to leadership was less due to his taste for personal power than to his skill at fitting his actions, consciously or not, to a complex and fluid situation. He emerged from his group to take its leadership, which he consolidated by responding to the group's needs. At the peak of the *patriote* leader's personal power, in 1835, Frederick Elliott, secretary to the Gosford commission, wrote:

Others, again, hug themselves with the notion that Papineau is their *Instrument*. Heaven help their wits! That being the most audacious among them, they place him in the front of the battle, but voluntarily, and with power to set him aside at pleasure.... He is, in truth, their Master. Their natures crave for support, and they will always seek it in characters more vigorous than their own. I never saw any one who seemed better versed than the Canadian Speaker, in the arts and demeanour by which one man wields dominion over the minds of many, and he is daily becoming more confirmed in his sway, as they are in their obedience. Such is the man that a few of his followers have the presumption to suppose that they can set aside, when no longer serviceable.[6]

There were those, however, who considered Papineau's leadership to have been deliberately and artificially created. Élisée Mailhot, a *patriote* disappointed in the contradictions he found in his leader, observed that human beings are capable of creating idols and then turning about and destroying them. In 1839 he wrote, "Mr. Papineau has grave faults. But I myself blame those who have flattered this gentleman and supported him in all his acts of folly and persecution; the flatterers have corrupted him. We had in Mr. Papineau's person a man who might have brought us glory; we have sacrificed him in our personal interest; we have given preference to a modicum of honour over that of our country."[7] Yet Papineau the leader should be regarded neither as an irresponsible man acting in blind obedience to collective imperatives, nor as the sole artisan of French-Canadian destiny. He was in fact far too inclined to picture himself in the former role, offering himself as the sacrificial lamb on the altar of *la patrie*.

But in 1815 Papineau had yet to be placed on a pedestal. His personal power grew with the *patriote* movement and unrest in the Montreal region.

The crisis of 1805-10 did much to polarize the vote along ethnic lines. In the decade before the turn of the century no such tendency is apparent (see Table 57), but by the election of 1816 it is unmistakable. In Quebec's Upper Town, for instance, 92 per cent of French-Canadian votes (96 per cent of French-Canadian merchant and professional votes) were cast for French-speaking candidates (see Table 58).

Despite the War of 1812, the Canadian party had a firm hold over the rural lower classes. It was still at a disadvantage in the cities and in the rural ridings with rapidly growing English populations or strong English control, such as Gaspé, Dorchester, Warwick, and York. In 1814 Bédard wrote from Trois-Rivières:

> Here everyone is against the House and for the English party. That comes, I believe, of their always having had puny representatives. The heads of the clergy here are strongly against the House.... Accustomed to receiving all their impressions from the English and being led by their influence (being absolutely nil themselves) they have no strength to resist and are swept up by the current.... It is an untenable position to have against oneself the English Party in which are all the government people.[8]

In 1830 the Canadian party set out to break these pockets of resistance.

For all its pretensions, the Canadian party was not a party of or for the people. The people did not dictate its objectives or the thrust of its tactics. In 1810 the English party, trying to attract the working-class vote, decided to back a tanner by the name of Gauthier. The Canadian party reacted immediately by trying to take control of a working-class meeting. Wrote J. Viger, "Still masters of the battlefield, our people ventured to address the workers. But it was useless.... They [the workers] do not realize the situation in which they are placing themselves by acting thus; in this way they are dividing the vote and are risking the defeat of the two Canadians and the election of the two English. A trap is being laid for them."[9] National imperatives were not necessarily social imperatives for the élite group who were the leaders of the Canadian party. It was first and foremost a French-Canadian middle-class party, and so it was to remain until 1837. The social composition of the legislative assembly, with its overwhelming Canadian party majority, reflects this fact. Between 1815 and 1824, 36 per cent of the members were merchants and 38 per cent professionals (31 and 34 per cent respectively in 1805 and 1814). The members who were farmers or tradesmen, by virtue of their wealth and status in the community, were closer to the middle than the lower classes (see Table 7).

The absence of financial qualifications for candidates allowed anyone of any class to run for election. Both French and English, moved by the idea of devotion to the common cause, accepted the absence of remuneration for assembly service as laid down by the 1791 constitution. This, however, resulted in much absenteeism, and particularly among the French Canadians. Every bill designed to correct the situation after 1800 was defeated, some members fearing a House filled with peasants and others an increase in the already crushing majority of French Canadians. In 1821 Papineau's leadership was still in the balance and, in opposition to one of these bills favoured by rivals with strong rural support, he wrote:

> I admit I begin to doubt the validity of the theory which I held that the good sense of the habitants and their lack of ambition for public office would make them useful representatives. They are not enlightened enough, and they are just as much influenced by their selfish interests as are men of other classes, and just as easily misled. The payment of tithes and seigniorial dues begins to irk them, and they don't see that their jealousy for their superiors is the same as the jealousy of the landless for them.[10]

Papineau's attitude was very different after 1830. By then his leadership was assured and he sensed a need for a more radical complexion to his entourage. Still, he was thinking more of penniless young professionals than of peasants; "it would be stifling to the best budding talents not to facilitate conditions for those who show enthusiasm for sitting in this house, but whom fortune has not favoured. Seeing them enter young and with brilliant capabilities and pure hearts and full of courage, we may conceive the greatest hopes." To opponents of the reform he replied, "It would be impossible to explain their motives unless by probing the deepest recesses of the human heart." And he concluded with democratic fervour, "To give a people full exercise of their rights, we must also give them self-respect, incite noble emulation, assure them freedom of choice."[11]

Payment of members might have changed the social composition of the house, yet peasants and tradesmen would not necessarily have chosen representatives of their own class. "All their hopes lie in their representatives," wrote de Tocqueville of the peasants.[12] Between 1792 and 1838, an average 77.4 per cent of the assembly's membership were merchants and professionals, which appears to reflect the progress and influence of these groups in the society. The merchants were at first the largest group representing the people, but they were soon overtaken by the professionals. The average age of merchants when first elected was 44.7 compared with 48.4 for farmers (who comprised only 12 per cent of the House in the period mentioned), and they stayed an average of 5.6 years. The professionals were 35.5 when first elected and stayed an average of 7.0 years. Half of these were advocates, first elected at 33.5 years of age and staying an average of 8.4 years. There were even twenty-three physicians, relative newcomers to the society. In the same period, only an average of 8.6 per cent were aristocrats. Those who became professional politicians were mostly young and ambitious professionals, particularly advocates. The English population, despite its rapid growth in certain areas, was less and less adequately represented in the House.

The Canadian party's disarray around 1815 was not due to lack of popular support. In 1817, J. Viger wrote his wife that among the people the House of Assembly was known as "The Great Inquiry of the Country."[13] Pierre Bédard followed the political situation closely from Trois-Rivières where he was a judge; he was gravely concerned for his party's future and wrote to Neilson in 1814:

The [English] party has astonishing strength and regards itself as the government and the governor is not part of the government. There was a time when I believed that the governors had great influence over them; I believe now that they have none unless they are of the party. If they were in great number a governor would be unable to do anything with them; they would be quite ungovernable; they must of necessity govern the governor; and things being as they are, even the Canadian party cannot counterbalance them and sustain a governor who might take sides with the Canadians. Only the present circumstance of war could make a governor take the side of the Canadians; without such circumstance, a governor will always find it in his interest to take the other side unless things change greatly and the necessity to make things go otherwise is seen in England.[14]

Some months later Bédard returned to the same theme. "If the governor is recalled it will be a bad sign for us. I believe that this year particularly, there are many different feelings in the House: many persons who wish to lead."[15]

The leadership crisis which began with Bédard's imprisonment in 1810 had deepened by 1815, enflaming personal quarrels and rivalry between the cities and country districts. It was clear that Quebec was losing the party leadership to Montreal, which was now the focal point of economic malaise, demographic pressures, and ethnic friction. Bédard wrote to Neilson:

It seems to me by the few debates that I have seen published by the *Spectateur* that there is division among the members and that partisanry between those of Quebec and Montreal is growing. The debates seem to me to be published in this spirit. Much good is heard of the one side and much ill of the other. Besides, the Quebec members each have their own particular feeling. It is true besides that if each works to his own end and without common goal [the House] will not be in condition to profit by the advantages it could have. Is it true that Lee spoke against the clergy as it appeared in the *Spectateur*? If it is true, he has acted very foolishly and should make every effort to repair his error.[16]

The internal crisis did not come to a head until the years 1827-30, but in the meantime it greatly affected the party's ideology and strategy.

There was no dearth of aspirants to succeed Bédard. Obviously there would have to be losers among the bright, ambitious young men in the House in the first decade of the century. Joseph Robitaille and J.-B. Fortin, wealthy farmers who were to sit in the House for twenty and thirty-one years respectively, were strong only in their rural ridings. The physician and seigneur François-Xavier Blanchet, the advocate Joseph-Louis Borgia, and the notary and merchant Thomas Lee were all in line for the leadership, or so they thought, and had strength both in Quebec and the rural areas of the district. The notary Taschereau was another of Bédard's former entourage. Louis Bourdages, notary, and P.-D. Debartzch, seigneur, were rivals with much rural support about Montreal, and neither intended to remain local "cocks of the roost." D.-B. Viger and L.-J. Papineau, cousins with vast family ramifications in the cities and country districts, were elected in 1809; both were advocates and both were ambitious for distinction. D.-B. Viger, the senior by twelve years at thirty-five, was beginning a long political career. Until 1837, however, he remained in Papineau's shadow.

Louis-Joseph Papineau was born in Montreal in 1786. His father Joseph, son of a cooper, had been part of the movement which had agitated for the parliamentary system, and was first elected in 1792. He was both notary and surveyor, had built mills for the Seminary of Quebec, and was manager of a number of seigneuries. Early in the century he purchased the seigneury of La Petite Nation on the Ottawa River, which proved a good investment over the long term. Like the Bédards, the Papineaus were moving up the social ladder, hence the perpetual interplay of peasant, aristocratic, and bourgeois values in Louis-Joseph. Commonly in this milieu, the family was perceived as the principal source of prestige and values, and a framework of security against outside forces judged to be hostile. Papineau the younger never questioned the family's institutional role. The mother was the traditional guardian of family and religious values. Such was Papineau's own mother, as can be seen from her letters in ill-spelled French to her sons when they were boarders at the Seminary of Quebec. To Benjamin she wrote in 1807:

> ... but this is not enough. you must do well in your religious duties which are the essential thing. For no religion, no virtue. Remember that in you I prefer virtue to science, for virtue will lead you to Heaven and science without virtue and the succour of religion will never lead you to this happy end to which the true Christian must aspire. thus my dear make every effort and pray the Lord to give you the grace necessary for your salvation and save you from the reefs on which so many Catholics founder, that is, falling into irreligion. to my dear son, let us pray God to save us from such misfortune....[17]

Rosalie Cherrier-Papineau's prayers and exhortations did not prevent her husband and several of her sons from becoming deists, like many intellectuals of the period. Even then, Louis-Joseph remained profoundly influenced by the religious and moral climate of his upbringing. For this sensitive man, ambition, greed, and sexual desire were always forbidden and unmentionable. In the depths of his being, he believed that purety, unselfishness, and affection—if they existed at all—were not to be found in politics or even in the practice of a profession, but only in family life, pastoral surroundings, and intellectual pursuits. He created a kind of mythology around his political activities, no doubt in an effort to cleanse and excuse his entry into the kingdom of evil. His penchant for a kind of exorcism, which intensified as his political career progressed, was probably reinforced by his experiences at the Seminary of Quebec, where he distinguished himself in oratorical debate, worked for the Congrégation de la Sainte-Vierge, and read voraciously.[18]

On leaving the Seminary in 1804 he considered becoming a notary like his father, but he found notarial practice boring and complained of too little time to read. He then turned to the study of law under the wing of his cousin, D.-B. Viger, but was no happier in the world of what he called "squabbling." In 1816 he wrote to his brother, "In truth I am enslaved at this time and this does not give me much attachment for a condition I was [already] sick of, but what can I do[?]"[19] A pastoral life was seemingly what he yearned for. He launched into politics without waiting to complete his legal studies, elected in 1809 in a rural riding where his family was held in high esteem. Not until 1815 was he elected in the city of Montreal. He seems to have been seized immediately by what he termed "the demon of politics." Despite his father's warnings about demagogues, he joined the party led by Bédard.

Like many others, after Bédard's downfall he accepted the leadership of James Stuart, an advocate, who was elected in one of the Montreal ridings in 1808 at the age of twenty-eight. Stuart, despite admirable qualities, a gift for oratory, and skill at the law, was not without shortcomings for the party. He was the son of a Presbyterian minister, became an Anglican, and in fact had more affinity with the colonial bureaucracy and the English business community than with French-Canadian politicians. He had studied under Attorney-General Jonathan Sewell, through whose influence he became solicitor-general in 1805. He was ambitious and looked for rapid advancement, but was destined for bitter disappointment. He not only did not succeed Sewell when the latter became chief justice, but in 1809 was dismissed from his post by Governor Craig. After that he drew closer to the leaders of the Canadian party.

That Stuart should be leader of the party which spoke for the nationalist movement is somewhat astonishing. Bédard, however, had drawn about him a number of English individuals whom he considered almost French-Canadian. The most important of these, John Neilson, was his political adviser, friend, and confidant. Andrew Stuart, advocate and brother of James, was another close friend. Alexis de Tocqueville expressed concern over the possible outcome of this coalition of interests:

> There exists already in Quebec a class of men who form the transition between French and English; they are the English allies of the Canadians, Englishmen discontented with the administration, [and] French placemen. This class is represented in the periodic press by the *Gazette de Québec*, in political meetings by Mr Neilson and probably several others unknown to us. It is this class that I fear most for the future fate of the Canadian population. They excite neither its jealousy nor its passions. On the contrary, they are more Canadian than English in interest because they oppose the government. Basically, however, they are English in customs, thinking, and language. If they should ever take the place of the upper classes and the enlightened classes among the Canadians, the nationality of the latter would be irretrievably lost.[20]

But for the moment, James Stuart's leadership of the Canadian party gave it credibility as a liberal party in the eyes of the English-speaking. He appeared to be a pragmatic continuator of Bédard's work in constitutional theory. He certainly had personal motives in launching the impeachment of Judges Sewell and Monk, but his strategy had much wider implications. The ultimate objective was to give power to the legislative assembly. In their resolutions calling for the dismissal of the two judges, the majority raised the legal responsibility of judges in the execution of their duties, but also attacked Sewell as political adviser to Governor Craig. They demanded the suspension of the two pending the decision of the British Privy Council, and voted 2,000 *louis* to enable Stuart to argue the case against them in London. The legislative council refused to allow the allocation. But Stuart had other than financial reasons for not making the voyage. Wrote Bédard, "Mr Stuart is not going to London. He is afraid, Bourdages had told me, that the new House of Assembly will undo what has been done by the last; this should merit consideration. But I do not believe the new House to be so opposed to the first."[21]

More to the point, though Stuart had strong support in the Quebec region, he felt his power as leader to be fragile. The party's assembly members from the Montreal region were not averse to attracting the English vote and accepting certain Englishmen in the upper echelons of the party, but wanted a leader who was both a French Canadian and a Montrealer. On February 18, 1815, Bédard wrote to Neilson:

I am vexed with the treatment suffered by Mr Stuart. Jealousy is a powerful tool to use against those who have had some success in the House of Assembly. It is the tool used by those who need to work outside the House to preserve their influence—a person of Quebec writes here that Mr Stuart would leave the House; it would be a pity for him to be lacking in patience. The House will not go well as long as there is no press that publishes all that happens there, and which removes it from the influence of the gallery and charlatans and places it under that of the entire Province.[22]

When Governor Drummond announced to the assembly at the opening session of 1816 that Sewell and Monk had been acquitted by the Privy Council, the violent reaction, led by Stuart, caused the governor to dissolve the House. Stuart's influence declined thereafter.

The Montreal assembly members' disaffection for Stuart stemmed less from local rivalry than from realization of a need for greater appeal to the French-Canadian population and unanimity in the upper echelons of the party. Bédard, who liked to consider Stuart a "Canadian" and sensed the leadership slipping away from Quebec, saw it differently. In 1818 he wrote to Neilson:

I saw Mr Stuart for about a minute coming up; he is not happy with the House: Viger and the Montrealers carry everything with them. I see that the same humbug continues. The House now feels only the influence of the entourage about it, which is stirred up outside by Viger's practices. There is no remedy to that I believe but a good press which brings everything to light, and forces the House to act on a stage with the whole Province as audience and which will bring all the entourage of the House and all the Montrealists themselves under the influence of all. . . .[23]

Papineau had succeeded Jean-Antoine Panet of Quebec as speaker of the House in 1815, and with his self-assurance and skill as an orator was increasingly popular with the Montrealers. He also had a sharp eye on his own advancement; he was quick to take advantage of Stuart's obstinacy in trying to revive the impeachment question, and of the benevolence shown him by Sir John Sherbrooke, the new governor. He had a keen instinct for compromise at this time, broke gently with Stuart, and in 1817 obtained salaries for the speakers of both houses of the legislature. The Quebeckers accused him of treachery and lack of principle. He was bitterly reproached in *Le Canadien*: "In this session you abandoned the question of chief judges and you betrayed Mr James Stuart to whom you were committed and whom you were honour

bound to support [,] to plunge the country into disrepute and igno-
miny because you had arrears to receive and were expecting a thousand
louis from the Executive."[24] Another detractor wrote, "I will ask again
if it is the intention to count the Speaker of the House of Assembly
Mr Louis Papineau among the members of the leaders of the opposition [,] the one who receives £1,000 from the Executive, and if it has
ever been heard in England that a man who received such a sum from
the Executive... has been one of the leaders of the opposition."[25]

In 1817, with financial security and prestige as speaker of the
House, Papineau travelled to the United States, and the following year
purchased La Petite Nation, his father's seigneury. The same year, at
the age of thirty-two, he married Julie Bruneau, daughter of Pierre
Bruneau, a Quebec merchant and member of the assembly. He had
entered the second stage of his political career. But his position as
party chieftain was a source of anxiety, for he felt he had a mission to
accomplish and must sacrifice himself for his country and his fellow
French Canadians. He identified with the French-Canadian nation. In
his thinking, the legislative assembly and the party he led must above
all defend the national heritage of the French Canadians. With this
prime objective went protection first of French-Canadian middle-class
interests, and next, of those of the clergy and the seigneurs, from
which should flow ideological unanimity among all the component
groups of the nation. The interests of peasants and workers were seen
through the eyes of the élite, in other words. Referring to a debate in
which he and James Stuart were opposed, Papineau wrote:

> He has insulted, flattered in trying to win a few partisans, told the
> habitants how odious is feudalism, that I was speaking as a seigneur
> for the interests of two hundred individuals opposed to the interests
> of half a million men, and at half past one in the morning we
> divided, thirty against him, his brother who is his timid slave, the
> idiot Borgia, and Taschereau who has not a thought in his head, a
> movement of which he is supposed to be the master.[26]

Papineau had not only to deal with his party's internal dissensions, but
also to parry the clergy's campaign against a brand of nationalism they
considered to be sullied with liberalism. He realized the curés'
influence with the electorate and knew that Bishop Plessis's appointment to the legislative council gave him more than symbolic power.
The bishop, a powerful persuader, was now in a position to sway the
members of the council, and indirectly the members of the assembly as
well. Anti-clericalism could be politically damaging, Papineau realized. He distrusted Plessis but met with him frequently. He wrote to

his wife, "If this man always could act as well as he can talk, he would be really very estimable; but vis-à-vis the great he will be lacking in firmness to the end of the chapter, and I doubt that even the pope has sufficient power to absolve him of such a grave fault."[27]

On the education question which was so dear to the bishop's heart, he and the other party leaders bent over backwards to be amenable, and supported the church in its fight against the Royal Institution. Not as totally as the church might have wished, however; Papineau expressed the opinion that the curé but not the church wardens should be consulted on the choice of a schoolmaster, and that each school should be governed by trustees, one of them the curé and the rest elected by the *habitants*.[28] In conciliating the clergy, Papineau was not merely following electoral or personal expediency. He was convinced, and wanted others to be convinced, that the clergy, as one of the constituent elements of the nation, must make common cause with the Canadian party. The quarrel over the creation of the diocese of Montreal presented an opportunity for a rapprochement. About Lartigue, Papineau's cousin and the centre of the controversy, Papineau wrote: "I admit, however, that as a neighbour I would like Mgr Lartigue only slightly, for fear he should take it into his head to make me preach. But to advance the establishment of the Canadian clergy, because their interests are allied to all other Canadian interests, I would still resign myself to this inconvenience as to all others which I would not tolerate as a private man, but which I tolerate as a public man."[29]

The uncertainty over party leadership and the need to conciliate the clergy kept the party's ideology from turning too radical. In Papineau's judgment the circumstances demanded great moderation, all the more since he was intent on dividing the English-speaking vote. He was not disposed, however, to give in to the clamour for roads and electoral ridings in the townships, land registry offices, and local administration of justice; such concessions would not only increase English electoral representation but defeat one of the party's objectives, which was to reconquer the townships, turn them into seigneuries and keep them for French-Canadian possession. As to the townships settlers, he agreed with Bédard, who wrote in 1818: "Is it possible that the House not perceive the absurdity, the baseness of using the province's money to have roads built for these yankees and then have them kept up with [more] money? People will buy land thirty leagues from habitations, where they will get it cheap, and then the province will have to use its funds to give it value, to fourfold perhaps tenfold its value."[30]

When in 1821 commercial stock-raisers asked the assembly to prohibit importation of animals from the United States and thus assure them the Lower-Canadian market, Papineau told them that free trade was best for agriculture: "The agricultural class ought to be satisfied with the prerogatives which the legislature has obtained and preserved for them and ought to be happy not to be subject to taxes with which all others are charged."[31] On the economic problems affecting English city-dwellers, he made a point of showing more flexibility. When supporting a petition protesting reductions in British protective tariffs on timber, he cast doubt on the utility of the timber trade but—his eye on the urban English electorate—justified his stand by accusing the mother country of attempting to tax Lower Canadians indirectly.

> It was not that he considered the lumber trade as the most profitable branch of our commerce. The five or six thousands hands employed in felling and squaring timber and preparing staves, might be more profitably employed in reducing them to potash and in tilling the soil. But our ports, particularly Quebec, would materially suffer by the loss of this branch of trade which must fail unless powerfully protected, although even the real loss which the merchants, proprietors of Quays, Saw Mills, lumber yards, etc., in which millions of money are vested, were not very great, would they have not much cause to complain of ministers who in imposing duties on foreign timber induced them to embark their capitals in their colonial trade....[32]

Papineau counted most of all on John Neilson to rally Quebec and English-speaking support. Neilson was born of a Presbyterian family in Scotland in 1776, came to Lower Canada in 1790 to work for his uncle, then owner of the bilingual *Quebec Gazette*, and in 1796 inherited the paper and became its editor-in-chief. He married a niece of Bishop Hubert, and had excellent relations with French Canadians, both lay and ecclesiastic. He was a large property owner and seigneur of Cap Rouge, and perceived "the connexion of good offices and gratitude between rich and poor as one of the chief cements of society, the main support of order."[33] He believed in moderation and patience. "Time and patience are powerful workers in politics. We are children; time with patience will make men of us."[34] Though apparently progressive in economic matters, he was a defender of the seigneurial régime and church privileges, was anti-American and a believer in liberally interpreted British institutions, perhaps the first Canadian to anticipate a lengthy evolution culminating in independence for a Canadian nation composed of two ethnic groups. He was considered by Papineau "the friend of my country," and despite their different temperaments became Papineau's political adviser and confidant, a collaboration which endured until 1830. In 1817 he stood for election but withdrew in protest against the "goon squad" tactics of his opponents, McCallum and Lee. In May, 1818, he stood again in the same mixed rural and urban Quebec riding and won narrowly, thanks to rural support.[35] His presence in the assembly helped strengthen Papineau's leadership.

Papineau and his followers attempted not to set the peasants and urban and rural proletariat against the clergy and the seigneurs, but to unite all against the English merchant bourgeoisie. By almost totally anaesthetizing the social aspirations of the masses, they were able to capitalize on popular discontent, turning it to the pursuit of conservative goals. They idealized traditional institutions as national institutions, building a mythology by playing on long-standing lower-class anxieties. Papineau stoutly resisted both regionalism and urban-rural rivalry:

> ... the unfortunate dissentions fermented by a few artisans of deceit, by persuading the country habitants that they were despised and their interests sacrificed by city representatives.... No, if it were not my sense of duty, which sets me the task of serving, amidst the most intense aversions and most discouraging prospects, the cause of my country and thereby the interest of our dear children, in common with that of our compatriots in general, I would not have the courage to live so long far from you and from them.[36]

Fear of the United States also inspired respect for the British political system and the advantages of the colonial régime. On the death of George III, Papineau gave a speech in praise of English parliamentary monarchy and the benefits realized by the French Canadians since the conquest. "Suffice it then at a glance, to compare our present happy situation with that of our fathers on the eve of the day when George the third became their legitimate monarch."[37] For all that, the Canadian party's major objective was still to achieve supremacy for the legislature over the executive. With Papineau the strategic priority was no longer ministerial responsibility, though it remained an objective in principle. The new priority was winning control of revenues.

Governor Sherbrooke arrived in 1816, when the British government was urging frugality. His impression was of having inherited a chaotic financial situation in Lower Canada. After 1760, the British government had arranged for colonial revenues deriving from crown lands. Annual deficits were made up through "army extraordinaries." In 1774 duties were imposed on certain imports, which helped reduce the deficits. The Constitutional Act of 1791 gave the legislative assembly the exclusive right to impose new taxes, but not control of the revenues previously provided for by imperial legislation. With the turn of the century, revenues deriving from provincial statutes increased far more rapidly than those at the disposal of the crown, and the governors, to escape assembly control, continued to dip into military funds to overcome annual deficits. In 1810 the assembly, by now determined to counterbalance the executive, proposed that it take charge of all the colony's expenditures, which the executive judged premature and dangerous. During the War of 1812, with the extreme difficulty of obtaining currency from Britain, the governor began to make up deficits from funds provided by provincial statutes. Thus, Governor Sherbrooke discovered that the crown owed £120,000 to the legislature, which the imperial government was unwilling and indeed unable to repay. On January 7, 1818, he requested the legislative assembly to "vote the sums which will be necessary for the ordinary and annual expenditures of the province," but without recognizing the assembly's right to control all forms of revenue. On February 26 he presented his budget to the assembly.

Pierre Bédard was probably the first to recognize the significance of the governor's request. He wrote to Neilson suggesting insistence on the assembly's right to vote the civil list, "each year and item by item,"[38] which, he said, would permit the people's representatives to control the civil servants, do away with the executive's unwarranted patronage, and establish the supremacy of the House of Assembly. In appearance it would have been a struggle over principles, liberalism versus conservatism, not an ethnic confrontation. Dalhousie wrote some years later, "It has always been my anxious study to find out the real cause of the feverish and fretful temper which has disturbed the session of the legislature year after year—the real cause in my idea is a wild desire to grasp at power, but ignorant at the same time of the extent to which they would grasp." In 1818, however, Papineau, despite pressure to the contrary, displayed a remarkable sense of conciliation, which Governor Sherbrooke's sympathetic attitude largely justified, and proposed the granting of supplies and generous increases in salary for the governor and his civil secretary. "Our governors ought to be entire strangers to every party or local interest and jealousy, and to enable them to be so, it was requisite to make a liberal provision for the personage occupying the important post of governor."[39] But he also demanded the abolition of certain unnecessary posts and the withdrawal of salaries of certain absentee civil servants unless they returned to their posts. The assembly in effect voted a sum equal to the budgetary deficit, thus obtaining indirect control of the entire public purse. It was now in a position to exert pressure on the executive and the civil servants, and to assert its supremacy over the legislative council in financial matters.

Sherbrooke proposed the appointment of Papineau, as leader of the Canadian party, to the executive council, hoping to restore the people's confidence in that body; in effect this would have opened the door to an orderly progression toward ministerial responsibility. But the Canadian party's opponents were appalled at the idea, particularly the merchants who foresaw even greater power falling to a majority which was hostile to economic development and social change.

Sherbrooke's successor, the Duke of Richmond, was a man of very different stamp. He presented a budget which ignored the ground won by the assembly, a much larger budget which included a round sum of £8,000 for pensions. The assembly claimed its right to eliminate sine-cures and unjustified pensions, declared its opposition to the budgetary increase, and voted to adopt the civil list annually and item by item. Seven out of eight English-speaking members voted against the major-ity, Neilson alone voting with it, and four French Canadians voted with the minority. The supply bill was rejected by the legislative coun-cil:

> The mode adopted by this bill, in effect according a supply to His Majesty for defraying the expenses of the civil list is unconstitu-tional and unprecedented, and a direct usurpation by the Assembly of the most important rights and prerogatives of the Crown. Should the bill become law, it would give to the commons of this province, not only the constitutional privilege of providing supplies, but also the power to prescribe to the Crown the number and description of its servants and to regulate and recompense their services indi-vidually.[40]

The governor reprimanded the assembly members and sent them home. A general election was held in 1820, followed by a second due to the death of George III.

The Canadian party wasted no time making political capital of the supply dispute, assisted by the difficult economic situation of the period. Depending on the kind of electorate being addressed, the cam-paign issues were either principles or taxation, for or against. Thirty-nine candidates were elected to the assembly by protesting exaggerated increases in public expenditure and government wastefulness, three with moderate platforms, and only six English and two French Canadi-ans by advocating budgetary increases.[41]

So effective was the appeal to the popular dislike of taxes that even certain English party candidates used it. Louis Moquin, organizer for

Neilson and his running mate Gauvreau, wrote to Neilson of his fears of a new ethnic polarization: "It would be possible and even probable that the English electors, if they see the Canadians voting for two Canadians, will league together against Mr Gauvreau. Another reason to forget nothing in order to have the support of the [rural] parishes for tomorrow at the latest.... I do not believe them [the English electors] to be in good humour and I always fear them because when they set to work, they have courage and unity."[42] In stressing the control of revenues, the Canadian party tacticians hoped to win Irish and liberal English votes in the cities, but not to divide the French vote.

Lord Dalhousie, who became governor on June 10, 1820, exacerbated the crisis unleashed by Richmond. Without recognizing the control obtained by the assembly over crown revenues, he asked the House to vote supplies in a total sum and for the life of the king, and demanded the legislative council's participation in their allocation, thus defending crown prerogatives, the independence of the administration, the rights of the legislative council, and the position of the governor, including his right to recommend all allocations of public funds. The Canadian party held to its stand on the civil list. Each side used the pressure tactics at its disposal. The assembly announced its intention not to renew certain fiscal statutes, and informed the receiver-general and the governor's advisers that it would hold them responsible for unauthorized expenditures. The battle raged uninterrupted until 1828. If the crisis had only limited effect it was because the government still had control over crown revenues, and by dipping into the military funds was partially able to cover deficits and avoid total paralysis of the political system. The assembly began to demand total control over all categories of revenue. In this stand, the *patriote* movement gave the appearance of being a truly liberal movement basing its actions on the best parliamentary traditions and liberal doctrines.

Despite serious internal friction in its upper echelons, the Canadian party had maintained the initiative since 1815, keeping its adversaries on the defensive, with the quarrel over impeachment and then supplies as the principal political issues and polarizing factors. The townships inhabitants' demands had been rejected and negotiations between the agents of Upper and Lower Canada over the division of customs revenues had reached a total impasse. With the results of the 1820 elections showing even broader popular support than ever, total victory for the Canadian party seemed close at hand. On February 15, 1821, J. Viger wrote to H. Heney:

Well, brother, there has been clamour against foreign influence in the House (I do not speak of elsewhere). Rightly. There has been much clamour against ministerial influence, rightly again. But when all has been said and done, I believe it the greatest present ill that we have defeated these influences or nearly. These English, these ministers held the Canadians tied, on their guard, constantly vigilant; they are no longer so, or at least their voices are silenced. What will follow? Division and the most bitter division. Ill-feeling among brothers, relatives, old friends, in reverse proportion to their ill-feeling of the past.... It is unrelenting. Poor compatriots! Yet we must not declaim too much against them; especially not too loudly.[43]

Many of the party's members in the Quebec region felt at the time that Papineau was not showing the aggressiveness called for by the circumstances. "We are very glad to hear that ... the speaker of the House of Assembly has resumed his practice at the Bar. His practice as advocate will do more to make him independent in the House of Assembly than the thousand *louis* he was receiving at the king's pleasure. The money which the House of Assembly had voted was well motivated. It was imagined that, with the money, importance and independence were conferred. But this was a serious mistake."[44]

Tactical errors by the Canadian party's adversaries won much sympathy for the party in the eyes of the electorate. In their alarm at the prospect of finding themselves at the mercy of the French-Canadian middle classes, the bureaucrats and English merchants decided to carry their cause to England. The union plan of 1822, prepared in the greatest secrecy and submitted to the British House of Commons, not only expressed their dismay and concern but revealed ethnic and religious prejudice in certain elements of the colonial civil service. The British authorities somewhat cautiously expressed support, but when the Whig James Mackintosh indicated to the House of Commons the irregularity of the unionists' procedure the plan was withdrawn.

Rumours of the union plan and its sponsorship by the British authorities first reached Lower Canada in June, 1822. The day following Henry Caldwell's return from England, Papineau wrote to his brother, "The present moment is a moment of cruel anxiety for all the friends of this country which is threatened with seeing instantaneously destroyed everything [done] to prevent the ruin of its establishments and the overthrow of its laws, by the union of the two provinces leaving Upper Canada which has only 120,000 inhabitants with forty representatives and fifty only for Lower Canada which has 500,000."[45] The rumours became more persistent in the course of the summer and only in September did the existence and details of a plot become known. The public protest was immediate. The clergy was aghast at the plan to require the governor's consent for the appointment and pay of curés; in political union they foresaw greater Protestant influence and the abolition of the seigneurial régime, tithing, and French civil law, on which Catholic Church economic and legal privileges reposed. When the plan was discussed by the legislative council in January, 1823, Bishop Plessis and the seigneurial aristocracy, including the English, voted *en bloc* against the English-speaking merchants and civil servants. Elated, L.-A. de Salaberry wrote to Viger, "Victory, victory, victory.... The Canadians were obliged to deploy all their fearlessness. It was almost like Châteauguay.... Never has the Upper House seen such an uproar."[46] The next day J. Bélanger wrote to Neilson: "Caldwell in particular distinguished himself with his honesty and candour: he was lavish with praise for the Canadian people for their loyalty, spirit of obedience to the government, their charity, their good moral and religious conduct; he declared that he believed no people on the surface of the Globe to be more virtuous and more charitable. His speech was much savoured and gave much satisfaction."[47]

Citing among other reasons the unionists' attacks on the seigneurial régime, Papineau proposed P.-D. Debartzch, seigneur and legislative councillor, as the anti-unionists' delegate to London. "The nature of his properties, all landed and seigneurial, which binds him in affection and interest to so great a proportion of his compatriots, [will] tend to give weight to his opinions in Europe which the same opinions would not have from the mouth of one who did not have such numerous, such close relationships with the Canadian farmers."[48]

For the French-Canadian middle classes, the union question was part and parcel of their struggle for power. Papineau wrote to Neilson:

The country does not wish to submit to the injustices planned against us all by the handful of intriguers who would sacrifice the happiness of Canadians to their boundless ambition. These men whom chance has made so great in this country, who would have remained so unknown elsewhere, why do they not enjoy in peace the innumerable preferences which are theirs without undertaking to strip the habitants of the province of their rights[?] Actuated by the most unjust prejudices against the establishments which are most dear to us, harbouring as great disdain as that which they display against all that is particular to the customs and usages of Canada, can it be overlooked that if ever they should seize all the power to which they aspire, they will abuse it to the point of endangering the tranquillity of the country?[49]

Neilson agreed entirely, and told Papineau: "The real purpose of the authors of the plan is to make themselves masters of the country for their own profit, and to rid themselves of the veto power ... which the existing constitution has given to the majority of the inhabitants, and which has often defeated their hostile projects. This veto power is all that the constitution has given the Canadians after thirty years in operation."[50]

In his union plan analysis to be submitted to the British authorities, which was co-signed by Neilson, Papineau attempted to show the differences between the communities of Upper and Lower Canada. He was careful not to use the word "nation" when speaking of the French Canadians, but represented Lower Canada as the natural habitat of the French Canadians who composed, he claimed, 95 per cent of the population; geographically, economically, and culturally it was a distinct unit, with institutions and habits of thought peculiar to it and for which it alone was responsible. On the problem of Lower Canada's control of access to the sea, he wrote, "It is neither necessary nor feasible that the inhabitants of different countries, situated near great rivers forming their natural and common exit toward the sea, be united under the same government." In short, political union "between two provinces, whose inhabitants have nothing in common, unless it is the title of British subjects," would be an absurdity as well as an injustice. He applied the same reasoning to the townships of Lower Canada which, in other circumstances, he made no secret of wanting to annex to the "national" territory:

> These townships are still in part separated by waste lands from the ancient establishments of Lower Canada along the St Lawrence. They have few relationships and few interests in common with the mass of His Majesty's subjects in Lower Canada. They manufacture in these townships, or receive from the United States as in Upper Canada, a portion of the articles [otherwise] paying an entry duty at the port of Quebec. They have more affinity with the population of Upper Canada than with that of Lower Canada.[51]

The hostility of most Upper Canadians to the Union Bill of 1822 was viewed by Papineau as confirmation of this perception of space. But the bill would make English the official language, give the same number of representatives to Upper Canada and the townships combined as to the seigneuries, regardless of population, and place the appointment of curés under government control.

The French-Canadian middle classes, Canadian party leaders in the forefront, led the opposition to the bill. Anti-unionist committees were formed in each of the three districts, public meetings were held, and petitions were circulated on which Papineau was sure of obtaining 50,000 names. "Messieurs, the unionists say that this will serve their purpose because Parliament will make sure that it will make no allowance for the representations of a population as ignorant as that of this country, who cannot write, and make crosses...."[52] His anxiety was extreme, for he was perturbed by the moderates' coolness over sending agents to London, and feared not only plots among the English-speaking to sow dissention among the Canadians, but most of all renewed personal and regional rivalries threatening his own leadership, particularly in Quebec. Neilson wrote to him in December, 1822:

> The wretched district jealousies have erupted. Your committee should not, in my opinion, have asked us to concur in your nomination as delegate to London, considering that it has been opposed due to the necessity of your presence in the House as speaker; asking us besides to concur with you in the nomination of two other agents has caused it to be said that you wish to decide everything alone.... Nothing in the world must unsettle you now. Above all avoid showing the slightest ill-humour with us; defend us and hide what you find to blame in us for the good of the country.[53]

After refusals by Debartzch and several others to go to London, and Bédard's inability to obtain leave from Trois-Rivières, Papineau persuaded Neilson to accompany him: "We must have a good Englishman to belie the atrocious calumnies trumped up by the blindest hate against us."[54] They left Canada in January, 1823.

While in England they conferred with James Mackintosh, the Canadians' champion in the House of Commons, and met with R.J. Wilmot and Lord Bathurst. Papineau was quite astonished at the easy manner with which the colonials were received at the Colonial Office. Gradually the two became convinced that the plan had been set aside. Wrote Papineau to his wife, "If messrs Stuart and Ellice were not encouraging each other to persist in their representations, the whole would be consigned to oblivion and that I hope will be the result although these Gentlemen give assurances that they are fully confident of a contrary result."[55] Edward Ellice, seigneur of Beauharnois, was the unionists' principal spokesman in England and James Stuart was one of their leaders at home. The latter's rupture with his former associates was now obviously complete.

Neilson returned home but Papineau remained in England. With much time on his hands he kept company with both French- and

English-speaking Canadians in London: "The English are always surprised at the cordiality and eagerness with which we hasten to meet and the pleasure we take in being together...."[56] He saw something of the English countryside and planned a journey to France. "If their condition is in effect much inferior to that of England's inhabitants, as I am much inclined to believe, I shall be more and more convinced that we are fortunate in America not to know how defective is European legislation; how oppressive the governments and powerless the Peoples...."[57] He was struck, indeed, by English social inequalities and the poverty of the lower classes. Later he was to evolve a new perception of the role of European institutions in North America.

During Papineau's absence, competition for the leadership of his party resumed, and with new contenders: Augustin Cuvillier, F.-A. Quesnel, Andrew Stuart, George Vanfelson, Vallières de Saint-Réal. The speakership left vacant by Papineau was sought by D.-B. Viger, Saint-Réal, and Louis Bourdages. The latter, losing out, was furious to see a relative of Papineau's still in the running. "He railed against him personally and all his family," wrote H. Heney.[58] The speakership in fact went to Saint-Réal, first elected to the House in 1814 at the age of twenty-seven; but the new speaker still had his eye on the party leadership. Andrew Stuart, now ostensibly the leader, worked closely with Viger.

Despite vehement speeches, the party's leading lights pursued a moderate line to avoid provoking dissolution of the House by the governor over the supply question, or to engage in all-out warfare over the new Canada Trade Act which raised serious constitutional problems. Andrew Stuart instigated a series of inquiries to show the superiority of the seigneurial régime and the ineptitude of government land administration. With a mixture of vote-seeking, liberalism, and a desire to weaken the "Anglican establishment," described by Papineau as "the ally of persecution against the Canadians," a campaign was launched favouring Methodists, Jews, and the Church of Scotland. Large sums of money were allocated for the St Lawrence and Richelieu canals. Vallières de Saint-Réal drafted a bill for the establishment of land registry offices (based on Napoleonic Code principles), which was never passed. D.-B. Viger pointed to this as further proof of its author's "triviality of mind."[59]

Papineau's popularity gained with his role in Canada and England over the union crisis; he expected perhaps to return to undisputed leadership, but it was not to be. Saint-Réal took advantage of Andrew Stuart's voyage to England to advance himself to the rank of leading pretender. Papineau was now financially embarrassed, having lost his speaker's salary and not having been fully reimbursed for the expenses of his voyage. So was Neilson, and both considered retiring from politics. But Papineau was persuaded to run in the hotly contested general election of 1824, when the principal issues were union and supply. Only nine English-speaking candidates were elected, four for the Canadian party. Bribery was widespread on both sides. In the rural Richelieu riding and Quebec's Lower Town this is well documented.[60] Signs of liberalism versus conservatism began to appear, ethnic alignment appearing to lessen. In Quebec's Upper Town, the Canadian party obtained 71 per cent of the vote but only 53 per cent of French-speaking electors voted for a French-speaking candidate (see Table 59). The ethnic basis of party support overall was still in evidence, however. The Canadian party obtained 73 per cent of its votes from French Canadians (86 per cent of the working-class vote and 89 per cent of the merchant and professional vote), and 63 per cent of the English party's vote came from English-speaking electors. The Canadian party, however, won 66 per cent of the English merchant and professional vote. Its attention to the urban English-speaking electorate was bearing fruit.

The inevitable confrontation between Papineau and Saint-Réal—the Montreal-Quebec confrontation in other words—occurred following this election. At stake were both the speakership of the House and the party leadership. The Montrealer Bourdages wrote in *La Canadienne* (not to be confused with *Le Canadien*) that "the speaker must be the people's friend and not the tyrant, . . ." and that the party chieftain must be a man of moderation.[61] But most of the members were still for Papineau and he was elected speaker by 32 to 12.[62] That day Papineau wrote to his wife, "Bourdages is furious. . . . He is grumbling at the Quebeckers; it is not enough, he says, that the damned clique is doing much harm to Montreal, it will dupe the Quebeckers too and will want to run everything. Bah! All my old friends here greet me with much confidence and friendship."[63]

Despite urgings by Bédard, the *patriote* movement still had no newspaper capable of diffusing its messages and policies. In 1824 Bédard wrote once again to Neilson, "You are lacking a paper to support the House. When there are good reasons for doing something there are always ways to make them felt and bring light to opinions. The speeches given in the House by the members are not enough. They are good to serve as base, but things must be chewed over for the rest of the year. . . . I remember well the Montreal members' fears of [public] opinion. . . ."[64] The newspapers not controlled by the "Scotch" were too unstable or conservative. *Le Canadien*, after 1831, gave the Quebec party members' views, but was considered by the Montrealers to be hostile to theirs. *La Minerve*, founded in 1826 with Ludger

Duvernay as its first editor, was to help fill the void and became the party's principal organ. Later, other papers began expressing the various tendencies of the movement: *The Vindicator*, an Irish paper which was soon being financed by the *patriote* leaders; *L'Echo du Pays*, a rural Catholic paper; and *Le Libéral*, which was somewhat radical. In the townships, where the party was trying to make headway after 1830, a number of papers espoused its democratic tendencies.[65]

With fears of union of the Canadas and of English machinations against "national" institutions, and then talk of annexation of Montreal to Upper Canada, the French-Canadian masses appeared in great majority to be solidly behind the party. Many of the clergy and aristocrats seemed reassured by the direction being taken by the *patriote* movement. In the cities, considerable numbers of English-speaking liberals and Irish Catholics were supporting the government's opponents. Sir Francis Burton, administrator in Dalhousie's absence, had accepted a supply bill which complied with the assembly's wishes and was trying to persuade the legislative council to agree to it when Dalhousie returned. In Papineau's words, "It seems to be fated that each time a governor revives order some accident revives trouble."[66] Dalhousie was furious and obtained repudiation of Burton's conduct by London. He reaffirmed the government's stand on supplies and began to take reprisals against his political foes. Having decided to break all opposition he prorogued the legislature. This meant new elections in 1827, in which the *patriotes* made the most of the governor's excesses; not only revenues but more or less all Lower Canada's problems were in issue. The *patriotes* won overwhelmingly; fifteen of their candidates were elected by acclamation and their opponents in the House were reduced from nine to four. They even won in Dorchester, until then an English party stronghold, and in the "rotten borough" of Sorel, where they ran the veteran campaigner Wolfred Nelson against James Stuart, a stroke of genius in their opinion. In Quebec riding they garnered 85 per cent of the vote, 91 per cent of the French-Canadian vote. In the Upper Town their candidates Amable Berthelot and George Vanfelson were defeated, however, by Andrew Stuart and Vallières de Saint-Réal, who had switched parties. Berthelot accused Stuart of corruption and also contested his right to refuse the vote to women as such.[67] Saint-Réal won with French-speaking votes and Stuart with English votes; Vanfelson was considered an English-speaking rather than a *patriote* candidate (see Table 59).

In the *patriote* camp there was wild rejoicing at the sweep. Papineau declared to his own electors, "There is not a riding, not a city, not a town which has not condemned this pernicious pretention, since even in the two or three [ridings] where a partial or dominant influence caused the choice of a representative favourable by conviction or necessity to the views of the present administration, the popular ascendancy and strength of principles caused him to have an associate of contrary opinion."[68] During his campaign in Montreal West, Papineau had paid special attention to the Irish and other English-speaking voters. He had spoken of the party's efforts for Protestant "dissidents," but he had been careful to avoid appearing merely opportunistic. "I do not recall these circumstances for attracting their favour—far from me such artifice . . .[;] the freedom I claim for myself, for all my compatriots, for all who think as they, I allow for all who think otherwise."[69] He spoke of creating ridings in the townships, of equal laws for all citizens, of according equal but not greater value to the men of the frontiers and townships, and of increasing the representative body, despite the lesser value of land in the newer areas in comparison with that already improved and better situated on the banks of the St Lawrence. After the election he thanked his electors of all origins and outlined the significance of his party's victory:

> In the universal enthusiasm of my compatriots which preceded, accompanied throughout [my] progress, and followed the elections in general as in yours, the country's friend observes with unmixed satisfaction, what principle of strength [my compatriots] will find in this spirit of indissoluble unity whose bonds each day they draw closer and cultivate more and more. He will give them, as soon as a judicious administration is presiding over the province, that weight and that influence in the direction of its affairs which their number, comprising nine tenths of the population, the value of their landed properties, the undying interest they have in the prosperity of the native soil, the superior knowledge of the leading classes among them, should have assured them long before this day. . . .[70]

His party's spectacular success inspired Papineau to take the debate to England, one of the chief objectives being to obtain the recall of Governor Dalhousie whom he held personally responsible for most of the ills afflicting Lower Canada. On August 20, 1827, long before the governor committed the blunder of refusing to accept him any longer as speaker, he wrote to his brother:

> I have not yet completely emerged from the torment of the elections. . . . The general result of the elections which has put J. Stuart, Simpson, Dumont, Davidson, and Desprès out of the House is good beyond what could have been expected. But our task is far from accomplished. We absolutely must obtain the removal of the

governor; we must send someone to England; we must not be content with an opiate to soothe our pains as long as the cause of the ill still subsists; reform in the Augean stables, which is to say in our councils, is essential. . . .[71]

As in 1822, the party set about creating riding and district committees, circulating petitions to be signed by the electors at large, preparing an address to the king, and choosing delegates who would go and argue "the cause of the country" in England. On December 15, Papineau sent Neilson the list of resolutions drawn up "in private assembly" and asked him to set up a committee to assure liaison with Montreal. Despite renewed Quebec-Montreal rivalry, the delegates were chosen; Neilson, D.-B. Viger and Cuvillier agreed to take the petition bearing 80,000 signatures to England. J.-M. Mondelet wrote to Viger, "All our habitants now take part in public affairs, know about, and discuss them. This unfortunate crisis in which we find ourselves will at least have the effect of opening their eyes."[72]

The new government in England was receptive to any complaint proffered against the past administration. The circumstances were therefore most favourable for the *patriotes*. Their delegates, thanks largely to Neilson, were able to brush aside the accusation that they were representing a nationalist movement bent on having power for itself alone. Their arguments for the seigneurial régime and the Coutume de Paris and against registry offices appeared reasonable. They were especially effective in incriminating the colonial administrators, the judges, and the legislative council as responsible for the progressive paralysis of the political system. The House of Commons committee appointed in 1828 to consider the state of government in Canada agreed that the receipt and expenditures of the entire public revenue should be placed under the control of the assembly, but recommended that the salaries of the governor, the executive councillors, and the judges be independent of annual votes of the assembly.[73] The Commons committee was in fact in agreement with almost all of the *patriotes'* contentions. Dalhousie was recalled and sent to India. Neilson's image in particular was greatly enhanced.

Not only the *patriotes* but the reformists in Upper Canada were elated. M.S. Bidwell wrote to Neilson:

There are many people in the province . . . who have looked with much sympathy upon your noble struggle for constitutional rights and who rejoice at your success. . . . We have indeed good reason to regard with interest the proceedings in your province, for you have really defended our rights while defending your own. I know this to be the sentiment of those of this province who care for our rights. They wish to cultivate a cordial and confidential friendship with the patriotic members of your House of Assembly and to act in concert with them, upon those great questions which involve principles equally important and equally applicable to both provinces. . . .[74]

William Lyon Mackenzie also wrote to Neilson, stating that he was in favour of a confederation of the British North American colonies, but above all desired "to see us more our masters in regard to our local concerns."[75] He proposed the immediate creation of joint committees of Upper-Canadian reformists and the *patriotes*. Papineau was evasive, remarking to Neilson that "the method of acting separately in the two assemblies, in the same spirit, in the same purposes, is perhaps the most effective; [it will] excite the least jealousy and distrust from England."[76] He was determined to preserve his movement's autonomy and avoid any situation which might justify the union of the Canadas, yet he considered the sympathy of the Upper-Canadian reformers a valuable asset for his party, which was so constantly accused of extreme nationalism by its opponents. Relationships with British radicals were cultivated in the same spirit. H.S. Chapman and John Arthur Roebuck served the cause of French-Canadian nationalism, but also used the Lower-Canadian situation for their own ends.

CHAPTER 9

The Paralysis of the Political System, 1828-1837
(Part Two)

The *Patriotes*: a Radical Turn

Around 1828 Papineau sensed a need for change in ideology and strategy for the *patriote* movement. Popular discontent had reached such a pitch that it looked to be getting out of hand. Growing resentment in the population against the seigneurs and the collectors of tithes, the Canadian party leaders felt, could well turn the *patriote* movement in a direction opposed to their own interests; they could no longer count on diverting the attention of the masses. Continuing economic distress, demographic pressures, the arrival of more and more immigrants, and increasingly shrill propaganda from the politicians all served to intensify nationalistic fervour in the popular milieu. The principal villains both in the cities and in the country districts were seen to be the immigrants, everywhere more and more in evidence. The Canadian party was faced with a dilemma: it could alienate the English-speaking element if it responded too readily to the fears of the native-born. The party was still determined to appeal to the Irish and liberal English vote, which in fact, from 1827 on, it was gradually losing.

The English voted massively (80 per cent) for Vanfelson in the Quebec Upper Town by-election of 1829. Vallières de Saint-Réal, the incumbent, had become a judge; J.-F. Duval was running as his protégé and drew 74 per cent of the French-speaking vote (see Table 60). Vanfelson was the Canadian party candidate but was regarded by the electorate as an English candidate, and his party therefore was obliged to soft-pedal the immigration question. Saint-Réal had been reflecting the confusion of many *patriotes* when, before becoming a judge, he wrote to Neilson, "The trouble is that the country is poor and so am I. If one of us were rich, all would be well."[1]

A new, younger generation, more nationalist and liberal—radical even—was exerting pressure in the upper levels of the Canadian party. Louis-Hippolyte Lafontaine, Augustin-Norbert Morin, Charles-Ovide Perreault, and Edouard Rodier were respectively 23, 27, 25, and 32 when first elected to the assembly; and Dr Cyrille Côté, the most radical, was 25. The brothers Wolfred and Dr Robert Nelson and the Irish-born Edmund Bailey O'Callaghan were in their thirties. Together, this group succeeded in bringing a more vigorous and radical focus to the activities of the movement and of the party (see Table 7).

The party leaders, uneasy to see a potential overweighting to the left and seeking a controlled expression of unanimity among the masses, attempted to strengthen their hold on the rural areas. In this, the years 1828-30 were crucial. Because of the English-speaking minorities in the seigneuries, reworking the electoral map was a difficult and delicate task, but an essential one long sought by the townships inhabitants. In any event, in 1829 the number of ridings was increased from 27 to 46, 8 new ones in the townships; the number of representatives increased from 50 to 87, with 13 for the townships (most ridings had two representatives but some only one). Wrote Papineau, "The government will reap the fruits of its negligence and poor treatment it has so long given the townships, which will send it only yankees. They were good subjects a year ago . . . but they have been forced to become bad subjects."[2] Still, in this period he was confident that the Canadian party could establish firm roots in the townships. To his wife he wrote, "At last they have adopted our bill for the increase of representation. . . . That is an incalculable benefit. Destroyed forever the idea of union between the two provinces; [we will] fortify the representative system, announce determination to remodel the Council. . . ."[3] Considerable sums of money were voted for road construction between the townships and the urban markets, but since the law on road upkeep remained unchanged, the road construction money looked like rather blatant vote-seeking. Wrote Bédard to Neilson, "I see as you say that each is out for his own end and that *good patriotes* are not beyond that temptation. You cannot know how proud and pleased I am to see that you were not one of these good compatriots when the construction of the Valcartier roads were in question, and that you did not wish those funds that were voted."[4]

The failure of the party leaders to espouse universal suffrage giving the vote to the rural and urban unlanded at the time of the electoral revision demonstrates that, though they sought sympathy from that quarter, their prior concern was landowners. The dominant group before 1830 was also inclined to avoid creating conditions which might bring confrontation between the landed and unlanded, and so considered the existing suffrage provisions entirely satisfactory. The Assembly Schools Act of 1829, which gave the House a new source of patronage, the bill of 1831 on parish council administration, and the post-1830 programme of administrative and judicial decentralization were all similarly motivated. Only after the beginning of the *patriote* movement's revolutionary phase did the radical wing of the party start to press for universal suffrage. In 1829 the reformists' proposals in favour of generalization of the elective principle envisaged the right of vote only for landowners, and the practical goal was to win maximum power for the lay élite sympathetic to the party. In fact, party leaders paid increasing attention to the elective principle with a view to winning power for the French-Canadian middle classes; it was to be the major tool in the party's strategy and ideological restructuring in the years after 1828.

The supplies question remained contentious, but cooled as the principal focus of political attention. Following the British Commons committee report, Parliament had adopted measures allowing the legislative assembly conditional control of crown revenues, the assembly meanwhile having voted supplies according to the principles it had adopted itself. Then, in 1831, the British government proposed giving the assembly entire control of crown revenues in return for a civil list equivalent to half the revenue granted. The following year it modified this, offering to limit the civil list to the sum of the salaries of the five principal personages of the colonial government.[5] The assembly continued to ignore the British offer, though in 1828 it had promised to guarantee the independence of the governor, the lieutenant-governor, judges, and executive councillors, if it were given total control of revenues. The supplies question in any event remained a powerful weapon in the assembly's hands, though control of the public purse was only one of the expedients at the disposal of the Canadian party leaders in their quest for power.

In 1829 Papineau wrote to Neilson that the legislative council was "a body between which and the assemblies, it is impossible that there be any rapprochement. Therein is the origin of all the abuses which impose strain on the provinces. The administrations insult the assemblies when they do not dominate them, instead of which in principle, it is for the assemblies to influence the executive, to direct it."[6] Thus, when the assembly was on the point of total victory as regards supply, its attention was shifted to the legislative council as the source of all ills.

The legislative council, it will be remembered, was originally conceived as an aristocratic counterbalance to the popular branch of the system; domination of the assembly by the nationalistic French-Canadian middle classes had forced a new function on the legislative council, namely counterbalancing the nationalistic as well as the democratic elements. The Canadian party had come to regard the council as the servile tool of the bureaucracy and the English-speaking merchants who controlled the executive; the council members and those whose interests they espoused were depicted as individuals with no real roots in the society. Hence the determination to change the composition of the council. The party leaders demanded that it include more French Canadians and that judges be excluded from it. In 1823, J. Bélanger wrote to Neilson that there could be no hope of harmony if, while Neilson were in England, he could not obtain a change in the composition of the council with the addition of many important French-Canadian seigneurs, who, while those he named might not be men of great talent, were honest and more truly attached to the land than others.[7] The *patriote* leaders realized that these individuals had more in common with the government than with the French-Canadian middle classes, but nevertheless considered them to be reliable defenders of the seigneurial régime and the Coutume de Paris and opponents of the union of the Canadas.

In 1829, the *patriote* leaders changed their strategy, and Papineau began to talk privately of the necessity of making the legislative council elective. He wrote to Neilson:

> The petitions of the people would not have the Constitutional Act changed; it would be most daring so soon after to ask for this change, but the petitions so strongly indicate that the source of all abuse is in the councils that it would be acting in the spirit though against the letter of the petitions to ask for this improvement. In Lower Canada we cannot go further at the moment without making ourselves ridiculous, in view of such unanimous protestations from the people not wanting alteration of the Constitutional Act....[8]

The previous year, in fact, the *patriotes* had declared, as they had been doing ever since 1810, "We consider our Constitutional Act as the most solemn and inviolable pact which the Imperial Parliament could give us to assure the preservation of our rights."[9]

In the Canadian party's upper echelons, restructuring ideology was first a matter of readjusting principles and rationalizing to fit a changing situation. In the context of an all-out struggle for power, the old reform concept seemed outdated. In January, 1829, Papineau wrote his wife, "The two houses bear each other mortal grudges. The council assuredly detests the [elective] system because it is necessarily to the advantage of the Canadians.... Besides, I do not believe it possible to be happy and well treated under the colonial régime. Even with the greatest will to be just, how can a governor surrounded by so many scoundrels always be so?"[10] Governor Kempt was the last in whom Papineau was disposed to recognize a modicum of good faith. The role of the colonial system and British institutions as protectors of French-Canadian and middle-class interests was being re-examined.

In Papineau's political career, these were the years of his greatest power. Sceptics could only remain silent, so successfully had he, for twenty years, projected among his admirers his desired image of unselfish devotion, incorruptibility, and denial of all he loved most in order to serve his country and its people. To accusations of personal ambition he retorted, "For many years I have occupied in this house, without having asked it and without intrigue, a post to which the good will and confidence of the members of the House have raised me, not just simple merit.... I am, it is true, in apparent situation, more visible, but I have only shared and followed public opinion, without desire to rule anyone...."[11] With his function as the translator and interpreter of the national and popular will overriding the more sordid aspects of his role as party leader, he became the living symbol of the national desires of French Canadians: "... if my name is more often cited, exposed to the greatest animosity, defended by the truest friends, it is not because my sentiments are mine, but because they are those of all, at least of those who have common interests with the people."[12]

Yet he did not frequent the humble. In 1834, André Lacroix, a rural party organizer, wrote to Duvernay, "If Mr Papineau, as I have several times said, were to address a few little lessons to the country folk occasionally on the affairs of the province, as O'Connell has done in Ireland, great benefit would result and before long our country districts would be prepared for anything."[13] But Papineau was in his element in the assembly and had made himself the reputation he believed he deserved, that of a great philosopher. Morin observed to Duvernay that a journalist sent to report the assembly's debates would be justified in giving Papineau the limelight, so superior were his speeches despite the other great talents present in the House.[14] Papineau was both the principal artisan of ideological evolution and the guardian of orthodoxy. He sanctioned the thinking of others, corrected the ideological deviations of his friends, and pointed the finger at the unfaithful. His personal power verged on a kind of intellectual and moral tyranny which was accepted because of the intensity of the social and political climate and the needs it satisfied among the party faithful. The circumstances favoured the emergence of a "national hero" myth surrounding this exceptional man, simultaneously pure, eloquent, and vigorous, God-inspired, perfectly in tune with the popular aspirations he so unerringly understood; a myth which was a collective creation with Papineau himself among the most fervent creators. Firmly established as the prophet, by turns announcing and denouncing, he gave long, inspiring, and exhausting speeches; but once they were over he found time and again that much goes on behind the scenes in politics.

In 1828 Papineau stepped up the virulence of his attacks on the legislative council, which later he described as "a putrid cadaver,"[15] and began to demand election of its members. The strategy implied extension of the elective principle to all levels of power; the very foundation of British institutions was therefore being called into question, demanding a redefinition of the position of French Canadians in the imperial context. Papineau was here drawing on the thinking of Rousseau, Jefferson, the Jacksonian democrats, and radical English writers in his desire to follow justifiable principles, and also in the hope of giving the *patriote* movement a liberal, democratic, and republican image abroad. "They pretend to believe that our demands are the fruit of our differences in origin and our Catholicism, when always and everywhere in liberal ranks there is a majority of men of every belief and every origin. But what can be said in support of such a posture when one sees Upper Canada [,] where there are few Catholics and where almost all the inhabitants are of English origin [,] denouncing the same ills and requesting the same reforms[?]"[16]

Papineau's contention was that the French-Canadian nation was and had always been of unique character in North America, due not only to its French origin but to its particular institutions which had determined its land-oriented vocation and the nature of its élite classes. Yet its existence as a national entity had been constantly threatened from without by the United States and from within by the colonial bureaucracy and the English-speaking merchants. The obstacles to advancement for the French-Canadian middle classes and repeated attacks on the national institutions had been engineered by the English-speaking minority, who had succeeded in duping the governors and the British authorities. Britain itself, and British institutions, therefore remained unsullied. The Constitutional Act, which had reconfirmed the Quebec Act and created a "national" assembly, was tangible proof of the mother country's good faith: "It was intended that the legislative assembly should be influential, since the province of Quebec had been divided in order that the old population might protect its own institutions."[17] Thus the colonial system gave military protection to the French Canadians, while the 1791 constitution provided the framework which, in theory, gave the lay élite the power necessary both to defend the nation's interests and to pursue its particular objectives. All this justified a reformist strategy based on a liberal interpretation of the 1791 constitution in order to obtain all that the English constitution could provide. The theory underlying the struggle for the control of revenues was complemented by the concept of ministerial responsibility. This pattern of thinking, however, changed with the political developments and confrontations from 1828 on.

The French-Canadian society was now seen as living an intensely hazardous existence, not only as a French, Catholic, and agrarian society in a hostile English-speaking world, but also as a normal North American society in the British Empire. Papineau adopted the currently modish Jacksonian democratic thinking which in that period was also espoused by Alexis de Tocqueville, who made it the framework of his three-volume work, *La Démocratie en Amérique*, published from 1835 on.

In February, 1831, Papineau declared: "It is therefore not in the mother country, nor in the rest of Europe, where social organization is entirely different, where the sharing of wealth is very unequal, that we should seek examples; it is rather in America where one sees neither colossal wealth nor degrading poverty, where a man of genius has the run of the different social ranks without obstacle."[18] Central to his political thinking now was the notion of America as the natural habitat of democracy and equality of opportunity, where European heritage had no place. Having re-read the history of the American colonies, he concluded, "The unanimous consent with which all the peoples of America have adopted and extended the elective system, shows that it conforms with the wishes, customs, and social condition of the inhabitants."[19] Furthermore, the relentless advance of democracy in North America was a reflection of basic conditions of life for men of the frontier. In a speech in 1834 Papineau said: "But what has been the procedure in the United States? As new agreements have been made, all has tended toward democracy. . . . When, therefore, all the changes in this part of the world have tended to establish the democratic system, and those of the United States which are in the west, the last established, are the most democratic of all, it is evident that this is an order of things peculiar to America and there can be no aristocracy created there."[20] A few weeks earlier he had prophesied in the assembly:

It is certain that before very long, all America should be republican. . . . We need only to know that we live in America and know how people have lived there [before us]. England herself has founded powerful republics there, where liberty, morality, and the arts are flourishing.... The fallacious system that has reigned in the colonies has only given greater vigour to the people to make themselves republican.... All the opinions, the prejudices of old Europe fall away in the presence of republicanism in unity.[21]

For all his admiration of the United States, Papineau was not envisaging annexation to the neighbouring republic, but rather a redefinition which likened the French-Canadian society to the rest of the essentially democratic North American societies. For him, the Coutume de Paris and the seigneurial régime engendered equality of opportunity, the first because it stipulated equal sharing of property among descendants, and the second because it offered an equal sharing of land among individuals; the seigneur was simply the neutral guardian of that equality of opportunity. In 1836 he proclaimed in the House: "The ministers have wished to put into action and into force aristocratic principles in the Canadas [,] whose social constitution is essentially democratic, where everyone is born and dies a democrat; because everyone is a property owner; because everyone has only small properties...."[22] The extent of Papineau's own seigneury, it might be said in passing, was a paltry 178,000 *arpents*. Over half the farmers had less than fifty.

The mythology, proclaimed constantly after 1831, began to have an air of reality. The picture of a French-Canadian nation torn between a supposedly democratic social condition and a monarchistic and aristocratic political régime imposed by England was fostered by a great deal of intellectualizing, with hints that only political revolution could rectify such a grievous contradiction.

In fact, the British government was showing signs of being ready to make concessions when Papineau began to throw doubt on its good faith and to accuse it of being and always having been party to the imagined conspiracy against the French Canadians. "I believed at first that it was through ignorance; I have since perceived that it was perversity..."[23] he proclaimed in 1834; "... for years, this House and the people had nourished hope and professed faith that His Majesty's government was not knowingly participating in the political demoralization of its colonial servants...."[24] A year later, when he had decided finally that the principal target must be the mother country, he stressed that the situation "must convince the most spineless, the most half-hearted Canadians that the government is organized to persecute them; that only in a change of constitution may they find a government which will act in accordance with the law...."[25] Yet in Papineau's mind the perversity of men was less at fault than the political system: "We have only a delusive shadow of the English constitution...."[26] "The government of Lower Canada is corrupt in its head and in its limbs; the constitution is defective in most of its provisions except those concerning the Constitution of the House of Assembly."[27]

If England had not given Lower Canada a representative system until 1791, as it had to its other colonies, "It was [because of] a systematic exclusion of the French, the Canadians, and the Roman Catholics. Pernicious, narrow, and persecutive counsel prevailed against us. This evil initiated then still endures and, combined with this bad constitution, continues to weigh upon the country."[28] When finally England, under pressure from the French Canadians, resolved to grant a parliamentary system, Papineau maintained, she did it in such a way as to impose on it a monarchical and aristocratic character; the constitution of 1791, in his mind at this later time, was designed to neutralize the legislative assembly, which was logically the voice of the French Canadians, and to give strength to those bodies which allowed an English-speaking minority without real ties in the country to control power and patronage. Thus, it was now England which was principally responsible for the rising tide of ethnic tensions in Lower Canada. "Give [us] institutions in which there are no motives for adulation and national distinctions will cease."[29] Furthermore, the 1791 constitution, as he saw it, embodied a policy of assimilation of French Canadians:

> A wise government would not seek to destroy as important a re-source as that which it could still find in the Canadians' sense of nationality.... Arrogant pride and insult give offence daily; they will reap the fruits. How can the Canadians endure at every hour and every day the preferences and insults proliferated against them? As if for us it were a sign of censure to be descended from one nation rather than another.[30]

Papineau's outbursts became increasingly bitter: "... it seems that the [lady] liberty they hold so dear in England loses her attraction for them here, and she seems to them only a prostitute to be rejected if she has to be as much our friend as she is theirs...."[31] "Keeping the present form with its vices means perpetuating national distinctions.... Only in a general elective system is each on a perfectly equal footing with another, has his rightful degree of influence in the country and does not borrow from outside."[32]

But for all his talk of equality, Papineau was really thinking of a power mutation for the benefit of the French-Canadian middle classes. He also talked much about "European and British aristocracy." When he denounced "the aristocracy of the banks, the government, and trade," he meant that the bureaucrats and English-speaking business-men owed their political power and economic supremacy to favourit-ism of the most arbitrary kind. "One nation," he said, "never was able to govern another. British affections for Ireland and the colonies had never been more than affection for pillaging Ireland and the colonies, [which had been] abandoned to exploitation by the British aristocracy and its creatures."[33] All government posts would invariably go to Englishmen of questionable talent and outright hostility to the local population: "... it is simply to 'faire des jobs'," he said flatly, "which term has no synonym in French since the act is more English than continental; it is simply to make room in the colonies for younger sons no one knows what to do with at home, to assure a European influence, that the old colonial system is preserved...."[34]

If [the governors] have talents and knowledge of affairs, the arro-gance of the Europeans surrounding them, in their pride of being such, as if they bore all the knowledge and all the progress of the nation they have left, corrupts them, flatters them [as they] buzz attentively about them. Brought into the councils, these people have interests contrary to those of the people [of the country].... It is hence clear that the system which gives most patronage is the most contrary to the endurance and permanence of the colonial régime.

Similarly, "the aristocracy of bankruptcy," as Papineau termed the English-speaking business community, had no roots in the local society and owed its success to government protection; "the commer-cial cabal which thinks it runs everything here is not the strength of the country."[35]

It was therefore a repellent image of the English-speaking minor-ity which Papineau created and propagated, evoking "... their repug-nant passions, violently and openly manifested against all that is Ca-nadian," their hostility to the assembly over twenty years, their in-difference to real land ownership in the province, and their mercurial and unreliable trade, "as mercantile enterprises ordinarily are when managed with capital invested outside the country." There was "no longer hope of seeing them in harmony with the House,"[36] he con-cluded. Constitutional deviations, furthermore, were caused by the colonial system and its propensities for discrimination: "... we are called to defend the cause and rights of all the English colonies against a colonial system containing in its essence all the seeds of corruption and disorder."[37]

The governors themselves, maintained Papineau, were natural promoters of European monarchistic and aristocratic values, and were
motivated besides by personal interest. "When I think that a Duke of
Richmond who had governed as viceroy in Ireland... came here to
make good his losses of fortune; and that he was succeeded by another
noble who came also seeking the wherewithal to repair his dilapidated
old castle, I begin to doubt the impartiality of the English nobility."[38]
In 1831 he declared:

> Where will we see so malevolent a contrivance as that formed by an
> executive council without responsibility, whose life and [malig-
> nant] outgrowth is found in the legislative council. The king cannot
> do wrong: the ministers who counsel him are punishable [in Eng-
> land]; but here ten or twelve individuals hold all the royal prerog-
> ative, with no responsibility whatever; they enjoy inviolability and
> can with impunity impede useful measures or by surprise obtain
> sanction of laws dangerous to the country's well-being...[;] Eng-
> land must be told that [the assembly] cannot support or defend a
> factitious aristocracy which is loathsome and insufferable in Amer-
> ica, that the appointment of executive councillors to the legislative
> council [to allow them] to obtain their ends, succeed in all their
> iniquitous designs, is an anti-social contrivance which leads to giv-
> ing us not a king but twenty tyrants assured of impunity in all their
> excesses.[39]

At this date, the only aspect of the British constitution to which Papineau held staunchly was responsible government, the supremacy of the
legislative assembly over the executive. In 1836 he reiterated his view
"that the only essential principle of the British constitution applied to
its colonies is the absolute control over revenue by the representation
and its preponderant and direct influence over all the acts of the
executive."[40] He was certainly bent on breaking the close ties between
the governor and the executive council and their systematic opposition
to the assembly. The composition of the council was a persistent sore
spot. In 1830 he observed that only one of the ten or eleven members of
the council was a native-born French Canadian.[41] As late as 1837 he was
saying, "If the government had a responsible executive it might enjoy
some consideration; there is no right as long as it is not subject to this
condition for the existence of any constitutional government."[42] Papineau's attitude to responsible government is indeed not always clear; his
recommendations for the principle were less frequent than his outbursts
against the irresponsibility of government. In 1834, for instance, he
said:

The regular ministers [in England] had power, and on the part of the people carried on the business of the government in the Commons; they were responsible and they acted everywhere.... It was in fact [in Lower Canada] the members, on their own responsibility, who proposed all government measures, supplies and the rest, while in England it was the ministers who shared the responsibility.... The comparison between an Executive Councillor, a member of the House, and the Ministry in England was most strange. What member? The porter, the messenger of His Excellency, charged to tell us to do what he cannot prevent us from doing.... If the Executive wish to seize hold of our functions, let them have the responsibility and not make us mere tool[s].[43]

In 1832 he replied to Governor Aylmer, who had just been lecturing the assembly: "In the mother country the king is so far from being able to censure the Commons that he can express only their sentiments and not his own, since his government, his responsible ministers, are those he designates, and despite him give him the will of the Commons.... The king is subordinate to the House of Commons, though invested with the privilege recognized by the English constitution, that he can do no wrong."[44]

It must be admitted that when Papineau forbade assembly members to accept government posts he was closing the door to a smooth evolution toward responsible government. J.-M. Mondelet accepted an executive councillorship while an assembly member and was condemned as a traitor. John Neilson refused a similar post, whereupon Abbé J. Demers, who was worried by the radical turn being taken by the *patriotes*, wrote to him:

I am still expecting you to make a sacrifice of your manner of thinking to procure the happiness of the habitants of the country. The entire Province wishes you to be called to the Executive Council. If you allow the government to propose this place to you a second time, our Friend from Montreal will have no reason for aversion to being called to it himself, and I am convinced that he could be persuaded to join. If you stop saying, like the valet in the Comedy, *I do not wish to join the army*, before six months have passed you will form the majority of the council; then it will be that abuses may easily be made to vanish, and the necessary and effective measures may be taken to bring happiness and tranquillity to our poor Canada. If on the other hand you persist in refusing, we shall have to live many years more in trouble and unrest, and that unhappy state we shall owe to a friend of the Country.[45]

In this period Papineau did not seem interested in winning responsible government as a principle, and even less in obtaining it pragmatically. He was already in hot pursuit of independence, or at least total overturn of the political system. Yet in 1834 he was ready "to sacrifice for commerce a few natural rights of lesser importance" which were already enjoyed by the Americans.[46] But certain reforms constituted an acceptable minimum: "A local, responsible, and national government for each part of the empire, for its local interests, with supervisory authority in the imperial government, to determine peace and war and trade with foreigners: that is what Ireland and British America are asking; that is what in a very few years they will be strong enough to take, if [the English] are not sufficiently just to give it to them."[47]

All Papineau's theoretical reconstruction and criticism now came to be focused more or less directly on the legislative council, as the symbol of every imaginable kind of exploitation and oppression, the refuge of an artificial aristocracy, and the pillar of monarchy. In monarchical Europe there had to be a king, Papineau allowed, but in Lower Canada there could be no aristocracy with its "magnificent attributes," for the country could not afford "the appanage of a brilliant Canadian empire." What was needed was simple government, like that of the United States.[48] Between the local legislative councillors and the lords of England there was "all the distance that there is between man and monkey."[49]

Wishing to preserve the rachitic pseudo-aristocracy, which an act of parliament placed on bare rock in 1791, [would be] to give the power of our politicians to the legislative council, to that Ahriman, that evil spirit, that father of shadows, which for over forty years has engendered only evil, killed all that was good, and has seemed desirous of inundating the society once more in chaos and anarchy, judging by the pleasure with which it destroys all it can of the works of good principle: the bills of the assembly.[50]

The truth is that Papineau saw the legislative council as the symbol and instrument of English-speaking power. Writing to his wife in 1831, he attributed the councillors' behaviour to their "passionate hatred of Canadians and unbridled love of money.... Of gold which they have made their god, on which they have gorged themselves and would continue to digest without restraint or control."[51] The reform of 1832, which added several French Canadians to the body, he virtually ignored; nothing short of a fully elective legislative council would do. To the British government's rejection of that principle, he retorted that what it wanted was "a council to defend a part of the population which could not be in majority in the assembly.... Each time it appoints an Englishman it does so from among the enemies of the House and the majority[,] to support the council; and most of the Canadians that it buys are to support the council's policy...."[52] Extension of the elective principle, he concluded, would prevent the administration from monopolizing the power and the fruits of office. On the other hand, "United by the elective system, they [the councillors] would be the apostles of the rights of man; their sentiments would conform to those of the people."[53]

Thus, Papineau's reworked ideology would make all seats of power elective: the governorship, executive and legislative councils, assembly, school boards, and *Fabriques*—even the proposed local administrations. "Spreading political instruction among the people," said the *patriote* leader, "will place them in a condition to act with wisdom, with unity: a compact mass which will rise with strength...."[54] But the democratic republic which he had in mind would be a democracy of landowners, at a time when at least 38 per cent of heads of families in the Montreal region had no access to land ownership. He optimistically held, however, that there was so much land that only an infinitesimal part of the population would be excluded from the vote by the qualification requirement. "Those who are not landowners today will become so soon."[55] The immediate beneficiaries, of course, would be the French-Canadian middle classes.

The evolution from nationalism in liberal and reformist guise to a democratic and republican nationalism (dedicated, for all that, to the seigneurial régime and French customary law) took place by stages. Papineau began his attacks on the legislative council long before the 1830 election, easing the question of supply to second place; finances were now neither the most important nor the most urgent of issues. "If it were an independent and true council," he wrote, "we might have scruples over refusing the supplies...."[56] The election of 1830 took place in a period of transition accelerated by rumblings from France, which culminated in the July Revolution in Paris.[57] Neilson, who lost no opportunity to urge calm and wisdom,[58] was worried most by the flocks of opportunists entering the Canadian party ranks. "I see many persons proposing to enter the House purely to satisfy their vanity and their personal interests, and they are the more dangerous that in past crises they have marched in the direction of the mass."[59] As soon as the election and the attendant uncertainties were over, Papineau began to proliferate his expressions of republican and democratic faith, as well as his condemnations of monarchy and aristocracy, which greatly perturbed the clergy and *patriotes* who were still traditionalists. One such was A.-N. Morin, who wrote in 1829: "... the

Canadian people still have [the advantage] of discovering all their historical background allied to their belief. Religion created and still preserves the patriarchal customs of our good habitants... so that in fact as in law, the Catholic religion is the religion of the Canadian population of the country and the safeguard of its customs and its liberty."[60] But Morin knew the essential difference between rhetoric and ideas that counted. In the autumn of 1831, when the Canadian party and the clergy were in open opposition, he defined the essence of the *patriote* movement's strategy:

> Under Dalhousie only good was said of the authorities in England and ill of the colonial administration. All is different now.... It is England's conduct which must be censured; and we run no great risk of mistake in holding on in opposition and remaining Canadian: as long as only partial justice is rendered to us, and the councils are not entirely changed, as long as crown lands are not opened to the Canadians, as long as attempts are made to anglify us and stifle us with the immigration, which seems to be in the programme. That in general is my view; and yet the majority of the members and of the people as well are so easy to satisfy, that it is a poor moment to raise one's voice and talk of revolution. Poor souls, if only they knew they are so little liked....[61]

In 1832, economic conditions worsened, immigrants kept pouring in, and there was the cholera, all favouring radicalism in the *patriote* movement. Papineau was already voicing the question of independence: "... we do not want a forced separation, but we might discuss the reasons and causes which could lead us to it...."[62] Clumsiness on the part of the governor and legislative councillors raised the political tension to an even higher pitch. In January, Daniel Tracey in *The Vindicator* and Ludger Duvernay in *La Minerve* attacked the legislative council so bitterly, demanding its abolition, that they were called before the council, condemned, and imprisoned for thirty-four days. There were popular demonstrations, and when the Irishman and the Canadian were released they were paraded through the streets as heroes, victims of the legislative council, and presented with gold medals. There was a vacant assembly seat in Montreal West and *patriote* strategists decided to test the election of legislative councillors as a vote-catching issue. Duvernay had been the obvious candidate, but since 42 per cent of heads of families were French, American and Irish voters had the balance of power. The English party put up Stanley Bagg, a merchant of American origin. At the *parti patriote* nomination meeting, C.-S. Cherrier introduced Tracey as the party's Irish candidate and reminded French Canadians that Dr Tracey had always been their friend and that his was the only English paper in the province which defended their cause. The Irish, he said, had claims on them for their support, for they had always been friends to the country in the worst moments of crisis.[63] Tracey's candidature can only be seen as pure expediency, a device to fan the quarrel over the legislative council and exploit the prevailing conditions in Montreal West. On that, Amury Girod's remarks leave no doubt:

> Tracey was undoubtedly a man as violent as he was gifted and talented; . . . without the opposition of a man such as Bagg, a citizen of the United States, affiliated with all that is opposed to the interests of the majority of the people, I do not believe that the strongest adversaries of the bureaucracy could think of sending him to parliament. . . .[64]

This by-election of 1832 is one of the most celebrated in Canadian history. It lasted from April 25 to May 22. Violence in words was followed by physical violence as soon as the poll opened. Of the 1,533 electors who turned up, 1,378 registered a vote; the candidates objected to 595, made 486 take an oath, and demanded 416 property descriptions. Not a stone went unturned. Rural property owners were brought from their parishes in the riding to vote; of the 61 who came, 37 voted for Tracey. Of the 199 women electors, 104 voted for Bagg. This had happened too often; on presentation in 1834 of a bill denying the suffrage to women, Papineau said, "As for the custom of having women vote, it is right to dispose of it. It is odious to see women dragged to the hustings, wives by their husbands, daughters by their fathers, often even against their will."[65] The violence throughout the election was such that 335 special constables were sworn in to deal with it; finally troops were called in, and on May 21 three Canadians were killed. As the count of votes went on from day to day the candidates were running virtually neck-and-neck. At last, on May 22, Tracey won by four votes (see Table 61). "The national party carried the day over the anti-Canadian faction . . .," was the characteristic comment in *La Minerve.*[66]

The French Canadians and Irish voted heavily for Tracey, and the English, Scottish, and Americans even more heavily for Bagg. As early as May 9, the *patriote* party leaders noted defections among the French Canadians. "If they had been unanimous," remarked *La Minerve*, "they would have easily won the victory. . . ."[67] French Canadians who were well established economically indeed tended to vote for the merchant side (see Table 62). The English papers noted this and *La Minerve* denied it, though not with great conviction: "We are far from believing or wishing to insinuate that the Canadians opposed to Mr Tracey are not respectable; we have among them friends whom we respect and esteem highly."[68] Socio-economic conditions certainly carried weight in this, while in the Irish vote the factors at play were religious, economic, and ethnic. The reactions of certain of the working class are difficult to judge, owing to a lack of information regarding non-voters, voluntary or by non-qualification. The by-election of the same year in Quebec's Lower Town between Vanfelson and Dr C.R. McCulloch shows more distinct ethnic partiality among the upper- and middle-class French Canadians (see Table 63).

The death of the three Canadians and the intervention of several legislative councillors in the Montreal West by-election were exploited to the full by the *patriote* leaders. Papineau had directed the campaign from his house but had otherwise remained out of the fray and was therefore well placed to act as arbiter. He immediately wrote the governor demanding that he come to Montreal to oversee the punishment of the Canadians' killers. The villains of the entire piece, of course, were the military, officers of justice, functionaries, and particularly the legislative councillors, all in league against the interests of the people. In one of the most violent speeches of his career, Papineau said, "Mr Tracey suffered a cruel persecution and long imprisonment from the legislative council. The vanity of this body[,] such a power for evil, so opposed and so fatal to the good of the country, for its own sake would not allow any mark of esteem or confidence for its victim."[69]

The campaign to arouse public opinion against the legislative council was soon interrupted by the cholera epidemic, and the "affair of May 21" was revived later only to be more or less dissipated in a long inquiry by the assembly. But the Montreal West by-election had served to enflame nationalist passions and open the eyes of the élite to the legislative council problem. In Quebec City, Papineau's supporters eventually won a degree of unanimity on the latter. In 1833, Edouard Glackmeyer wrote to Neilson:

Opinion on the eligibility of the council is not yet as fully formed as we have wished to believe; it is a very ticklish question, and yet I see no other remedy. I hoped that more time might pass before the country should come to a decision; we would have had longer experience in opposing the present council but as it happens the meeting in the Lower Town has started trouble and put an end to that indifference which many of the public had on the subject. . . .[70]

Papineau realized the rapidity of the change of feeling and sought to accelerate it further. In January, 1833, he proposed holding a convention for the purpose of formulating the necessary constitutional changes; this idea of a convention became a favourite theme for him, one which he had evolved through reading Jean-Jacques Rousseau and the history of the American colonies; "... it could introduce an entirely new system.... For under this system the governor, the council, the representatives, under the English monarchy as under a federative union, have been elected by all the people annually...."[71] A year later he declared in the House "that in the neighbouring countries there is a more universal and stronger attachment for the national institutions than anywhere else, and there exists a guarantee of progressive improvement in the political institutions through their revision, at frequent and determined intervals, through conventions of the people, to meet without commotion or violence the needs of all periods...."[72]

Papineau's convention project did not distract him from preparations for the next general election, which was to test the new ideological orientations and strategies envisioned for the future. It was to be an important test, for the sympathy of certain individuals and groups for the *patriote* cause had cooled somewhat, particularly among the clergy. Curé Viau cancelled his subscription to *La Minerve*, remarking that he had for some time been displeased with the paper, as were others, especially members of the clergy.[73] Curé Brassard did similarly, exclaiming, "God keep me from approving its principles!"[74]

The end of an alliance which had always been one of convenience, and precarious at that, was hastened by the dispute over the election of the *Fabriques* or parish councils. Lartigue wrote in 1832 to D.-B. Viger, then in London:

> ... when you have reflected and learned how things have gone on in our House of Assembly, you will see that the clergy has done only its strict and stringent duty with regard to the bill on the Fabriques. It can be said that Papineau and several others have behaved shamefully in this affair, and that they could not have done better to make their enemies laugh [than] by detaching the clergy from the popular branch of our legislature....[75]

The clergy felt the same revulsion over the parish councils dispute as the *patriotes* felt over the legislative council: the symbol of irreligion and power in the hands of the laity juxtaposing the symbol of colonial dependence and power in the hands of the English-speaking. In 1834 Lartigue again deplored the assembly's deceitful behaviour over the parish councils, and also Papineau's vehement and clumsy outbursts against the clergy and church rights.[76] What the clergy was really attacking was the *patriotes'* ideology in general, the threat it posed to the church, and the stratagems employed. To D.-B. Viger, Lartigue noted the turbulence of riding meetings and the fact that, even in rural areas, thugs were being used to assist in winning arguments. "I am afraid that [this practice] will make the next general elections of representatives exceedingly heated, and perhaps bloody."[77] Papineau, while deploring the clergy's failure to understand that their true interests lay with those of the nation, seemed to accept the defection as inevitable. In March, 1835, he wrote to his wife that, if they persisted, they would discover what protection they would get from the English government. "If they can open their eyes to the light, they must immediately understand where their real friends are."[78] Yet he still feared the curés' influence with the electors.

Between 1829 and 1834 there were other significant defections. Augustin Cuvillier, for instance, a merchant and auctioneer, had been closely associated with the Bank of Montreal; he was one of the few important French-Canadian urban merchants in the *patriote* ranks, had become the party's financial expert, and in 1828 had gone with Neilson and Viger to England. He was certainly ambitious and had perhaps hoped to replace Neilson as Papineau's lieutenant, perhaps even to succeed Papineau as party leader. Papineau maintained that the party really no longer needed a financial expert. In any event, Cuvillier, in frustration, joined the opposite camp and played a major role in the Montreal West by-election of 1832. At a public meeting he declared:

> There were already too many advocates in the House. They were too dangerous with their talents. Often one would see a client voting alongside his advocate and see the danger in this influence. If there were a preponderant class of physicians, the laws would smell too much of medicine. One could say that there was not a single Canadian merchant in the assembly and it was important to elect one....[79]

Also virtually complete at this time was another significant break, that between Papineau and Neilson. Neilson described himself as a moderate and a "radically disposed" reformist. With his substantial influence among both French- and English-speaking electors, he had been Papineau's "man in Quebec." But he could not accept the excessive republicanism, anti-clericalism, and nationalism which was becoming the party's feature, and even less its increasingly extremist behaviour. These developments he blamed on the influence of Girod and the Nelson brothers over the party leader.

In 1834 he wrote to Joly de Lotbinière:

> Since several members of the House have been bent on attacking the country's institutions and the constitution which we had all been united in defending, my position as representative has been most distasteful to me. I have no longer been able to act together with many among the members with whom I was once in agreement. I have seen the fruit of our work of many years and great personal sacrifice on my part practically lost....[80]

Neilson was also greatly dismayed by the political and economic consequences of the direction being taken by the *patriotes*; they "have produced attempts to alienate the affections of the people from the British government, a consequent feeling of insecurity, and an actual diminution of the value of property and of the rewards of industry to the amount of 25 to 50 per cent."[81] In 1831 he dissociated himself from the party over the parish councils question. The breach widened subsequently, and in 1833 Papineau wrote to his wife, "Neilson has deserted the cause of the country far more than he appears to have done, and he alone is harming it because he has credit and influence. He will, I fear, draw us into a monstrous blunder."[82] Papineau was both hurt and angered by Neilson's defection. In 1834 he said in the House, "Mr Neilson had the generosity to make himself Canadian and unveil these plots of iniquity and today he has not the strength to repeat [it]...."[83] Soon he was treating his former friend as a traitor. "Neilson must return or go to waste in the public as in the House...."[84] The Upper-Canadian reformist leaders regarded this rupture with great alarm, fearing a backlash in informed British opinion against reform in general, and a resurgence of division among the *patriote* leaders and the Lower-Canadian electors.[85] Neilson continued to oppose the idea of an elective legislative council and increased his appeals for caution and wisdom.

When, early in 1834, Papineau proposed a kind of strike of assembly members, the Quebec *patriote* leaders refused to follow him, in fear that the peasants, embittered by famine, would turn against the party. "The inside story," wrote Papineau then, "is that [Etienne] Parent [editor of *Le Canadien*] controls [Elzéar] Bédard and [P.-G.] Huot and those [control] a portion of the members of Quebec. That he is owed £1200 to £1500 for printing, that if there is no session he may not be able to sustain such a failure, that his paper may fail...."[86] Neilson took advantage of all such circumstances and became an encumbrance in the assembly.

This was the background to the general election of 1834. Papineau and the Montreal leaders were hoping it would bring renewed unity in the upper echelons of the party and a massive demonstration of popular support in their favour. They decided to use the same strategy that had proved so successful in 1822 and 1828. The Ninety-two Resolutions were to be the key. Basically reflecting Papineau's thinking, they comprised all the grievances of the *patriotes* against the established régime. The threat of secession they contained was less significant than their vehement denunciation of the legislative council, which was made to appear the symbol of all ills. The document was a nationalist manifesto which also could be read by English-speaking radicals, American democrats, and liberal and Catholic Irishmen as a democratic manifesto: a wordy text which could in fact be read in many ways. On March 3, J. Viger wrote to his wife, "Well! Who will go with Mr Speaker tomorrow to the Château, to present the address to the king; patriotic according to some and revolutionary according to others?"[87]

And so, instead of holding a strike, the party leaders decided to devote the final session of this "parliament" to a detailed discussion of all the resolutions, of which Elzéar Bédard, Morin, and Papineau were the authors. Papineau gave Bédard the task of placing them before the House, a procedure which would make it possible to distinguish among the believers, the luke-warm, and the opponents. Papineau himself delivered most of the oratory, opening the debate with a speech of more than three hours. Patriotic enthusiasm reached a fever pitch. Debartzch wrote to Viger:

> ... it is a victory which will mark an epoch in the country and in all America.... A people who can through their representation express their rights and their needs, give their reasons for their complaints and assert their grievances as is done through these resolutions, must inspire the respect of their rulers, the esteem and admiration of neighbouring countries, and then prepare for a future happier than the present....[88]

Papineau won some converts, but the final vote showed, of the total of eighty members, twenty-four who opposed the ideology advanced by the resolutions, some of them *patriotes* (three absentees were also opposed). Wrote J. Viger of F.-A. Quesnel, one of the dissidents who was nevertheless respected, "I have heard several say: he is a *patriote*, he is Canadian; what a shame he cannot think as we or we vote as he."[89] Naturally, the party organizers determined to deal with the recalcitrants at the coming elections; seventeen of them eventually decided not to run for re-election. Meanwhile, petitions were prepared to be signed in all parishes at all levels of the society. A.-N. Morin was designated to carry all the relevant documents to England.

This pre-election mobilization yielded excellent results. The *patri-ote* party's organization was remarkable for that day and age; it had a defined ideology, a programme constantly modified to fit the condi-tions of the moment, a complex hierarchy in the smallest of localities in all regions, a well-tried strategy, and a dazzling leader who was both a creator of myths and symbols and an authoritarian. Papineau confined his activities to his own riding and the assembly, but he had able lieutenants. Louis-Hippolyte Lafontaine was not the most con-templative of these, but he was already showing an innate political sensibility. Most seem to have been guided largely by instinct. The party's most effective leading figures were almost all Montrealers and closely connected with the Papineau family. This was to lead to re-newed friction over leadership. But the party was entering the 1834 electoral campaign with confidence and a sense of engaging in a deci-sive battle.

The three ridings of the city of Quebec attracted lively political attention. Quebec riding was the stronghold of Neilson, now the man to beat. Papineau had already begun to undermine him by raising Dr E.B. O'Callaghan to assistant leader of the party, with a view to replac-ing Neilson and also to keeping the Irish vote. O'Callaghan had suc-ceeded Daniel Tracey as editor of *The Vindicator*, had done much to rally the Irish of Quebec to the *patriote* banner, and had achieved prominence in Montreal. Since he would almost certainly be beaten in Montreal West, the party "parachuted" him into a safer rural riding. He was "the new friend of the Canadians."

Neilson's electoral defeat was therefore being busily prepared. Joly de Lotbinière urged him to run in Quebec, assuring him that he should be elected without difficulty, having the clergy firmly behind him and also the support of the riding's most influential figures; he should also have considerable support for his stand against the radicals in the House.[90] Neilson seemed less convinced, for he ran both in Bellechasse, where he won no votes, and in Quebec riding where, after only three days of voting, he suffered a humiliating defeat. The vote in his favour was 66 per cent English-speaking, in contrast to 1827, when it had been 84 per cent French-speaking (see Table 64).

The nationalistic character of the entire 1834 election is unmistak-able, despite efforts to make it look otherwise. The worsening eco-nomic crisis was more than ever before interpreted in ethnic terms, and inter-ethnic tension had never been so strong. In the city of Quebec, stagnation in shipbuilding, the end of work on fortifications, and quarrels over public expenditures and investments had resulted in a climate of depression which was reflected in property values (see

Table 65). Continued massive immigration and a second cholera epidemic increased the gravity of the social and economic instability. A contemporary observed, "The unjust outcries against the Irish and against emigration have driven away to a man even that class which on former occasions acted numerously with the House of Assembly."[91] Ethnic political alignments clearly showed a correlation with the economic and demographic context.

In Quebec's Lower Town the *patriote* candidates won easily over the lumber merchant B. Pemberton, who received only thirteen French-speaking votes.[92] In the Upper Town the candidates made no attempt to veil their ethnic appeals. One of the English party candidates, Duval, certain of his defeat, withdrew, and *The Mercury* stated, "The affair has now become a national one."[93] The other, Andrew Stuart, redoubled his appeals to English-speaking voters of all origins. Amable Berthelot, a *patriote* candidate, remarked, "The interests of the English population are protected and defended in England, by the legislative council and by the governor. We ourselves have only the House of Assembly and we may be sending to it persons who will support our political enemies."[94] He failed to mention that the *patriote* programme included election of the legislative council and even the governor. He and his associate candidate, R.-E. Caron, formerly mayor of Quebec, declaring this election to be "one of national importance,"[95] solicited votes from the Irish as friends of the Canadians or enemies of the English. There were brawls in the streets as the election continued for six days, and then Stuart, too, withdrew (see Table 66). The French Canadians had responded almost unanimously to the ethnic appeal. The *patriotes* won all six seats in the city of Quebec, which is the more significant for the fact that Stuart had acted as the Canadian party leader while Papineau was in England.

In Montreal there were similar confrontations. Of the Montreal West election, Papineau wrote, "Among the subscribers of funds [in 1832] for Mr Bagg, in two and a half years there have been more than £200,000 in bankruptcies, ..." and wondered how many more millions the candidates Donellan and Walker would steal from widows and orphans in the next two and a half years through further bankruptcies. Advances from banks and British sources, he declared, allowed such immoral subscriptions and *gentilles violences*, which were neither customary with nor available to the Canadians.[96] The site of the key contest was once again Montreal West, Papineau's riding, which the powerful English bourgeoisie was determined to take. Papineau, to avoid unnecessary risk, also ran in the half-urban, half-rural riding of Montreal, where he and his cousin C.-S. Cherrier were elected by acclamation. In Montreal West, the English party was running an Irish tradesman, John Donellan, who, it was hoped, would attract the Irish vote. Papineau's comment reveals the intensity of the ethnic feeling:

> The aristocracy of the banks, the government, and trade was no doubt initiated in secret before becoming as strongly democratic as it has, yielding to the marked superiority of knowledge and influence above it, which it attributes to John Donellan, the new idol whom it has placed on a pedestal. [As] for the public, it has seen in these prostrations of British nobility at the feet of an illiterate gardener only saturnalia and demagogy. As for me, from the abject nature of the measure alone, I have believed it to be truly aristocratic, monarchistic, loyal, and British, and derived from our colonial government's maxim: divide in order to reign.[97]

According to Papineau, the *patriote* party feared another May 21 incident, and proposed a compromise in the election of one French-speaking and one English-speaking member. The English party having rejected the proposal, Dr Robert Nelson, son of a loyalist family and a well-known radical, was persuaded to stand along with Papineau. The election lasted fourteen days, and was marked with violence from beginning to end. On the fifteenth day, the chief returning officer, faced with a frighteningly riotous situation, declared Papineau and Nelson elected, though their majority was only forty votes. Papineau, naturally seeking to clear his partisans of blame ("Guile and violence were the aristocratic tactics, confidence and patience to the point of gullibility the popular tactics"), gave his personal version of his opponents' behaviour:

> ... these cannibals shouted, danced, threatened, struck in all the sidestreets, and British gentlemen [,] directors of banks and commercial offices and the Walker committee [,] shouted hurrahs amid the cannibals.... The gentry who had led the movement, seeing determination among the honest electors, who were reproaching their infamy, to regain the lost terrain the following Monday, and being warned that they would lose temper not with the hired assassins but with the hiring assassins, found that it was painful to pit their tender, soft, aristocratic parlour skins against the hard, leathery plebeian skins of the bourgeois and tradesmen....[98]

With the election over, Papineau denounced not only the powerful English bourgeoisie and the legislative council, but also the electors of American origin.

They are mostly American tories, those who have had the good fortune to see[,] more than men of other nations of the earth, how the reign of liberty is suited to elevating and ennobling the human spirit and giving birth to a happy State, those who on crossing the forty-fifth parallel have lost all other sentiment than that of flattering Scottish pride to make money, and whose particular nature is so low and grovelling that the sublime spectacle offered by their government, today the terror of kings, the hope of the nations of Europe, has failed to make them admire the free man's dignity....[99]

The excess of Papineau's tone at this time was no doubt responsible for defections among the Irish, which were considerable. Defectors were now "tories" in Papineau's terminology.

They are Irish tories, those who have seen at close hand all the natural advantages that can be destroyed by an oppressive government, bigoted by religious intolerance, grasping, cruel in timidity, because it has been against nature, because it is [a government] of a minority to whom detestable laws have given detestable ascendancy over the majority; who have seen thousands upon thousands of robust, industrious men cultivating a soil which is one of the richest in the world... and starving on the fertile ground they cultivate with skill and diligence.... Those who have seen thousands of men leave their country....[100]

The *patriote* candidates took all twelve of the Quebec and Montreal seats, and also the old English party fiefs of Trois-Rivières and Sorel.

In the rural seigneurial ridings the *patriote* party's sweep was such that, in twenty-one ridings, forty-one *patriote* candidates were elected by acclamation. Only in Gaspé were the party's two opponents, both moderates, elected without opposition. All the new *patriote* members were French Canadians, with the exception of O'Callaghan in Yamaska, whose candidature, it will be remembered, had been imposed by the party. In nine ridings the contest had been lively, this most often due to a large and active English-speaking electorate. Beauharnois and Deux-Montagnes are cases worthy of note.

Beauharnois riding included the seigneury of that name and several townships, with French majorities in the seigneury and Scottish, English, American, and Irish majorities in the townships. Ellice was the seigneur and his influence was exerted through his agent, Brown. The incumbents were both *patriotes*, Charles Archambault, a merchant, and J. de Witt, whose family was American of Dutch origin. De Witt was a landowner, operated a sawmill, and owned a steamboat. Earlier, he had worked in Montreal as a blacksmith and in the hat trade. He was one of the founders of the Banque du Peuple in 1835. His political role in the riding was partially due to his basic liberalism, but even more to his dislike of Ellice and the powerful English bourgeoisie that controlled the Bank of Montreal and the transportation sector. A third candidate, J. Perrigo, merchant, was also running under the *patriote* banner. The sole English party candidate was W. Bowron. De Witt and Archambault were elected by a comfortable margin after thirteen days of polling, De Witt with 73 per cent of his votes in the seigneury and Archambault with 45 per cent of his in the townships, which made him more fully representative of the riding. The English-speaking vote appears to have been much more divided than the French-speaking. This appears also to have been the case in two other ridings, Rouville and Lacadie, where the winning candidates were similarly all *patriotes*.

Deux-Montagnes is even more interesting because it shows clerical influence at work throughout the riding, though in varying degrees. A number of curés were violently anti-*patriote*. Curé Paquin was said to have had "the infamy to use, as unfortunately did several of his confrères, the anathema of his Ministry, and abuse the most sacred things to persuade his parishioners...."[101] P. Boucher-Belleville, a clerical *patriote* and intransigent nationalist, wrote to Duvernay, "Tell me then: what have we to fear or to hope of the pétraille [priestly rabble]? They are a privileged class like the ministerial gang. They are and will invariably be here what they have been in France and elsewhere.... The curé of Laprairie, my uncle,... no longer replies to my letters."[102] The riding included the seigneury of Argenteuil, where the population was mostly English and Scottish. The two *patriote* candidates, Notary Girouard and W.H. Scott, a young Scottish merchant with a French-Canadian wife, tried to have themselves elected by acclamation when the poll opened at St-André, but a group of electors would have none of it and proposed Globensky and Brown. The candidates' fortunes swung violently, with Globensky and Brown leading by 300 votes on the sixth day. There were a large number of French-Canadian defections, which alarmed the *patriote* organizers. With the help of a group of Irish Catholics, they finally gained control when the poll was transferred to St-Eustache. For two days there were no votes for the English party, and on November 14 Globensky and Brown withdrew, though they were still the leaders by some thirty votes. Girouard congratulated his electors for having "defended with courage and steadfast patience the noble cause of liberty."[103] An anonymous commentator pronounced on the victory throughout the province:

Canadians, your enemies have provoked you and given you the opportunity to show your strength: you now know your value; ten times theirs.... They have taken off their mask; act in consequence and repel force with force, holding to an honest defence like your compatriotes of Deux-Montagnes.... As for the cowardly among you, who have had the infamy to join our enemies; as for these traitors, who live in your midst from the fruits of your labours, your attentions, your pains... let them beware! The people sense their importance and will avenge the wrongs done to them. They will no longer allow themselves to be cheated with impunity by giving arms [to be used] against them....[104]

Rural electoral motivations were complex and are difficult to pinpoint. In the fundamental reality of rural community life, the seigneurial and parish framework undoubtedly figured strongly, but the family, in the broad sense of the term, seems to have been an even stronger force. In certain parishes certain families were dominant, had been the traditional pillars of seigneurial and clerical power in the past, and still seemed capable of welding cohesion among differing interests and values. There were certainly rivalries within and between family groups, and also between rural communities. The creation of electoral ridings had given a measure of perpetuity to this kind of interaction and a new focus for collective identity which, pushed to the limit, could overshadow other motivations. This was apparent in by-elections in Portneuf and Saguenay (see Tables 67 and 68). A study of the 1834 election in Orléans reveals powerful family influence in parish electoral results (see Table 73).[105]

Such rural peculiarities made the choice of party candidates a very sensitive problem. Parachuting a candidate, even after 1830 when tension was running high, was a dangerous practice. Wrote A.-N. Morin to Duvernay in 1832, "Unfortunately we do not hold the electors dependent on us, particularly in this riding of Rouville where the electors always want a local inhabitant."[106] The local leading citizens did not always provide the backbone of the *parti patriote.*

There were regionalisms to be considered as well. In 1841 the riding of Dorchester included Dorchester and La Beauce. Two of the Taschereau family were the *patriote* candidates; one of them took 77 per cent of his votes in Beauce and the other 74 per cent of his in Dorchester.[107] Localisms and regionalisms tended also to be expressed in more or less strong hostility toward the cities. If it suited their purpose, candidates often had no scruples about arousing rural prejudice against "ladder-jumpers." In the 1833 by-election in Quebec riding, which included urban and rural sections, the urban vote went almost exclusively to Besserer, the city candidate, and the rural vote to the rural candidate Rainville. Besserer won only twelve rural votes and Rainville only forty-one urban votes. The English-speaking simply abstained that year, but in the general election of the following year there was a realignment of the vote according to ethnic origin (see Table 69).

In the context of agricultural problems, over-population, English economic control, and heavy immigration, there was much rural instability at both parish and family levels; the *patriote* party was well placed to capitalize on the consequent fears and discontent. Its ideology, stressing the values of the past and proposing acceptable solutions to present ills (at least on an emotional level), pointed a finger at elements outside the community to fix blame for local discontent and another finger at actual or potential allies within the community.

In 1830 in Lotbinière riding, the party had indeed penetrated deeply. There were three candidates: Lachevrotière, an English party supporter of aristocratic background, J.-B.-I. Noël, seigneur, physician, and moderate *patriote*, and Louis Méthot, merchant, a more radical *patriote*. Méthot and Noël were elected, but Méthot was by far the more representative, having dominated the vote throughout the riding and at all social levels (see Table 70).

The forty-one members elected by acclamation in 1834, however they came to be elected, were certainly not simply representatives of isolated localities, yet it cannot be assumed either that they represented the full range of interests found in the parishes. Rural parishes did not necessarily react as units to external constraints or stimuli; they had their traditional élites who inevitably suffered by the intrusion of new men who had their own connections in the community and were in competition for community leadership.

The riding of Beauce is interesting in this regard (it later became part of the riding of Dorchester, which gave rise to the situation described above for 1841). It was the stronghold of the old Taschereau and De Léry families. The latter were strongly traditionalist whereas the Taschereaus were remarkably adaptable to changing circumstances (see Table 71). In 1830 two Taschereaus were *patriote* candidates, probably because the *patriote* party stressed safeguards for the seigneurial régime and the Coutume de Paris, and were elected. In 1834 both were re-elected sweepingly over W. Henderson (who obtained only seventeen votes), G. Desbarats, and W. De Léry. Of all the candidates, only A.-C. Taschereau had support throughout the riding. The English-speaking electors apparently gave one of their two votes to him and the other to a candidate of their own origin. The French-speaking electors did likewise. The voting pattern therefore had both local and ethnic dimensions. This is also apparent in the 1835 by-election when

Desbarats took 92 per cent of the English-speaking vote and a large proportion of the total vote in a number of localities, leaving J.-A. Taschereau with only 69 per cent of the French-Canadian vote. A by-election in the following year produced similar results.

Whereas in Beauce the Taschereau family's adaptability and identification with the *patriotes* tended to mask the old élite's loss of influence, the phenomenon was more apparent in Dorchester. Here Henry Caldwell was active both as seigneur and entrepreneur. In 1827, J. Davidson, Caldwell's son-in-law, ran against two Lageux and Joseph Samson, and obtained 60 per cent of the English-speaking vote but only 17 per cent of the French vote. The winners were Samson and L. Lageux (who was a radical but was considered a moderate by the English). In 1830 Caldwell ran himself and won with support throughout the riding and almost twice the vote for L. Lageux, the other winner, whose support was heavily agricultural.[108] Caldwell, who represented all three economic sectors—commercial, agricultural, and industrial—was indeed an exceptional candidate. The true *patriote* strength lay in the most agricultural parishes, which had been sorely affected by a series of poor harvests. The curé of St-Henri wrote (quoted in English):

> ... hardly a third are able to sow their lands and even this third will be obliged to sow the bad seed grain which they reaped last fall, and they are consequently exposed to lose their crops entirely, or to reap bad grain and in small quantity. According to the statement of honest farmers, the crops during former years of distress when the Legislature came to their assistance were not so bad as last year; half the parish is without bread, and many are fortunate to have potatoes. Upwards of fifty families are dependent on parochial relief, and which relief is very limited....[109]

The most radical candidates were favoured by the economic conditions. L. Lageux followed Papineau even on the question of parish councils. In 1832 he said, "The parishioners supplied these funds and one [priest] had the effrontery to say that these funds belong not to those who supplied the funds, but to those who contributed nothing, that the former do not have the right to protect these funds."[110] He died the same year and his successor, Notary J. Bouffard, won against P. Lageux in the by-election. By the 1834 general election the *patriote* candidates had achieved such favour that Caldwell did not run. P. Lageux was again defeated, though he obtained 61 per cent of the English vote. The winners were Bouffard and J.-B. Beaudoin, a farmer (see Table 72).[111] In Rimouski, Saguenay, Bellechasse, and Orléans similar tendencies were apparent (see Table 73).

Outside the cities, the *parti patriote* encountered strong opposition only in those areas where the population was ethnically and religiously mixed and where the economy was diversified. Newly arrived immigrants were urgently seeking land. Large-scale stock-raisers and potato producers were preoccupied by American competition. Forestry, potassium production, and small manufacturing broadened the range of interests. Here the *patriote* party could not present the same image that was proving so successful in the old seigneurial parishes with their overwhelming French-Canadian majorities. Candidates were therefore not parachuted in from the outside but sought locally.

Megantic is an interesting example of ridings of this type. In a by-election of 1832, the merchant W. Henderson won over A.C. Buchanan, an immigration agent, because he obtained two-thirds of the professional, merchant, and trade votes, though only 50 per cent of the agricultural vote. There is little local polarization apparent.[112] On April 5, 1832, the *Quebec Mercury* reported, "... a meeting held in Inverness accused Anderson [sic] of introducing a foreign influence into the country to trample the rights of resident voters."[113] The lesson was not missed by the *patriote* party, and in 1834 its candidate, Layfield, declared:

> ... it is the bounden duty of every one having the welfare and prosperity of the country at heart, to return a resident member on this, as well as on all future occasions. ... There is a strong necessity of maintaining inviolate the independence of the county, and for preventing it from becoming prey to the intrigue of strangers and political speculators, who are utterly devoid of all claims to the confidence and support of the people of Megantic. ...[114]

He lost, nevertheless, to Graves Clapham, a large landowner and Quebec merchant, though there was a strong polarization of the vote according to locality. Together with appeals to local sentiment, there was much denunciation of government land policy and appeal to the republican leanings of settlers of American origin (see Table 74). Missisquoi, Shefford, and Sherbrooke elected opponents of the Ninety-two Resolutions, but in Stanstead the winners were *patriote* party candidates. In the Ottawa Valley, where there was less political tension, two moderate English party incumbents were displaced by two moderate *patriotes* whose principal concern was money for roads.

In the new assembly after the 1834 election, the English party was left with only nine members, a number of them considered moderates. The *patriote* party had captured 77 per cent of the votes throughout the province, and had besides their forty-one candidates elected by acclamation. Papineau expressed an almost sadistic satisfaction, speaking of "the sorry spectacle of the idiotic arrogance, bloodthirsty sympathies, and conceited pretensions of the tory party, conservator of the status quo, [of] the Scots of the Banks, of bankruptcy and of the government,..." whose discomfiture he had so relished as the results of the election had rolled in. The minority, battered and beaten and in ruins, had "given to His Majesty, [in the persons of] George Auldjo, John Molson, and a few other precious relics of the British party, only a miniscule and pitiable opposition. The censure of the wicked is the panegyric of the good...." These elections, he went on, head filled with visions of the coming republic of which he would surely be the uncontested leader,

> ... impose on the elected representatives the obligation to pursue with redoubled fervour the punishment of the guilty,... reform of abuses, correction of a faulty constitution, extension of the elective system, the sole refuge of a persecuted people [who would only thus], since the fateful and bloody May 21, 1831,... escape the murderous fire of their assassins and the revolting partialities of the courts. I accept this mission with all my heart. I shall devote every instant of my life to fulfilling this mandate....[115]

Papineau was now convinced that all the aces were in his hand, that he was engaged in a movement of universal scope which would inevitably and in short order give independence to all peoples and make all men free and democratic; even in England, the radical movement would soon emerge triumphant. The election results in Upper Canada led him to believe that the reformists there must henceforth follow the same policies, aims, and strategies as the *patriotes*. When he met with Mackenzie in 1835, this is what he urged. But Mackenzie, like Roebuck and Chapman, thought of the *patriote* movement quite simply as a liberal and reformist one. As he wrote to Neilson in 1835:

> ... the idea of a French Canadian State, Province or Republic controlling the St. Lawrence and the commerce of the great countries situated on its banks is too absurd to be seriously credited. I think that freedom of trade, the free navigation of the St. Lawrence, the gradual abolition of the timber exclusive bonus, and a better and more responsible system of government in Upper and Lower Canada would prove beneficial to the population, united with general education and the abolition of monopolies....[116]

Papineau's image of himself was no longer that of spokesman only for the French-Canadian people, but also, if the occasion should arise, the voice of a minority ready to engage in much more radical action on a larger scale. Many of his followers now were taking the idea of revolution for granted. As early as 1832 a letter published in *La Minerve* declared that the party was heading in the wrong direction by seeking its objectives through peaceful means. Having criticized in particular the party's obsession with election of the legislative council, the writer continued:

> And let us think well on it: it is not simply a political question, it involves our possessions, our institutions, our language, our laws, our religion and our liberty.... After that it can be seen that there exist here two sides entirely opposed in interests and customs: the Canadians and the English. The first, born French and having French habits and character, have inherited from their forefathers hatred for the English, who detest them in their turn. These two sides will never unite and will not always remain tranquil: it is a bad amalgam of interests, customs, language, and religion which sooner or later will produce a collision; the possibility of a revolution is thought of but is thought far off. Myself, I believe it is near.... A nation subjected, unless protected by some extraordinary law, thinks not of obeying this sovereign, but the nation of the sovereign; no nation will wish to obey another for the simple reason that no nation can command another.... [117]

Papineau was convinced of the necessity of total or at least partial independence for Lower Canada, perceived as the national territory of the French Canadians, but he still believed that it could be achieved without violence. In November, 1835, *La Minerve* dutifully reported:

> We shall not desist from our requests for the plenitude of our political powers and rights.... We hope but with anxiety that the British government will eventually do justice to us. In this hope, we shall do nothing to hasten our separation from the mother country, except by preparing and leading the people toward that era, which will be neither monarchist nor aristocratic. Mr Papineau hopes with all his heart that America will give republics to Europe....[118]

A month later, when a gang of young English hoodlums had been creating trouble in Montreal, Papineau wrote to his wife: "Some of our friends in the countryside have not wanted us to hear of it because, they told themselves, so much the better if they start, we shall finish with it the faster. Some think that constitutional means alone cannot obtain us the necessary reforms and are not the least grieved to obtain them otherwise, if they are thrown on the defensive....[119]

Emerging from his heady victory of 1834, Papineau immediately set about bringing an end to the existing legislative council. His strategy was to paralyse the political system and at the same time destroy the politico-economic foundations of the bureaucracy and of the English-speaking business community. He did not abandon his defence of the traditional institutions, but rather tied it into an all-out offensive aimed at impoverishing his opponents and forcing the British government to grant the political changes demanded by the *patriotes.* The strategy was not new, only the intensity with which it was to be pursued; he had perhaps given up hope of keeping an English element in his party. In any event, his attacks on the English were concentrated on what he called their "passion for money."

His road construction programme, substitution of the Chambly Canal project for St Lawrence canals, and his sanction of the private Laprairie—St-Jean railway suggest that he had in mind a north-south orientation as an alternative to expansion toward the west, a beneficial one for French Canadians. The truth is that before 1829 his party had done its best to block British immigration to the townships. After 1825, however, the Lachine Canal had given stimulus to Montreal and Upper Canada, and also to the massive immigration and to the concentration of the English-speaking population in the cities, to say nothing of the growth of economic disparities between the ethnic groups. Efforts to encourage north-south development continued from 1829 to 1832, though it was the English-speaking who were obtaining the most benefit from it. In all this, political expediency weighed far more with Papineau than rational economic policy.

Despite his free-trade philosophy, obtained from Adam Smith, the physiocrats, and liberal economists, Papineau's economic vision was still "agriculturist," centred on population growth, access to land ownership, land-clearing, and agricultural development, on which base all development in trade and manufacturing should repose. He did not conceive that breaking the powerful English bourgeoisie might imperil the French-Canadian nation as it was at that time. His most powerful weapon, he thought, was refusal of supplies, which would bring public works to a halt. He seemed unable to realize that it was a weapon which struck not merely at the enemy but at all classes of an entire economy that already was weak. In 1836 the surveyor Louis Legendre wrote to Neilson:

... the outrageous pretentions of the majority of the provincial assembly to having immediate redress of supposed grievances [by] refusing supplies... is ruining the habitants of the country in general.... For when it comes to selling goods and chattels and land by order of justice all is sacrificed for less than a quarter of their value.... In my opinion, if there were less advocates and notaries in the House and more habitant farmers things would go infinitely better....[120]

Papineau exhorted not only his party but also the entire French-Canadian population to participate in paralysing trade and the political system, by breaking all ties with those whose interests and aspirations were not theirs, by refusing to buy English woollens and other textiles, by building breweries and distilleries so as not to drink imported and English-manufactured beverages, which, he pipe-dreamed, would stimulate crop rotation and restore land fertility.[121]

He attacked the British American Land Company for refusing new land to French Canadians. He attacked the banks, threatening to refuse renewal of their charters and urging *patriotes*, who formed the mass of their small clientèle, to withdraw their money from them, because, he said, they were the tools of anti-French-Canadian elements, favoured the English-speaking over the French-speaking, and aided big business at the expense of small. He called on every *Canadien* worthy of the name to participate in the campaign against the legislative council, the symbol of colonial and English-speaking power: "You are the most numerous consumers; buy only from your friends; urge the country merchant and the farmer to buy only from your friends. Be assured that these methods [if] continued for some time, will suffice with the constitutional opposition that your representatives will offer a corrupt government to have it quickly replaced by that which you have asked for...."[122]

Reacting to circumstances and goaded by the revolutionary elements of his party, Papineau closed his mind to compromise and pictured his movement succeeding through systematic organization "of discontent and agitation." It was a policy of blackmail, boycott, and political obstruction intended to keep socio-political tension at a maximum. Governor Aylmer's recall and the arrival of Gosford as both governor and head of a royal commission of inquiry brought no change in his state of mind. After meeting with one of the commissioners he wrote to his wife that he foresaw the approach of a time of terrible crisis and suffering: "We have never had justice in the past[;] we shall never have it in the future.... Thus, from those English who wish to give us justice we learn over the years that for us our nationality has disadvantages...."[123]

There were moments of optimism for Papineau; when, for instance, he saw the Upper-Canadian reformists modelling their activities on those of the *patriotes*. But the untimely disclosure of the royal commissioners' instructions, the publication of their report, and Lord John Russell's Ten Resolutions virtually removed all hope of obtaining the reforms by constitutional means. Following the publication of the report he declared:

> If the liaison with the mother country could bring good fortune to the colony, if it could bring it prosperity, it would be right to continue a liaison which nevertheless ought inevitably to cease in time. But such refusals have shown that a kind of loyalty is demanded which would require the renunciation of the good fortune of Canadians [in favour of] the fallacy, pride and greed of the civil servants in the mother country and in the colony. Loyalty thus understood has received its death blow with the reports of the commissioners ... and loyalty for Canada always and in all circumstances has received the greatest stimulus and an irresistible vitality....[124]

Without being basically a believer in revolutionary action, Papineau was engaged in a strategy which obliged him to become used to the idea of revolution and to accept its necessity, should methods of ordinary political usage fail. The hour of truth was approaching. He hesitated still, but by the spring of 1837 he found himself virtually imprisoned in a situation which demanded revolutionary action. Henceforth constitutional methods were a mere cover for more radical action.

After the 1834 election the *patriote* movement lost much of its following; English-speaking sympathizers, alarmed by the virulent nationalism of the most militant *patriotes*, deserted to the other camp, and even certain influential French-Canadian *patriotes* desisted. Lafontaine himself, who was ambitious but not one of the doctrinaire radicals, developed serious doubts about the emphasis on the defence of the seigneurial régime. In February, 1837, he wrote to Chapman:

> Peoples have reconquered their natural independence, by recourse to arms and spilling the blood of their oppressors.... To arouse the people we cannot simply wave the banner of purely abstract questions. There must be something more substantial. We must touch the sensitive spot: the purse. As long as a question of this nature is not raised, agitation cannot be constant and lasting. In the circumstances, I see nothing better to achieve this end than the question of the abolition of seigneurial rights. The seigneurs and the government excepted, everyone wishes it, whatever their political shade. I

am therefore firmly decided to bring forward the proposal at the opening of our next session. The government, the seigneurs, and *the important little aristocrats of both parties* will no doubt oppose it; but the masses will unite and act in concert...."[125]

The radicals, because the developing situation was serving them well, did not share Lafontaine's doubts. Some other *patriotes*, however, began to denounce Papineau's dictatorial power and the grasp of his family on the party, even talking of a "Family Compact." In 1836 Papineau was worried over the defections and wondered "if there were new circumstances in the political situation of the country which might justify those seemingly deserting the cause of the homeland, and separating themselves from this immense majority of their fellow citizens...."[126]

In Montreal the desertions little troubled the *patriote* movement. Apart from the English-speaking, the instances were isolated and without immediately profound effect. Dissidence among the leaders of the Quebec region, on the other hand, was significant. Papineau himself remained very powerful there; he had managed to discredit Andrew Stuart and Neilson in 1834 by claiming that their attacks on abuses and corrupt men had been contrived, that their short-lived friendship for the Canadians had in fact been calculated to serve their own ends and their hearts had not really been in it.[127] Beginning in 1835, however, the defections of Quebec region leaders began to be serious and led finally to a rupture which served the *patriote* movement ill at a time when it needed strength throughout the province. Papineau attributed the conflict to the poisoned atmosphere of Quebec where everything turned about the Château St-Louis, for him a hotbed of corruption, patronage, and every kind of opportunism. In February, 1836, he wrote to his wife, "Will the heated division at the beginning of the week have vexing consequences for all the rest of the session? Will all our advocates be pandering beyond conscience to our elegant commissioners in their desire for the three-cornered hat [of King's Counsel]? Their ladies too would like to see them have it. It is so nice to be in the glittering first rank at the balls at the Château St-Louis...."[128]

Patronage may well have had something to do with the disunity in his party, but Papineau seems to have forgotten that one of the principal goals common to the élite leaders of the party had long been to control and benefit by patronage. The friction between Quebec and Montreal was more fundamental; tensions and the sources of radicalism were more severe in Montreal. The Quebec leaders, among whom Etienne Parent, editor of *Le Canadien*, was a moderating influence, began to feel that Papineau was going too fast and too far. They had been quick to suggest sending him to England in 1835. The Montrealers had smelled a rat. Boucher-Belleville had written to Duvernay:

> Is there in the House, apart from Papineau, a man so outstanding above the other members, that a speaker may be elected without division among the patriotes? What is to be feared [is that] those of Quebec will want Bédard or Caron elected and those of Montreal Morin or Lafontaine. Four or five cliques could form among the patriotes and then all would be lost.... Besides, are not a great number of patriotes retained by the great name, the great talents, the immense influence of Mr Papineau[?] I would fear Papineau's departure more than a governor like Dalhousie or Aylmer, more than a tory ministry. In short, we are in a sorry state, yet there are still great chances of success. But in my opinion, with Papineau gone there would be none....[129]

Papineau flattered the Quebeckers, tried to fan their patriotic flame, even threatened to stir up revolt among their electors. Yielding to the pressure, Caron resigned as member for the Upper Town. There were reconciliations but they did not last, and the gulf between the factions kept widening, with the Quebeckers even drawing the Montreal dissidents to their side. In February, 1836, Charles-Ovide Perreault wrote to Duvernay, "If you could see how men like Vanfelson, Bleury, Huot, Caron, Dubord, etc., cry victory to see Mr Papineau in a majority of 1 or 3 on such an important question! The fools, they think they are as great as he because they are by his side."[130]

In the 1836 by-election to replace Caron, the *patriote* camp was in such disarray that it could run no better a candidate than an ineffectual Dr J. Painchaud against Andrew Stuart, who won because so many French-Canadian electors abstained. In contrast to the 1834 election, only 58 per cent of the French-speaking electors voted, while 76 per cent of the English-speaking went to the polls. The abstentions were most marked among the French-speaking élite, whereas the English-speaking élite turned out in force. The small French-Canadian vote was undoubtedly due to confusion and uncertainty created by the friction in the leading ranks of the *patriote* party (see Table 75). A similar situation was produced the following year in the Lower Town when Vanfelson was defeated by Munn, a wealthy shipbuilder. This time Irish abstentions determined the result.

The concentration of the French-Canadian vote in the 1836 by-election remained extremely high (92 per cent), particularly among businessmen and tradesmen, suggesting that the élite and not the masses were responding to the conflict between the Montreal and

Quebec *patriotes*. Since the conflict turned more on strategy than fundamental convictions, Quebec dissidents chose to stand back rather than to defect to the other side. The result was that the region was left without real leadership when revolution came, a deficiency for which the Montreal leaders were unable to provide an adequate remedy. Significantly, the English-speaking voted massively for Stuart in 1836. Apparently the Irish and liberal English were now seeing in the *patriote* movement nothing but French-Canadian nationalism.

CHAPTER 10

The Paralysis of the Political System
(Part Three)

The Defence of the Imperial System

Despite its internal crises over leadership, the *patriote* party appeared to be constantly on the initiative and to be moving triumphantly from victory to victory. None of the governors succeeded, as Craig had done, in breaking its strength through divisive tactics. The *patriotes* had the power to paralyse the political system and also to force their adversaries to commit blunders, or at the very least to endure the odium of obstruction. Their electoral successes allowed them to proclaim their representativeness at every opportunity and point with derision at their opponents' lack of it. Said Papineau in 1831, "We see here in this House property immovable and movable, trade, manufacturing, in a word all social interests represented. The Legislative Council represents what other interests? None but self-interest, the greed of people in power."[1] He and his lieutenants, who were often accused of being mere errand boys of a social minority pretending to represent an entire ethnic group, identified the "bureaucratic party," as they termed it, with a minority spawned by political patronage, the ooze, so to speak, of the imperial system, a minority with no roots whatever in the local society. With such a caricature of the enemy, so useful as the image of evil in diverting popular attention, they saw cohesion and total identity of interests where the reality of situations was often more fluid and complex, and underestimated the enemy's resilience to both political and economic pressure. The *patriote* leaders' principal error was indeed their persistence in seeing economic power as a pure emanation of political power.

Frederick Elliott's analysis seems more realistic.[2] He discerned two factions within the English party. One, comprised of senior government functionaries, appears to have been approaching the terminal phase of decline:

> The Official—or as the French term it—Bureaucratic party is com-
> posed of a few old men, holding the highest offices. They seem to
> be fond of privilege, jealous of interference, and ready to take
> offence at any inquiry into the popular allegations. Most of them are
> dull, and those who are the reverse, are said to be interested. It is of
> very little consequence what they are. Whatever influence they may
> have formerly exercised, through the instrumentality of weak Gov-
> ernors, they are now destitute of any of the real elements of power,
> having neither connections at home, nor weight in the Province.

In the merchant arm of the party Elliott saw no such decline:

> Very different from this feeble Corps, is the real "English party." It
> is composed of almost all the Merchants, with an admixture of
> considerable Landholders, and of some of the younger and more
> intelligent Civil Officers. It possesses much intelligence, much
> wealth and still more credit, and in addition to these, it has all that
> mutual confidence, and that precision and unity of purpose, which
> to do our countrymen justice, they know better than any other
> people how to confer on political associations.

Far from considering the English party as a coalition of interests con-
ciliable in all matters, Elliott had distinct doubts about the solidarity
of the ties uniting the merchants to the government and the empire; it
was their economic interests, he conceived, which conditioned their
loyalty, and he was not optimistic for the future.

> Yet I do not like the English party. It is fully as ambitious of domin-
> ion as the French party, and, in my opinion, prepared to seek it by
> more unscrupulous means. Whenever either of the two, at the pres-
> ent moment, speaks of separation, I look upon it as mere bombast,
> or artifice to bend the course of Government, but depend upon it
> that if ever these heats in Lower Canada should go so far as to
> hazard the connection with the Mother Country, the English will be
> the foremost to cut the tie. They, of the two parties, are the best
> disposed to sympathize with Republican principles; and, I must
> add, the most capable to wield Republican Institutions. They are
> the most rancorous, for they remember the power they have lost,
> and hate their rivals as a sort of usurpers.

There is no doubt that the party was first and foremost an English-speaking party, and drew its support from the English-speaking population. Yet its social composition as described by Elliott had an appeal for certain of the French Canadians. And in 1835, after its crippling electoral defeat of the year before, it was still fighting doggedly to recover the political power it had lost twenty years earlier.

By 1815, the party had become the tool of social groups which, by virtue of their interests and values, were firmly attached to the imperial system and held conservative views regarding the operation of political institutions in the colonial milieu. The civil servants, most of them English-speaking and many of them English expatriates, felt genuinely threatened by increasing French-Canadian claims to government employment, and most of all by the growing strength of the Canadian party with its political theories envisaging the ultimate conquest of power and control of patronage. Many were clever and competent, but, with an increasing number of others aspiring to join their ranks, they were both envied and distrusted for their arbitrary behaviour, particularly concerning their self-perpetuation. Along with the military "establishment," they were the hard core of political conservatism, the most susceptible to ethnic and religious prejudice, the most inclined to look down on the local population, the most committed to monarchy, aristocracy, and Anglican Church privileges. For those French Canadians dedicated to authority, monarchy, and aristocracy, their conservative attitudes exerted a strong appeal.

English merchant conservatism was of different source. In the difficult context following the Revolutionary and Napoleonic wars, this group's preoccupation was economic development based on Lower Canada's forest resources and cultivation of new farmland in the townships and in Upper Canada. This would require large-scale immigration, infusion of considerable capital, road construction, and above all a St Lawrence canal system. Easing prices and intense American competition, particularly with the completion of the Erie Canal, emphasized the urgency of economic development in an east-west direction, if Upper Canada were not to turn toward the United States. For such development a continuing British market, with preferential tariffs on timber and grain, was essential, as was a banking system; major obstacles were seen in the seigneurial régime, old French customary law, and the absence of land registry offices. As long as capitalist interests failed to gain strength in the legislative assembly, realization of such development, and the defence of preferential tariffs which were then under attack in England, appeared impossible. With its dependence on the colonial system, the English-speaking business community simply could not subscribe to political theories designed to change the colony's relationship with the mother country. Perhaps most stimulating to this group's conservatism and British loyalty was its impotence in an elected assembly dominated by a party hostile to its vision of economic development.

In 1815 only 20 per cent of the assembly were English-speaking and only 25 per cent were English party members; only in the cities, in the two minor urban areas, and in certain seigneurial ridings was the party able to elect members. Through the Taschereaus and Caldwell it was strong in Dorchester, and in Trois-Rivières through the Bell and Hart families; in Sorel and Bedford the Joneses were still in control, as were the seigneurs Cuthbert and Dumont in Warwick and York. Thus, the party that was committed to the balance of powers theory was virtually bound to seek intimacy with the executive and with the legislative council.

Craig and Prevost, with their emphasis on the balance of powers, had undoubtedly been seeking that balance in their appointments to the legislative and executive councils. In 1811 there were ten English and only four French executive councillors; the French were all seigneurs and the English were senior civil servants, judges, important merchants, and the Anglican bishop. Prevost's seven appointments did not change the ethnic ratio. Some of the executive councillors were also members of the legislative council, which comprised six French-Canadian seigneurs and aristocrats and seven English senior civil servants and judges.[3] Prevost's appointments increased the aristocratic character of the body. Clearly, even the governors who were considered liberal and sympathetic to the French were preoccupied with neutralizing the popular tendencies of the Canadian party, the majority in the assembly, though the community of interests linking the English party leaders, the legislative council, and the governors was neither automatic nor complete. That conjugation of powers, however, was insufficient to force the hand of the majority in the assembly; in fact, each of the two power blocs could only stall the initiatives of the other, for the system reposed on compromise and conciliation.

Since the English party could not rely on wide distribution of electoral support, even among the English-speaking, its quest for power was always precariously based, and the legitimacy of that power open to question. When Governor Sir Gordon Drummond dissolved the assembly in 1816 on instructions from London, the English party was in fact the loser, for the English electorate was even less cohesive than before and though the new assembly differed little from its predecessor in composition, its tone was more radical. Drummond's successor, Sir John Sherbrooke, wrote, "I cannot avoid submitting to Your Lordship my humble opinion that, in this country, where there is no room for the exertion of Salutary government influence such as exists in

England, the strong measure of a dissolution must in almost all possible circumstances of the country produce rather evil than advantage...."[4]

Sherbrooke would use neither dissolution nor the legislative council against the Canadian party. For him, diplomacy was by far the more effective measure. Like Prevost, he saw a moderating influence in the clergy and appointed Bishop Plessis to an enlarged legislative council, hoping to profit by the prelate's influence both there and with the assembly, and to restore the council's respectability in the eyes of the French Canadians. Turning to the Canadian party, he encouraged Papineau's rise to leadership, for he considered James Stuart to be the principal fomenter of current political problems. In his eyes, Papineau was sincere, malleable, and moderate; he even proposed his appointment to the executive council. Having analysed the financial situation, he recognized that the colonial government could not function normally without the co-operation of the party in control of the assembly, and in 1818 proposed a compromise involving the civil list. In fact, so concerned was he for conciliation that he missed the real significance of the struggle for political power and played straight into the Canadian party's hands. Papineau's amenability proved to be only skin-deep and short-lived.

Sherbrooke was forced by illness to withdraw. His successor, the Duke of Richmond, in whom the English party had cause to have greater confidence, had powerful connections and a pressing need to repair the state of his coffers. He held himself and his prestige as the king's representative in high esteem, but was all too susceptible to pressure from his entourage. He espoused the cause of the English party entirely, arrogantly, and perhaps without forethought. Against the Canadian party he used the traditional weapons of recourse to the legislative council to block dangerous bills and dissolution of the assembly to obtain modification of its composition. The two elections he provoked, however, did nothing to improve the popularity of the English party, even among English and Irish voters. And when Lord Dalhousie became governor in 1820 the climate of confrontation worsened even further, with both sides making reprisals.

Dalhousie had been administrator of the peaceful province of Nova Scotia. Of Lower Canada he said, "I find it a country most sadly distressed by party spirit, national jealousies, political speculators and general poverty in all classes and conditions of people." He was a Presbyterian Scot, serious and intelligent, and a man of good intentions but cold exterior. He perceived many abuses and at first hoped earnestly to correct them with complete impartiality. He determined to take control of the distribution of local patronage away from London and assure its equal distribution between the ethnic groups. He envisioned reform of the executive council, to which Papineau was appointed, in order to gain the population's confidence in it and make it work. He expected to obtain like results with all government institutions. In a situation free of conflict he might have done well, but he was not prepared to compromise where he encountered antagonism. The slightest opposition or even hesitation would throw him into a towering rage. He took too many things personally, as demonstrated when he discovered Receiver-General Henry Caldwell's prevarication over accounts. He and Papineau regarded each other with mutual dislike. The balance of powers was once again the governor's preoccupation;[5] he expected each individual to fulfil the role which he, Dalhousie, would assign, and if peace and harmony did not ensure, ambition and ill-will were responsible. He was due for bitter disappointment, of course.

Dalhousie's hatred of opponents of any ilk took on a strong ethnic tone as opposition came regularly from the Canadian party leaders. Soon he realized that the quarrel over money votes was part of the political power struggle. He was horrified by the pretensions of the Canadian party, which he considered a rabble of illiterate and ignorant peasants led by the nose by a handful of ambitious, dishonourable, and dishonest advocates. All very French, thought he, and completely foreign to British respectability. His hostility toward Papineau, whose native intelligence he recognized, became particularly intense. Failing to perceive the weaknesses in the enemy's ranks, he came to view the French-Canadian society as a virtually monolithic bloc, with the clergy united firmly with the Canadian party agitators. In a great many intrigues he even suspected Monseigneur Plessis's hand at work. Nevertheless, he negotiated at length with the prelate, particularly over the Royal Institution, but without observing or profiting from the many points of common interest between the clergy and the government. By now practically a party faction leader himself, he suspected the curés of intervening in elections and attributed many defeats to them. Monseigneur Lartigue, in his eyes, besides being cousin to his two *bêtes noires*, Papineau and Viger, was especially hateful, a religious and political agitator busily sowing discord in a society already over-endowed with demagogues. In fact, Lartigue, Papineau, and Dalhousie had much in common psychologically.

Despite Dalhousie's initial intention to remain impartial, the supply question drew him to the English party camp, and even there he found enemies. His sympathy lay mostly with the Scottish merchants of Montreal.[6] In the circumstances, he was obliged to seek support from the two councils, and his appointments to them increased their partisan and English character. Papineau attended a few executive council meetings and then withdrew, partly perhaps because he did not want to live permanently in Quebec. Charles De Léry was Dalhousie's only other French-Canadian appointee to the body.

New members were appointed to the legislative council in the same ethnic proportion, contrary to tradition; only Toussaint Pothier and J.-T. Taschereau found favour with the governor. To Dalhousie's annoyance, he found the French and even some of the English legislative councillors lacking in appropriate docility; a number of them were distressed and alarmed both by the governor's attitude and the extremism of their "bureaucratic" colleagues. The legislative council therefore divided into two factions, whose positions hardened during the crisis of 1822, and the division was to remain. The individuals who had the governor's full confidence were all strongly partisan. C.R. Ogden was one of these; he controlled the town of Trois-Rivières electorally and had powerful connections in business and government circles. It was he who drew up a long list of accusations against Judge Pierre Bédard, probably in reprisal for Canadian party accusations against Judges Monk, Sewell, and Foucher. Patronage came more readily than ever before through association with the English party; Vallières de Saint-Réal, for instance, had to show himself to be the very model of moderation before being made a judge shortly after Dalhousie's departure.

It would not appear that Dalhousie had any substantial part in the preparation of the union plan of 1822, or even its arrival in London, but he was certainly in agreement with its purpose. The idea of political union was not new; frustration among the English-speaking had already brought it to the surface on occasion. Economic depression and political imbroglio in 1822 led many to attribute virtually all the post-war economic and social problems of Lower Canada to the Canadian party. The unionists condemned the 1791 constitution for permitting control of the political system to fall to an anti-commercial, French, and procedure-bound majority. The legislature of the province, they said, had been so embroiled in dissention and procedure that commerce, agriculture, education, and other matters had been neglected; there was no law for registration of property and mortgages, or to deal with insolvent debtors, or for representation of the townships, and the petitioners had little hope of obtaining these and many other measures.[7] Further, they blamed the majority in the assembly for blocking east-west development, and deplored the power of the assembly over import duties (which effectively taxed both provinces), its inflexibility over division of these revenues, and its reluctance to accept the massive investments necessary to improve transportation, thus retarding the economic expansion of the two provinces.

It [the division into two provinces] has also, from the control which the geographical situation of the Lower Province enables it to exercise over the trade of the Canadas placed the export trade of the Upper Province at its mercy being subject to such regulations and restrictions at the Shipping Port, as its Legislature may chose [sic] to impose. From this circumstance, and from the feeble attempts made to improve the grand natural channel of the Canadas strikingly contrasted with the enterprise and energy evinced by the neighbouring State of New York in the rapid formation of Canals, together with the indifference manifested on this subject by the Legislature of the Lower Province; Your petitioners have just reason for alarm that if a similar system be persisted in, it may tend in a most injurious degree to increase the Commercial Intercourse of the Upper Province with the United States and divert the enterprise and trade of its inhabitants into a foreign channel and from these causes Your Petitioners not only apprehend the immediate loss of beneficial Trade, but that the gradual effect would be to interweave the interests of Upper Canadians with those of the neighbouring States, thereby alienating their minds from Your Majesty's Government, notwithstanding their present known and tried loyalty.[8]

The importance of economic considerations to the unionists is clear. A petition from the inhabitants of the Eastern Townships expressed the local frustrations over the lack of roads, registry offices, local courts, electoral ridings, and their necessary submission to French law, which, they complained, deprived them of the instruments of development and the possibility of political action. The purpose of the dominant party in the assembly, they maintained, was to prevent development of the townships, block canalling of the St Lawrence, and force the immigrants to assimilate.

The present crisis therefore offers this alternative to Great Britain, either by uniting the Provinces to hold out inducements to the French to become English, or by continuing the separation to hold out inducements to the English in Lower Canada to become French, and the question is not whether a country already peopled is to renounce its national feelings and characteristics as the French Canadians may endeavour to represent, but whether a country for the most part waste, and to be hereafter chiefly peopled by a British race is to assume the character, language and manners of a foreign nation.[9]

The townships petitioners clearly anticipated that union of the provinces would lead to assimilation of the French Canadians by the larger group of British origin.

For all categories of unionists, whatever their particular objectives, the purpose of union was to break the Canadian party's stranglehold on the legislative assembly. The proposed bill, in its clauses on representation, shows this without a shadow of doubt. The Roman Catholic religion was to be allowed full freedom, on condition that clerical appointments have royal approval, which provision would allow stricter control over the bishops. English would be the sole official written language and eventually the sole language of debate. The old social régime was to be preserved, except that future legislators would be empowered to change it.

The English-speaking population does not seem to have been won over by the plan. Many in Lower Canada disliked the secrecy of its preparation, its punitive nature, and, for a variety of reasons, its objectives. The results of the 1824 elections suggest sharp division among English-speaking electors. The English membership in the assembly dropped from eleven to nine, six of them Canadian party members or moderates. The number of "bureaucratic party" English members was reduced from nine to three. The English-speaking vote in Quebec's Upper Town, with a large proportion of the English professionals and businessmen supporting Canadian party rather than English-speaking candidates, tends to confirm the impression (see Table 76).

Since 1815, the English-speaking population had lost much of its cohesion. The authoritarian governors Drummond, Richmond, and Dalhousie had undoubtedly helped separate the liberals from the staunch conservatives. The union plan had all too clearly shown the hand of functionaries and wealthy businessmen. Not even the majority of Upper Canadians were enthusiastic; only the businessmen of Kingston were in favour, because of their connections with the merchants of Montreal. The rest seemed to prefer to keep their political autonomy, fearing domination by the Montreal merchants and increased political dependency on Lower Canada. The British authorities knew that the French Canadians were opposed, but not that the opinion among the English-speaking was so divided.

The bill met with unexpected opposition in the British House of Commons and was set aside "for the moment," as Bathurst wrote to Dalhousie. The government considered it suitable and wise in theory, but inopportune in view of the lack of support hoped for and in the light of ensuing events.[10] What killed it was vigorous opposition in both the Canadas and from a few members of the British House.

The unionists turned to Dalhousie. In 1824 a group of Montreal inhabitants petitioned the governor to preserve at all costs the rights and prerogatives of the crown, declaring their conviction that these had safeguarded the English character of the province, and were essentail to good government and even more so to the petitioners as their principal refuge in case of danger, their protection against the French Canadians, and their sole hope of averting anarchy and chaos.[11]

The governor hardly needed urging. In his eyes the future of monarchist and aristocratic institutions depended on the outcome of the struggle for control of the public purse. He departed for England to bolster support there, leaving the diplomatic and conciliating Sir Francis Burton in charge, who, during his absence, manoeuvred a bill almost exactly corresponding to the Canadian party's demands through both the assembly and the legislative council. James Richardson announced the news to Dalhousie, stressing the powerful role played in the operation by Bishop Plessis:

> The Canadian Bishop mustered a phalanx to support the Bill whatever it might be, and to rescind my resolutions, as they are generally called. He succeeded in the former but failed in the latter, it being alleged that the Bill did not touch upon them. . . . He brought down Messrs Cuthbert and De Bartzch, got up Mr. Turgeon from below and old De Salaberry and Colonel Taschereau were brought from the brink of the grave to be present—neither having attended at any part of the sessions. . . .[12]

Dalhousie felt he had been betrayed by his entourage and by the Catholic and French-Canadian legislative councillors. On his return, which some had thought unlikely, he mobilized his forces, had Burton censured and repudiated, performed a few other imperious acts to impress the élite and the electorate in general, and prorogued the legislature, which of course meant a general election. Control of supplies, the election issue, by now clearly symbolized the defence of rights and interests—French-Canadian and nationalistic on the one side and English and bureaucratic on the other. In the election of 1827 the Dalhousie forces suffered a humiliating defeat: Simpson and the Seigneur Dumont were beaten in York; Morrison in Warwick; Hart in St-Maurice; Davidson, James Stuart, McCallum, and Després in Dorchester, Sorel, and Devon; in the three Montreal ridings, Molson, McGill, Grant, and Delisle. Outside Quebec and Montreal, the only survivors were R. Christie in Gaspé, Ogden in Trois-Rivières, and the moderates Mousseau and Cannon. In Quebec riding, Ryland was defeated by the *patriotes* Neilson and Clouet, obtaining only 10 per cent of the French vote and 49 per cent of the English, which suggests that almost all the English electors gave him their first vote and divided their second between Neilson (31 per cent) and Clouet (20 per cent) (see Table 77). Quebec's Lower Town elected one *patriote* and one English party candidate. In the Upper Town, Andrew Stuart, former *patriote* and now a moderate "bureaucrat," was the only English-speaking candidate; he and Vallières de Saint-Réal were the victors (see Table 76). The ideological positions of the candidates were unclear, but the English liberals and Irish Catholics were beginning to lean toward the English party. Stuart received only 12 per cent of the French vote and Berthelot only 6 per cent of the English; Vanfelson received 63 per cent of his vote from the English. In this riding, 99 English electors were military, civil servants, Protestant clergy, gentlemen, and merchants; they had a right to 198 votes and yet they cast only 150, 87 for Stuart, 37 for Saint-Réal (considered a "bureaucrat"), 24 for Vanfelson (judged to be reassuring) and only 2 for Berthelot (viewed as a dangerous *patriote*). The *Quebec Mercury* pronounced:

> Never have we witnessed more devotion on the part of a committee than that shown by the gentlemen who supported Mr. Stuart. The cause is obvious, independent of the esteem in which he is personally held, and the approbation due to the principle on which he grounds his public conduct, the electors of the Upper Town were indignant at the attempt made to deprive them of the power of returning one member to represent the British portion of the city....[13]

The English party emerged from the election in disarray and quite incapable of exerting any influence in the assembly. If Dalhousie had been less personally involved, he might even have felt contrary winds blowing from England. As early as July, 1827, Lord Goderich wrote him to point out that in the United Kingdom the civil list was granted for the life of the king, and the arrangement would be reasonable also in Lower Canada. He proposed that Dalhousie announce to the assembly that His Majesty did not wish the question to be a cause of discord and that Parliament would be asked to give the assembly control of all currently collected crown revenues in the province which were not already under its control.[14]

But Dalhousie seems at this point to have lost all capacity to appreciate the evolution of the political situation. He refused to accept Papineau as speaker of the House, declaring him unfit as the leader of a party with violent propensities. Papineau, considering it degrading to have a governor become *de facto* a party leader, resolved thereupon to have Dalhousie's head. Reorientation of colonial policy and further blunders by Dalhousie resulted in his recall in the spring of 1828, when he described Lower Canada as a country divided against itself, torn by racial hatred and jealousies of every sort.

His successor, Sir James Kempt, was a conciliator and compromiser and as such could not identify with the English party. Its leadership of necessity fell to a collegium, John Richardson being a member of both councils and not free to function fully as leader. The report of the British Commons committee of 1828 agreed almost entirely with the Canadian party's view on control of supply and suggested a reform of the two councils, which provided additional consternation for the English party. In conjunction with reformist thinking in England, there loomed the spectre of a total overhaul of the existing colonial system on which the hopes of the civil servants and merchants of Lower Canada were pinned.

But at least one sure source of support remained, and that was the legislative council left by Dalhousie, a body of twenty-seven of whom twenty-one were English-speaking (judges, civil servants, merchants, and the Anglican bishop) and the rest French-Canadian seigneurs and aristocrats. Its support was indeed vital to the English party during the transition period of 1828-32, when the party's influence was at a low ebb in Canada and in England, and when the majority party, now known as the *parti patriote*, was bent on disqualifying judges from both the councils. But its efficacy in obstruction and counterbalancing had been undermined by *parti patriote* strategy, for the party had shown a conciliatory attitude to some of the business community's objectives and had won a measure of sympathy from English electors. Now there were banks, the Lachine Canal had been financed, and some funds had even been voted for the Welland Canal. Between 1828 and 1831, the *patriote* party further mollified its critics by giving representation to the townships and voting considerable sums for roads and education. The projects launched, however, gave the assembly an executive function and also its own source of patronage. And the legislative council could hardly obstruct projects of such clear advantage to the business milieu.

Governor Aylmer came to Quebec in 1830 imbued with optimism and the spirit of reform and complete impartiality. "The country itself far surpasses my expectations," he wrote. "Its resources are every day unfolding themselves, with such rapidity and to such extent that it is impossible for the imagination to prescribe limits to them."[15] To Goderich he wrote, "My first and principal object has been to produce in the minds of the Canadians whatever of French or English extraction, a conviction that I am determined to act upon the principle of strict impartiality and to remain a watchful spectator of ... those party views which have caused so much strife and bad feeling in the colony."[16] He also showed great indulgence toward the old French-Canadian institutions which the English-speaking were so determined to abolish or reform. But his lack of experience and eccentricities were perplexing to many.

In his first year he tackled the complex and difficult task of reforming the two councils. He appointed Philippe Panet to the executive council and then attempted to lure Papineau to it. Having been rebuffed, he wrote to Goderich:

> It is quite impossible to go further, than I do, in condemning the Public conduct, and language of that gentleman in the House of Assembly and he must himself be well aware of this, for I have expressed myself without reserve on the subject to some of his most intimate friends, and altho as an individual I live on good (I may say cordial) terms with Mr. Papineau, whose private character I must esteem, I studiously avoid all conversation with him on the conduct of the public affairs of the Province. My recommendation of him therefore to be a member of the Executive Council, could not have proceeded from any favourable disposition towards him, as a public character, but I felt desirous, I confess, to shew Mr. Papineau, and all those who participate in his political sentiments, that the administration of the Province was free of all party connections.[17]

Papineau charged all his supporters to follow his example and resist the governor's attempts to corrupt them. Neilson obeyed, but Dominique Mondelet accepted the invitation, partly because of pressure from clerical circles, and earned himself scorn and rejection from the hard-core *patriotes*. He was followed shortly by H. Heney, another disenchanted *patriote*, to whom Aylmer wrote, "I have nothing more at heart in my administration of this government than to surround myself with every thing that is respectable and talented in the country *de toutes les couleurs*."[18]

Aylmer also tried to change and improve the legislative council. In 1831 D.-B. Viger and Louis Guy were appointed to it along with two English merchants. Two years later, eleven new members were named, eight French Canadians, all seigneurs and aristocrats, and three English merchants, and the following year François Quirouet and Joseph Masson, both merchants, were named. Papineau promptly pronounced that the new council was worse than the old. On revenues, Aylmer met with obstinate silence from Papineau, who declared that their control was no longer a priority.

Aylmer was not unaware that his attempts at reform were failing because the *patriote* movement was steadily assuming a more radical stance; in 1831 he attributed its leaders' behaviour "to a latent desire to dissolve the existing connection with Great Britain."[19] Two years later when their ideology and purpose had become more clearly defined, he wrote to Glenelg:

> It is very evident that Mr. Papineau and his party have taken up new ground, for they no longer confine themselves to false or exaggerated statement of abuses in the administration of the existing government; their avowed object is now to alter the whole frame of the Constitution and Government of the colony; to render the former purely democratic and the latter purely elective.... Mr. Papineau indeed goes a step beyond his coadjutor the Hon. Mr. Debartzch for, according to him, the office of governor like every other office in the colony should be elected.[20]

In 1834 he wrote to Spring-Rice: "It is now evident that His Majesty's Government will have to encounter fresh opposition from the House of Assembly, which I cannot refrain from repeating, is not to be satisfied with any concessions on the part of the Mother Country, short of the total abandonment of the Government into the hands of Mr. Papineau and Company."[21] In November he wrote bluntly that the 1834 elections had "assumed a feature of nationality unknown on former similar occasions,"[22] and a month later he saw a crisis fast approaching: "I believe the line of separation between the contending parties here has never been so thoroughly marked as at the present time...."[23]

Though Aylmer had grasped the nature and characteristics of the power struggle, he failed to appreciate the extent of the *patriote* party's hold over the population, assuming that it depended only on the leaders' ability to delude the lower classes. His arrival had coincided with the party's period of revision of ideology and strategy, and the internal party tensions had registered with him as being of great significance. He was convinced that the deceit which bound the people to the party's oligarchy was about to be revealed for what it was. As early as 1831 he was predicting disintegration of the party, writing to Kempt: "Circumstances which occurred during the Session just terminated had very much lowered the party who hitherto has been paramount in the House of Assembly.... Certainly the House of Assembly has taken up a new character and I am much mistaken if the members will suffer themselves any longer to be led by the nose as they have hitherto been by a few individuals."[24] In June, 1832, he wrote to Goderich in the same vein:

Upon a careful review of passing events I am much disposed to entertain favourable anticipation in regard to the tranquillity of the Province. The Ultra Liberal party (or as it is termed here the Papineau party) are going to great lengths and will probably in the end disgust, or estrange from them many who have hitherto acted with them. They are discountenanced by the clergy and as they seek to draw a line between the British inhabitants and the Canadians of French extraction, the former will unite and rally around the Government.[25]

In the autumn of the same year he was foreseeing the possibility of a third, more moderate party:

... there is good ground to hope that a *third* and most powerful party may be created. One that shall combine all that is respectable and talented amongst the French Canadians and the British established in the colony; and which if once declared would soon extinguish the influence of the Ultra's on either side. It is to be observed however that in endeavouring to accomplish this desirable object the prejudices and feelings of the French Canadians require to be treated with great delicacy.[26]

The increasingly radical stance of the *patriote* party, Aylmer was convinced, was merely revealing desperate efforts by the party leaders to keep their organization alive and moving. In late November, 1832, he told Goderich, "The fact is, that Mr. Papineau and his party felt that they are daily losing ground in Public estimation; and their only chance of recovering it is to provoke a prorogation...."[27] This interpretation was held by many in England until late 1834 and even after. Wrote James Stephen, Under-Secretary of the Colonial Office, in September:

It is, I apprehend, to this circumstance, and to the consequent apprehension that their Power was in danger, that the more recent proceedings of Mr. Papineau and his associates are to be ascribed. They perceived not only their stock of grievances but the number, the weight of their adherents, rapidly diminishing, and it became necessary to find means of fomenting a quarrel, which might otherwise have been extinguished to the entire overthrow of their own importance.[28]

Aylmer held to his interpretation throughout his term of office, and remained unperturbed by increasing calls to arms and talk of revolu-

tion in 1835. He was sure that the people were loyal to Great Britain
and had nothing in common with the Americans, and that the agitators lacked the strength to undertake a revolution. Inevitably, since he
opposed the *patriote* ideology, he was drawn into party politics and in
his appointments gave serious consideration to political affiliation. His
appointment of Samuel Gale to the bench was approved by the British
authorities, who felt it necessary however to remark: "... that when
any future occasion may arise for recommending an appointment of
this kind, your Lordship will weigh [scrupulously] the claims of those
who may be considered as the fitting candidates, and that you will not
allow any circumstances to interfere with the fair pretensions of the
French Canadian portion of the Bar whenever they can be satisfactorily
supported."[29]

Two weeks later, Aberdeen asked Aylmer to withhold the an-
nouncement of Gale's appointment until he could announce a French
Canadian as successor to Judge Kerr: "This just and equal distribution
of office will afford a practical proof of your impartiality.... "[30] The
governor had in fact, despite his original intent, become too politically
involved. As Stephen remarked," ... when, as in Canada, the distinctions of national character and descent coincide with those of parties
in the State, the observance of [certain] maxims assumes the sem-
blance and incurs the reproach of national antipathy and prejudice."[31]

As the *patriote* movement became more and more radical, it was
inevitable that the English party, the legislative council, and the governor would renew their alliance. Individuals in favour of preservation of
the monarchy and aristocracy and opposed to the idea of independence,
however acquired, were bound to rally round the government and the
party which supported it. The "bureaucrat" leaders quickly grasped the
real implications of *patriote* party strategy; behind talk of abstract principles there was, as always, thought of other things. Thus, John Richardson opposed the incorporation of Montreal, which he might have
welcomed as a normal development, because, he said, whereas he admired all the constitutional branches when they worked together, in the
province there seemed to be a disposition and determination to gather
all the power of the country to the popular branch.[32] In other words, he
was alarmed at the thought of the administration of Montreal and all the
local institutions falling into the hands of the *patriote* party. It was not
the peasants and working classes but the French-Canadian middle
classes which the English milieu dreaded finding in control of all the
real political power. This is reflected in the results of the by-election in
Quebec's Upper Town in 1829, and also in the Lower Town vote in
1832 (see Tables 78 and 79).

When the *patriote* party began openly to show its partiality for republicanism and to demand election of the legislative council, political debate became even more violent than ever. B.C. Gugy, the member for Sherbrooke, a moderate who voted occasionally with the *patriote* party and one of the few assembly members who could stand up to Papineau, replied vigorously to the attacks on the council, as reported in *La Minerve*:

> Men, when gathered in a body, cannot invariably have the same sentiments, and though the idea might here appear heretical, it lent support to his argument.... That the king should create peers was an integral part of the English constitution. But the king was only the regulator between the two other principles comprised in a limited monarchy: democracy which was represented by the commons and the aristocracy by the lords, and these elements had been so well placed that, for over a century, the veto had never been exercised by the royal authority.... Experience in all countries proved that an intermediary body was necessary, but if this body becomes elective, it will be under the control of the people and thus the balance will be broken. It has been said that the people had the influence [ultimate power]: yes, undoubtedly, but that influence must have limits. In a word, the democratic branch must be held in check by the wealthy and educated class which always has an interest in the prosperity of the entire State.[33]

With his traditional view of representative institutions, Gugy accused the *patriotes* of cultivating ideas which would lead inevitably to armed revolution:

> When they laud their republican institutions to us, I prefer this [our] paternal and protective government which does not produce disorder and anarchy. Republics cannot survive for long. Excessive liberty gives rise to riots, defiance in the populace, and soon there come revolutions, butchery, and anarchy. The United States already gives a thousand examples that their system cannot be a durable one and is inadequate.[34]

Neither the seigneur Gugy nor the merchant Richardson were political theorists, but neither entertained any illusions regarding the *patriote* leaders' intentions. "Thirst for position has made this warfare," Gugy said bluntly.[35] He accused Papineau of wanting power for himself, for the leaders of his party, and for French Canadians to the exclusion of all others. Replying to the *patriote* leader on the Ninety-two Resolutions, he said in the House:

Passion sometimes dominates public men; [and it] makes them say: move over so I can take that place, I want to rule, I want to dominate, I want to occupy the rank of that miserable, lily-livered, despicable English faction.... Is there any more convincing proof of our liberty than the venomous and insulting terms he [feels free to use] against what he calls an English faction, when it curbs his plans of aggrandizement... [?] I say that the passions of a man who believes that everything is made for him, that the sun and the moon shine only for him are dangerous and deadly.[36]

Gugy, who proclaimed himself a *Canadien* of English origin, assumed the role of spokesman for the English-speaking, both native-born and immigrant: "They say those of English origin are few. Those of French origin are not the only Canadians, though. I grant that they are virtuous; I allow them what is theirs; I am ready to come to their defence on occasion; but I do not consider that I should be the object of persecution if I venture to believe that those who do not think as the hon. speaker have rights as inhabitants of this country."[37] On the *patriotes'* insistence on election of the legislative council he said:

... I would be convinced that the elective council would have disadvantages. In a country where we see the speaker of one of the branches of the legislature appeal so often to passions and where the majority of inhabitants are of French origin, if the council were elective, who would represent our fellow subjects who come from England, who have the same rights as we and are Canadians like us[?] There would be a council and a house which would [both] be motivated by the same sentiments, sentiments like those already stated, when it has been made a crime for a very respectable public servant to have an English name and he has been dismissed for that reason.[38]

The idea of an elective legislative council was regarded with great alarm by the English-speaking. "The Canadians of British origin," wrote James Stephen, "have been... accustomed to look to the Legislative Council for defence against the partiality which they ascribe to the members of the House of Assembly...."[39]

From 1832 on, the English party made concerted efforts to obtain unanimity in the vote of the English-speaking and any others concerned for the rights of minorities. During the 1834 election campaign in Quebec's Upper Town, Andrew Stuart made undisguised appeals for such unanimity.

The questions were, first, if those of British origin (and he had not yet learned to be ashamed of such a name) should have any share in the representation? The second was, whether the circumstance of his vote against the 92 resolutions (It is only because you have an English name? [question from an elector]) was alone sufficient to deprive him of his election? If such were the case a man must go to the House and move like an automaton.... He would say that it was a great national effort of the Canadians to deprive the English portion of society of their moderate share of the representation....[40]

Significantly, English-speaking voters each cast only an average of 1.3 votes of the possible 2.0 (the first undoubtedly for Stuart), whereas the French-speaking cast 1.9. The other two candidates were both French-Canadian *patriotes*: Caron, former mayor of Quebec, who had earned much gratitude for his efforts during the cholera epidemic, obtained roughly a third of the second English-speaking vote, and Berthelot, the radical *patriote*, only 5 per cent. It would seem that there was still some confusion among the Irish working class over the issues at stake (see Table 78).

The 1834 general election was disastrous for the English party, for not a single one of its members was returned to the assembly from the cities or the seigneuries. Its only members were returned by the townships, and most of those were moderates. On the other hand, a relatively large number of English-speaking candidates were elected under the *patriote* banner. The royal commissioners sent to Lower Canada in August, 1835, to try to resolve the constant troubles observed that the French-Canadian-dominated assembly had been defending popular rights and liberal institutions, while the predominantly English legislative council seemed to have been upholding arbitrary power and outmoded political doctrines; this, they were convinced, was why most former Americans had been siding with the French rather than with the English. The members for Stanstead and Missisquoi had been sent to the assembly not to defend the feudal system, protect the French language, or oppose land registry, but to aid the defenders of popular rights and oppose a government which found American emigrants irksome and had neglected them.[41]

Since it could no longer even pretend to speak for urban interests, the English party could hope for a measure of credibility only in identifying with the defence of English-speaking interests in general. The wind was in fact beginning to blow in the direction of stronger ethnic polarization; English-speaking liberals and Irish Catholics appear to have been returning to the English party fold. In the 1836 by-election in Quebec's Upper Town, for example, 96 per cent of the English-speaking electors voted for Stuart and 92 per cent of the French voted for Painchaud. In the autumn of 1834, James Stephen, who tended to overemphasize the ethnic factor, analysed the political situation:

> Parties in Canada have followed to a great extent the original division of the inhabitants into the French and English races. Some few of the leading opponents of the Provincial Government were indeed Englishmen by birth, and, on the other hand, some French names were to be found in the list of its adherents; but the opposition which, under other circumstances, Lord Dalhousie's measures would have incurred from English settlers, was silenced by the deeper motives which separated the two races from each other. The electoral divisions of the country had thrown into the hands of the French almost the whole representation, while the English held a large proportion of all the places of honour and emolument. The one were all powerful in the Assembly and the other in the Legislative Council. The French held, as seigneuries, all the finer parts of the province, while the English settlers formed a distinct community in that region which is called the townships. The French were in possession of all collegiate and ecclesiastical endowments, while the English had seized upon every lucrative branch of foreign commerce.... The feelings of repugnance were probably at first confined very much to agitators on either side, who, however, of course drew the mass of population after them.[42]

At least the crippled English party could count on support from the governor and the legislative council. In retaliation for the assembly's refusal of money supplies and threats of strikes, the council could block the assembly's bills and did so, for instance, in refusing renewal of the Assembly Schools Act. But in the meantime, civil servants were not getting paid and the economy was going from bad to worse. Neilson and Stuart set to work founding constitutional associations in as many localities as possible with a view to promoting a new political party. In 1835 Neilson went to England. H. Heney, ex-*patriote* and now executive councillor, wrote to him:

> I know that you will ask nothing that is not reasonable. You consider, as we considered in 1828, that there are abuses, that there are abuses in all man's institutions; that by the very fact that [institutions] are human it is legitimate to correct and do away with abuses by all decent and honest means, without recourse to sedition and revolt; that we must repair the House [we live in] and not demolish

it; that young men are not the best counsellors on serious matters; that the elective principle, though good in itself, will be very injurious when exploited for purposes of national hatreds, religious disputes or other interested motivations.[43]

Neilson's mission was to convince the British authorities that the plight of Lower Canada was a result of the policies of the *parti patriote*, to urge continuance of the preferential tariffs. and particularly to plead for a solution to the impasse over control of revenues along the lines suggested by the British Commons committee in 1828. He was also to recommend an executive council composed of government department heads, which should be representative and yet independent of the assembly, and a legislative council whose control would not be allowed to fall into the hands of the major landowners and which would act primarily as the voice of commercial interests. His instructions from the Quebec constitutional association stated in part:

The members of the Constitutional Association claim no privileges over their fellow subjects of another origin; but the experience of the late years has shewn a determination on the part of the majority of the Assembly of that origin to make of the power which this repeal has vested them with, an instrument for controlling the metropolitan government, and for reducing their fellow subjects of British and Irish origin to a condition of inferiority without regard to the public utility or the principle of equal justice.... In considering the public affairs of this country it can never be lost sight with any safety that the population is not homogeneous, and those rules which may be pursued with safety in a country whose population is homogeneous will lead to dangerous consequences in a country whose population is composed of two large and unequal and heterogeneous masses of people.[44]

Besides the constitutional associations, there appeared clubs founded by hotheads, which contributed to political tensions. A "British Rifle Corps" of ultra-loyalist young men sowed great alarm in the population and was promptly dissolved by Gosford; it was succeeded by the Doric Club, of slightly less bellicose mien. French and English newspapers engaged in virulent verbal warfare inciting violence.

The political paralysis had reached such a state in 1835 that the British government recalled Aylmer and replaced him with Lord Gosford. Gosford came both as governor and as chairman of a royal commission of inquiry, whose other members were Sir Charles Grey and Sir George Gipps. The new executive head's role was to conciliate, temporize, and inform the authorities on administrative matters yet to be decided. The British government had a fairly clear picture of the situation, and though not disposed to go as far as to allow an independent French-Canadian republic, made it known that it would accept all reforms possible, providing they were within the framework of British institutions and compatible with the maintenance of the colonial tie. In short, it would stand by the reformist policy adopted after 1828. The *patriote* movement's radical turn, however, had changed the complexion of the situation.

The commissioners' reports were faithful to the reformist outlook. Their observations *in situ* confirmed their prior conviction that the Lower-Canadian conflict was basically of nationalist cause. Gipps, in his comment on the second report, noted that the majority leaders in the assembly had to a point succeeded in making the quarrel look like a contest between aristocratic and democratic principles rather than one of nationality, for among members from the townships, where there were many residents of American origin and none of French origin, almost as many voted with the French party as against it; adding the English representatives of French ridings to those elected by American or democratic interests, of the twenty-two with English names or of English origin, thirteen voted generally with the French party and nine against it.[45]

This simply reflected the view of most other observers, and bore decisively on the commissioners' examination of the grievances of the *patriotes.* While recognizing that the principles they invoked were equally applicable to Upper Canada, they kept in mind the ethnic reality of Lower Canada. The conception of responsible government, the notion of an elective legislative council, the absolute control of revenues and land grants: all pointed toward the impending establishment of a French-Canadian republic independent of the mother country.

Since they identified ministerial responsibility with national independence, the commissioners judged unacceptable the request for responsible government in the colonial milieu. Application of the principle, they considered, would destroy all dependent relationship with the mother country because it would remove real power from the governor and place it in the hands of a ministry responsible to and chosen by the legislative assembly. "The progress of affairs," they said, "would depend exclusively on the parties succeeding one another in the province. All union with the empire through the channel of the executive head would cease; the country would shortly be virtually independent."[46] They followed the same line of thought in their final report:

There are other demands, too, which we believe to be so incompatible with the unity of the Empire as to be almost equally inadmissible. One of them is the demand, that the whole local affairs of the Province shall be conducted by a Ministry responsible to, or, in other words, removable at the pleasure of the House of Assembly. They do not indeed ask that the Governor should be made directly and professedly responsible to them, but they require that he shall be supposed to be always acting under the advice of his Ministers; by which means it is sufficiently plain, that though shielded from responsibility to the Assembly, neither could he remain responsible to the King and the Imperial Parliament. We trust that we have, in our separate Report on the Executive Council, sufficiently exposed the impossibility of granting this request, and maintaining, at the same time, the dependence of the Province on Great Britain. There might continue to exist a sort of federative union between them with some degree of duty annexed to it from the weaker to the stronger power; but the relation of dependence one on the other, would, in our opinion, be destroyed.[47]

They therefore proposed retention of the traditional political régime in which the governor, as the king's representative and executive head, was responsible to London. They suggested, however, that the executive council "be composed in such manner as to merit the confidence of the people as much as possible." Their position on revenues followed logically from their constitutional postulates. The surrender of all revenues of the province to the assembly was to have its *quid pro quo* in the grant of a civil list guaranteeing the independence of both the "executive government" and the judiciary. As for the granting of crown lands, the assembly might pass laws and lay down rules but it could not take over a managerial role, for that belonged to the executive.

The election of the members of the legislative council, the *patriote* leaders' principal demand, appears to have been a question of far greater importance to the commissioners, for whom the notion was antithetical to the fundamental principles of the British Constitution. They realized that the aristocracy was not as strongly rooted in North America as in Europe; their objections were based less on political theory than on the local context. The second report observed that with an assembly and council both elective Lower Canada would be rather similar to the neighbouring independent states, and that its administration would be concentrated slightly more within the province than it already was. The commissioners were not prepared to say to what degree such a state of affairs would be either incompatible with good government or prejudicial to continuance of the union with the mother country, even for a colony inhabited by a homogeneous and undivided people, which, in Lower Canada, was unfortunately not the condition of the populace.[48]

In discussing the implications of ministerial responsibility, the commissioners curiously did not attempt to examine the motives and reactions of the opposing groups; perhaps they felt that the population did not really understand responsible government. Not so in the case of the election of legislative councillors. Far from inferring that those demanding this reform would like to free the province of dependence on the mother country, they declared it more natural to suppose that the French Canadians' desire was to continue to benefit by Great Britain's protection in order to develop their resources and ensure their national existence—and to do so more effectively than would be possible through immediate independence or annexation to another state. But possession of the totality of real power in the country by one group was out of the question, and this would be the certain result of the measure under consideration, for no equitable and impartial manner of popular election could be devised to allow the majority in the council to be other than of the dominant party in the assembly.[49]

The commissioners had grasped exactly what was really at stake in Lower Canada's political and constitutional tussles, whether over ministerial responsibility or the election of legislative councillors. Opponents of an elective legislative council, they noted, that is to say, almost all the merchant class and the great majority of persons of direct British descent, feared that if the powers of the assembly were increased and consolidated by a council drawn from the same source, they would be exposed to every kind of injustice and oppression. While loath to speak of the profound distrust reigning in the province between the different populations, the commissioners felt bound to express the opinion that the English portion of the inhabitants, particularly the merchant classes, would never agree without resistance to the establishment of what they regarded as a kind of French republic in Canada.[50]

The commissioners criticized the role played in the past by the legislative council and recommended changes in its composition. Gipps suggested that it should be, not an organism of more or less aristocratic pretensions, but one comprised of representatives of intermediary bodies: former mayors of Quebec and Montreal, the rector of the university, representatives of the bar and chambers of commerce, and farmers from the three districts, some to be elected and others to be appointed by the governor, and with a seven-year term of office.

While the commissioners pursued their inquiry, Gosford kept

working to persuade the *patriote* party leaders to accept his policy of compromise and conciliation. In the Quebec region he met with some success. Defections among Quebec *patriote* leaders who were urging moderation suggest that weak spots were appearing in the party, and that Papineau's hold over it was not as strong as it had been. But the untimely disclosure of the commissioners' instructions forbidding an elective legislative council infuriated most of the militant *patriotes*, who took this as further irrefutable proof of the British government's duplicity. The *patriote* leaders thereupon issued an ultimatum to London, and to demonstrate their determination called a strike of assembly members until such time as the election of legislative councillors should be recognized as a matter of principle. Gipps wrote of this impasse that without the unfortunate disclosure, and if supply had been obtained, there might have been a good chance of having an agreeably disposed majority in the next session of the House. Circumstances having changed radically, however, in his opinion the only hope for any measure of acceptable reform, short of suspension of the constitution, lay in its imposition on the assembly by a unanimous or insignificantly opposed vote of the British House of Commons.[51]

So grave had the situation in Lower Canada become that the British government asked Parliament to intervene. The royal commissioners' full report was placed before the Commons on March 2, 1837. On March 6 the firm and official response to the Ninety-two Resolutions was submitted to the House in Lord Russell's Ten Resolutions, which were adopted after three days of debate. Suspension of Lower Canada's constitution was clearly in the wind. The Ten Resolutions not only rejected the *patriotes'* principal demands, but authorized the governor to take whatever funds were necessary to pay arrears in civil service salaries, without the assembly's consent. In short, the British government was more disposed to risk a revolt by the French Canadians than one led by the English-speaking minority; besides, they were convinced that the people were still loyal and would refuse to follow their leaders into a revolution. But the Ten Resolutions, far from resolving the crisis and forcing the *patriotes* into the approved process of reform, touched off an explosion of nationalist reaction. In September, 1837, Gosford wrote despairingly:

The violent and unjustifiable attacks which have been made by the ultra-Tories against the French Canadians in general have created an animosity of which M. Papineau has not failed to take advantage, and I attribute to this cause much of his influence on a great many members of the house. M. Papineau has emissaries in all directions, and although I do not know that there is cause to take alarm, there is need of much precaution and vigilance to prevent and check the disorders which might take place, as a result of the efforts made to excite discontent among the people by the most abominable representations.[52]

Of the *patriote* party he wrote:

> It is evident that Papineau's party will not be satisfied with any concession which will not put it in a more favourable position to realize its ultimate intentions, that is to say, the separation of this country from England and the establishment of a republican government. M. Papineau has gone so far that he must persevere, or submit to a defeat which would destroy all his influence; the plan that he follows shows that he has decided to risk everything to reach his goal.[53]

Gosford terminated his dispatch with a warning that the constitution might have to be suspended and that his government needed to be invested with the fullest power.

Ever since 1815, the English party had become more and more disorganized, for it never really had achieved a suitably diversified structure, nor had it devised adequate strategy or adapted its ideology to its society's moods and colour. Thirty years of successive electoral defeats had undermined its energies and capacity for resistance, and with each election its credibility as defender of urban interests had faded. The party was not even very credible as the defender of English-speaking interests, since many *patriote* candidates and party supporters, even some of the *patriote* leaders, were English-speaking. The English party's representativeness of the English-speaking in general began to revive only after 1830. Its real strength lay in its ties with the holders of economic power, and this was the reason it received the support and protection of the British authorities. If the English-speaking of Lower Canada had been as anaemic economically as they were politically, Britain's attitude to the *patriotes* and their demands might have been very different.

CHAPTER 11

Rebellion, 1837-1838 (Part One)

The insurrections of 1837-38 were the culmination of a conflict which began at the turn of the century and deepened steadily with succeeding developments. The idea of revolution emerged after 1830 from a context of mounting stress, and came to inhabit the daily lives of a growing number of fervent *patriotes*.

In the spring of 1836, Julie Papineau (who seems not to have understood the constitutional issue) wrote to her husband of the atmosphere in and around Montreal:

> ... we are more and more uncertain what will happen over the supply bill and then we cannot foresee what effects will follow. I keep saying that if Montreal's state of mind is not changed, there will be dangerous times after the session; but we cannot tell until then. You can see that the country districts are preparing and are very willing, but we must hope that the reforms will be brought about without recourse to such unhappy methods.... Thus we are convinced that our only resources are in our own strength. It must be begun by firm resistance to constitutional reforms [sic] and if we can obtain nothing [that way] we shall of course have to have it by violence.[1]

For some, this kind of thinking was exhilarating, for others depressing. The feeling of being on the brink of armed revolution was increasingly common and by 1837 was widespread indeed, and deep-rooted. The social climate deteriorated even further with a sudden and prolonged aggravation of the economic situation, adding fuel to popular discontent and hardening the attitudes of those most directly involved in the political and social conflict. In this tinder-box atmosphere, the imperial Parliament adopted the "coercive" Ten Resolutions proposed by Lord John Russell. The *patriotes'* reaction was immediate and violent: they would not bow to a set of decisions which ended practically all hope of attaining their ends by peaceful means. The irresistible force meeting the immovable object.

A new strategy would have to be devised, and whether or not it was to have a legal guise it was bound to be influenced by the most extremist elements of the *patriote* movement. The more cautious leaders, those anxious to elaborate and follow careful and complex tactics taking account of all aspects of the situation, were at a disadvantage; the initiative for action fell to the more impatient, the authentic revolutionaries with radical objectives. The necessity for action as well as a changing revolutionary ideology attracted new members but also provoked defections, for *patriotes* of certain social categories and interests, as events unfolded, began to see an ugly side to revolution.

I The Economic Situation during the Revolutionary Period

The surge of revolutionary thinking coincided with an economic crisis which peaked in 1837-38 and subsided only partly in the succeeding years. It occurred in England as well as in Lower Canada. It coloured and to a degree oriented the revolutionary events, even formed a part of their fabric. Its part in the total context was central, though its impact on social groups and regions was uneven in timing and intensity.

The severity of the 1837 economic crisis was principally due to a coincidence of particularly bad agricultural conditions. In 1836 the harvests had been exceptionally poor in Lower Canada and England, and, aggravating the problem, in Upper Canada and the northern United States as well. The failure of production throughout the area of supply, together with sharply higher demand from England, left Lower Canada deprived of grain for local consumption; prices and the cost of living soared, affecting all social groups directly or indirectly. In October, 1836, Julie Papineau-Dessaulles, seigneur of St-Hyacinthe, wrote that due to heavy frost damage to crops the peasants were unable to pay their *rentes*: "... I shall not have a quarter of the usual yield of lesser grains for the harvest: we run the risk this year of paying very dear for all our food, the winter setting in so early and boding to be long and harsh."[2]

The poor harvest of 1836 was simply another episode in the decline in Lower Canada's wheat production, despite the exceptionally harsh weather and the wheat fly epidemic; the major contributing factors were the same that had been at work since the beginning of the century, namely deficient agricultural methods and subdivision of farms. The year's hardships were certainly not regarded by the peasants as a temporary phase. In the Quebec district the harvests had been very poor for years, and they had been almost as bad in the Montreal district; only the Trois-Rivières district seems to have been spared disaster, but even there the respite was short-lived. Production declined again in 1837, and in the Montreal district this was accentuated by pillaging and devastation on the part of government troops. In the following two years it shrank still further, bringing hardship everywhere.

Descriptions of the rural situation after the 1836 harvest are virtually identical to those given by the curés after that of 1833, when, in the parishes east of Quebec, there were calculated to be 2,243 indigent families. At St-Henri de Lauzon, for instance, the curé estimated 380 families in distress, half of them living on potatoes and having no bread at all; fifty families were entirely dependent on the parish.[3] Conditions were similar in a great number of parishes in the Quebec and Montreal districts as the year 1837 began. Exorbitant prices made the purchase of grain for food and seeding onerous indeed. Furthermore, on the pretext of discouraging peasant dependency, the *patriote* leaders were firmly opposed to money-lending and the governor, to avoid provoking deterioration of the political climate, refused to give any aid. From one year to the next, then, the number of farmers incapable of seeding their fields increased. Sheer poverty and discouragement explain the successive production decreases from 1837 to 1839. The rural population became more and more deeply in debt to merchants, seigneurs, and curés.

The crisis in the Trois-Rivières district seems to have appeared later and to have been less widespread. Tithe reports of the curés of Nicolet and Ste-Anne de Yamachiche suggest a relatively slight wheat crisis[4] (see Table 80). Yet despite good soil fertility, when crisis came to Yamachiche it was a wheat crisis, developing over a long period. Production fell from 31,000 *minots* in 1802 to 26,000 five years later, and to 7,800 in 1829, a particularly poor crop year. Between 1784 and 1831 the population of the parish rose from 1,427 to 3,605, and by 1844 to 4,638. In 1831, 70 per cent of heads of families were farmers, 7 per cent craftsmen, and 14 per cent labourers. The farmers of Yamachiche paid increasing attention to potatoes—44,670 *minots* in 1831—and to oats, whose production rose from 7,800 *minots* in 1802 to 16,900 in 1807 and 33,800 in 1829. But by 1831 the local wheat production, an average of 38.1 *minots* per family, was already insufficient for local consumption, and the quality, according to reports, was no better than elsewhere (see Table 81).

The new crisis beginning in 1836 led to almost total abandonment of wheat-growing in the area, entailing also a temporary fall-off in oat production, which, however, recovered after 1840. Defections of peasants discouraged by poor yields and fragmentation of farms were no doubt largely responsible for this. The beginning of the final wheat crisis in this parish can in fact be detected in 1834. Between 1831 and 1839, the number of wheat producers diminished from 392 to 226, from 60 per cent of heads of families to 32 per cent. The number of consumers was therefore greater and production volumes were smaller (see Tables 82 and 83). Of farmers still producing wheat, those failing to raise sufficient even for their families' subsistence (50 *minots* and less) averaged 40 per cent from 1831 to 1835 and 48 per cent from 1836 to 1839; an average of 31 and 32 per cent in the same periods were able to feed even large families (raising between 51 and 100 *minots*) but not necessarily to reseed adequately. Taking these categories as well as non-producers into account, we see that at least 92 per cent of the parish families were obliged to buy wheat. In 1835, 69 per cent of the total production was raised by the 39 per cent of farmers able to produce more than enough for their own needs; however, in 1837, 1838, and 1839, these proportions dropped to 31 per cent of total production harvested by 11 per cent of producers. The strongest producers, those with the most land and heaviest commitment to wheat, therefore suffered sorely along with the weakest. The harvest record of François Lesieur dit Désaulniers, perhaps the leading wheat producer, is indicative of the vulnerability of even the most fortunate. His wheat harvest rose from 611 *minots* in 1831 to 806 in 1832, then fell to 156 in 1839. In 1838 and 1839, only 4 per cent of producers harvested more than 100 *minots* of wheat, and their share of the harvest was 11 per cent (see Table 84).

At Yamachiche as elsewhere, small landowners survived by growing potatoes, but there again production was anything but on the rise. In general they earned virtually nothing from selling oats, whereas the large landowners reaped large oat harvests even in the poorer crop years and sold their surpluses relatively well to offset their losses on wheat. Though the number of oat producers in the parish declined, the average production per farm increased from 148 *minots* to 155.

Production failure in an agricultural scene already suffering a structural crisis brought lower revenues and new importance to the potato in the rural diet; it also brought greater indebtedness and greater resentment, reaching the mass of local consumers who were by now the great majority of the population. Shortages of produce and money and spiralling prices brought distress everywhere. From Lotbinière, the surveyor L. Legendre wrote expressing the almost universal lament in

Lower Canada during the period of insurrection: "The farmers are extremely poor this year for lack of harvest and lack of money."[5] From Rivière-Ouelle, C.-E. Casgrain painted a more explicit picture:

> We are here in state of alarming poverty. The needs are such that I fear we will not be able to provide sufficient for the winter for all the poor who grieve us and sear our souls with their stories of hardship. The harvest has been so poor that a good half of the habitants will not have enough for themselves. Most of these are in debt and without [further] credit. The rest are little better in consequence of debts contracted in hope of good harvests which have been lacking for several years. It is a sad state of affairs partly the fault of the people themselves who have unwisely indulged in expenses beyond their means and conditions due to the excessive eagerness of merchants to make them advances and long-term credits which have brought if not ruin, at least great penury to many. To all I preach reform as much as I can to make them understand the necessity of denying themselves any object of luxury and of obtaining everything with the produce of their land and animals without turning to the merchants.[6]

The incomes and profits of seigneurs, merchants, curés, tradesmen, and labourers also fell. In 1839 the seigneur of St-Hyacinthe, Papineau's sister, wrote that no one dared undertake or invest in anything. The crisis was felt by the mass of urban consumers, too. In 1837, with so little Upper-Canadian and American produce arriving, the price of wheat leapt 51 per cent (flour 81 per cent) at Quebec, and 38 per cent at Montreal. The following year, with supplies from outside improving, wheat still rose 8 per cent at Quebec, though at Montreal it declined 5 per cent. In 1839 imports were sufficient to bring a further 5 per cent decline at Montreal, but did not stop an even greater increase of 13 per cent at Quebec.[7] That city was obviously disadvantaged by its greater distance from the centres of production. All Montrealers dependent on the transport of agricultural produce were in difficult straits in 1837, though less subsequently. In the cities, perhaps even in the rural areas, speculators were playing liberally on food shortages.

The year 1837 also saw a crisis in the financial and commercial sectors, felt first in the cities and then by diffusion in the rural areas. The financial crisis began in England, deepening rapidly toward the end of 1836 and culminating in a series of bank failures. Trade and manufacturing were the next victims. By the spring of 1837 the British crisis was affecting the American economy and in May the American banks suspended cash payments in an effort to avoid disaster. In

Canada the reaction was instantaneous; in Quebec and Montreal there were meetings of merchants and on May 18 the Quebec Chamber of Commerce reported, "That in consequence of the suspension of cash payments throughout the United States, the Banking institutions of this province have been compelled to adopt the same course in order to prevent the whole of the specie now in their vaults from being drawn out for transmission to the United States."[8] The business community's decision, ratified by the governor as proposed, caused a serious but inevitable reduction of credit and currency in circulation.

Commercial activity, already slow, came to a halt in those localities most affected. In August, 1837, a contemporary wrote from Montreal, "An excessive languor pervades nearly every branch of commerce, and our streets have, so far as relates to business, the appearance they are wont to exhibit on a close holiday or a sunday."[9] The following April Joseph Papineau wrote to his grandson in exile in the United States, "There is no imagining the difficulty found in carrying on business; there is no money to be found by anyone, [and] nothing to be found to sell; yet something must be sold in order to pay debts. Madame Cavelier is in the most dire straits, [and] I cannot myself obtain money for my own needs."[10] Even after cautious resumption of banking activities, severe credit restrictions and currency shortages continued. In November, 1838, the Quebec Chamber of Commerce requested and received a renewed suspension of cash payments, citing "an unusual demand upon the banks of the city for specie."[11] In 1839 there were signs of improvement, but the financial situation remained precarious throughout the revolutionary period.

Lower Canada's economy, with its great sensitivity to factors at work in Britain, was bound to suffer repercussions from economic troubles in the mother country. As early as February, 1837, Lafontaine wrote to Chapman, "Perhaps the almost general distress both in commerce and agriculture will cause discouragement in many minds. I admit that shortage is great and hardship total in Canada."[12]

Timber was the sector least affected by the poor conditions reigning in the British market. Certain forest products, such as deals and potash, suffered hardly at all; exports of these products in fact rose slightly, one per cent and 5 per cent respectively in 1837. Exports of staves, squared pine, and ships built for the imperial market declined, 7, 11, and 6 per cent respectively. In the sector overall, since the local lumber market was depressed, the crisis was still real and caused serious problems, but without touching the depths reached by other sectors. The following year, sales of squared pine, deals, and squared oak improved by 6, 3, and 32 per cent, though the recession persisted in shipbuilding and staves, sales dropping once again by 11 and 12 per cent respectively. In 1839 all categories of forest products, with the exception of potash whose production had long been in decline, were stimulated by a vigorous recovery in the British market. Shipbuilding tonnage increased 80 per cent and squared pine 21 per cent.

The forest industry's resilience was particularly important in the circumstances. The city of Quebec, though not a protected haven, suffered the period's misfortunes less severely than other localities. In June, 1837, a contemporary wrote, "Besides, continued port activity, and the employment which the timber trade continues to furnish to part of the population, is contributing to neutralizing seasonal effects and other unfavourable circumstances."[13] Thus, in 1837 activity in timber and shipbuilding continued (though perhaps less in 1838) to soften the effect of the crisis, despite high unemployment and hardship for many. Its immediate impact on the rural area around Quebec, the Ottawa Valley, and the townships is difficult to evaluate in view of the gravity of agricultural problems.

Indeed, though the 1837-39 economic crisis was partly financial and touched even the forest industries, its crux was agricultural production. It involved all agricultural produce, but wheat most severely. The Montreal region was the hardest hit, due to the extent of the local failure coinciding with smaller supply from the West, which had been supplementing the meagre wheat harvests in Lower Canada since 1830. In Montreal, the financial and grain trade centre and therefore the commercial link with Upper Canada and the neighbouring American states, the situation was very grave. In the years 1837-39, annual shipments of wheat and flour bound for Great Britain were 67 per cent below the level of the period 1832-36; arrivals in Montreal from the west dropped by 56 per cent (71 per cent in 1837 alone). Inevitably, there was a fall-off as well in other imports; 1837 saw a total import value decline of 26 per cent at the ports of Quebec and Montreal and 17 per cent at St-Jean.

Such was the background for the rebellions of 1837 and 1838. Hardship, distress, poverty, misfortune were words on all lips, voicing the depressed mood of the population. Those least affected might feel and express pity for the mass of truly suffering souls turning toward them for relief, but it was not a situation which fostered brotherly love. On the contrary, the frictions and conflicts already existent intensified abruptly. The notion of economic warfare against the alliance of English merchant bourgeoisie and English government emerged naturally, as in 1834, evoking a picture of two sides, each out to destroy the other. All this was timely for the *patriotes'* designs of mobilizing the masses against the English government and particularly against a governor whom they accused of "robbing the people of their money," of intending to drive the French Canadians from their farms in order to give them to foreigners, and of seeking to deprive them of their rights. These accusations resounded all the louder in the hollow depths of the crisis. The economic situation served the radical *patriotes* especially well, those who would turn peasant hostility against tithe-hungry ecclesiastics and grasping seigneurs.

But what began as a national independence movement and might have been converted into a popular and social revolution when economic conditions were deteriorating, in fact alienated the peasants from the revolutionaries as the economic crisis began to recede and to make the English merchant bourgeoisie and the clergy appear to be the victors. In December, 1838, the Lotbinière surveyor Legendre wrote of certain incidents which were stirring public opinion: "Some little country doctors and notaries rejoice in these incidents, but the mass of habitant farmers, in this parish and others about, is very loyal.... These poor people now see the frightful state in which the great Papineau has placed the country."[14] Despite thirty years of economic problems, the rebellions can hardly be regarded simply as a manifestation of economic crisis. Economic crisis, demographic crisis, political and social crisis had for so long been interwoven that it would be difficult indeed to draw up a list of causes in order of responsibility. Yet certainly the economic crisis was the spark that set off the explosion over Russell's Ten Resolutions.

II Revolution in Legal Guise

News of the adoption of the Ten Resolutions reached Lower Canada in April; on the 13th *La Minerve* commented:

The anxiously awaited news of the Commons proceedings relating to this country has arrived at last. The story we have to tell is one of new acts of oppression, this time sanctioned by the [supreme] authority, by a majority of the representatives of the British people. The ministry has resolved to pay the arrears due to the public officers of this colony from our own revenues. The mother country is putting its hand in our coffers and will distribute these sums among its servants in this province and meet the official debt without the vote and against the will of [our] representatives. Is it considered that we must succumb to the weight of this force, bow our heads shamefully under the yoke? No, our position as a people is simply strengthened, since such measures should help us pursue more actively than ever this struggle which will end in success for

American principles. Let the mother country pass what laws it pleases, let it lean its heavy arm on us, its decrees can never remove us from [this] continent where free institutions are part and parcel of the beliefs and political existence of the inhabitants....[15]

This firm but moderate tone was far from reflecting the boiling resentment of the *patriote* leaders who already knew what Russell's resolutions contained and were busy preparing their reply. Revolution was unquestionably at the core of their discussions, and unquestionably the firebrands would have liked to rouse the masses and take up arms at the earliest possible moment. But the movement was still controlled by men who, while capable of strong indignation, were accustomed to calculating, to working out strategies. This small group knew that mobilization of the masses to obtain revolutionary objectives would demand far more than would the most critical of electoral campaigns. They knew, too, that their territorial base must be broad, and for that they must regain their hold on the district of Quebec. They were also anxious not to frighten the moderates, the weak of heart, and in general those hoping still for a peaceful resolution of Lower Canada's problems.

Stirring up the masses, but not too much; bringing the Quebec region back to the fold; reassuring those who hoped by legal means to pressure the British government into surrender; making sure that any aggression would be perpetrated by the British government: these seem to have been the components of the strategy which took form in the month of April in the minds of the *patriotes* of Montreal, a strategy whose ultimate goal was revolution. On May 10, 1837, Papineau wrote two wills, the first in favour of his wife, the second, in anticipation of her death, leaving his possessions to his children; on December 20 of that year he again appointed her his sole heir.[16] On November 22, Dr. R. Kimber, a Trois-Rivières *patriote* leader who was not privy to the Montrealers' secrets, wrote to Lafontaine:

Every day I hear such curious news of your district that finally I have begun to believe you to be in a state of total insurrection.... If you expect the majority of your representatives to be in step at present with the rebels, that will be the end: we must await events and resign ourselves to living under a provisional government or under martial law. What treachery, what ulterior motives there were in the driving force, the father of the 92 resolutions! They were unknown to us, we participated in good faith, and I still hold firm to reform of the government and not to its overthrow, as I see was the intent at the beginning. I congratulate myself for having opened my eyes in time and remained a reformist in the midst of so many revolutionaries.[17]

There was certainly premeditation. Wolfred Nelson, who was among those better informed of the *patriotes'* intentions, wrote, "I am vexed by Mr. Papineau's and Mackenzie's admission that we had decided to rebel. It gives justification to our adversaries and denies us the right to complain of having been attacked."[18] Papineau, like others, may have believed in the workability of resistance within the bounds of the law, which might explain much of his contradictory behaviour, but the fact remains that he did at an early stage agree to or even urge a plan which included ultimate recourse to arms. The rebellions did not result from a spontaneous uprising of the masses against government aggression. The mysterious secret mentioned later by the Abbé Chartier was shared at first by a small élite of Montrealers, who leaked it bit by bit as circumstances seemed to warrant. Incontestably, events unfolded according to a plan which was pre-established though it was modified substantially as the moment of armed confrontation approached.

There were two phases to the plan. The first was to be legal agitation, so-called; it would include economic warfare against the merchants and the government and also the organization of great public meetings in all the counties, supplemented by parish meetings, whose purpose was to draw the masses into a protest movement strong enough to force the British government to back down unconditionally. These monster rallies were to culminate with a convention of representatives of all the counties of the province. If the British government still refused to bow to the *patriotes'* demands, the armed uprising would become inevitable. The moment appointed for this second phase would be "after the ice had taken," following a general convention planned for December 4, which would produce a declaration of independence and establish a provisional government. The pretence of legality, as the developments showed, was a cover for a genuinely revolutionary plan. In the illusions created and reflected, there appears to have been more preoccupation with tactics than with any authentic objective.

The *patriotes'* Permanent Central Committee, formed in 1834 in Montreal, was the body which did the planning and framed resolutions, directives, and slogans. Its members, the true leaders of the *patriote* party, no doubt drew inspiration from their own experience, but the American Revolution was more their model than the French. On May 23, 1837, the body was enlarged to include the region's *patriote* assembly members and a fair number of radicals. The great public rallies were initiated by these Montreal leaders, who hoped thus to involve the sympathetic élite of the various localities and the humble folk as well.

The first of the great rallies was held on May 7 at St-Ours in Richelieu county; in his "Journal d'un Fils de la Liberté," Amédée Papineau wrote, "The county of Richelieu was the first to raise the banner of ferment, just as it was the first to triumph on the field of battle."[19] It had been called a week earlier by an influential group from St-Charles, St-Denis, and St-Ours, which was composed of professionals, merchants, a few farmers and tradesmen, and, unusually for such a group, two schoolteachers, P. Boucher-Belleville (who was also a farmer and practiced journalism) and Siméon Marchesseault. The latter was to write from prison in 1838 that they had all been political pupils of Debartzch; "... even in these last troubles, all we did was to water the grain he had so long been sowing."[20] The twelve resolutions adopted by the crowd of 1,200 who attended the meeting appear to have been prepared in Montreal, but no city men rose to speak; the prominent orators were Wolfred Nelson of St-Denis and Dr. Cyrille Côté of Napierville, both of the party's radical wing.

Thus was launched the campaign of protest and mobilization of the people. The *patriotes* pronounced it the test of strength into which they had been forced by the oppressive and Machiavellian policies pursued by the British government since the conquest of 1760. "In the circumstances," went one of the St-Ours resolutions, "we can only regard the government which would have recourse to injustice, force, and a violation of the social contract to be an oppressive power and a government of force, to which henceforth the measure of our submissiom should be only the measure of our numerical strength, together with [whatever] sympathies we may find elsewhere."[21] Papineau was hailed as the personification of the national rebirth, the Daniel O'Connell of French Canadians. As for concrete action, the *patriotes* for the time being merely announced an assessment, "Papineau's tribute" (inspired by the Irish "O'Connell's tribute"), and the establishment of an association with province-wide ramifications whose members would pledge themselves "to consume only products manufactured in this country, or imported without the payment of duties." Non-consumption of dutiable goods, they maintained, would deprive the state of revenue and encourage local industry; but in going a step further, calling outright for contraband trade with the United States, they had already overstepped the bounds of legality.

A week later two more rallies were held on the same day. At St-Marc-sur-Richelieu the meeting closed with the declaration, "Better a bloody but just and honourable fight than cowardly submission to a corrupt power."[22] At the rally in Montreal which was attended by the party's leading lights but drew a crowd of only 700, Papineau himself gave the keynote speech:

> The English have always considered it just to draw swords against those violating the law by seeking to break the doors of the public treasury, the keys to which they had given their representatives. In this just and legitimate defence, they have at times driven out governors who were violating equally cherished rights; a few times they have beheaded them.... History tells us that the English were right to detest their oppressors to the point of imprisoning, driving out, [even] killing them.

He compared the Lower Canadians' situation in 1837 with that of the Americans as they launched the drive which led them to independence. But it was not yet time for revolt, said he; more effective for the moment was the ruination of British trade through non-consumption and smuggling. Then almost in the same breath: "If they take the road of unlawfulness and injustice, let us proceed at the same pace or faster on the road of resistance. They have taken a step along their road, and today we shall take two along ours; that will suffice for the moment, and will subsequently make other steps easier if they become necessary."[23]

In the latter half of May the *patriotes* held many parish meetings. On May 23 the Permanent Central Committee prepared a request to the American Congress asking for adoption of a policy of free trade and decided to create vigilance committees in all parishes. From then on, the number of county rallies multiplied. Three great public meetings were planned for June 1 alone, at St-Hyacinthe, Chambly, and Ste-Scholastique. Of the three, Ste-Scholastique in the county of Deux-Montagnes generated the most revolutionary atmosphere, with songs, banners and signs bearing symbols and slogans, and Canadian and French flags. It also left the most turmoil in its wake. The organizers, the county's *patriote* chiefs, had invited Papineau to attend with O'Callaghan, who was now his constant companion. Some English-speaking individuals, mostly Irish, had been brought in to help call for unity among all ethnic groups against an oppressive power, but there was no mistaking the event's real purpose, which was a demonstration of French-Canadian nationalism. The innkeeper Noël Duchesneau recalled later that "since M. Papineau of Montreal has been coming to parish meetings in the county of Deux-Montagnes there have been disturbance and animosities caused by a certain party called patriotic against the inhabitants from the old countries."[24] In July there were complaints that French Canadians, besides breaking contact with the English-speaking, had been pillaging their properties and doing all possible to drive them out. Declared R. Hall of Ste-Scholastique, "I have always lived on the best terms with my neighbours the Canadians, but since political meetings have been held in that parish, and the adjoining parishes of St-Benoit and others, the Canadians have ceased to have any contact with the inhabitants of English extraction."[25]

Papineau's nationalist message had clearly been taken to heart, and the *habitants* were demonstrating their animosity toward the English, the English government, and French-Canadian "traitors." By now they were convinced that the British government and its supporters intended to abolish the French language, the Catholic religion, and the French civil law, and furthermore to seize their farms for the benefit of immigrants. Some even read into Papineau's words encouragement for the abolition of tithing. A farmer of St-Benoit was reported as having declared that he was obeying Papineau's directions to use threats and cruelty to bring individuals to join the *patriote* ranks, and that Curé Paquin's barn had been destroyed because Papineau had told the *habitants* that the curés were too rich and did not need farms and had too much in tithes.[26] For all the emphasis on non-consumption and smuggling, the Ste-Scholastique rally left not only fear that "the Canadian race was in danger of death," as another peasant put it, but also a suggestion of revolutionary action to come. Papineau had said, "we must let the plum ripen, and when it has we may pick it."[27] The plums were ripening more rapidly in Deux-Montagnes than elsewhere in the district of Montreal. A few days after the rally, Dr Jean-Olivier Chénier and the merchant W.H. Scott called on the postmaster D. Mitchell and threatened to destroy his house. Mitchell told them, "There is none property in this house which belongs to me; there is King's property," to which Scott rejoined, "as to the king and the law—the law consists in the will of the people."[28] On July 9, the farmer A. Drouin told the blacksmith J. Choquette of St-Eustache, "I'm off to revolt [and] to buy guns to kill all the Chouaguens [traitors]."[29]

After July 1, revolutionary organization in Deux-Montagnes was taken over by a local permanent central committee, with parish vigilance committees reporting to it. The regional *patriote* leaders met often in private houses, and on Sundays after mass held public meetings on the steps of the churches. As reported by a farmer, at one of these meetings Scott, Chénier, the surveyor Féré, and Notary Berthelot "called his excellency the Governor-in-Chief a robber and sought to incite the habitants to revolt, telling them that if they did not resist the authorities, the government and the English would put yokes on their necks and harness them like oxen to the plough." This was confirmed by two joiners, who reported that the leaders urged the *habitants* "to organize to rebel against the government" and told them they were numerous enough to succeed and must get themselves guns to fire at the troops.[30]

By September, unrest and excitement were at such a pitch among the masses that the regional leaders attempted to control the local militia and magistracy. At a public meeting, following the American example, they replaced the government-appointed militia officers and magistrates with men elected by the people, although "the people" in fact simply accepted those chosen by the party leaders. Scott, the dominant figure at St-Eustache, was chosen to be a colonel, and Chénier became a major. Scott gave a speech saying nothing about economic warfare but railing against government-appointed officers and magistrates, who he said were nothing but scum and filth; then, carried away with himself, he exhorted the *habitants* to ready their arms and save their money for ammunition to oppose the enemy, assuring them that the government or parliament of England was nothing but a bunch of old women, that no justice could be expected of them, and that the *habitants* themselves must try to overthrow the scum and filth.[31] Notary Girouard, supreme chief of St-Benoit, not to be outdone, said a provisional government could be established that would be as good as the British government; he announced that anyone who could serve but refused to accept a post as captain or magistrate when appointed by the people would be regarded as an outcast from the whole Canadian society, would be deprived of all public office, and would be despised and disgraced, and his name would be posted on the church doors of all the neighbouring parishes.[32]

While events developed most rapidly in Deux-Montagnes, in the other counties north of Montreal there were numerous and tumultuous rallies. A Terrebonne county meeting at Ste-Rose on June 11 was attended by over 1,000 people. A week later, 3,000 flocked to listen to Papineau in the county of Berthier. A joint rally of the counties of l'Assomption and Lachenaie drew 4,000 on July 29. Papineau was now less cautious when speaking. He told his listeners how the Americans had succeeded "in becoming a great nation through their energy." Having talked of the advantages of creating small local industries, he then declared, "The Americans began with passive resistance before taking to arms. Love for a good government and hate for a bad one is natural to man; this feeling is engraved in his heart and he can always uphold his right to change his government when it no longer fulfils the purpose for which government is instituted.... Our cause is much more just than that of the old colonies." He roundly denounced the English monarchy, vested in a young woman of eighteen whose only thought was of marriage, and the House of Lords, dominated by the aristocracy and a clergy corrupted by money and privileges of every kind. He reminded his audience of the killing of the three Canadians on May 21, 1832, "not because the people were guilty of poor conduct but because they were Canadian." On the suppression of the Assembly Schools Act: " [The colonial government] saw that with the diffusion of education, the Canadians were becoming so enlightened and superior that they would understand all the Machiavellianism of their oppressors." On the question of land distribution: "you sowed for the good of your country and foreigners have reaped your harvests."[33] On this July 29 the plums were just about ready to be picked.

The last rally north of Montreal was at Vaudreuil on August 6. The local leaders were joined for the occasion by leaders from Montreal and neighbouring counties.

South of Montreal the rallies began again in the third week of June. A crowd of 800 turned out at Yamaska and a revolutionary atmosphere was whipped up and maintained by the local élite. At St-Grégoire there was a meeting in front of the church, during which J.-B. Proulx, an assembly member and prominent farmer, declared that the English government was a corrupt one which must be got rid of, a yoke to be shaken off before it became too heavy; that the governor and his staff were stealing the people's money; that the land company was stealing the lands that should belong to the *habitants'* children; that if they did not hasten to shake off the yoke it would be too late; that the American government was a free one, unlike theirs which enslaved them; that at a mere whistle the Americans would fly to their aid and help them become independent.[34] Similar speeches were given by the Pacaud brothers of Nicolet, who owned a steamboat; they declared themselves "ready to help Papineau overthrow the English government and give Canada an independent government like the American government."[35] On June 23, 1,000 to 2,000 people attended a great meeting at St-Hyacinthe, and the next day there was a rally at Longueuil. On July 4, the American Independence Day, the *patriotes* gathered at Missisquoi, calling for support from former Americans. On July 17, Papineau drew a crowd of 4,000 at Napierville. L. Thonin reported having spoken to Papineau on that occasion: "I can get from your speech you would recommend the inhabitants of this country to rebel against the government of England: would it not be a dangerous thing for us to disobey the commands of our sovereign, [for] it may happen that we will be served in the same way that the inhabitants of Acadia of Nova Scotia were, when they rebelled against their sovereign. Mr. Papineau replied and said this had nothing to do with the affair of Acadia; this does not molest the sovereign, but the ministry and parliament who are a band of robbers."[36]

Clearly these rallies were not intended merely to alarm the British government; they were part of the strategy in pursuit of the party leaders' goal of destroying the established political régime, generating increasingly radical activities and attitudes in the people. J. Dodelin, bailiff of St-Charles, who reported having attended a number of meetings in the house of the merchant J.-B.-E. Durocher during the summer, stated "that the purpose of all those great rallies was to get rid of the English government and find ways of becoming independent."[37] The blacksmith Foisie declared that Durocher and his clerk and also Marchesseault often urged him that summer to "hurry and get the weapons in good order so the rebels will be ready to fight the English troops, overthrow the English government, and become independent."[38] The Henryville merchant J. Gariepy, described as having "a bloody-minded mind," was said to have maintained that there would be no peace until all the "bureaucrats" had been beheaded.[39] In Pointe-Claire, a similar note was rung by the innkeeper L. Charlebois, "who asked and gave seditious and revolutionary advice and opinions against the British government," and exhorted all of good will to aid the then-existing revolutionary party at Pointe-Claire by supplying all the necessary money for powder, shot, guns, and other necessary things to ready the rebel party to go out at the first possible moment to fight the British government.[40] At Varennes, Dr. Perkins Nichols was reported to have said "that he was working to overturn the government of this province to establish a republic."[41]

The final great rally south of Montreal took place at St-Constant, attended by some of the *patriote* party's star performers, namely Girod, Brown, Cherrier, Pelletier, Lacroix, and Cardinal. A banner emblazoned with the word *Independence* was carried by C. Duquette. Cherrier and Pelletier, though not the most violent in their speeches, were reported to have incited the *habitants* "to revolt if the English government did not grant what had been demanded in the Ninety-two Resolutions."[42]

There were also great rallies held outside the Montreal district. At Portneuf on July 6, a crowd of 600 reprimanded their assembly member for his moderation. Close to 3,000 people attended a rally in St-Maurice county on July 16. The Quebec district, where Augustin-Norbert Morin had become the principal *patriote* organizer, was beginning to have considerable importance under the circumstances. Its rural areas in general seemed enthusiastic enough, though patriotic fervour was less intense there than around Montreal. Flanked by Lafontaine, Girouard, and Morin, Papineau made a special effort to participate personally in the region's protest campaign. At St-Charles de Bellechasse, Lislet, and St-Thomas—with attendance at the latter between 1,500 and 2,000—he was enthusiastically received. At Kamouraska, however, where the dominant figure was Amable Dionne, seigneur, merchant, and dissident *patriote*, Papineau decided in the end not to speak for fear of rebuff. Morin continued the campaign alone, crossing the St Lawrence and achieving huge success in the Charlevoix parishes. In mid-July a final rally was held at Deschambault. But, except where the local leadership was ardent and energetic, the campaign in the Quebec rural areas had not acquired real impetus.

The city of Quebec, more than the town of Trois-Rivières, continued to be a pocket of resistance that hampered adequate organization, even in the rural areas. Assisted by the urban leaders Bouchette, Hunter, and Drolet, Morin had been trying since May to re-establish the party's hold on the region, with some measure of success; the rallies were well attended, the people even going as far as to repudiate those assembly members who were urging moderation. But Etienne Parent observed that Morin, while strong on ideology and action, had yet to acquire skill in leadership.

Parent, editor of *Le Çanadien*, had no hesitation in warning his readers of the dangers inherent in the party leaders' strategy, which, from the time of the St-Ours rally, he denounced as leading by stages to armed insurrection. On September 13 he wrote, "For a couple of years now we have been going from aggressiveness to inflexibility and from inflexibility to aggressiveness, marching on and on, and we cannot march on this way much longer without finding ourselves at a stop somewhere, but stopped between a hail of shot on one side and dishonour on the other."[43] In October, when the boiling point had been reached in the Montreal district, Parent attacked the advocates of violence, the moot provisional government proclaimed at St-Eustache, and the manifesto of the *Fils de la Liberté,* which he likened to a declaration of independence. After the six-county rally on October 23 at St-Charles on the Richelieu River, there were no longer any doubts about the real intentions of the *patriote* leaders; they kept talking about industrial revolution but were in fact preparing for political revolution. Parent accused them of aggression, instigating anarchy, and provoking the government. His writings certainly influenced the élite of Quebec City and, indirectly, the lower classes. He convinced the timorous, the hesitant: all those who shrank from radical action. Morin, having failed to create a group of *Fils de la Liberté* in Quebec on the Montreal model, wrote of his disappointment to the *patriotes* of Deux-Montagnes: "My efforts would have succeeded without the influence which the local leaders, intrigue, and ignorance have had, unfortunately, on those predisposed or most susceptible.... With persistence and courage we shall destroy a passing evil, unmask our enemies and some formerly presumed friends."[44] At Quebec the plums were slow to ripen.

At each of the mass meetings the *patriotes* took care to have representatives elected to participate in a general convention planned initially for late summer. Difficulties in the capital and the governor's calling of the assembly, however, forced them to shelve the convention for the time being. When the Montreal assembly members arrived in Quebec on August 17, almost all dressed in home-made, rough homespun clothes, their mood was anything but peaceful. The session of August 18 to 26 was marked by confrontation between the extremists and those willing to give the government a last chance; essentially between Montrealers and Quebeckers. Taschereau's dissidence suggests that formerly sympathetic seigneurs had begun to dissociate themselves from the *patriote* movement as it was evolving. By the end of August, the movement's leaders had little hope left of carrying the Quebeckers with them and so began to concentrate on the Montreal district.

The last mass meeting in Montreal was on June 29, drawing a crowd of 4,000, and its success encouraged the formation of a revolutionary organization. In July the advocate André Ouimet gathered together some small groups of young *patriotes* and the association of *Fils de la Liberté* was founded in September. "In principle," wrote Amédée Papineau, "the association... had been formed to diffuse political awareness among the young and give them an early taste for public affairs. But soon the plan had been modified so as to make it a society both civil and military."[45] The "civil"aspect was a cover which did little to hide the real activities of the group. When Dr Robert Nelson addressed the public founding meeting, as recounted by the young silversmith C. Lemoine, he told his audience "to try to overthrow the government if we considered ourselves strong enough and that if on the contrary we considered ourselves too weak to stay quiet.... The association then believed itself strong enough to overthrow the government."[46]

The association had six military sections. Its leaders, a group of professionals, merchants, and shopkeepers, held both large and small meetings whose purpose was to motivate and give military training to the members. At the meetings Montreal newspapers were read, "and Books in the French language that treated of the French Revolution

and the manner in which the plans of the insurgents had been prepared and executed[,] and [how] on occasion the people in order to
prevent the troops from advancing on them prepared a quantity of
straw which they carried with them and on the approach of the troops
they set fire to it."[47] T.S. Brown, a leader of the *Fils de la Liberté*, was
reported to have advised his listeners "to arm themselves and to hold
themselves all in readiness as the country was fast advancing with
rapid strides towards independence of Great Britain," and not to be
afraid of the Queen's troops.[48] According to other witnesses, R. Ples-
sis-Belair, a member of the association and of the Permanent Central
Committee of Montreal, declared, "That the principal object of a radical meeting he had attended was to devise means to attack and destroy
the City of Montreal."[49] After such meetings, some attended by 800 to
1,000 persons, the *Fils de la Liberté* generally engaged in military exer-
cises on land owned by D.-B. Viger. These meetings and parades, often
noisy, soon created an atmosphere of confrontation. On November 6
there was a clash between the *Fils de la Liberté* and members of the
aggressively loyalist Doric Club. Wrote Amédée Papineau, "... the
sections went one by one to the place of assembly... marching in
ranks two by two, and in silence, each member carrying a stick in his
hand, and under his clothing a cutlass, dagger, or pistol, and ammunition."[50] After the incident, each side accused the other of responsibility for it, but whose it was is not important; it was no simple
accident regretted by either group in the aftermath, but rather another
step in the ripening of the revolutionary movement.

Until the St-Charles six-county rally of October 23, the movement's
operations had been carried out within the parishes and counties; but
now Papineau's cherished convention, or constituent assembly, came
to the forefront. St-Charles was to be a preparatory step toward a
general convention at which there would be a declaration of independence, the creation of a provisional government, and the issue of coin
bearing the insignia of the *patriotes*.[51] Papineau was invited and agreed
to speak; his wife wrote on October 17 to her son Lactance, a student
at St-Hyacinthe, that his father was to go to it;[52] yet a few days before
the battle of St-Denis on November 24, Papineau told J.-T. Drolet and
Dr F. Duvert, vice-chairmen of the meeting, that "the St-Charles
meeting had been their affair and he had come only in passing."[53] In
any event, he was met by fifteen armed and mounted men when he
crossed the St Lawrence at Longueuil.[54] On the eve of the rally, he and
O'Callaghan, at the house of a *patriote* by the name of Ducharme, at
St-Marc on the Richelieu, drafted the resolutions which were the sub-
stance of the Address of the Confederation of the Six Counties to the
People of Lower Canada.[55]

The rally, originally including five counties, opened in an atmosphere of revolutionary festivity. There were armed militiamen, a liberty pole, and flags and banners bearing inscriptions of every kind, announcing to the 4,000 attending that the moment of great decisions was approaching. Speakers had come from Montreal: L.-M. Viger, President of the Banque du Peuple, E.-E. Rodier, C.-O. Perreault, and T.S. Brown; Notary Girouard had come from St-Benoit. As the meeting began, a delegation from l'Acadie asked to be admitted to the confederation, and so it became a rally of six counties. The tone of the speeches was violent in the extreme. Wolfred Nelson, who was presiding, Rodier, Brown, and Côté openly called for revolt. The latter, as later testified, said that "it was useless to send petitions to England, that America was there ready to help them, that Upper Canada was rebelling and Prince Edward Island too and their example must be followed...."56 The people were impressed.

The applause of the crowd from which there came not a single disapproving voice showed clearly that already a revolution had taken place in [their] hearts and all that was left was to proclaim it by some more overt act of opposition to the government. During this meeting, many donations were made for buying arms and munitions of war for defence in case of attack. This meeting brought the period of armed opposition being prepared considerably closer.57

Dr Kimber, one of Chamby's foremost leaders, declared on the following day:

As soon as the ice on the river has taken, we shall go with 40 or 50,000 armed men to seize Montreal; all the habitants are well armed and supplied with ammunition and firmly resolved, and after Montreal, we shall take Quebec. I was at St-Charles and never in any country has there been seen such an assemblage determined to be rid of the English government.58

The St-Charles resolutions and Address of the Six Counties clearly expressed the rebellious mood of the time in the district of Montreal. There was a declaration of independence drawn directly from the American Declaration; containing no formal reference to the seigneurial régime or the Coutume de Paris, it begged the question of acceptability to either the friends or the enemies of the old social régime. But besides stating principles justifying Lower Canada's independence, the *patriotes* at St-Charles adopted concrete revolutionary resolutions;

government-appointed militia officers and magistrates were to be forced to resign and would be replaced by men elected by the people, this transfer of power to take place in December. Papineau wrote to Mackenzie in February, 1838, "If navigation had been closed on November 20 as normally, if the election of the magistrates had been organized without violence and only in December as recommended, then communication between the north and south shores of the Saint Lawrence would have been blocked and there would have been better chances of success."[59] But the Six Counties Address demanded immediate action in that domain, and Papineau was one of that resolution's authors. There were misgivings. François Mailhot, seigneur and legislative councillor, objected to it and finally withdrew from the meeting. T. Franchères, a merchant of St-Mathias, claimed later to have disputed the resolution with Papineau after having been asked to second it, and to have declared it to be too strong and to be encroaching on government rights, while Papineau held to the contrary.[60] But otherwise the dissidents, if they were there, remained silent, and even Franchères's opposition was weaker than he later wished it believed. There was no objection to the formation, in each parish, of vigilance committees as in Deux-Montagnes and sections of *Fils de la Liberté* as in Montreal; nor to a resolution to incite desertion among English soldiers. The radicals spoke violently, and even Papineau's relatively moderate speech favoured radical action. Ideological differences remained in the background; there was no confrontation between the leftists and Papineau, who, his mission accomplished "in passing," continued on to St-Hyacinthe to visit his son.

To working-class minds, land and immigration were still uppermost in the economic context, and this the militant élite did not lose sight of. Early in November, Eustache Cheval of St-Eustache was sent to the village by Jacques Dubeau "to take the necessary measures to resist the English government which intended to drive them from their farms . . . ."[61] Another farmer declared "that he would rejoice in killing thirty or forty [English] enemies."[62] Still another, J. Longpré, told the merchant W. H. Scott of St-Jérôme, "Woe to the English, if the Canadians win,"[63] and urged J. Léveillée, after a military camp was established at St-Eustache: "Come with us; we're well armed, we have fun; it's like at a wedding; we drink, eat, play fiddles, dance, we're free, we do what we want . . . . It's our right, we poke fun at the King, the Queen, and the Clergy . . . ."[64] Independence, for most of the peasants, tradesmen, and labourers, was the symbol of the struggle to safeguard their traditions against the English and the Protestants. There was much harassment of Protestants by groups led by François Molleur, a merchant of Lacadie. Eloi Babin complained of being tormented by them and being told to "go back to the Roman Catholic Religion."[65] Moyse Marchesseault, describing the organized harassment of all the Protestants of his village, said he had been told, "We don't want M. Roussy [the Protestant minister] here, we want only one religion, he must go, if he doesn't go this week we'll come and tear down his house."[66] The French-Canadian Catholic clergy, too, was subjected to hostility, but this was because of the clerics' resistance to the *patriote* movement, not because of anti-Catholicism.

The left-wing *patriote* leaders, however, were bent on real social revolution. Dr Cyrille Côté, one of the most active, told the farmers "that they would be independent and free and would pay no rents to the seigneurs or tithes to the curés."[67] Among the masses, wherever this message was spread, it won some converts. The Laprairie notary J.-B. Dupuy went as far as to blame the peasants' seigneurial obligations for the rebellions: "They are so prejudicial to the inhabitants, that I can say with safety that, if we have had an insurrection in this country, we may assign the seigneurial tenure as the cause of it ... [;] I asked them [the habitants] for the reasons they had ... they answered me that it was to bring down the seigniors, who were their ruin, and that by this means they hoped to do away with the seigniorial tenure."[68] The real impact of radical propaganda on the lower classes is difficult to evaluate; land scarcity and immigration certainly stirred more popular resentment than tithing and seigneurial dues, but anti-feudalism did become a significant source of popular unrest. The farmer A. Boudrieux of St-Valentin, explaining his revolutionary attitudes, "began by saying that the Canadians were much abused by the English and went on to show by various ways that the British had no right in this country, that the British took the money belonging to the Canadian Public and paid their officers and likewise the clergy of the Church of England without their consent. He then complained of taxes, seigniorial rent, Romish clergy's dues ... and hoped he would have an opportunity of shooting some seignior and if killed in combat his children would bless him for it."[69] Though radical propaganda fell on deaf ears in certain regions, its effect among the lower classes, even when not repudiating traditional values, was enough that the clergy and seigneurs began to be seriously alarmed, particularly after the St-Charles rally.

St-Charles also unleashed an escalation of revolutionary activity. South of Montreal, there was organized harassment of magistrates, officers of militia, and others not of *patriote* persuasion, beginning in Lacadie parish and spreading throughout the area by early November. The blacksmith J. Palardie recounted having been approached several times by a number of élite individuals first asking, then commanding him to take the leadership of a group of which they were members, even threatening him most alarmingly if he did not; he added that he had never seen persons of their rank so determined to overthrow the government.[70] Subscription campaigns were conducted by *patriote* leaders for the purchase of arms.[71] On November 10, the *patriotes* of St-Jean gathered for an attack on the garrison there, led by B. Dupuis, a farmer, and A. Gervais, an innkeeper, who used "abusive and threatening language towards the Queen and Government declaring that they would be independent."[72] W.H. Scott travelled from St-Eustache to Montreal on November 12 to ask Papineau if the revolution had really begun in the south: "He [Papineau] said that it was the case but that leaders, he thought, could not prevent it as it was a spontaneous movement of the inhabitants. To the best of my knowledge, I replied the leaders might supply it if they chose. It strikes me that in our conversation Dr Côté's name was mentioned as being the principal agitator in this part of the country."[73]

The fact is that neither in Deux-Montagnes nor south of Montreal was there a spontaneous uprising of the people against English oppression. Though there were some lower-class individuals among the *patriote* leaders, revolutionary activity was guided and fuelled by élite laymen. Two St-Césaire cobblers declared that "Mtre Ambroise Brunelle was a rouser of the people against our sovereign... and that he made off after having aroused the feelings of the common people."[74] At St-Edouard a merchant, R. Robitaille, urged the Canadians to choose their officers and procure arms.[75] At Longueuil in November, the merchant François Charron, "an independent man having much influence generally," was selling powder and shot for the purpose of killing the "red pigs."[76] Beyond question, the middle-class rabble-rousers and the lower classes they were attempting to arouse were not identically motivated. On November 20 the steamboat owner J.-N. Pacaud told the blacksmith J. Trudel of Nicolet that the *habitants* of the Chambly River had risen *en masse* to shake off the English government yoke, and that it was good, since he (Pacaud) had suffered enough from the damned English and had not had enough justice from them.[77] By the time the *Fils de la Liberté* and the Doric Club were battling in the streets of Montreal in the first week of November, revolutionary agitation in the surrounding rural areas had reached uncontrollably feverish proportions, causing first the clergy and then the government to intervene.

CHAPTER 12

Rebellion, 1837-1838 (Part Two)

III   Church and Government Intervention

What the Catholic Church deplored in the *patriotes* was not only their theories justifying recourse to arms, but even more their democratic ideology, most specifically that part of it which called for separation of church and state and an end to the clergy's economic and social privileges.

The agitation in the Montreal region was particularly alarming. By July, Bishop Lartigue was convinced he smelled revolution in the wind. On July 25, at a banquet celebrating the consecration of his auxiliary, Monseigneur Bourget, he launched his counter-revolutionary campaign. With six bishops present, he instructed the 150 priests of his diocese who were in attendance on the attitude preachers and confessors must take toward those bent on overthrowing the established order: "... they must remind their parishioners that it is never permitted to rebel against the legitimate authority, nor to transgress the laws of the country; that in their confessionals they must absolutely not absolve anyone who teaches that [such] is permitted."[1] The *patriotes* were infuriated. In a letter of July 29 to the Bishop of Quebec, Lartigue wrote that "the so-called patriotic newspapers" had begun to assail him for this, adding, "but they will tire of it."[2] But the *patriotes* and their newspapers did not tire of it. When the curé of Quebec preached submission to the established order, doubtless following the directive, the radical paper *Le Libéral* retorted: "They would much better quietly receive their tithes and the thousand other contributions exacted through the ignorance of the people, as long as they can preach in return the moral doctrines of Christianity to their flocks, than come down into the political arena, prompted as they always are in these questions by their private interests."[3] *La Minerve*'s reaction was no less sharp: "M. the curé of Quebec preaches passive obedience, which is to say, servitude.... one would say... that giddiness in government and sacerdotal heads is carrying them pell-mell into the vortex of human passions."[4]

The clergy's entry into the scene, while it cooled some elements, was widely resented in both rural districts and the cities. When, on Queen Victoria's accession to the throne, the bishops praised the British sovereigns in pastoral letters and ordered the *Te Deum* to be sung, many churches were almost empty. Some curés, out of personal conviction or fear, refrained from reading the letters or mumbled them hastily. A great many, after delivering fire-and-brimstone sermons, retreated into their presbyteries, cutting off all contact with their parishioners. But they were not left in peace by the *patriotes*. Curé Blanchard of St-Lin recounted being visited by a group led by J.-B. Foisy: "... they threatened me and finally told me that if they did not blow my brains out that afternoon they would come and do it after dark, and other things."[5] Some seemed to be counting on the magical fear they could inspire in their flocks. Others, like Curé Crevier of St-Hyacinthe, were braver and made their influence felt not only in their pulpits and confessionals but at mass meetings. Crevier mustered all his "metaphysical powers" against the violence proposed by the *patriotes*, participating actively at rallies in an attempt to keep his flock from yielding to the traitorous agitators.[6] He felt that certain *patriote* claims were "just," but that the assembly must not "demand so hotly nor immediately the redressment of all grievances." His opinions, it was reported, pleased the "peaceful" *habitants*.[7] Peaceful *habitants*, however, were in the minority at St-Hyacinthe. The clergy's intervention in fact failed, at least temporarily. Curé Blanchet of St-Charles, one of the few priests sympathetic to the *patriotes'* nationalist objectives, wrote to the governor: "I believe that the excitement is at its peak.... I must say further that the gentlemen of the clergy must not be counted on to stop the popular movement in this area. Moreover you know that the pastors cannot separate themselves from their flocks. Which leads me to believe that soon there will be but one voice requesting correction of grievances among the Canadians, whatever their state and condition."[8]

On October 24, the day following the St-Charles rally, Bishop Lartigue, judging the situation to have reached a most critical point, issued a strongly-worded *mandement*, or pastoral letter, condemning the *patriote* élite's political conceptions as he saw them. Invoking the Scriptures, the Encyclical *Mirari Vos*, and Gregory XVI's papal brief to the Polish bishops, he reaffirmed with the utmost vigour the divine right of kings and unity of church and state, fulminated against the heretical notions of sovereignty of the people and separation of church and state, and declared the dogma of absolute power to apply even to British institutions. Anyone not adhering to his doctrine was a "heathen and publican," and Catholics must either uphold the laws of their religion or abandon them. "The Catholic Church, the advocate of peace," he wrote in his *Défense du Mandement*, published anonymously in November, "will never sanction a doctrine which, instead of giving some stability to government, would overturn in perpetuity the strongest monarchies of Europe." He described the anti-clerical and unbelievers as hypocrites and manipulators of the people. "Cease calling yourselves Catholics.... Then at least you will not be deceiving your less educated compatriots... [by pretending] to belong to a religion whose most characteristic practices most of you had already abandoned before dissociating yourselves from the doctrine of the bishop and his clergy."[9] He did not deem it necessary to reiterate that, for the disobedient, insurrection would incur refusal of absolution, as already announced on July 25, and refusal of religious burial. In December he wrote that since his pastoral letter he believed none were any longer "voluntarily blind"; a Catholic's duty toward the secular power, he had written in his *Défense*, could no longer be in any doubt.[10]

The extreme severity of the *mandement* and its implications, added to the parish clergy's fears in the circumstances, awakened the curés to the need for a certain caution; some were even inclined to a degree of casuistry. For the vast majority, including the indefatigable Curé Paquin of St-Eustache, it was impossible not to yield, if only a little, to the pressure of the events unfolding about them. Curé Demers of St-Denis, although one of the most knowledgeable about theology and church discipline and obedient to the bishop, when it came to refusing religious burial began to find it difficult to categorize all combatants equally. Some curés even felt the *mandement* would cause more harm than good. Though it caused no rupture between the high and the low in the church hierarchy, there were certainly reservations at the parish level. Curé Blanchet, torn between his bishop and his flock, went to the *patriote* camp on the morning of the battle of St-Charles. "I tell you again, I do not want to mix in politics," he said, "... but as [your] priest, I have come here to beg you think of your last moments, and for that let us call on the Holy Virgin with five *Paters* and five *Aves*." Each should make his penance, he said, which was done, and then he withdrew with heavy heart.[11] After the battle he buried the dead in the parish cemetery. To the great distress of their families, Lartigue ordered him to fence off their graves from the rest. At La Présentation the curé hesitated until November 21, and then, at a revolutionary meeting in the presbytery, declared himself a *patriote, comme vous autres,* having signed a day or two before. This gesture convinced the group that the authorities must be resisted, particularly the witness who reported the event, such was his confidence in his curé.[12] The parish clergy could bring their influence to bear, but in fact could rarely make spectacular converts as in this case. Curé Tessier of Pointe Olivier sang mass on November 25 for the *patriotes* who were to fight at St-Charles, "... that they might succeed in their endeavours against the government," told them to do their best and not be cowardly, and gave them his blessing.[13] Abbé Chartier, curé of St-Benoit in Deux-Montagnes, rejected Lartigue's doctrine completely and encouraged his parishioners to revolt, virtually making himself a commanding officer of the *patriote* army in the north, it was said.

In their rage at Lartigue's *mandement,* the *patriotes* accused the bishop of having betrayed the national cause after having so long used the strength of the *patriote* movement for his own ends. A group of political prisoners later wrote him a rebuke: "Monseigneur, we have not yet finished with you; we admired you, protected you too much to let you take our disdain and disaffection to your grave. There was a day when you were the subject of all conversation, your cause had become national...."[14] The *patriote* leaders, hoping to minimize the impact of the *mandement,* declared it to be the "second edition of the Gosford proclamation,"[15] and claimed that there was collusion between the clergy and the government. Dr Léandre Dumouchelle of St-Jérôme told the *habitants* that the bishop was on the government's side because he received from it a thousand *louis* per year, though he had been a *patriote* before; he asked them if they wanted to become boot-blacks for the English, and said that if not they must defend themselves.[16] Lartigue was not paid by the English at that time, but he did try to use the situation to remove the last obstacles blocking incorporation of the diocese of Montreal and to obtain a salary equal to that of the Bishop of Quebec.[17] The *patriotes'* stress on the materialism of the clergy did bear some fruit, but mostly among peasants hoping to be freed of seigneurial dues and tithes. Moyse Danis of St-Jérôme was reported to have declared that if the *patriotes* could win, the *lods et ventes* and tithing would be abolished by Papineau.[18] In the eyes of all the *patriotes,* liberation, whether national or social, was personified in Papineau, an ambiguity which was never really clarified for the lower classes.

Church intervention having failed, the government began to take action in November. On June 15 Gosford had by proclamation forbidden public meetings, but this stimulated rather than tempered revolutionary fervour. Gosford's calling of the assembly in August brought a temporary and relative calm with renewed promises of reform. At this stage the government was still regarding the *patriote* agitation as bluff intended to force the British government to capitulate; this despite warnings aplenty from the English in rural areas. Even when Gosford proceeded to purge the magistrature and militia with dismissals, he felt he was not countering a revolutionary design but simply a strategy of disobedience. Lartigue was no doubt better informed than Gosford. The English population began to protest the governor's inaction. On September 8, Gosford wrote to London: "As I have told you in my previous letters, I do not expect a serious movement, yet when I see in action so many agents, so devoid of principles and blindly obedient to the orders of such a man as M. Papineau, it is impossible to place bounds upon the calamities which they could cause."[19] He also mentioned "jealousy between the two races." Though his convictions were being sorely tried, Gosford continued to resist the counsel of his entourage and the exhortations from beyond it. But finally, after the St-Charles rally, considered by Attorney-General Ogden "as the first public and open declaration of an intention to revolt...,"[20] and then the November 6 street fight in Montreal between the *Fils de la Liberté* and the Doric Club, he was obliged to take stern measures, calling in troops from the other colonies and preparing warrants for the arrest of the principal *patriote* leaders.

Now the *patriotes* could accuse the government of aggression. Papineau declared later, after his defeat,"I defy the English government to contradict me when I assert that none of us had prepared, wished or even considered armed resistance.... We were not conspiring to overthrow the government by force. We wished to cure it with a restricted and controlled diet. We did not know that it was conspiring against us to crush us, to start a civil war against the people."[21] The government had certainly made its move before the moment chosen for an armed uprising, before the revolutionary organization was ready. Papineau wrote to Mackenzie in February, 1838, "You complain that the rich have made no sacrifice to arm the people. First, in Lower Canada the people possess only immovable property which is impossible to convert into money.... Secondly, if the attempt to introduce arms had been done earlier, the war against the people would have begun earlier because it was impossible to do it in secret."[22] Gosford's decision to arrest the leaders caught the *patriotes* off guard and sowed consternation in their ranks.

Papineau learned the rumour of his imminent arrest through D.-B. Viger. His first reaction was acute distress. Viger, trying to be reassuring, told him "that the sun shone for everyone and would shine again for them and perhaps he would see the day when they would be victorious and masters of the country;... that they must call on the supreme being to support their cause;... that he [Viger] would not be responsible for having the streets reddened with the blood of those who were not of their political persuasion [and] were only outcasts...." A. Labadie reported: "I also heard Mr Papineau say [to Viger] that he could never be satisfied until he was president in this country and so he would be soon.... Mr Viger then told Mr Papineau that he must go more slowly and wait for the ice to take; that then at a whistle from the habitants en masse thousands of Americans would espouse their cause and they would soon be masters of the country. He spoke also of the Indians who, he said, for a thousand louis would also join their cause."[23] For a few days Papineau remained in contact with the party's Montreal establishment, those who could finance an insurrection and would be the principal beneficiaries of independence. The Upper-Canadian radicals sent Jesse Lloyd to visit him. Amédée Papineau recounts in his journal, "My father told me never to breathe a word of it, that he was an envoy from our friends of Upper Canada."[24] An immediate intervention by British troops was not expected at the time; the appointed day for the planned convention was still December 4. On November 13 Papineau and O'Callaghan left Montreal, stopped at Varennes to see Girod and suggested he go to St-Eustache, then continued toward St-Charles. When the arrest warrants were issued on November 16, only five *patriote* leaders could be found, lesser figures at that.

With the departure of the Montreal leaders, the *patriotes* of the city talked bravely and performed a few acts of daring but did nothing to re-organize under new leadership, living and waiting in fear and indecision. On November 18, W. Kelly, an Irish peddlar, told J. Poet, a wood-turner, "that the Canadians would rise and take the country from the British government and butcher all the English."[25] François Rivet, a farmer of St-Paul de Lavaltrie, visited the Montreal blacksmith J. Gagné, perhaps to buy or have arms repaired, and told him, "We're more comfortable [safer] than here: we're well prepared, we have arms and, as soon as the ice has taken, we'll all come and fight [for] Montreal."[26] After November 16, the significant events took place outside the city.

The evening of November 14, Papineau arrived with O'Callaghan and Wolfred Nelson at the house of T. Drolet, a merchant, in St-Marc. At this time the leaders were thinking less of taking refuge in the country than of organizing in preparation for the great convention of December 4, to be held at St-Charles. Fear and disorder in the rural areas demanded the presence of firm leadership. A *patriote* leader who had been beating the drum for the convention through the parishes reported, "I had little success for my part because the people I met first were seized with terror."[27] A number of leaders, he reported further, had already gone to the United States.

The new revolutionary organization was to have the same structure as the *Fils de la Liberté*, with a civil section directed by Papineau and O'Callaghan and a military one whose leader would be Nelson. The civil section was in fact simply a cover for Papineau, who remained the supreme chief in every sense. Nelson's authority extended only to St-Denis and the neighbouring parishes. But the succession of events was accelerating. On November 16 Constable Malo was ordered to St-Jean and St-Athanase to arrest Doctors Davignon and Lionnais and Notary Desmaray. He had an escort of fifteen cavalrymen. On the return journey from St-Jean the prisoners were liberated by a force of 150 Longueuil *patriotes* commanded by Bonaventure Viger and Joseph Vincent, both farmers.

Heartened by the Longueuil success, the *patriotes* hastened to set up camps at St-Denis and St-Charles and to organize rallies of peasants. The leaders knew now that the army would be intervening soon. As early as November 17, E.-E. Rodier and Dr André Lacroix alerted the militia captains, telling them to arm and hold themselves ready, "because there would be a row very soon."[28] Notary Moreau, in fact, believing that Malo had been sent to seize Dr Côté, had begun to assemble a veritable army. At Pointe-à-la-Mûle a group of well-armed men, already 150 strong and growing daily, was commanded by Côté and Lucien Gagnon. When the government troops began their campaign on November 12, the *patriotes*, while not ideally ready, were not entirely unprepared. On the 20th, Toussaint Drolet promised S. Lesperance command of all the St-Hyacinthe *patriotes* "who could be put on the march," adding that "things had got to a point where there was no turning back," and that "things would be decided in two or three days at most."[29] The *patriote* organization clearly had no choice but defensive strategy.

At St-Denis, Wolfred Nelson had 800 men, perhaps half of them with guns. They were not all brave men; the blacksmith Modeste Roy described his part in the battle, positioned in the St-Germain house: "... then fear took me and I hid in the cellar where I stayed until it was all over."[30] As he mobilized his men for battle, Nelson had threatened to cut the throats of any who dared take off. At five o'clock in the morning of November 23, a messenger brought news of the approach of English troops; Colonel Charles Gore was in command. While Nelson prepared the resistance, Papineau and O'Callaghan stayed in his house, where they were visited by E.-R. Fabre, a director of the Banque du Peuple; the bank's president, Louis-Michel Viger, had been arrested. By nine o'clock, when the battle began, the two men had left St-Denis. They were seen in the vicinity of St-Charles by Luc Etier, a tanner, who learned from Papineau that "the troops had attacked St-Denis, that nothing would come of it, he thought."[31] Michel Vilbon, a spy, also met them; Papineau told him in English that he feared the Canadians would lose at St-Denis, and to gather all the men he and others could find in the houses "and bring them along with us."[32] The battle was a victory for the *patriotes*, and many were the expressions of surprise that Papineau had not been at their head, "along with all the other leaders whose threats had made them obey."[33] The reasons for his leaving, or his flight, are not known for certain. He may have been committed to remaining aloof from all fighting; but the supreme chief's inability to assume his role as leader at the crucial moment was to create mixed feelings at all levels of the revolutionary organization. At St-Denis fear had been overcome, anarchy prevented, and local rivalries silenced by Wolfred Nelson with his energy and determination.

The camp at St-Charles was established on November 19 when the *patriotes* seized the Debartzch manor house. During the election of leaders, T.S. Brown arrived from Montreal, a diminutive, mercurial shopkeeper, very active in the *Fils de la Liberté*. He had distinguished himself and been wounded in an eye during the street fight of November 6. Brown had been extremely ill-treated in Montreal and was very happy to be at St-Charles, he said, and everyone must get to work making entrenchments.[34] Papineau and O'Callaghan came the following day, found Brown buoyant and full of confidence, and conferred on him the title of general. Through a Montreal carter, the new general sent "his compliments to the general of Montreal," adding that he was ready any day to have him visit his camp.[35] General Brown issued orders and talked a great deal but could not instil his own optimism in his men or maintain discipline; the complement in his charge varied in a single day between 400 and 1,000.[36] A labourer, O. Lussier, reported seeing Papineau in the Debartzch house on November 24, the day before the battle of St-Charles, haranguing some forty men, telling them to stand firm and not retreat; after that Papineau disappeared and he had not seen him since.[37] The same day Wolfred Nelson came and told the men at St-Charles that a victory there would give the *patriotes* total control of all the parishes south of Montreal, and the city would then be vulnerable. He offered Brown 300 men and two cannon, but Brown in his overweening confidence refused the offer. Mailhot and Côté at St-Mathias, who had 1,000 men, 500 of them with rifles, also offered reinforcements but did not press when turned down, for they shared Brown's optimism. J.-B. Tétro, tanner and innkeeper of

Ste-Marie, reported that the intent was to take the troops prisoner after their defeat at the battle of St-Charles.[38] But Brown proved incapable of standing the heat of battle. A deserting labourer, François Darche of St-Hilaire, recounted seeing him "on horseback escaping toward Maska."[39] Nor was he the only leader to take fright and flee. Darche also recalled seeing J.-M. Tétro, who commanded forty-five armed men and called himself a captain of the Canadian republic, reviewing his men before the battle, urging them, "mes enfants, be brave, pay close attention, don't miss those scoundrels, aim well and truly, aim at their hearts, stomachs, heads, no mercy or quarter"; they had not seen him since and Darche supposed he had fled.[40] The brunt of the battle fell finally on a much reduced contingent. The *patriotes* were defeated, because of the failure of leadership.

Following the rout at St-Charles, the *patriote* force at St-Mathias melted away in a few days. Wolfred Nelson made heroic efforts to fortify St-Denis but soon realized that all hope was lost. Early in December, he and his lieutenants set out for the United States, as did Papineau and O'Callaghan. On December 6, Côté, Gagnon, Bouchette, and Rodier, leading some hundred men and with two cannon and eighty extra rifles, invaded Lower Canada from across the border. They were repulsed by English volunteers from Missisquoi. Having broken the *patriote* resistance south of Montreal, the English troops and volunteers turned their attention to the *patriote* camps to the north.

The formation of these camps, as in the south, had been hastened by the issue of arrest warrants. At Vaudrueil, *patriote* meetings had met with some success. H. Roebuck, a farmer, proposed a resolution abolishing seigneurial rights; there was silence on the question of tithing, but the clergy was denounced for its lack of sympathy for popular liberties.[41] In November, the merchant W. Witlock distributed a home-printed pamphlet. "Do not believe," it said, "that the Canadians are so vile as they have been represented. The sacred flame of liberty may have taken possession of their bosoms.... Liberty! Do you enjoy it here! No. A tyrannical seignior will tell you that you shall not dispose of your property without his consent, and if you do he will fine you to the amount a twelve part of the fruits of your industry. He will tell you that you must send your grain to his mill to have it destroyed. He will compel you to make his road. In fact you are considered as villains."[42] Neither this nor other similar appeals seem to have had the desired effect. When the merchants and professionals who were the local leaders learned that they were to be arrested, they tried to mobilize the local people. The merchant J. Racette, who was making shot around November 12, declared "that all he had and the other leaders had done for [the people] was solely for their benefit and welfare, and that he trusted that now they were in danger of being apprehended they would arm and defend them and themselves to the last."[43] There were about 125 armed *patriotes* at Vaudreuil, who agitated but did little else. At Rigaud, which was vulnerable like Vaudreuil, the situation was similar. A number of leaders departed to take refuge at St-Eustache, for which the Vaudreuil peninsula was little more than an outpost.

Attempts had been made early in November to establish camps at St-Eustache and St-Benoit. There and at Ste-Scholastique and St-Jérôme there was better protection and more advanced revolutionary organization, and the defensive reaction to the issue of arrest warrants was less marked. Amury Girod came from Varennes and also four advocates from Montreal, but this had little immediate effect on local *patriote* leadership; and since no coherent strategy evolved, the scope of operations remained parish-oriented. Obtaining arms and munitions was the major preoccupation. Shot was being made by many individuals. About November 20, some St-Jérôme *patriotes* descended on New Paisley and ordered the Scottish settlers to hand over their arms, failing which their village would be burned; they told the villagers "that the war was begun in the South, that the troops had been defeated, that Mr. Papineau was riding on a grey horse at the head of his troops, and that they were all going to attack Montreal, where the flag of liberty was already hoisted."[44] On an expedition to Lac des Deux-Montagnes, arms and ammunition were seized from the Indians and also material stored in the Hudson's Bay Post. J.-J. Girouard's recounting, as though he had been there, of the successful skirmish at Longueuil and the victory at St-Denis bolstered morale and set strategic planning in motion. St-Eustache would be the main camp, it was decided, with St-Benoit secondary, possibly to fall back upon from St-Eustache.[45]

News of the defeat at St-Charles was brought by A. Spinard, a Montreal innkeeper; the troops had returned with many prisoners and the liberty pole, he reported.[46] Now the leaders realized the danger and morale fell very low. Girod reacted angrily, declaring "that all those who brought news like Spinard were imposters." Girouard, whose prestige in the region was great but who avoided taking command, maintained that the cause was good and must be supported, and with five hundred *livres* he believed he could take Montreal. For the benefit of rank-and-file morale, the leaders decided to spread the word that St-Charles had been a victory,"that all the troops had been killed or taken prisoner."[47] Other leaders showed less bravado. W.H. Scott resigned as colonel, saying that his political beliefs had not changed but he saw the *patriotes* were too weak to resist;[48] the surveyor E. Féré soon followed, and there was great dismay in the *patriote* ranks.

At St-Eustache Girod emerged as leader. He was an immigrant of Swiss origin, something of an adventurer, who claimed expertise in just about everything, including military strategy. Girouard and Dumouchelle took charge of the St-Benoit camp, where there were 300 men. Girod took the title of general of the "united *patriotes*," and Dr Jean-Olivier Chénier became colonel. Richard Hubert, a young Montreal advocate, was Girod's aide-de-camp; the three other Montreal advocates, F. Peltier and the de Lorimier brothers, also played major leadership roles. All were radicals who, reported Abbé Paquin, curé of St-Eustache, "were still promising to give their soldiers the choice of the best land and the abolition of tithing and seigneurial rents."[49] Local farmers and tradesmen were captains, lieutenants, and sergeants, and were responsible for recruiting. But Girod and Chénier were quite incapable of maintaining discipline over their forces, which from day to day varied in number between 200 and 1,500, according to certain witnesses; Hubert mentioned a maximum of 900 men, only half armed with rifles. Although Girod issued notes in the name of the provisional government to pay for provisions taken from individuals, the *patriotes*, it seems, really lived by pillaging the storehouses and farms of their political foes. Weak leadership and idleness gave rein to disorder, which would disappear to some extent only in cases of alert. On December 13, when the leaders had held a council of war and were pondering adoption of an offensive strategy, they had, it was said, between 800 to 1,000 men; that day Abbé Chartier of St-Benoit gave a speech "encouraging them to revolt."[50] When the moment of battle arrived, their manpower was between 500 and 600 armed men.

Against this ill-disciplined and ill-led rabble at St-Eustache, General Sir John Colborne, expecting determined and even formidable resistance, moved slowly and systematically with a force of 2,000, including a detachment of cavalry and eight artillery pieces. The *patriotes'* supreme commander, after the first skirmish, fled in terror toward St-Benoit, using a pre-prepared *carriole*, a sleigh of a type favoured by the well-to-do. Abbé Chartier was not long in following. A farmer who took him to Girouard's house reported seeing General Girod there.[51] The other leaders from the city did likewise, and many of the rank-and-file began to slip away too. Chénier made efforts to rally those leaving, then repaired with some fifty diehards to the church of St-Eustache, where he held out until the building was in flames. He was killed while attempting to escape through the cemetery.[52] Some lesser unidentified leaders prolonged the resistance for a time, barricaded in houses. Girod, after many wanderings, eventually shot himself when faced with capture. The defeat at St-Eustache ended the 1837 rebellion. When the troops reached St-Benoit the local leaders and refugees were already gone and the *habitants* had lain down their arms.

The failure of the insurrection may be attributed more to the inefficacy of the élite who were the *patriote* leaders than to the might of the British army and clerical intervention. In April, 1838, Ludger Duvernay wrote from the United States to Dr J. Robitaille, "The people in general were not ready for the fighting, which came earlier than expected[;] no one expected these incidents. The government acted with trickery in causing them when they were not expected. It knew our weakness then in our want of organization."[53] But there is no certainty that the *patriote* organization would have been much the better by December 4, the day appointed for the insurrection's launching. Elisée Mailhot wrote bitterly to Duvernay in August, 1839:

> That is the old system of Canadian leaders, old for you because for twenty years you had occasion to know the knavishness of these great potentates, new for me because only two years before I had placed myself under them aboard the revolutionary galleon; but I embarked just in time to learn their generosity. Those people are good at pushing others to the front and keeping back themselves, always ready to blame those they have pushed ahead if they do not succeed, and if they do, always ready to take the benefit and glory themselves. Thus are our leaders.[54]

This judgment contained more than a grain of truth, hardly belied by the second revolutionary attempt.

IV   The Failure of the 1838 Rebellion

The first insurrection left several hundred dead or wounded, many villages burned, 515 insurgents in prison, and the province under martial law. But restoration of peace by force did not restore peace in hearts and minds.

The clergy, fearing that this period of anarchy would result in union of the Canadas, recommended that all the people not only take government-imposed oaths of allegiance but also sign addresses of loyalty, to which the widespread response was that these were "oaths from the mouth and not from the heart,"[55] as a peasant remarked.

Initial dejection among the *patriotes* soon gave way to new hopes and expectations. Rumours, both credible and wildly fantastic, were rife. In St-Laurent on the road to St-Eustache, two labourers, Jean-Baptiste and Etienne Ouellet, aroused excitement with talk of Papineau's return in force to take revenge on the *sacré bande d'Anglais*.[56] At Ste-Scholastique, the innkeeper Louis Charette declared shortly after the St-Eustache debacle,"that the affair was not over, that if the Choyens had won [that] day, they would not win a second time, that Papineau was coming with 50,000 men and fifty cannon, some of which could shoot a ball seven leagues, and that Papineau would come and lunch in Montreal on New Year's Day."[57] A St-Jérôme puppeteer named Deschamps showed even more fertile imagination: "In France there are a great number of Turks in ambush for the English troops; they have killed about forty thousand men of English troops; the queen has no more to send. If America comes, it will take the Canadians like a pack of sheep."[58] Throughout Lower Canada, Papineau was awaited as the saviour who would come and avenge the Canadians and "destroy all the English."[59] Predictions of his coming at the head of an army were heard at Contrecoeur and Nicolet[60] and elsewhere. Sergeant McDermott, sent to feel out the mood in the Beauce region south of Quebec near the American border, wrote, "... the general feeling in this place is that Papineau will rally in the Month of March next and proceed from the State of Maine with a considerable force. I proceeded from St. Mary's to St. Francis where a similar feeling pervaded all classes and as far as I could observe seems to them very desirable."[61] The rumours, however distorted and swelled, were often nurtured intentionally by *patriote* refugees to test public opinion. Early in January, Zacharie Bourdeau, a St-Philippe farmer, slipped back across the American border to his parish and announced an imminent invasion, arousing "terror and alarm" and "almost universal sensations or movements" in a number of parishes, and the local magistrate, F. Hart, concluded that it was "very dangerous for all loyal subjects living in this place to be exposed to being murdered by people so hostile to the government."[62]

The Canadian refugees, determined to carry on their struggle, met with widespread sympathy from the Americans for the emancipation of the Canadas. The *patriotes* soon realized, however, that mobilizing Americans to join in an invasion would take some inducement. Around December 5, Côté had begun to promise 200 acres of land to his soldiers. Trying to persuade the American generals Wool and Scott to join them, the *patriotes* talked of "a recompense of 10 or 20,000 acres of good land partly improved and having on it already built several mills saw and grist. Locality for the present must not be named...."[63] Perhaps it was the hated Ellice, seigneur of Beauharnois, who was to pay the price. There were problems in procuring arms and ammunition, beyond those of obtaining donations. Wrote G.M. Bioren to the *patriote* leaders: "Mr Henry Deringer of Philadelphia is prepared at the present time to furnish 6,000 of the best muskets with bayonnet, steel ram rods and wipers at $5. delivered at the City of New York."[64] But on December 16, Papineau, who had been moving about under an assumed name, was so confident of being able to return to Lower Canada at the head or in the van of an invading army that he wrote to his son, recently arrived in the United States:

> But far from having such a horrible perspective before us, we have one which, I believe now, assures us full success for the future, however many victims will be offered in the holocaust, to ensure the triumph and emancipation of the two Canadas. We shall soon be able to come back, I hope. But I must say nothing more, while important plans are being coordinated on various points. Simply tell Dr Bouthillier that I pray him not to lose courage. To keep faithful to the views and principles which we have openly professed together.[65]

A month later, rumours of this plan, embellished by popular imagination and gossip, reached St-Lin. The climate of the time and the manner by which information was diffused in the popular milieu are illustrated by Papineau's letter and the report passed by J. Gagnon, a farmer, to J. Hunter, a New Glasgow cobbler, that Papineau would be in Montreal on February 15, arriving by the Côte des Neiges route, with an army of 8,000 men commanded by young Bonaparte, and that the priest of St-Eustache had 500 men to join Bonaparte and the priest of St-Charles the same number, and Mackenzie of Upper Canada would also join Papineau with 5,000 men; the forces on arrival "were to commence burning three miles in rear of the city of Montreal."[66]

Early in January, 1838, however, a rift developed between the Papineau refugees and those of more radical leaning, led by Robert Nelson and Dr Côté. By the end of the month the rift was virtually a rupture. Côté wrote to Duvernay:

> I do not know if you have had news from Albany. I can tell you for my part that I am utterly disgusted with that source. Our friend Dr Nelson has been there and has not brought back very pleasant news. On the one hand Maître O'Callaghan wailing that all is lost and looking for work in a print-shop; on the other, the great chief pacing from one end of his room to the other, barely willing to receive Dr Nelson whereas many strangers are admitted to his company.[67]

A month later, Robert Nelson wrote to J.B. Ryan: "Papineau has aban-doned us for selfish and family motives regarding the seigneuries and his inveterate love of the old French laws. We can do better without him than with him. He is a man fit only for words and not for action."[68] Abolition of tithing was also one of the bones of contention between the two factions, not only among the refugees but, to a lesser extent, among *patriote* leaders still in Lower Canada. As late as March, 1839, just before the *patriotes'* hopes finally collapsed completely, Abbé Chartier went, as secretary-treasurer of a new revolutionary committee, to attempt to moderate the anti-clerical and anti-seigneu-rial fever among the refugees. Julie Papineau wrote to her husband in March, 1838, expressing worry that it was the two Nelsons, Protes-tants and not *Canadien* in origin, who were to head this new commit-tee, that Robert was so unreasonable about the clergy and religious institutions, and that the rest were so incompetent and so heedless of religious interests.[69]

But the rupture between the factions was never total; though each seemed to be going its own way, the conservatives kept trying to regain control of the movement in exile, or at least to influence its direction. When, on February 28, 1838, Nelson and Côté crossed the border at the head of a force of armed men (300 according to some, 600 to 700 according to others), they did so independently of Papineau, but avoided going so far as to brand him a traitor. The incursion was brief and its only accomplishment was the proclamation (no more than symbolic under the circumstances) of an independent republic, declaring complete separation of church and state and aboli-tion of the seigneurial régime and the Coutume de Paris; other fea-tures were restriction of the death penalty to murder, recognition of human rights for all including Indians, recommendation of universal public education, and, in principle, establishment of universal suffrage and a secret vote.

While the refugees kept up their sword-rattling and prepared inva-sion plans just beyond the border, the governments in Quebec and Lon-don took measures to calm the people and ensure internal security. Gosford had requested his recall in mid-November and was replaced by Colborne on February 27. Shortly after, the new governor was informed by London that the constitution was suspended, and that he was to govern with a council of an equal number of French- and Eng-lish-speaking members. This régime ended in late May, 1838, with the arrival of John George Lambton, first Earl of Durham, as governor of all of British North America; his instructions were to conduct an inquiry into the problems of both the Canadas. His reputation as a reformer and radical was reassuring rather than disquieting, and everyone was impressed by the pomp and splendour with which he surrounded himself.

Durham endeavoured to give his mission an authentic tone of impartiality. He dismissed his predecessor's council for being too strongly identified with one particular group, and made up his entourage of men foreign to the colony and aloof from its quarrels. He quickly formed a number of research groups whose task was to bring to light everything involved in the conflicts besetting the two Canadas. When he left in November, 1838, his report was still to be written; it was submitted in February, 1839.

The most delicate problem for Durham was what to do with the political prisoners. Of the original 515, Colborne had already released all but 161, seventy-two of whom seem to have been prominent instigators of the 1837 rebellion. Durham pursued the policy of pacification already begun. He realized that juries would either condemn or acquit regardless of guilt or innocence; by June 28 he had decided to proclaim a general amnesty for all but eight, who were to be exiled to Bermuda, while twelve refugees in the United States were forbidden on pain of death to set foot in Lower Canada. This act of mercy was acclaimed by both French and English moderates. The British government, however, declared the decision arbitrary and illegal and disallowed it. At the news, Durham immediately packed up and returned to England, leaving Colborne once again in charge. On that very day, November 3, the second insurrection began.

The 1838 rebellion was no more a spontaneous uprising of the masses than that of the previous year. It resulted from the mournful deliberations of refugees who were not from the lower classes. "The uncertainty of my future, the variety of my plans made and abandoned so often according to alternating hope and despair for the regeneration of our country, does not deter me from the unalterability... of my principles," wrote Papineau to his wife.[70] He had become convinced that revolution in Lower Canada was impossible without outside help—American, French, even Russian. But his diplomatic efforts proved disheartening. The French ambassador to the United States was bluntly cool to his approach: "what has [France] to gain?"[71]

Despite friction between refugee factions, a new nucleus of organization appears to have been forming, at least according to J.B.E. Fratelin, an exiled Hungarian army officer, who declared:

I saw Mr. Papineau in the month of June. He does not communicate much personally but generally by a third person. He warned me not to depend upon Nelson and those connected with him. The central committee of New York and Philadelphia referred me to Mr. Papineau who referred me both to them. The committee of Philadelphia proposed to me to form one of military committee of which general San Martin, Colonel Baubitch, Colonel Murat and two other colonels being of New York and a young Pole named Doroskin were members with many others to consider and report upon the best plans of campaign in Canada.[72]

The location of the Maine-New Brunswick boundary seemed the only potential source of conflict between Britain and the United States. Papineau, despite his erratic moods, followed all such situations closely and kept in contact with *patriote* leaders in Montreal and also in Quebec, where A.-N. Morin was still dominant; the Quebec district seemed more sympathetic to the cause than a year earlier. In June, 1838, a self-designated former *patriote* warned Durham of a revolutionary plot in Quebec.[73] Though Papineau held himself apart from Nelson and Côté, confusion over his relationships with the various revolutionary groups indicates that he was not inactive; though he refused to be involved in the insurrection of November, 1838, he did not object to the radicals using his name. T. Bruneau wrote to Duvernay on October 11 that he had told Papineau, his brother-in-law, that he had sworn fidelity to Nelson's provisional government and was a member of the Albany secret societies, "that we shall use his name freely everywhere, except in money matters," and if it were done with discretion in New York he was sure he would not object.[74] Bruneau was one of those who followed the radicals for strategic reasons and looked toward settlement of ideological differences once victory had been attained.

After the aborted invasion of February 28, 1838, the radical leaders adopted and then dropped a multiplicity of further invasion plans; fifteen according to Mailhot, who wrote on April 6 of the fifteenth, which was to be launched that evening: "I must take part in it, but not gladly . . . ," not for fear of dying or of hardship, but of another abortive exercise, "and yet, I am so to speak forced to support it."[75] All of which reveals the frustration and sense of failure reigning among the refugees. Côté and Nelson considered Papineau's flight from St-Denis and apparent inactivity since to be the principal cause of their troubles; they itched to unmask him, but most of the eminent refugees resisted doing so. Some felt that denouncing him would irreparably damage the *patriote* cause, while others maintained that, for all his faults, he could be a Franklin without being a Washington. When asked in October what role Papineau was playing in the revolutionary organization, Glackmeyer replied "that he was not at all a warrior and would return when all was over, adding that he was a man [fit] only for office work."[76] Elisée Mailhot wrote that one Dickenson, "a man full of good sense" who knew everything that went on, was pained to see that many *patriotes* had descried Papineau's conduct, but he felt that "we ought to hide it in the interest of our cause."[77] Only when the refugees began to rally about a single invasion plan did the radicals realize the positive value of the man, even the necessity of using his name as the very personification of the revolution.

Nelson and Côté organized the new revolutionary movement around a secret society, founded and directed by them, known as *Les Frères Chasseurs*, or Hunters' Lodges. Members were recruited with the help of rumours and gossip spread among those chosen to share the "secret." Michel Meunier, a farmer of Ste-Marie Monnoir, was told by Notary Mathias Meunier that the Americans would invade Lower Canada on November 3, that for the capture of Chambly alone they had 8,000 rifles and nine cannon, and that an attack on Sorel would be made under equally advantageous conditions.[78] The leaders also claimed to have caches of arms hidden at points throughout the territory, and spread the word that local forces would support an invading army moving on St-Jean. What they were hoping, in reality, was to mobilize the country folk for attacks on St-Jean, Chambly, Laprairie, and Sorel. With these strategic points secured, the next objective was the capture of Montreal, with the help of *Frères Chasseurs* from the city and from parishes to the north. Simultaneously, an attack would be made on Quebec by *patriotes* of that city and region.

Rural groups of *Frères Chasseurs* multiplied rapidly, aided by the allure of mystery and horror enveloping the revelation of the secret. J.-B. Desmarais, a farmer, declared that during his initiation he had "learned things for which he would gladly have given 1,000 francs."[79] Certain informers spoke of a minimum membership of 10,000 to the north and south of Montreal; in the city itself there were reportedly 2,000. The society's success in the Trois-Rivières district was mixed, but many members were recruited in the rural Quebec district. Dr P. Taché appears to have been particularly active in Kamouraska, and a rumour reached Beloeil, south of Montreal, that he "was to seize the lower River [St Lawrence]."[80] Morin, who seems to have kept in touch with agitators in Maine, was the chief recruiter in Quebec City. The Hungarian Fratelin visited the Quebec leaders in August on Papineau's recommendation. "They generally discoursed," he wrote, "upon the means of taking Quebec and the means of organizing people in Quebec.... I understood there were two thousand persons initiated in Quebec and vicinity.... They are ready about Quebec but I do not think they will move until some success is caused elsewhere. They are more cautious than in Montreal."[81] Plans were sufficiently advanced that Notary Meunier of St-Damas knew that "Quebec was to be taken by men of the faubourg St-Roch."[82] The exact relationships between this organization and Papineau, Côté, and Nelson are difficult to ascertain.

In Côté's and Nelson's objectives, abolition of the seigneurial régime and tithing had a certain priority. On November 4, when they reached Napierville, fifteen miles inside the border, their first act was to "read a proclamation declaring Lower Canada independent and exemption from all seigneurial dues and abolition of tithes."[83] At Beauharnois, the farmer J. Dumouchelle, having given himself the title of colonel, called on the peasants to revolt "to abolish tithes [and] lods et ventes."[84] As in the year before, the *patriotes* plundered stores and warehouses belonging to English merchants and their French sympathizers; in several localities they were belligerent with the seigneurs and even the clergy. They ransacked W. McGinnis's stores and a number were determined to seize, tear up, and burn his papers, those of the de Léry seigneury.[85] J.-B. Lague, a St-Mathias farmer, set out from his parish "to take prisoner several black pigs [priests]."[86] Almost certainly, such radicalism was not dominant among the majority of the leaders or of the rural people. In this second rebellion, as in the first, the controlling influence was exerted by the conservative nationalists. The merchant F.-X. Prieur of Beauharnois said to his rural followers, "have no fear, my friends, we shall overthrow the English, and if we pull together, we shall succeed in bringing M. Papineau into the country."[87] The Montreal merchant C. Beausoleil recruited *Frères Chasseurs* "to safeguard our religion, our wives, our children, and our properties."[88]

Patriote professionals and merchants, fearful that an explosion of popular discontent would destroy the traditional institutions, continued to try to channel the movement toward protection of those institutions, and thereby the promotion of their own interests. For them, winning political power by force would give them control of patronage,[89] and, they thought, control of the economy. The Montreal merchant Glackmeyer, when seeking to entice individuals into the *patriote* ranks, contended "that Dr Nelson should demand of John Molson a sum of 80,000 *louis* . . . that the Lachine canal and the Laprairie-St-Jean railroad should be confiscated for the benefit of the provisional government. That the sieur Benjamin Hart and the other Jews should be strangled and their property confiscated. That the Water Works also be confiscated and the Montreal banks pillaged (excepting the Banque du Peuple which will be the government's)."[90] Such were the motives, expressed more or less openly and with some variations, which inspired the revolutionary élite and appealed also to a great many of the prominent farming landowners.

Among the rural populace, land was still the dominant preoccupation, related closely to the agricultural crisis and fears aroused by English immigrants. W. Brewster reported a conversation with the farmer C. Laplanche of Lacolle "respecting the intended rising of the French Canadians":

> ... deponent asked what motive they could have as they were untaxed and enjoyed the same laws as the English. He replied that the English have no right here at all and that the country belonged to the French Canadians and that they were sufficient to occupy it. I endeavoured to convince him that an Englishman purchasing a farm and having plenty of capital to spend would be a benefit but he would not hear of it; the country was theirs and they wanted all the land for themselves.[91]

The responsibility of government, the English merchants, and the immigrants for the rural malaise, so long harped upon by the *patriote* leaders, was restated in more violent terms than ever during the period of rebellion. In La Présentation, the leaders incited the *habitants* to attack Sorel, "to destroy all the bureaucrats and divide up what they had in property and not less than 500 arpents of land to each of those who would give their aid."[92] Nelson himself aroused greed in the country folk, saying, "that soon we would be in comfort, that all the poor Canadians would have land."[93] Notary Têtu of St-Hyacinthe, exasperated by the hesitant parishioners of St-Simon, declared, "... they want to put the rope around their own necks, I cannot understand how they can be so blind. They have been told in vain that before long they will be driven from their property by emigrants who will treat them like slaves and drive them into uninhabited country and hardship will pursue them to their graves."[94] Speculators, large and small landowners, rural proletariat, and impoverished former landowners were united by greed or frustration in the darkest designs. At Laprairie, Hubert Lefêbvre urged his men "to murder all Bureaucrats as they called the English population and destroy their properties."[95] When all was over and done, I. Lavoie of St-Philippe unhesitatingly declared that "if they [the *patriotes*] had taken Laprairie at the time they would not have left a single person of English, Irish, or Scotch extraction living without distinction of sex or age."[96]

The day appointed for the launching of the second rebellion was November 3. Elisée Mailhot, with the title of general, arrived at St-Hyacinthe the day before. He was to take Sorel, attacking by land and water, and was to obtain his forces from sixteen parishes. In each locality there was agitation, but the *patriotes* seem not to have been following any clear plan. The leaders at St-Damas, the merchant J.-B. Bourque, Notary Meunier, and Dr Consigny distributed 300 rifles. To a group of ill-armed *habitants* arriving at La Présentation, Meunier told a most unlikely story: "that there were as many arms as needed.... That there were sixteen hundred in the St-Charles hatmaker Joachim Jacques's cellar; that the parishes of St-Charles, St-Marc, Verchères, St-Césaire, St-Damas were all organized and armed. That there were arms depots at St-Ours, St-Denis and Maska."[97] But the local insurgents at St-Charles, finding too few arms to go around, protested noisily and then went home. Arriving there the following day, Toussaint Gagnon of La Présentation found neither men nor arms and, "learning that they had taken off, each to go home, I decided to go back home myself."[98] The other *patriotes* of La Présentation went to St-Ours, where they cooled their heels awaiting Mailhot until November 7. There ends the tragi-comic tale of the assault on Sorel.

On November 10, General Mailhot and Celestin Beausoleil decided to set up camp on Mont Montarville between the St Lawrence and the Richelieu behind Boucherville. Beginning with a nucleus of 150 men, 200 rifles and 3 cannon, they hoped to rally a force of 2,000 to 3,000 men and seize Chambly. On November 13, on news of the approach of troops, the Montarville *patriotes* dispersed. Beausoleil, according to J. Ménard, "the better to escape, took and stole by force a black horse from the manor-house stables."[99] Yet the rural people were aroused and ready to answer the call; at Nicolet the mood was such that Lieutenant Ford asked for more troops.[100] Mailhot's failure to provide leadership seems to have been partly due to rivalry with the radicals, but the *patriote* leaders in general were simply inept, which destroyed all possibility of concerted action.

The seizure of Chambly and St-Jean was to be directed from the Montarville camp, with the assistance of *habitants* from ten or twelve parishes. The principal agitator at Beloeil was Dr J.-B. Allard; "... when he talked politics," reported a farmer, "all his heart and senses were brought to it."[101] But when offered command of the local *patriotes* by J. Préfontaine, Allard declined on the grounds that under fire, if he were needed as a doctor, "it would interfere with the command and all I can do is accept a rifle so that when I have nothing to do as a doctor I can pass the time shooting."[102] On November 3 he tired of awaiting orders from Robert Nelson or from Beausoleil, the new commander, and left to find out what was happening. He turned up later at Chambly "in an appalling rig: it was frightful, the state of that poor animal, it had hardly the shape of a horse left ..."; he told the local leaders, "Gentlemen, we have all been taken in by Dr Nelson; he was to meet us... and from there come and breakfast with us at Chambly this morning, but he has betrayed us[;] let us all go home until further notice."[103] The St-Mathias *patriotes,* already on the march, dispersed too. So ended the planned seizures of Chambly and St-Jean. The supposed leaders for these various localities were at Mont Montarville.

Another target for attack was Laprairie, but once again the scene was one of confusion. A band of 150 men was assembled at St-Rémi by a shopkeeper, H. Lefebvre, and was joined by others recruited by peasant leaders as it moved toward Laprairie. René Pinsonneau, a wealthy farmer, took the title of colonel, distributed ammunition, encouraged his men to "hold yourselves ready to defend yourselves and let us march ahead," and then disappeared.[104] Now several hundred strong, the force continued, led by Lefebvre. Shots were fired at F. Singer's house on his orders, a number of English-speaking prisoners were taken, and the Vitty house was attacked, during which a man named Walker was killed. The advance ended when a scout returned "with the alarming intelligence that it was no use to advance, that there was a cannon placed on Laprairie wharf and a strong patrol in the village."[105] Another band led by the bailiff P.-R. Narbonne of St-Edouard, who was burning "to slit the throats and bellies of all the tories," came no closer to conquest; near Laprairie it met "a few mounted dragoons and thereupon the deponents and their companions were afraid and fled."[106] The plan of an immediate attack on Laprairie seems to have been abandoned, for most of the *patriotes* involved turned toward Napierville on Nelson's orders. Notary Médard Hébert was their general.[107]

Napierville thus became the principal rallying point for the insurgents south of Montreal. Dr Côté and the farmer Lucien Gagnon, both as generals, had begun to assemble forces there on November 2. The following day they announced the approach of Nelson at the head of a great army.[108] On November 4 Nelson arrived, accompanied only by two young men formerly of the French army, Hindeland and Tourvey. That day he addressed a force of 1,000 in the town square, assuring victory, introducing the French generals, and then proclaiming independence for Lower Canada, with himself as president of its provisional government. Within a few days the insurgent army had swelled to over 4,000. Its organization was relatively simple, since the rebels were already grouped by parishes and often by concessions and ranges. The lower ranks of command were given to or taken by tradesmen and the more aggressive farmers; the situation indeed facilitated usurpation of power, and generals, commanders, and colonels abounded. Tourvey was cavalry commander and Hindeland brigadier-general; Narbonne and

Lefèbvre were commanders, as were François Nicolas and four others of little or no military experience. Notary Charles Huot, quartermaster-general in charge of supply and pillaging, distributed notes in the name of the provisional government.

The leaders' promises turned out to be hollow. There were no American troops and no new arms. Barely 800 of the 4,000 insurgents had guns. On November 5 Nelson sent Côté and Tourvey with a detachment to bring back arms deposited just beyond the American border. On their way back the *patriotes* were accosted and beaten at Lacolle by English volunteers, and the arms, a much smaller supply than expected, were lost. This was a most distressing development, and yet the *patriote* leaders kept promising their forces quick and decisive victory. News of the imminent arrival of the English army under Colborne was a further blow. On November 8, Nelson gathered his general staff and insurgents, particularly those who were armed, and set off with the intention, as Côté told a prisoner at Napierville, "to clear the way to enable an armed body of Americans, that is to say the citizens of the United States, to enter this province for the purpose of cooperating with himself."[109] But the rebels were not all taken in by this story. Since the second day of the insurrection, Côté, Nelson, and Nicolas were suspected of duplicity by a number of peasant leaders, who made plans to seize them and turn them over to the authorities. But, reported one of the doubters, "the said arrest could not take place in view of word at the time that a quantity of Americans and arms were on the point of arriving and that we must take courage."[110] As the expedition of November 8 began there was even greater distrust and the plot was revived. The farmer L. Défaillette said, "I believe and believed at the time that Nelson's design was to use us to protect him on the route to the States and to clear the way for him."[111] A small group of insurgents did in fact seize Nelson, along with Trépanier and Gagnon, and would have turned them over to the British had not other *patriotes* prevented it. At nine in the morning on that November 8 a battle began at Odelltown, and the *patriotes* were defeated. The president of the Lower-Canadian republic left the battlefield shortly after the fighting began. L. Lussier, a farmer, corroborated by several others, declared that "Dr. Nelson then took flight and retired from the battle.... The day before I saw something which made me suspect that Dr. Nelson would cheat and betray us. In consequence I watched closely what he was doing."[112] By that date, it would seem that the leaders foresaw the inevitable failure of their movement, and the march on Odelltown was indeed to secure their escape. They left command of the insurgents at Napierville to Guillaume Lévesque, a Montreal clerk, who "then and there admitted that he was such commander with this limitation that although he was left in command by the said Robert Nelson that he... did not possess sufficient experience to take command in the battle."[113] The insurgents were then advised by Notary J.-B. Lukin and others to disperse, to which "they replied that all their leaders had abandoned them and they would follow our advice."[114] Colborne entered Napierville without a shot being fired.

At Châteauguay the rebellion collapsed even more quickly than elsewhere. Notaries Joseph-Narcisse Cardinal, P.-P. Desmaray, the bailiff M. Lepailleur, the notary's clerk J. Duquette, Dr H. Newcombe, and the blacksmiths Graveline and Lesage mobilized about 200 *Frères Chasseurs* the evening of November 3 and decided to go the next day to seize arms from the Indians at Sault St-Louis (Caughnawaga). Cardinal, the leader of the group, said that "... we wished to seize a number of localities and declare independence there so that the Americans might then be able to come the more freely."[115] But the Indians, while the seizure was being discussed with them, surrounded the *patriotes* and took sixty-four of them prisoner, whom they dispatched by boat to Montreal. Action by the remaining Châteauguay rebels then lost all cohesion and dwindled away.

The Beauharnois *patriotes*, who were also expecting imminent arrival of an American army, were better organized. Their leaders were the merchants François-Xavier Prieur, the advocate O. de Lorimier, the bailiff L.-G. Neveu, the innkeeper T. Rochon, Dr G. Perrigo, and the farmer J. Dumouchelle. The night of November 3, with 400 men, they seized the Ellice manor house, and the next day requisitioned the steamboat *Henry Brougham* on its arrival. Awaiting orders from Nelson, they then formed Camp Baker not far away. The army of insurgents there numbered 800, three-quarters of them armed with guns.[116] On November 8 they repulsed a series of attacks by volunteers, but upon news of the defeat at Odelltown they dispersed before the British troops arrived.

In Montreal, calm reigned. The leader of the *Frères Chasseurs*, an Irish advocate, John Picoté de Belestre-MacDonnell, had left Montreal on November 2, as had Beausoleil and Lévesque. He went to Berthier where a large force of *Frères Chasseurs* were gathered and who were, it was said, to take part in the attack on Sorel. He finally left, accompanied by a local leader, Dr Lafontaine, and was arrested a few days later near Nicolet.

Once success had been achieved to the south, according to the plan, the *Frères Chasseurs*, of whom there were large numbers to the north, at Ste-Rose, Ste-Anne des Plaines, and Terrebonne, were to take part in an attack on the city of Montreal. Except for a brief encounter at

Terrebonne, however, nothing materialized resembling the earthshaking events predicted by the curé of Ste-Rose, who had spoken of "a general massacre...an appalling thing like to the general judgment."[117] The *Frères Chasseurs* of the city of Quebec, meanwhile, were still awaiting the promised turn of events.

The second rebellion left more tragic scars than the first. Marauding soldiers and volunteers looted and burned the *patriotes'* farms and houses much more savagely than the year before, the volunteers in a mood of vengeance, giving vent to fears of many years' standing. Wrote Colonel Charles Grey in his journal, "These men have certainly had a great deal of provocation, but now that they have again got the upper hand they are disposed to exact too severe a retribution and require to be kept in order."[118] The government resolved that this time there must be exemplary punishments. The prisons were filled to bursting, with a total of 850 *patriotes*; 108 were brought to trial before courts martial, of whom nine only were acquitted and ninety-nine condemned to death. Finally, twelve of them were hanged, fifty-eight deported to Australian penal colonies, two banished, and twenty-seven released under bond for good behaviour.

The reprisals and exemplary punishments established a reign of fear and of surface calm. Colonel Grey wrote ironically, "They are now the most loyal people in the world and in the different villages where I had them assembled to give up their arms they have been quite ready to give three cheers for the Queen."[119] Beneath the surface, all was by no means calm. The *patriotes* of Quebec still clung to their plan of seizing the Citadel with the help of suburban *habitants*, and of arousing the surrounding countryside. But an infiltrator revealed the plot, and toward the end of December the Quebec region *Chasseurs* were disbanded.[120] Meanwhile, the refugees in the United States were not idle. Amid much bickering, plans and strategies formed and faded one after another, though many were attracted to the idea of keeping the British in a constant state of apprehension with successions of small raids. After conversations with Mailhot, Decoigne, and Côté, the innkeeper J. Demers of St-Georges recounted that the only course left was harassment: that the British troops would burn all the buildings and afterwards would withdraw and then the rebels would have the country, which was the way the Americans had won their independence.[121] The American example of eight years of struggle for independence was especially reassuring. The surveyor P. Renaud of St-Hyacinthe was said to have declared that the *patriotes* must not lose courage despite their present plight and "he hoped that in two years the cause of independence for the Canadas would be obtained, that this was just a delay."[122] The notion of ruining Lower Canada so that England would give it up as a burden, however, was soon abandoned for more realistic plans.

Papineau appeared increasingly to the refugees as an encumbrance. Côté was still anxious to denounce him, but the rest had a better idea: they would send him to France to seek help from the French government. Once he was out of the way, they could get on with their invasion plans. In May, 1839, at St-Constant a farmer even felt compelled to inform the authorities that, "For about fifteen days past, rumours have been current in the parish that the Canadians intend to rise, in order to take revenge for the Canadians who have been executed and massacre all the old country people residing in it.... I have observed the Canadians became bolder and bolder and kept more distant from the old country people and specially since a number of them have returned from the United States."[123] But despite all, the refugees gradually yielded to discouragement, and the Lower Canadians still awaiting them succumbed to resignation.

The rebellions of 1837-1838 were the culmination of a nationalist movement instigated and guided by and for the benefit of the French-Canadian middle classes. The proposed republican style of government was intended to transfer social and economic power from the English-speaking into the hands of a French-speaking minority who saw economic power as deriving from political control, but for whom economic development presupposed land ownership. Agriculture was therefore of paramount importance and was idealized in *patriote* dogma, and it was necessary for trade and manufacturing to develop in response to the needs of an agricultural economy. Mastery of the native soil, that is, control and distribution of land, was therefore central to the preoccupations of this minority, and hence of the French-Canadian population in whose name they claimed the right to it. The political élite could then tailor the granting of land to population growth—French-Canadian, needless to say. Whatever capitalism might emerge in such a society must be authentic to it—consequently, French-Canadian.

The colonial system, in the eyes of most of the élite associated with the *patriote* party and the revolutionary movement, had been responsible for importing an artificial capitalism beneficial only to foreigners. The political power vested in the mother country and in the governors sent to exercise it, through the bestowal of patronage and various other forms of favoritism, it was held, had enabled the English minority to dominate the colonial economy, notably in the principal branches of trade and industry and in the financial institutions, and even to acquire considerable landed property through purchase of seigneuries and farms. The form of capitalism encouraged by the colonial authorities and manipulated by the English-speaking élite had corrupted the seigneurial régime and created a class of landless rural French Canadians, and was responsible, too, for the decline of the French Canadians in the cities. Colonial exploitation and ethnic discrimination, especially the refusal to reserve ungranted land for the native-born and the encouragement of massive immigration, had virtually locked the great majority of French Canadians inside the frozen limits of the seigneuries, stifling them. British policy, in short, was seen as one of political domination, economic subjugation, and religious and cultural assimilation.

The agriculturally-oriented nationalism which emerged in response was centred on the defence and promotion of the seigneurial régime and the Coutume de Paris as institutions essential to national survival; free and common socage would be abolished and the seigneurial régime extended to encompass all of Lower Canada; there would be a single agrarian régime and a universally-applied system of law. Many French-Canadian professionals and merchants were already seigneurs, and a still greater number dreamed of obtaining that status by retrieving the townships as well as by supplanting the English-speaking seigneurs, whose wealth derived principally from commerce and industry. Most professionals, the notaries in particular, depended on the operation of the old institutions. The Catholic Church was also regarded as a national institution, even by certain agnostics; its privileges were not really questioned by the majority of nationalists, and the widespread anti-clericalism rested not so much on an image of a new role for the clergy as on the desire for *un bon clergé national*. Even with the radicals in control of the revolutionary movement, most of the revolutionary élite continued to look to a future founded on an agricultural economy and the survival of the old social régime.

Independence, since it would have destroyed the two most viable sectors of the economy, namely the trade in grain with the west and the lumber industry, would have condemned Lower Canada to several decades of serious under-development and would have strengthened the seigneurs and the clergy. The nationalists knew this when they appealed to and mobilized the masses in 1837 and 1838, yet the call they launched was to "a nation in peril." The masses, feeling their existence and their values and traditions indeed to be in peril, responded in hope of saving their families, faith, language, and laws.

When in 1840 the British government formally made known its intention to unify the Canadas, the Catholic clergy took fright and attempted to take over the mobilization of the masses from the nationalists. As in 1822, the clerics saw the spectre of protestantism looming menacingly with the anticipated abolition of the seigneurial régime, the Coutume de Paris, and tithing.[124] Curés preached against it in their churches and the bishops acquiesced. Former *patriote* leaders fell into step behind the national clergy. At St-Benoit, J.-B. Jobin, long a prominent *patriote* figure, warned the *habitants* that "the government would deprive you of your rights, your religion and your priests, you have already been burned and pillaged and they are not content with that, they still want to seize the seigneuries... and take your farms from you."[125] The seigneur Maximilien Globensky wrote immediately to T.W.C. Murdoch in Montreal:

> We must recall that it was with similar discourses that the indisposition of the inhabitants of this province was begun [before], that they were inspired to defy the authorities and persuaded that the government wished to enslave them and that they were finally led to take up arms to overthrow the authority which according to them would subjugate them.... M. Jobin was one of the members of this provincial parliament, one of those who contributed to the revolt of 1837 and his discourse must have made a sensation, particularly in a parish which was one of the first to raise the banner of revolt.[126]

The new governor, Charles Poulett Thompson (created Baron Sydenham in 1841), met with the bishops, gave them reassurances, and prayed them to temper the curés' zeal. The nationalist élite continued to talk of independence, political liberty, and a republic, unwittingly continuing to strengthen the position of the clergy and the seigneurs.

The leaders of the radical wing of the *patriote* movement were a remarkably mixed bag ethnically and religiously. Their goal was "national" independence and the attainment of political power by the middle-class elements which had been victimized by the colonial system and which were comprised not only of French Canadians but of many English-speaking as well: "Canadian" in short. Furthermore, many of the radicals considered the seigneurial régime and church privileges (Catholic and Anglican alike) to be obstacles to a complete transfer of power and the thorough transformation of the society. In this their thinking was not far from that of the sprinkling of English-speaking farmers in the seigneuries and the English-speaking merchants, for whom there was a basic conflict between "feudal" heritage and the growing needs of a capitalist economy. Girod's and Côté's inquiries into the workings of the seigneurial régime in 1836 led to denunciation of "feudal exploitation," but did not budge the ideological line laid down by the *patriote* party. The radicals' attempts to direct popular discontent against the government, the seigneurs, and the clergy began to reach the lower classes in certain regions only after revolution became a reality, and even then the proselytizers were too few to produce the full effect hoped for. Thus it was a conservative nationalism that gave rise to the first rebellion.

The rupture between Papineau's conservatives and the radicals gave the latter the upper hand in the second rebellion. Nelson's declarations of independence in February and November of 1838 proclaimed abolition of the old social régime and also universal suffrage, appealing directly to the urban and rural proletariat. But the radicals were no more successful that year than their predecessors of the year before in controlling the middle-rank organization. Papineau remained the symbol of rebellion, and his shadow was long. In the recruitment of *Frères Chasseurs* there was much blustering talk of killing Englishmen and township inhabitants and confiscating their possessions, but little was said against seigneurs and tithing. The attempt to rouse the masses against the old social régime met with only partial success.

The failure of the rebellions can be attributed to obsession in the French middle classes with their own short-term interests, and perhaps also to a lack of true revolutionary spirit. They were simply undergoing a growth crisis and seeking recognition of their status in the society. The glaringly deficient revolutionary leadership can certainly not be laid to the crushing might of the British army, which itself was hardly a model of seasoned discipline. The fact is that the sometimes impressive concentrations of peasant insurgents rarely had any defensive strategy and simply disintegrated where they were, fear pervading their ranks in the absence of dynamic leadership to counteract it and channel it into orderly offensive action.

Clerical interdictions and troubled consciences may have had much to do with that fear. A farmer, P. Plante, was reported to have said "that he was so overwhelmed by distress to find himself with the rebel troops that he vowed, if he could be delivered, to keep absolute silence returning home, and to present himself in the attitude of a beggar at the door of every house he encountered on his way and once home to have two masses of thanksgiving said for his deliverance."[127] But fear and remorse, though no doubt widespread, did not prevent most peasants, labourers, and tradesmen involved in the revolutionary movement from surmounting the religious impediment, perhaps not without soul-searching. Isidore Carpentier testified: "... before leaving I went to confess and consult my pastor ... [.] he told me: you have done wrong and I cannot absolve you: however I was at St-Charles and St-Denis with my gun ... for the expedition whose goal was to take Sorel."[128]

The responsibility taken and leadership given by Wolfred Nelson at St-Denis, by Dr Chénier at St-Eustache, and on occasion by a few lesser lights did result in cohesive action, but these were exceptions. Accusations of cowardice were hurled in every direction once all was over. Premeditation or the lack of it has nothing to do with the fact that not only Papineau but also the revolutionary élite in general failed to provide leadership. This was the principal cause of the *patriotes'* weakness, for there could be no effective organization or action without leadership. In the absence of vigorous direction from the élite, the popular elements might have taken control and pursued the cause toward their own objectives. If they did not it was because they were lacking a class consciousness of their own, the conservative nationalists having long made so much of the perils hanging over the entire "nation" and of the protection inherent in the seigneurial régime.

CHAPTER 13

Conclusion

This analysis, an attempt to portray the many-faceted, complex, and changing society of Lower Canada in this period, centres on the emergence of a crisis that deepened and took hold of the entire society, and ended only after a thoroughly miscarried adventure in revolution. Attention to the crisis, its nature and components, necessarily becomes attention to the society's long-term evolution, for the crisis was the product of change in a community which had taken form in the seventeenth century and kept its essential characteristics until the end of the eighteenth century.

Introduction of the parliamentary system was primarily due to pressure from the local society. The dominant economic sectors, the fur trade and agriculture, had expanded throughout the eighteenth century, contributing both to the rise of the merchant bourgeoisie and to diversification in the rural society. A multitude of new villages sprang up and tradesmen gradually established a place for themselves alongside the merchants. These developments did not reverse the trend toward ruralization, for most of the manpower for the fur trade was seasonal and was obtained from the country districts; but the changes did create new and increasingly pressing demands. The merchants, both English and French, began to challenge the existing political absolutism and the concentration of power in the hands of the old aristocracy and the clergy. They were not revolutionary but reformist, and perceived the parliamentary system as a means of obtaining a share of political power alongside the traditional élites. The old aristocracy, weakened by improvidence and division of inheritances, stoutly resisted reforms which to them endangered the supporting institutions of the old social régime and the orderly hierarchical society which they conceived as essential. The constitution of 1791 was in fact a compromise which for a time at least served the interests of both old and new élites.[1]

The division of the colony into two political units, Upper and Lower Canada, was the result of an arbitrary decision by the authorities in London, not the wishes of the local society. Those who were demanding political reform, since they were active in an economic space extending from the Atlantic to the Pacific, by no means wanted a political frontier created, and English and French merchants were agreed in considering it artificial. The authorities in London, bearing in mind the cultural differences, were in fact obeying preoccupations similar to those that had led to the creation of New Brunswick in response to Loyalist immigration.

During the last decade of the eighteenth century, economic expansion and fears inspired by the French Revolution helped to unite the leading classes; together they were determined to preserve peace in the society at all cost. There was no question of one class trying to advance its own interests by channelling ethnic differences or popular discontent through a political party. The Militia Law, the reintroduction of the *corvée* for road construction, quarrels between certain seigneurs and their *censitaires*, and a measure of peasant distrust for the parliamentary system had provoked a number of demonstrations of popular displeasure. Since there was no class consciousness or nationalistic feeling among the masses, however, and since the élite groups maintained their attitude of solidarity, these eruptions were only isolated, short-lived incidents. But evidence of economic disparities between the ethnic groups, though it created little ill-feeling at the time, sowed the seed of discontent for future years. The English-speaking merchants in fact established their hold on the principal economic activities in the final twenty years of the eighteenth century. The French-speaking merchants lagged behind primarily because of their attitude to large-scale business; between 1768 and 1790, only 10 per cent of them participated in partnerships, in contrast with 49 per cent of the English. The French Canadians' inattention to technological change was also a telling factor. Whereas, along with amalgamation, replacement of the canoe by the larger flat-bottomed *bateau* became essential to cost-cutting in the fur trade after 1770, the change was made by only 28 per cent of French-speaking traders in comparison with 75 per cent of their English competitors. Furthermore, beginning late in the eighteenth century, an impressive number of French-speaking fur traders put their assets into seigneuries and became landed gentry. This pattern shows another facet of a society whose values and institutions, by encouraging unproductive investment, blocked the emergence of a powerful French-speaking merchant class.[2] Discrimination in patronage was a lesser impediment.

After 1800, external peril became more real. Besides the continuing threat from French revolutionary influences, there was now more compelling danger from the United States. But fear of enemies outside the colony was no longer enough to ensure peace within; that fear now served to exacerbate tensions in a society beset by conflicts of every kind. Economic change and a new imbalance among population growth, availability of land, and agricultural production brought deterioration of the political and social climate. This was the background for a developing three-way power struggle among the French-Canadian middle classes, the English merchant bourgeoisie, and the Catholic clergy. The imperatives of the struggle not only brought political parties into being but also forced ideological innovation or compromise on the classes involved.

The crisis that rocked the rural communities, even to that most basic of institutions, the family, was primarily a demographic one. The crux of the problem was not flagging vitality in the French-Canadian population, but the disappearance of available land in the seigneuries. Demographic pressure affected the country districts in a number of ways, one being the increased movement of people in search of land. Between 1800 and 1822, 20,000 individuals left parishes in the Quebec and Trois-Rivières districts for localities where land was still available. The migration was first into neighbouring parishes, then away from the home region entirely, even to the United States. The Montreal region, where the land was thought to be the richest, became the centre of attraction and eventually the centre of the most severe demographic pressure. In a society where the family was the most powerful institution and a wellspring of community life, departures were not undertaken lightly. The growing number of individuals without land formed a newly visible rural proletariat; in the rural Montreal district this class increased from 28 per cent of householders in 1831 to 38 per cent in 1844. The growth in the number of labourers is an excellent illustration of a change that owed more to scarcity of land than to economic diversification; in certain parishes, over 40 per cent of heads of families were labourers. Another consequence of demographic pressure was subdivision of landed property; in 1831, 51 per cent of landholders in the Montreal district owned 50 *arpents* or less.

These problems and their consequences for the rural people were worsened by seigneurs who took advantage of conditions to raise seigneurial dues and the price of land, held back on land concession, and developed a system of indirect sales with under-the-table commissions. Many seigneurs also profited from the expansion of the lumber trade by reserving rights to timber and sometimes even firewood on concessions they granted. Such behaviour limited access to land, made its price prohibitive, and generally added to the burdens borne by the country people. The existence of vast areas of unoccupied land in the townships exacerbated the frustration. Massive immigration from the British Isles was perceived as part of a plot to restrict French-speaking people to the seigneuries and to keep them out of the townships and cities.

The situation for French lower-class city-dwellers was hardly less dismal. Tradesmen and labourers inevitably felt threatened by the burgeoning urban immigrant population. In 1831, 45 per cent of the population of Quebec City was English-speaking. In Montreal the situation was even more disquieting, for the English proportion of the population rose from 54 per cent in 1831 to 61 per cent in 1842. In short, for the French Canadians—peasants, tradesmen, and labourers alike—immigrants were people coming to take away their land, their customers, and their jobs.

Peasant discontent deepened with the agricultural crisis. In the eighteenth century, land had been abundant and the rural people could produce enough food for their own subsistence and for the export market, too. With new land being put to the plough, wheat production increased; but after the turn of the century, outmoded agricultural methods, population growth, and scarcity of land hastened soil exhaustion and led to shrinking yields and rising production costs. In both export and local markets, Lower-Canadian wheat producers became less and less competitive with American and Upper-Canadian shippers on the St Lawrence, despite higher transportation costs for Americans and Upper Canadians to the port of Quebec (see Table 86). Only a revolution in agricultural methods could have maintained the viability of wheat as both a subsistence and a commercial crop, especially in view of the subdivision of farms. Localities where the soil was rich and land ownership was stable were the most successful at resisting the decline in production, but these pockets of resistance gradually disappeared and Lower Canada became a major importer of wheat and flour (see Tables 85 and 86).

The peasant, faced with meagre wheat harvests which reduced his income and in many cases made even subsistence precarious, was forced to diversify his production. His growing reliance on potatoes for food and new interest in stock-raising were dictated not so much by marketing possibilities as by his need to feed and clothe himself and his family. There was nevertheless an agricultural élite active in the cultivation of wheat and oats and in stock-raising for local and urban markets. The small and scattered number of French Canadians in this group, however, faced strong competition from English producers in the seigneuries and townships, as well as from Americans and Upper Canadians, who dominated the market in dairy produce, meat, potatoes, and oats. After 1830 the agricultural crisis that was manifest first and most severely in wheat spread to other sectors, including stock-raising. The most severely affected were French-Canadian farmers, because of their persistence in trying to grow wheat and their vulnerability to competition in all sectors (see Tables 87 and 88).

Demographic pressures, as well as crisis in the rural economy and in the seigneurial system, gave rise to a situation charged with enormous revolutionary potential. Rural discontent could have been channelled against the seigneurs, the clergy, and the state, leading to disaffection for the old social régime; but lack of class consciousness among the masses and manipulation on the part of a political élite opposed to social change served to focus hostility on the English-speaking merchants, "bureaucrats," and immigrants as the principal source of the perils hanging over the French Canadians and their culture. The intensity of this hostility was more pronounced in certain localities than in others. Between the early years of the century and the rebellions, the centre of this polarization of ethnic sentiment shifted from the Quebec district to the Montreal district, where the economy was most dependent on agriculture, particularly wheat, and where demographic pressures were strongest. Furthermore, Montreal was the city where the English presence was most keenly felt and where the continued existence of the French Canadians was most precarious.

The power struggle among the English business community, the French-Canadian middle classes, and the Catholic clergy may be seen as another facet of the Lower-Canadian crisis. The confrontation began midway through the first decade of the nineteenth century and became increasingly bitter, culminating in the rebellions of 1837-1838. Each group used the weapons at hand, altering alliances and strategies according to expedience. All of them made ideological readjustments, and the lay groups sought power through political parties.

At the end of the eighteenth century the English merchants, as the dominant economic class, played a crucial political role and exerted considerable social influence. As the economy diversified after 1800, their hold on it gained strength, and with immigration providing new blood their sphere of activity extended to cover both Upper and Lower Canada. Besides having access to the resources of certain American states, they maintained continuing contacts in the imperial markets to which they sold; the economic space in which they operated was therefore immense. In the cities, they were present in all sectors and at all levels, most strikingly in large business enterprises. While the English-speaking comprised 45 per cent of the population of Quebec in 1831, 57 per cent of the city's merchants were English. In Montreal the proportion was even greater, rising from 63 per cent of the merchant class in 1831 to 71 per cent in 1842. Even in the country districts, both seigneuries and townships, English merchants played a role far surpassing their numerical importance. In Papineau's seigneury, an area colonized by the nationalist leader, the only two merchants were English-speaking.

During the first forty years of the nineteenth century, the success achieved by this English bourgeoisie tended to obscure their difficulties and anxieties. Since they were vitally dependent on the adoption and continuance of British protective tariffs on timber and grains, political uncertainties in Britain and Lower Canada weighed heavily upon them. Their future depended also on the creation of banks and land registry offices, on road-building, and on canalling along the St Lawrence. Hence they needed whatever support they could muster in a legislative assembly whose majority considered Lower Canada to be the natural habitat of a threatened agricultural "nation." The vulnerability of the English-speaking merchant class was intensified by its determination to reform or abolish the traditional institutions it considered to be blocking economic and social progress, namely the seigneurial régime and the Coutume de Paris.

Not surprisingly, the English merchants created a political party, known as the English party, to represent their own and the colonial civil servants' interests—and, they claimed, those of the rest of the population, too. A long series of failures at the polls, however, prevented the party from playing a significant role in the legislative assembly in the years preceding the rebellions. For a time the party could legitimately claim representation of city and townships inhabitants, but after 1830, when it came to be known to the French-speaking as "the bureaucratic party," it could no longer pretend to represent any but purely English-speaking interests. Its attitude to the seigneurial régime reduced the party's support among the old aristocracy and many of the clergy. Even before 1830, its toadying to certain authoritarian governors alienated the Irish Catholics and liberal English, who were being enticed into the *patriote* camp. The political conservatism of the English merchants certainly owed much to the colony's economic dependence on the empire, but their conservatism resulted even more from their party's chronic failure to make inroads in the legislative assembly. As a consequence of that failure they were constantly seeking to strengthen their ties with the bureaucracy and the governors, and would even go so far as to appeal directly to London. After 1830 the imperial authorities turned an increasingly sympathetic ear to the pleas from an ethnic minority that felt it was being swamped by a triumphant nationalist movement. Understandably, the business community championed the balance-of-powers theory, the only one which in practice could guarantee it a share in decisions. Having been politically dominant as the century began, the English bourgeoisie, though still economically dominant, could only watch helplessly as its political power eroded.

The Catholic clergy played a determinant role in the class power struggle, which was also a confrontation with the nationalists. Despite their comfortable economic base of revenues from numerous and flexible sources, their support from a complex institutional network, and their powerful moral influence, the clergy did not escape the repercussions of socio-economic change. They were frightened by the French Revolution and its impious philosophy, by American democracy, and by the intrigues of the Anglican bishop, whose proposals won favour with certain of the governors. But a far greater worry was the growing political and social strength of the French-Canadian middle classes. The clergy saw in this element a new and dangerous force, working even in the remotest rural areas to bring radical transformation to the existing social hierarchies. The political activism of the French-Canadian professionals, implying conversion of the legislative assembly into a vehicle for social change, as well as their brandishing of liberal and nationalistic ideas straight out of the French Revolution, account largely for the clergy's vigorous reaction against the Canadian party in 1810. Bishop Plessis, convinced that the group was revolutionary, aligned himself with the state and followed its policy of confrontation. The end of the Revolutionary and Napoleonic Wars and the War of 1812 eased many tensions, however, and permitted the clergy to adopt much more subtle strategy.

As the Restoration began in France, the Catholic Church of Lower Canada was redefining its objectives and ideology. The influence of French theocratic philosophers was beginning to penetrate and undermine Gallican traditions, which recognized papal authority only in religious matters. Theocratic and ultramontanist thinking, which claimed papal and church supremacy in secular as well as religious matters, was adopted with a vengeance by Monseigneur Lartigue, and the bishops of Quebec were not unreceptive. This philosophy gave credence to an image of a church that was at once above the state and united with it, and of a clergy that would be the ideal leading class. Nationalism, with the clergy depicted as a "national" élite, was a concept popularized by Lartigue. The quarrel over the creation of the diocese of Montreal helped to spread the notion in the clerical ranks. This ultramontanist nationalism appealed to both the clergy and their flocks as a challenge to middle-class, liberal nationalism and as an invitation to nationalist forces to rally together behind the clergy.

With their redefinition of religious and social objectives, the ecclesiastical hierarchy began to give greater priority to education. Numerous classical colleges had already been created to recruit clergy primarily from local sources, although the hope of bringing priests from France was not abandoned. But ultramontanist ideology, stimulated by the perception of danger from Protestant and lay quarters, now led the clergy to seek control of primary education and its diffusion. Lartigue's dream was that new schools run by nuns or brothers would be a powerful factor in assuring that rising generations would be Catholic.

Around 1815, the Catholic hierarchy ceased to look only to the bureaucracy for support. Peace would have to be made with the dominant party in the assembly if the Royal Institution were to be defeated and control of primary education regained. An alliance was formed that produced the Parish Schools Act of 1824. The clergy and the Canadian party were drawn together by this and other questions, notably the 1822 plan for the union of the Canadas and the lengthy dispute over the establishment of the diocese of Montreal. But this alliance of convenience began to crumble as the *patriote* party took a radical turn. The *patriotes* attempted to take control of primary schools and parish council management, and declared their intention to apply the elective principle at all levels of power, even in parish affairs. This was too much for the clergy, who were nationalistic in their own fashion and remained fundamentally hostile to democracy, liberalism, and republicanism. After 1830 the breach between the *patriotes* and the clergy deepened. The clergy were now convinced that the two were bent on irreconcilable goals.

Among the middle classes, a schism occurred early in the nineteenth century. At its root were the French Canadians of the liberal professions. They derived their incomes largely from the operation of the old institutions, whereas their English colleagues, whose competition they felt keenly, derived theirs more from the business community. The French professionals were furthermore the group most sensitive to the growing economic disparities between the ethnic groups at all levels. As diagnosticians of social ills, they developed a class consciousness inseparably interwoven with the fermentation of a "national" consciousness. As a rising social group seeking status and power, they identified national interests with their own. Their image of the nation portrayed an ethnic community bound above all to the land and committed to agriculture as a vocation, a community whose institutions, traditions, and way of life were endangered. To them, their enemies were the immigrants, American or British, but most of all the English-speaking capitalists and functionaries who were using the political system to their own advantage and to the great detriment of the French-speaking people. This perception of reality had much appeal for the new generation of French-Canadian merchants who were restricted to Lower Canada and who resented the ever-growing hold of the English on the country's economic life. It had appeal as well for the lower classes who were troubled by instability and mounting rural problems. In short, the nationalism of the professionals, although centred on their own interests and aspirations, provided an all-embracing ideology, attractive to all French-speaking social classes and calculated to rally all behind the middle classes.

The professionals thus interiorized the problems of the French-Canadian society and gave outsiders a plausible explanation of the society's condition. They also built a mythology richly embellished with symbols. They appealed to the population and strove to mobilize it politically around the Canadian party, which became known as the *patriote* party in 1826. Since the party's goal was achievement of power for the defence and advancement of its leaders' interests and those of the "nation," it could hardly preach the political status quo. It had to advocate political concepts that justified a shift of power in its favour. In the circumstances, liberalism provided arguments that reconciled respect for British institutions with a new interpretation of how the parliamentary system should work. The party chieftain, Pierre Bédard, at the height of his confrontation with Governor Craig, the civil servants, and the English merchants, demanded implementation of ministerial responsibility and raised the prickly question of control of the civil list. Theoretically and in their practical implications, both demands were somewhat radical for the period. The party leaders, branded as revolutionaries by their English and clerical opponents, were imprisoned, and for a time their paper, *Le Canadien*, was suppressed.

The political crisis of 1810 brought to light the extent of popular support for the Canadian party, but it also unleashed an internal leadership crisis, with a throng of rivals vying to succeed Bédard. Papineau's accession to leadership did not put an end to it. At the time he was a compromise choice, and fully realized that he must consolidate his authority before trying to bring the party to more radical concepts and actions. He also realized that the growing English population in the cities could turn his party into a purely rural one. Since he hoped to attract the Irish Catholic and liberal English vote, he felt obliged to avoid antagonizing the business community too much over certain matters, and adopted a stance of moderate nationalism and liberalism. His choice of *un bon Anglais*, John Neilson, as his Quebec lieutenant is attributable to these preoccupations. His party was also obliged to step lightly with the clergy and the old seigneurial class in hope of rallying them to the nationalist movement on the party's terms. The concept of ministerial responsibility was shelved, being judged too radical, and control of revenues was brought to the fore as the major issue at stake. It was a very effective strategy. Developments such as the 1822 union plan, the quarrel over the diocese of Montreal, and Dalhousie's abuses of authority proved fortuitous; they won the party some powerful support in Canada and England and helped Papineau consolidate his leadership. The nationalist movement spread and deepened its roots during this period.

After his voyage to England in 1823, Papineau set in motion a thorough re-examination of the colonial system and British institutions. His change in attitude was accelerated by wrangles with Dalhousie, by pressure from his entourage, and by mounting popular discontent. When the British Commons committee report of 1828 agreed with the *patriote* party on the supply question, Papineau declared that this was no longer a priority for his party. Without totally abandoning the pursuit of revenue control, he then launched a new strategy that went hand in hand with a radical turn of thought and action in the *patriote* movement. The central feature of this strategy was application of the elective principle at all levels of power, and its purpose was to place all authority in the hands of the *patriotes*. The deliberate polarization of the power struggle around the issue of selection of legislative councillors was an attempt to focus attention on the misdeeds of an institution which, more than any other, symbolized the power of the English-speaking and the abuses of that power by an oligarchy. The idea of an elected legislative council symbolized the transfer of power to the French-speaking and the advent of a democratic society. Justification for the strategy was sought in American democratic and republican principles. As in the campaign for control of revenues, the symbolism and liberal rhetoric enabled the *patriotes* to advance the idea of independence without brandishing the banner of nationalism too alarmingly. The election of 1834 brought unprecedented success to the *patriote* party, with an extraordinary ethnic polarization of the vote; a minority of English-speaking voters remained faithful to the party, but generally speaking the English and even the Irish Catholics were no longer to be duped. The replacement of Neilson by O'Callaghan as Papineau's lieutenant was a vain attempt to retain the Irish vote. The strategy did, however, win continued sympathy from the reformists of Upper Canada and from radicals in England. Liberal rhetoric notwithstanding, the dominant tendency of *patriote* nationalism was still profoundly conservative, for it was as firmly committed as ever to protecting the institutions of the Old Régime, namely the seigneurial régime and the Coutume de Paris, and traditional privileges for the *bon clergé national*. A small, ethnically mixed element in the party, including the Nelson brothers, Brown, Girod, Côté, and Chénier, was bent on social revolution, not simply political independence, but for the time being this radical wing was content to postpone settlement of social goals and work for the common priority of independence.

Encouraged by his overwhelming electoral success of 1834, convinced that his course was irreversible and his objectives assured, and that revolution would occur in Upper Canada and even England, Papineau launched an economic war against his adversaries. His party withheld supplies, opposed the banks and the purchase of imported goods, and beat the drum for small manufacturing and for buying at home from friends. From 1830 on, many of the more militant *patriotes* held that trying to win independence through ordinary political channels was illusory and that the situation was leading to armed conflict. This seemed to be confirmed by the adoption of Russell's Ten Resolutions in March, 1837.

Russell's Resolutions were the last straw, goading the *patriote* movement to become a revolutionary one, although still pretending "opposition within the law." The strategy adopted in the spring of 1837 was designed to lead to armed conflict and did so. Even those still hoping that England would yield to legal pressure accepted that possibility and were eventually caught up in the exigencies of revolutionary action. The purpose of the great county rallies was to mobilize the local leaders and to complete the indoctrination of the masses. Continuing economic deterioration contributed to the extraordinary success the *patriotes* met with everywhere except in the city of Quebec, where the old leaders still exerted a moderating influence. Conditions were ripest for revolution and the situation was escalating most rapidly in the rural Montreal region. There the more militant called openly for revolt and independence, with the extremists proposing abolition of tithing and seigneurial dues. At the St-Charles six-county rally there was a declaration of human rights and the radicals talked of taking up arms. Even Papineau's relatively moderate speech proposed revolutionary measures. December 4 was set for the proclamation of Lower Canada's independence. In Montreal, meanwhile, the *Fils de la Liberté* were busy mobilizing tradesmen and labourers.

Rapidly intensifying rural agitation and the street fight of November 6 in Montreal did much to provoke the government's intervention. The clergy had already begun to react with strong warnings in July. The publication of Bishop Lartigue's *mandement* on the day following the St-Charles rally was a calculated move that showed the church's awareness of the mood of the people. The government, after the November 6 incident in Montreal, could no longer look upon the agitation as mere bluff. A few days later warrants were prepared for the arrest of the principal *patriote* leaders. Having received early warning of this, Papineau called together his immediate lieutenants and conferred with an emissary from Upper Canada.

Referring to the crucial decisions taken then by the small group that comprised the party's supreme command, Mackenzie wrote to O'Callaghan seven years later, in September, 1844: "When you yourself and friends sent up to Toronto in November, 1837, to urge us to rise against the British government it certainly would not have come into my thoughts that the men who did that would in the event of failure make a treaty with England for the patronage of Canada to themselves and our tory enemies."[3] Following the deliberations in the days leading up to November 12, 1837, the revolutionary leaders left Montreal to take refuge in the country.

Events developed rapidly. Soon after the formation of *patriote* camps, the governor sent out the troops. They were repulsed at St-Denis on November 23 but captured St-Charles two days later. Once resistance had faded at other centres to the south, General Colborne led his army against the *patriotes* to the north of Montreal. By December 15 the first rebellion was over.

Despite the magnitude of their failure, the *patriotes* who fled to the United States contemplated a return in force. But differences quickly arose between the Papineau supporters and the radicals, the latter attributing the defeat to the leader's flight and even more to the revolutionary programme's lack of attraction for the peasants. There developed a rupture over the abolition of seigneurial dues, the Coutume de Paris, and tithing—in other words, not over strategy but over basic ideology. Seen in broad perspective, Papineau's flight from St-Denis could be attributed to something more than cowardice. An influential minority of *patriotes*, many of them connected with the Banque du Peuple, were deeply worried over the danger of a social revolution and the safety of the man who could prevent it. In any event, the two factions in exile made separate plans for invasion. In February, 1838, the radical leaders led a small incursion into Lower Canada, just long enough to declare independence, to announce the abolition of tithing, the seigneurial régime, the Coutume de Paris, and the death penalty for theft, and to proclaim universal suffrage and separation of church and state.

For all that, the second rebellion, led by the radicals, did not bear the stamp of social revolution. Organized as it was around a secret society, the *Frères Chasseurs*, it did not give the radicals a real opportunity to popularize their goals. Besides, it was joined by many impatient Papineau supporters who were counting on settling ideological differences later. In rural Lower Canada, most local leaders held to Papineau's ideology. The radicals were therefore able to do little more than proclaim independence at Napierville and restate their objectives, and were obliged at that to use Papineau's name as a rallying cry.

Both rebellions were in fact directed from the beginning by the middle-class group which had given impetus to the Canadian and *patriote* movement since 1805. A total of 186 professionals (76 notaries, 67 physicians, 43 advocates) and 388 merchants took part in the rebellions. Their interests were confined to Lower Canada and, apart from individuals connected with the Banque du Peuple and some large landowners, in general they were not among the well-heeled. They were inclined to seize on the agrarian mystique and to dream of a society of small landowners in which they, of course, would have more land than others. Most being dependent on the operation of the old institutions and few being more than superficially anti-clerical, they laid their faith in the old social régime and idealized it as the "national heritage." Their image of the nation, although it embraced the people, began and ended with themselves. They therefore feared losing control of the revolution to the radicals, to the advantage of the common people and to their own detriment. In short, the revolutionary goal was to win for themselves political power and control of patronage, and also, they thought, the economic power that had been usurped by the English.

The role of the general populace is more difficult to measure, particularly in the cities. In Montreal the *Fils de la Liberté* mobilized some 700 to 800 tradesmen and labourers, who were motivated perhaps partly by dependence on a rural economy in crisis and partly by immigrant competition, and who were very early forsaken by their middle-class leaders. North and south of Montreal, however, the insurgent forces numbered between 4,000 and 7,000 farmers, tradesmen, and labourers, a military concentration which is more revealing of the relationship between the élite and the masses. Here, where the *patriote* movement provided organization and leadership, rural people were truly committed to it. Elsewhere, the prevalent feeling was hope and anticipation, more or less strongly expressed depending on locality. Those actively involved in the events of the rebellions revealed a rancour that was in a sense the voice of the rural masses everywhere; it was not merely personal or restricted to the Montreal region. They spoke from the heart of the harsh economic conditions of their existence, most specifically, and in clear and violent terms, of the land problem and English immigration. Their fears for their traditions began with the scarcity of land and the threat it posed to the stability of the family and the rural communities. Most of the insurgents possessed less land than the statistical average; those who had more tended to be closer to the middle classes. Since most were over thirty, their children's future was large in their minds. Above all, the rural masses were awakened to nationalism, and later to the idea of independence, by bread-and-butter problems. Belief in social change was neither profound nor widespread, for the radical *patriotes* were few in number and had been preaching abolition of tithing and seigneurial dues only in the later stages of the upheaval.

After the failure of the second rebellion, the refugees in the United States continued for a time to make plans for invasion and also continued to agitate in order to keep the people's hopes alive, but little by little they realized the futility of it all and began to drift back to Lower Canada. Thus ended the revolutionary adventure, leaving much bitterness among those who had been part of it. Lack of organization, weakness of leadership, covert or open conflict between left and right wings, the absence of real socio-economic goals, and opposition by the clergy were the principal causes of the failure of this experiment in revolution.

This book has borne essentially on the problem of social change and those factors inhibiting or contributing to it, namely the economy, demography, institutions, the equilibrium between classes and groups, ethnicity, ideology, political parties, and even group mentality. Evolution in Lower Canada in this period was the fruit of interaction among these various elements of human activity. Situating these determinants enables us to discern what ground for manoeuvre was open to the groups involved and what roles were played by individuals. Such at least has been the book's most specific intent.

ABBREVIATIONS

The following abbreviations are used in the Tables, Notes, and Select Bibliography:

AAQ	Archives de l'Archevêché du Québec
APQ	Archives de la Province de Québec
ASQ	Archives du Séminaire de Québec
BM	British Museum
BRH	*Bulletin des recherches historiques*
CHAR	*Canadian Historical Association Annual Report*
CHR	*Canadian Historical Review*
CO	Colonial Office
DC	*Documents Relating to the Constitutional History of Canada,* 3 vols., Ottawa, and their French version, *Documents relatifs à l'histoire constitutionnelle du Canada: 1759-91,* A. Shortt and A.G. Doughty (eds.), 1918; *1791-1918,* A.G. Doughty and D.A. McArthur (eds.), 1914; *1819-28,* A.G. Doughty and N. Story (eds.), 1935.
JHALC	*Journals of the House of Assembly of Lower Canada*
PAC	Public Archives of Canada
PACR	*Public Archives of Canada Annual Report*
P-B	Papineau-Bourassa Collection
QBT	Quebec Board of Trade
RAPQ	*Rapport de l'Archiviste de la Province de Québec*
RHAF	*Revue d'histoire de l'Amérique française*

In the agricultural statistics and throughout the book, the French measures *minot* and *arpent* have not been translated.

The counties created in 1791 served above all as electoral ridings. Most ridings elected two assembly members: therefore in most ridings each elector had two votes in general elections, and one in by-elections held to replace one member. Electoral statistics, unless otherwise noted, are from APQ, poll books (riding and year).

Production, population, and other social statistics for the late period are compiled mainly from the 1831 and 1842 nominative censuses, which list the householders, and which are held in the Public Archives of Canada. Despite certain blanks, particularly for 1842, they cover the cities and most of the rural localities. See also F. Ouellet, *Éléments d'histoire sociale du Bas-Canada*, (1972); and "La sauvegarde des patrimoines dans le district de Québec," RHAF (1972), 319-74.

1. Revenues from Lay Seigneuries, 1784

Currency (pounds)	French-owned		English-owned		total
	Seigneuries	%	Seigneuries	%	
10 and under	10	71	4	29	14
11-50	36	73	13	27	49
51-100	32	84	6	16	38
101-150	19	86	3	14	22
151-199	2	100	0		2
200-499	14	63	8	37	22
500 and over	4	40	6	60	10
total	117		40		157

SOURCE: Calculated from I. Caron, *La Colonisation de la P.Q.*, I, app. 8, 281-7.

2. Large Flour Mill Owners, 1788

	minots of milled wheat
Allsopp	65,000
Baker	15,000
Caldwell	40,000
Coffin	25,000
Duchesnay	30,000
Dennison	15,000
Day	5,000
Desbarats	5,000
Grant	40,000
Glenny	10,000
Jordan	50,000
total	300,000

SOURCE: I. Caron, *La Colonisation de la P.Q.*, I, 171.

3. Distribution of Rural Population, 1765-1831

Size of parish	1765		1790		1822		1825		1831	
	no. of parishes	%	no. of parishes	%	no. of parishes	%	no. of parishes	%	no. of parishes	%
100 and under	2	2	0	0	0	0	0	0	0	0
101-500	59	55	30	24	4	3	10	6	9	5
501-1,000	41	38	38	29	20	19	30	18	34	18
1,001-2,000	6	5	56	43	27	26	53	33	58	32
2,001-3,000	0		5	4	27	26	39	24	49	27
3,001 and over	0		0		27	26	31	19	33	18
total	108	100	129	100	105	100	163	100	183	100

SOURCES: Census of 1871, vol. IV; JHALC; I. Caron, *La Colonisation de la P.Q.*, I, 271-4.

4. Population Growth by Occupation, Quebec City, 1792-1805

	1792	%	1795	%	1798	%	1805	%
professionals	17	2	36	2	35	2	35	2
businessmen	192	17	278	19	288	19	370	23
tradesmen	470	41	665	46	700	47	662	41
labourers	180	16	178	12	163	11	248	15
carters	82	7	95	7	108	7	104	7
other	193	17	197	14	205	14	191	12
total	1,134	100	1,449	100	1,499	100	1,610	100
French-speaking								
professionals	13	1	18	2	20	2	24	2
businessmen	144	15	142	14	148	14	174	15
tradesmen	387	41	505	49	541	50	513	45
labourers	155	16	159	15	137	13	216	19
carters	80	9	86	8	101	9	99	9
other	168	18	124	12	127	12	112	10
total	947	100	1,034	100	1,074	100	1,138	100
English-speaking								
professionals	4	2	18	4	15	4	11	2
businessmen	48	26	136	33	140	33	196	41
tradesmen	83	45	160	39	159	37	149	32
labourers	25	13	19	4	26	6	32	7
carters	2	1	9	2	7	2	5	1
other	25	13	73	18	78	18	79	17
total	187	100	415	100	425	100	472	100

SOURCE: Calculated from RAPQ (1948-49), 9-214. See also F. Ouellet, *Éléments*, 176-202.

5. Tithe in Grain (¹⁄₂₆ of Harvest), Lislet, 1783-1802
(annual averages, *minots*)

	wheat	oats	peas	barley	rye
1783-1792	586	157	73	55	24
1793-1802	645	134	87	87	26

SOURCE: F. Ouellet, *Éléments*, 74-6.

6. Quête de l'Enfant-Jésus, Vaudreuil, 1773-1839
(annual averages)

	wheat		pork		
	minots	price (*livres tournois*)	lbs.	price (*sols*)	total value (*livres tournois*)
1773-82	60	5.6	192	12.8	506
1783-92	59	5.0	174	8.9	382
1793-1802	79	6.1	265	8.8	571
1803-12	62	8.8	158	16.2	762
1823-32	36	5.8	174	10.2	356
1833-9	31	7.6	119	12.0	374

SOURCE: Account book, Vaudreuil parish.

7. Assembly Membership by Social Class, 1792-1838

	1792-96	%	1796-1800	%	1801-05	%	1805-14	%	1815-24	%	1825-30	%	1830-38	%
merchants	30	59	26	49	19	37	63	31	74	37	33	33	60	32
professionals	9	18	13	24	15	29	71	35	78	39	38	37	83	45
advocates	6		6		11		43		49		23		44	
notaries	2		4		3		20		13		8		19	
physicians	0		0		0		2		11		6		15	
surveyors	1		3		1		6		5		1		5	
farmers and tradesmen	3	5	5	9	6	11	23	11	22	11	15	15	26	14
aristrocrats	9	18	2	4	3	6	25	12	12	6	9	9	7	4
other	0		3	6	2	4	0	0	2	1	5	5	5	3
unknown	0		4	8	7	13	21	11	13	6	1	1	3	2
total	51	100	53	100	52	100	203	100	201	100	101	100	184	100

SOURCES: Too numerous to be fully listed here. Those essential in order to identify the occupations of the members of the Assembly are PAC, Audet Papers, and F.-J.Audet's books on the members in the first parliament and on the representatives for Montreal and Trois-Rivières.

8. Vote by Parish, Orléans, 1834

parish	for Plante	%	for Godbout	%	total	heads of family (1831 census)
St-Pierre	17	11	125	89	142	149
St-Jean	146	94	9	6	155	202
St-François	66	99	1	1	67	93
St-Laurent	2	2	105	98	107	125
Ste-Famille	40	38	65	62	105	118
total	271		305		576	687

SOURCE: APQ, poll book, Orléans, 1834; PAC, nominative census, 1831.

9. Index of Wheat Prices, 1802-11

	Quebec	Montreal	Vaudreuil	St-Marc	Laprairie	Blair-findie	St-Denis	Ste-Marie Monnoir
1802	100	100	100	100	100	100	100	100
1803	131	100	125	87	126	139	150	100
1804	129	100	100	100	120	109	125	?
1805	159	150	176	202	230	225	200	?
1806	166	133	164	175	217	215	200	169
1807	161	141	164	220	189	200	200	172
1808	152	150	176	200	220	200	200	172
1809	191	158	210	248	246	140	250	?
1810	215	175	198	200	230	253	250	196
1811	239	175	244	300	257	250	275	240

Quebec price index reflects imperial market demand in relation to overall supply. Montreal price index reflects less the demand than the state of supply, i.e., production in the Montreal region (the richest source of wheat), in Upper Canada, and in certain American states. Statistical data for the rural parishes above are from the parish account books.

10. Quête de l'Enfant-Jésus, St-Denis, 1802-13

	wheat *(minots)*	price *(livres tournois)*
1802	305	4
1803	118	6
1804	120	5
1805	24	8
1806	49	8
1807	40	8
1808	43	8
1809	33	10
1810	30	10
1811	25	11
1812	56	8
1813	31	16 *livres* and 10 *sols*

SOURCE: Account book, parish of St-Denis.

11. Exports of Lower-Canadian Wheat (Port of Quebec), 1793-1842 (5 and 10 year averages, *minots*)

	volume		per head	
	5 year average	10 year average	5 year average	10 year average
1793-1797	326,921	405,663	1.9	2.3
1798-1802	484,406		2.5	
1803-1807	262,709	278,929	1.1	1.2
1808-1812	295,150		1.1	
1813-1817	30,551	72,120	0.1	0.2
1818-1822	113,689		0.3	
1823-1827	160,390	120,770	0.4	0.3
1828-1832	81,150		0.1	
1833-1837	*520,925	*685,303	*1.1	*1.4
1838-1842	*849,675		*1.6	

*No exports; imports for local consumption.
SOURCES: See especially JHALC (appendices) and PACR, 1888. Relevant data is also to be found in Tables 12, 21, 85, and 86.

12. Exports of Lower-Canadian Wheat, Best Years (Port of Quebec), 1763-1842
(*minots*)

best years	volume	per head
1774	467,370	4.5
1793	541,500	3.3
1802	1,151,530	5.5
1812	451,435	1.6
1825	732,360	1.9
1831	665,500	1.5

SOURCES: Same as for Table 11.

13. Tithe in Wheat, 1787-1838

	annual average under ¾ *minot* per communicant		annual average ¾ *minot* and over per communicant		
	no. of parishes	%	no. of parishes	%	total
1787-1802	122	58.9	85	41.1	207
1803-1817	131	83.4	26	16.6	157
1825-1838	203	97.1	6	2.9	209

SOURCES: Reports of the parish priests to the bishops, AAQ and Archives of the Archbishops of Montreal. See also F. Ouellet, *Éléments*, 52.

14. Tithe in Grains, Parish of Montreal, 1798-1850
(annual averages, *minots*)

	wheat	oats	peas	barley
1798-1802	293			
1803-1807	183			
1808-1810	255			
1821-1825	253	194	76	8
1826-1830	149	137	38	0
1831-1835	151	195	32	0
1836-1840	27	269	33	3
1841-1845	59	192	37	23
1846-1850	146	229	52	15

SOURCE: St-Sulpice Seminary Archives, Montreal, vol 6.

15. Contributions in Wheat, Quête de l'Enfant-Jésus, 1773-1832
(annual averages, *minots*)

	St-Denis	Varennes	St-Marc	St-Phillippe
1773-1782	95.5	138.4		84.5
1783-1792	93.7	132.8		54.8
1793-1802	94.3	100.8	61.1	
1803-1812	53.8	81.2	33.7	
1813-1822	46.7	132.0	26.6	70.2
1823-1832		69.2	33.3	

SOURCE: Parish account books.

16. Seigneurial rent in Wheat, Laprairie, 1799-1829
(annual averages, *minots*)

1799-1802	1027
1803-1808	681
1810-1819	690
1820-1829	492

SOURCE: APQ, Jesuit Estates Papers.

17. Agricultural Prices, 1805-34: Urban and Rural
(annual averages in French *livres*)

		1805-1814	1815-1824	1825-1834
wheat (*minot*)	St-Marc	10.10	7.10	5.90
	St-Denis	10.50		
	Varennes	10.60	7.80	6.20
	Rigaud		10.10	
	Quebec	11.70	8.60	7.00
	moving average	10.90	9.05	7.10
	Montreal	11.20	8.00	6.30
	moving average	10.20	8.60	6.40
flour (barrel) Quebec		25.70	18.20	14.90
eggs (doz.) Quebec		1.12	1.17	
	Montreal	0.95	1.04	0.81
oats (*minot*) Quebec		3.89	3.95	2.74
beef (lb.) Quebec		0.46	0.48	0.38
	Montreal	0.44		0.44
straw (100 bales) Quebec		38.00		
hay (100 bales) Quebec		69.60	74.80	
butter (lb.) Quebec		1.47	2.07	1.19
	Montreal	1.19	1.47	1.12
wood, mixed (cord) Quebec		19.20	19.80	14.30

SOURCES: For rural prices, see parish account books; for Quebec and Montreal, see J. Hamelin and F. Ouellet, "Le mouvement des prix agricoles dans la Province de Québec, 1760-1851," in C. Galarneau and E. Lavoie (eds.), *France et Canada français du XVIe au XXe siècle* (1966), 21-48.

18. Imports: Stock-raising Products and Tobacco, 1808-42*

	butter and cheese (lbs.)	pork and beef (barrels)	tallow and lard (lbs.)	sole leather (lbs.)	rawhides (no.)	tobacco (lbs.)
1808-12	287,838	16,750	42,925	106,647		217,707
1813-17	169,140	4,633	15,497			162,750
1818-22	432,965	20,554	63,385	100,646	2,489	63,708
1823-27	531,949	31,816	268,432	232,974	10,260	524,874
1828-32	506,680	42,681	435,506		37,851	595,237
1833-37	408,642	34,223	269,558		23,600	739,221
1838-42	451,636	31,948	225,884		40,870	836,925

*For the wartime period authorized imports were nil in some years; some official totals have been divided by the number of years of authorized importation. Since contraband trade continued at all times and was particularly prevalent in times of nil authorized trade, real imports from the USA are higher than the averages shown by 15 to 20 per cent in peacetime and considerably more in wartime.
SOURCE: Appendices to JHALC.

19. Outbound Shipping & Exports of Forest Products, Port of Quebec (annual averages)

	outbound shipping (tons)	ships built (tons)	squared pine (tons)	squared oak (tons)	deals (pieces)	staves (pieces)	potash (barrels) Lower Canadian	potash L. Can. & U. Can.
1808-12	100,188	6,742	38,945	22,178	292,740	2,590,184	18,335	24,706
1813-17	52,054	3,696	15,926	8,305	247,854	1,624,362	6,647	11,148
1818-22	130,485	3,123	60,175	16,505	939,095	3,799,316	10,131	31,378
1823-27	177,306	14,226	103,580	21,074	1,201,547	4,126,620	17,278	47,934
1828-32	242,773	6,345	162,734	20,841	1,648,944	5,469,648	13,631	40,481
1833-37	330,908	8,590	264,610	21,906	2,514,474	5,426,456	10,669	31,192
1838-42	403,048	17,122	310,982	24,980	2,732,645	6,083,686	9,345	25,823

SOURCE: Appendices to JHALC.

20. Imports, Port of Quebec
(annual averages)

	molasses (gals.)	sugar (lbs.)	spirits (gals.)	salt (min.)	wine (gals.)	coffee (lbs.)	tea (lbs.)
1808-12	38,658	1,653,375	721,876	134,456	164,215	123,782	9,691
1813-17	66,608	2,299,375	1,403,012	136,296	331,483	181,159	213,363
1818-22	80,625	2,027,945	1,339,255	170,183	194,492	63,469	219,361
1823-27	61,414	2,855,095	1,368,103	197,777	243,427	118,129	704,391
1828-32	90,135	5,400,448	1,440,375	260,266	302,914	158,726	593,924
1833-37	88,130	6,040,813	1,165,972	256,851	344,896	103,841	844,182
1838-42	104,265	8,778,441	1,020,819	278,550	335,465	236,207	1,054,952

SOURCE: Appendices to JHALC.

21. Wheat Imports to Lower Canada, 1818-1842
(annual averages, *minots*)

1818-22	288,411
1823-27	325,517
1828-32	731,502
1833-37	878,762
1838-42	2,251,330

SOURCE: Appendices to JHALC. See also Tables 11, 12, 85, and 86.

22. Notes Discounted, 1821-1830
(currency—pounds)

	Montreal Bank	Quebec Bank
1821	699,969	...
1822	1,120,649	43,411
1823	1,173,467	221,252
1824	1,705,763	317,948
1825	1,851,559	414,141
1826	1,354,024	456,538
1827	1,174,971	438,134
1828	1,377,483	430,094
1829	1,599,683	484,611
1830	...	526,870

SOURCE: Appendices to JHALC.

23. Revenues and expenditures, Government of Lower Canada, 1808-37
(annual averages, currency—pounds)

	revenues	total expenditures	public works
1808-12	57,046	54,882	314
1813-17	125,770	118,475	472
1818-22	90,546	79,849	3,452
1823-27	126,759	90,253	13,179
1828-32	173,202	144,911	41,599
1833-37	117,504	64,340	12,867

SOURCE: Appendices to JHALC.

24. Natural Population Growth
(annual averages per 1,000)

	births	marriages	deaths	growth
1760-1800	52.5	8.7	27.0	25.4
1800-4	51.9	8.8	27.8	24.1
1805-9	50.1	8.0	22.7	27.4
1810-4	49.1	8.6	28.1	21.0
1815-9	50.3	8.5	22.9	27.4
1820-4	51.9	8.5	25.9	26.0
1825-9	52.3	8.6	25.5	26.8
1830-4	53.9	9.5	31.1	22.8
1835-9	50.7	7.7	22.9	27.8
1800-1839	51.0	8.5	25.8	25.4

SOURCES: *Annuaire statistique de la province de Q.*, 1914; G. Langlois, *Histoire de la population canadienne-française*; appendices to JHALC.

25. Immigration from the British Isles

	annual average	England	% origin Scotland	Ireland
1818-22	8,041			
1823-27	10,867			
1828-32	31,541	54	10	33
1833-37	22,444	25	10	60

SOURCES: H.J. Cowan, *British Immigration to British North America*; appendices to JHALC.

26. Population Growth, Île d'Orléans, 1765-1831

parish		1765	1784	1822	1825	1831
St-Pierre	census	466	487	780	895	893
	estimated per L.C. average growth		745	1,994	2,165	2,548
Ste-Famille	census	456	436	752	781	750
	estimated per L.C. average growth		729	1,951	2,118	2,492
St-François	census	376	328	534	563	662
	estimated per L.C. average growth		601	1,609	1,747	2,056
St-Jean	census	518	493	1,300	1,023	1,275
	estimated per L.C. average growth		828	2,217	2,407	2,833
St-Laurent	census	469	466	677	760	769
	estimated per L.C. average growth		750	2,007	2,179	2,564

SOURCES: Census of 1871, vol. IV, and JHALC (appendices).

27. Population Change, 53 Parishes, 1790-1822

| | censuses | | natural growth | migration | |
	1790	1822	1790-1822	emig-ration	immig-ration
Kamouraska	1,706	1,492	4,510 (8)	1,234	—
St-André	—	1,784			
Ste-Anne de la Pocatière	1,316	2,200	2,626 (5)	426	—
Rivière-Ouelle	1,859	3,223	4,163 (4)	940	—
St-Gervais	1,180	5,269	4,594 (4)	—	675
St-Michel	1,337	1,889	2,266 (4)	377	—
Beaumont	561	1,003	726 (4)	—	277
St-Charles	1,406	2,350	2,756 (4)	406	—
St-Jean Port-Joli	1,103	2,520	2,407 (4)	—	113
St-Roch des Aulnets	1,458	2,470	3,278 (4)	808	—
Cap-St-Ignace	991	1,565	2,032 (4)	467	—
Lislet	1,297	2,082	2,418 (4)	336	—
St-François du Sud	1,030	798	1,899 (4)	1,101	—
St-Pierre du Sud	871	738	1,448 (5)	710	—
St-Vallier	1,160	1,940	2,362 (5)	422	—
St-François, Île d'Orléans	242	534	368 (7)	—	126
St-Jean, Î d'O.	652	1,300	1,166 (4)	—	144
St-Pierre, Î d'O.	643	780	916 (4)	136	—
Ste-Famille, Î d'O.	884	752	1,301 (4)	549	—
St-Laurent, Î d'O.	499	677	870 (4)	193	—
Deschambault	453	1,319	1,162 (4)	—	157
Cap-Santé	1,218	2,032	2,411 (4)	379	—
St-Augustin	1,998	2,048	2,886 (5)	838	—
Las Écureuils	311	462	510 (4)	48	—
Beauport	870	1,550	1,437 (4)	—	115
Ange-Gardien	478	655	683 (4)	28	—
Pte-aux-Trembles	847	1,004	1,251 (7)	247	—

Charlesbourg	1,854	_1,417_	2,473	(7)	1,056	—
St-Nicolas	696	_1,917_	1,771	(7)	—	146
Pointe-Levy	1,407	_3,566_	2,817	(4)	—	749
Ste-Croix	591	_1,230_	1,180	(4)	—	50
St-Antoine	774	_1,962_	2,024	(7)	62	265
Lorbinière	713	_1,936_	1,671	(4)	—	—
St-Thomas de Montmagny	1,598	_2,933_	3,067	(7)	134	—
Château-Richer	640	_1,013_	1,061	(4)	48	—
Baie-St-Paul	1,291	_2,464_	2,934	(7)	470	—
St-Joseph de Beauce	813	_1,725_	1,847	(7)	72	—
St-François de Beauce	518	_2,041_	1,426	(7)	—	615
Ste-Marie de Beauce	1,128	_3,763_	3,203	(4)	564	—
St-Henri	1,177	_3,520_	3,042	(4)	—	478
Gentilly	378	_1,375_	1,293		—	80
St-Pierre les Becquets	371	_1,553_	1,283	(3)	—	270
Nicolet	884	_2,700_	3,116		416	—
Bécancourt	1,027	_2,152_	2,417		265	—
St-François-du-Lac	840	_2,052_	1,892		—	160
Baie-du-Fèbvre	1,411	_2,680_	3,262		582	—
Yamachiche	1,669	_3,000_	3,403		403	—
Rivière-du-Loup	1,829	_3,256_	4,398		872	—
Maskinongé	1,155	_3,626_	2,943		—	683
Yamaska	1,324	_3,150_	3,832		682	—
Ste-Anne de la Prade	991	_1,880_	2,125		245	—
Ste-Geneviève	713	_1,260_	1,648	(3)	388	—
Cap-de-la-Madeleine	324	_469_	435		—	34
Pointe-du-Lac	456	_934_	890		—	44
total	52,942	104,206	113,899		15,340	5,747

SOURCES: Italicised figures are from the 1825 census, the 1822 records being lost; those in parentheses are the number of years of missing birth and burial records. Birth, marriage, and burial figures for these 53 parishes were published in JHALC, 1823, at the time of the land inquiry; births less deaths for each year have been added to the 1790 census figure.

28. Land Distribution, Seigneury of Laprairie, 1831 and 1837

	1831 census		1837 *terrier*			
		%		%		%
10 *arpents* and under	46	7	166	20	523	34
11-29	48	8	142	17	371	24
30-49	99	16	117	14	224	15
50-69	109	18	122	15	187	12
70-89	81	13	81	10	85	6
90-99	68	11	39	5	58	4
100-149	83	14	96	12	54	3
150-199	42	7	35	4	9	1
200-249	12	2	15	2	2	
250-299	12	2	6	1	2	
300 and over	13	2	0		8	1
total	613 land-holders		819 land-holders		1,523 land-holdings	

SOURCES: Nominative census of 1831 (PAC); APQ, Jesuit Estates Papers, Terrier de Laprairie.

29. Seigneury Revenues and Expenditures,
Seminary of Quebec, 1793-1842
(annual averages in French *livres*)

	revenues	expenditures	surplus	deficit
1793-97	66,310	53,863	12,447	—
1798-1802	82,579	63,772	18,807	—
1803-07	97,983	94,939	3,044	—
1808-12	86,381	72,363	14,018	—
1813-17	111,145	115,712	—	4,567
1818-22	91,970	98,157	—	6,387
1823-27	111,887	136,963	—	25,076
1828-32	136,462	137,318	—	856
1833-37	137,517	136,012	1,505	—
1838-42	128,762	134,643	—	5,881

SOURCE: ASQ, account books, Seminary of Quebec, 1760-1850.

30. Tithe, Parish of St-Laurent, 1791-1833
(*minots*)

	wheat	oats	peas
1791	800	600	300
1799	968	577	329
1801	1,000	492	211
1802	1,400	700	200
1804	900	500	200
1808	200	600	—
1827	650	—	—
1833	700	400	100

SOURCE: AAQ, reports from parish priests to bishops.

31. Population Change, St-Eustache Area, 1790-1842

	1790	1822	1825	1831	1842
Ste-Scholastique	—	—	2,684	3,769	3,683
St-Benoit	—	5,609	4,115	4,431	3,010
St-Eustache	2,385	4,476	4,833	4,830	3,195
St-Hermas	—	—	—	—	1,382
total	2,385	10,085	11,632	13,030	11,270

SOURCE: Calculated from JHALC; (appendices); census of 1871, vol. IV; I. Caron, *La Colonisation de la P.Q.*, I, 271-4; censuses of 1831 and 1842.

32. Land Distribution, St-Eustache Area, 1831 and 1842
(number of landowners)

	1831		1842	
arpents		%		%
50 and under	505	29	591	42
51-100	896	52	556	40
101-200	299	17	226	16
201 and over	41	2	34	2
total	1,741	100	1,407	100

SOURCE: Calculated from nominative censuses.

33. Agricultural Production, St-Eustache Area,
1831 and 1842 (per producer)

	1831	1842
wheat, *minots*	86.0	10.0
oats, *minots*	91.7	111.1
potatoes, *minots*	117.5	100.1
cattle	5.9	5.3
hogs	4.5	3.2

SOURCE: Calculated from nominative censuses.

34. Population and Occupations, St-Eustache Area, 1831 and 1842

	1831		1842		decline
		%		%	%
professionals	14	0.6	14	0.7	
businessmen	53	2.2	36	1.9	32
tradesmen	240	10.0	192	10.1	20
farmers	1,545	64.5	1,271	66.8	17
labourers	414	17.3	330	17.4	20
other	127	5.3	59	3.1	53
total	2,393	100.0	1,902	100.0	20

SOURCE: Calculated from nominative censuses.

35. Merchant Class, Quebec City, 1805-1842

	1805				1831				1842			
	French-speaking		English-speaking		French-speaking		English-speaking		French-speaking		English-speaking	
		%		%		%		%		%		%
merchants	64	42	91	58	237	46	270	54	306	54	248	46
innkeepers	17	21	58	79	46	36	81	64	32	25	94	75
butchers	22	70	9	30	18	45	22	55	34	53	30	47
bakers	50	80	12	20	54	67	26	33	63	70	26	30
clerks	2	40	3	60	11	17	53	83	18	23	59	77
brewers	0		4	100	3	42	4	58	3	37	5	63
other	19	50	19	50	29	20	112	80	60	35	107	65
total	174	47	196	53	393	43	568	57	516	47	569	53

SOURCES: RAPQ (1949-1950), 161-214; nominative censuses of 1831 and 1842.

36. Merchant Class, Montreal, 1819-1842

	1819				1831				1842			
	French-speaking		English-speaking		French-speaking		English-speaking		French-speaking		English-speaking	
		%		%		%		%		%		%
merchants	97	31	222	69	126	28	326	72	189	26	512	74
innkeepers	64	41	94	59	57	39	89	61	52	32	109	68
butchers	19	47	21	53	47	50	46	50	46	55	37	45
bakers	23	47	25	53	46	54	38	46	35	53	30	47
clerks	2	10	18	90	16	21	58	79	28	26	78	74
brewers	1	20	4	80	5	27	13	73	3	20	12	80
other	18	31	40	69	153	46	183	54	85	23	284	77
total	224	35	424	65	450	37	753	63	438	29	1,062	71

SOURCES: *Directory* of 1819 and nominative censuses of 1831 and 1842.

37. Merchant Class, Pointe Lévy, 1831 and 1842

	French-speaking		English-speaking (1831)		total	French-speaking		English-speaking (1842)		total
merchants	9	69%	4	31%	13	18	62%	11	38%	29
innkeepers	16		2		18	20		1		21
bakers	2		1		3	5		0		5
butchers	3		0		3	2		0		2
distillers	0		0		0	0		1		1
clerks	0		0		0	1		3		4
hotel-keepers	0		0		0	0		1		2
builders	0		0		0	1		1		2
agents	0		0		0	1		1		2
total	30	81%	7	19%	37	48	72%	19	28%	67

SOURCES: Nominative censuses of 1831 and 1842.

38. Merchant Class, Trois-Rivières, 1831

	French-speaking		English-speaking		total
merchants	29	74%	10	26%	39
innkeepers	11		3		14
bakers	10		2		12
grocers	0		5		5
peddlars	0		1		1
distillers	0		1		1
brewers	0		1		1
printers	0		1		1
agents	0		2		2
butchers	3		1		4
tobacconists	0		1		1
confectioners	1		0		1
furriers	1		0		1
total	55	66%	28	34%	83

SOURCE: Nominative census of 1831.

39. Merchant Class, Argenteuil, 1831 and 1842

	French-speaking		English-speaking (1831)		total	French-speaking		English-speaking (1842)		total
merchants	3	27%	8	73%	11	1	8%	11	92%	12
innkeepers	0		6		6	0		8		8
contractors	0		4		4	0		0		0
paper manufacturers	0		1		1	0		1		1
agents	0		1		1	0		0		0
butchers	1		0		1	0		1		1
clerks	0		0		0	0		3		3
distillers	0		0		0	0		1		1
total	4	16%	20	84%	24	1	3%	25	97%	26

SOURCES: Nominative censuses of 1831 and 1842.

40. Merchant Class, St-Eustache, St-Benoit, and Ste-Scholastique, 1831 and 1842

	1831 French-speaking		English-speaking		total	1842 French-speaking		English-speaking		total
merchants	10	45%	12	55%	22	10	58%	7	42%	17
innkeepers	17		3		20	5		3		8
butchers	3		0		3	2		0		2
bakers	4		2		6	4		0		4
brewers	0		1		1	0		0		0
clerks	0		1		1	0		0		0
secondhand dealers	0		0		0	1		0		1
total	34	64%	19	36%	53	22	68%	10	32%	32

SOURCES: Nominative censuses of 1831 and 1842.

41. Merchant Class, Soulanges and Vaudreuil, 1831

	Soulanges French-speaking		English-speaking		total	Vaudreuil French-speaking		English-speaking		total
merchants	6	55%	5	45%	11	5	56%	4	44%	9
innkeepers	6		4		10	7		2		9
bakers	1		1		2	1		1		2
butchers	2		0		2	0		0		0
total	15	60%	10	40%	25	13	65%	7	35%	20

SOURCE: Nominative census of 1831.

42. Merchant Class, Chambly, 1842

	French-speaking		English-speaking		total
merchants	3	30%	7	70%	10
innkeepers	1		6		7
contractors	0		1		1
evaluators	0		1		1
agents	0		1		1
butchers	1		0		1
bakers	2		3		5
clerks	1		2		3
total	8	27%	21	73%	29

SOURCE: Nominative census of 1842.

43. Merchant Class, Laprairie, Seigneury and Environs, 1831

	French-speaking		English-speaking		total
merchants	11	52%	10	48%	21
innkeepers	44	77%	13	23%	57
butchers	4		0		4
bakers	4		0		4
secondhand dealers	3		0		3
clerks	1		3		4
brewers	0		4		4
total	67	69%	30	31%	97

SOURCE: Nominative census of 1831.

44. Professional Class: Growth, 1801-38
(percentages-growth over preceding decade)

	notaries	%	advocates	%	physicians	%	surveyors	%	total	%
1801-10	88		34		57		47		226	
1811-20	145	64	64	88	77	35	53	12	339	50
1821-38	270	86	162	153	174	125	90	69	696	105

SOURCE: *Quebec Almanac.* These statistics, while not totally accurate, illustrate the trends.

45. Professional Class: Ethnic Breakdown, 1801-38

	notaries		advocates		physicians		surveyors			total
		%		%		%		%		%
Fr.-speaking										
1801-10	81	92	21	62	15	27	27	59	144	64
1811-20	135	94	38	60	23	30	28	53	224	66
1821-38	250	93	89	55	67	38	48	53	454	65
Eng.-speaking										
1801-10	7	8	13	38	42	73	20	41	82	36
1811-20	10	6	26	40	54	70	25	47	115	34
1821-38	20	7	73	45	107	62	42	47	242	35

SOURCE: *Quebec Almanac.*

46. Professional Class, Quebec City, 1805-42.

	1805				*1831				*1842			
	French-speaking %		English-speaking %		French-speaking %		English-speaking %		French-speaking %		English-speaking %	
advocates	7	58	5	42	23	52	21	48	26	50	26	50
physicians	5	71	2	29	9	34	17	66	13	46	15	54
notaries	8	80	2	20	16	64	9	36	18	69	8	31
surveyors	3		1		3		4		3		1	
architects	0		0		1		3		2		2	
engineers	1		0		0		1		0		2	
apothecaries	0		0		0		4		0		2	
dentists	0		0		0		1		0		5	
opticians	0		0		0		0		0		1	
chemists	0		0		0		0		0		1	
total	24	68	10	32	52	46	60	54	62	49	63	51

*English-speaking proportion of total population: 1831, 45%; 1842, 40%.
SOURCES: RAPQ (1949-50), 161-214 and nominative censuses of 1831 and 1842.

47. Professional Class, Montreal, 1819-42

	1819				*1831				*1842			
	French-speaking	%	English-speaking	%	French-speaking	%	English-speaking	%	French-speaking	%	English-speaking	%
advocates	12	48	13	52	30	48	32	52	20	40	29	60
physicians	3	12	22	88	8	32	17	68	11	28	27	72
notaries	14	77	4	23	17	73	6	27	16	69	7	31
apothecaries	0		0		0		6		0		6	
engineers	0		4		0		21		0		14	
surveyors	2		2		1		1		0		1	
dentists	0		0		0		1		0		2	
opticians	0		0		1		0		0		0	
chemists	0		0		0		1		0		0	
architects	0		0		0		0		1		4	
total	31	41	45	59	57	40	85	60	48	35	90	65

*English-speaking proportion of total population: 1831, 54%; 1842, 61%.
SOURCES: *Montreal Directory* and nominative censuses of 1831 and 1842.

48. Working Class, Quebec City, 1805-1842

	1805				1831				1842			
	French-speaking		English-speaking		French-speaking		English-speaking		French-speaking		English-speaking	
		%		%		%		%		%		%
tradesmen	513	77	149	23	1,102	61	686	39	1,479	66	794	34
blacksmiths	31	86	5	14	43	55	34	45	76	62	45	38
carpenters	71	79	18	21	190	76	58	24	391	85	64	15
joiners	87	90	9	10	245	85	42	15	321	90	35	10
cobblers	12	36	21	64	79	36	139	64	121	43	159	57
tanners	19	100	0		26	78	7	22	36	87	5	13
coopers	39	76	12	24	36	60	24	40	40	63	23	37
tailors	6	22	21	78	9	9	90	91	14	10	114	90
wheelwrights	9	90	1	10	29	87	4	13	41	82	9	18
cabinet makers	0		3		18	52	16	48	20	44	25	56
masons	58	93	4	7	115	63	67	37	67	69	30	31
other skills	181	76	55	24	312	61	205	39	352	56	285	44
labourers	216	87	32	13	427	49	433	51	760	60	501	40
carters	99	95	5	5	181	93	13	7	266	89	30	11
total	828	81	186	19	1,710	60	1,132	40	2,505	66	1,325	34

SOURCES: RAPQ (1949-50), 161-214; nominative censuses of 1831 and 1842.

49. Working Class, Montreal, 1831 and 1842*

| | 1831 | | | | 1842 | | | |
	French-speaking	%	English-speaking	%	French-speaking	%	English-speaking	%
tradesmen	984	47	1,107	53	911	45	1,107	55
carpenters	120	53	106	47	101	69	44	31
joiners	165	71	65	29	196	59	131	41
cabinet makers	1	4	30	96	16	19	66	81
cobblers	134	43	171	57	108	36	191	64
tailors	13	11	98	89	25	19	104	81
blacksmiths	37	28	94	72	40	33	81	67
tanners	55	70	23	30	13	41	18	59
masons	149	76	45	24	119	68	55	32
coopers	57	56	44	44	52	59	35	41
wheelwrights	17	77	5	23	25	69	11	31
other skills	236	36	426	64	216	36	371	64
labourers	526	50	517	50	559	37	915	63
carters	199	90	21	10	210	75	69	25
total	1,709	51	1,645	49	1,680	44	2,091	56

*Parish of Montreal included.

SOURCES: Nominative censuses of 1831 and 1842.

TABLES

369

50. Rural Population: Peasants and Workers, 1831 and 1842

	Dist. of Quebec, 1831	%	Dist. of Montreal, 1831	%	Dist. of Montreal, 1842	%
farmers	13,443	71	22,664	65	9,775	68
tradesmen	1,911	10	2,975	8	1,394	9
labourers	2,349	12	5,587	16	1,884	13
*heads of family	18,900	100	34,455	100	14,233	100

*Merchants and professionals are included in this category.
SOURCES: Nominative censuses of 1831 and 1842.

51. Agricultural Producers by District and Production Volume, 1831 and 1842

	Quebec, 1831	%	Montreal, 1831	%	Montreal, 1842	%
wheat (minots)						
50 and under	5,319	51	8,304	49	5,535	93
51-100	2,503	24	3,642	22	369	6
101-200	1,899	18	2,982	18	51	1
201 and over	714	7	1,826	11	17	
total	10,435	100	16,754	100	5,972	100
oats (minots)						
50 and under	4,981	52	8,751	51		
51-100	2,180	23	4,421	26		
101-200	1,779	19	2,953	17		
201 and over	628	6	1,115	6		
total	9,568	100	17,240	100		

51. Agricultural Producers by District and Production Volume, 1831 and 1842

	Quebec, 1831	%	Montreal, 1831	%	Montreal, 1842	%
potatoes (minots)						
50 and under	5,094	39	9,212	38		
51-100	3,527	27	7,161	29		
101-200	2,846	22	5,077	21		
201 and over	1,566	12	2,797	12		
total	13,033	100	24,247	100		
hogs (head)						
5 and under	8,501	61	18,331	67	8,244	86
6-10	4,252	31	6,573	24	1,210	13
11-15	1,007	7	1,772	6	114	1
16-20	162	1	448	2	10	
21 and over	40		175	1	5	
total	13,962	100	27,299	100	9,583	100
cattle (head)						
5 and under	7,858	55	15,301	58		
6-10	3,389	23	5,827	22		
11-15	1,984	14	2,918	11		
16-20	789	5	1,281	5		
21 and over	392	3	909	4		
total	14,412	100	26,236	100		

SOURCES: Nominative censuses of 1831 and 1842.

52. Wheat Production, 1831-44
(*minots*)

	1831	26 x tithe collected		1844
St-Hyacinthe	21,802	13,000	(1834)	8,034
St-Laurent	29,157	18,200	(1833)	3,414
St-Martin	31,920	15,600	(1833)	1,690
St-Ours	27,906	15,600	(1834)	3,719
Beloeil	44,959	28,600	(1834)	4,119
Boucherville	50,939	31,200	(1836)	3,149
Chambly	65,645	24,400	(1835)	12,209
Châteauguay	35,669	16,900	(1836)	6,085
Contrecoeur	17,564	15,600	(1836)	3,568
Île du Pads	7,143	6,500	(1834)	4,594
Lachenaie	11,491	9,100	(1832)	707
Lachine	15,399	7,150	(1833)	2,571
Longueuil	70,356	33,800	(1836)	9,179
Longue-Pointe	16,480	4,800	(1833)	315
St-Vincent de Paul	11,451	15,600	(1833)	2,802
Ste-Rose	21,015	16,900	(1833)	1,690
Sault aux Récollets	16,729	7,800	(1833)	2,221
Sorel	19,796	15,600	(1834)	6,691
Terrebonne	9,245	11,700	(1832)	807
Varennes	63,134	36,400	(1836)	4,084
Verchères	51,376	24,400	(1836)	4,022
R. des Prairies	8,799	9,880	(1834)	896
St-Charles	13,327	11,700	(1834)	810
St-Denis	25,803	18,200	(1834)	2,512
St-Eustache	39,393	15,600	(1832)	3,364
total	726,588	427,230		93,252

SOURCES: Censuses of 1831 and 1844; AAQ; Archives of the Archbishopric of Montreal: parish priests' reports to the bishops on the tithes.

53. Farm Animals, 1831 and 1842
(average number per farm)*

	French-speaking farmers		English-speaking farmers	
	1831	1842	1831	1842
cattle	6.3	5.7	9.7	9.2
hogs	5.1	3.2	7.1	3.3

*Three English-speaking townships, three predominantly English-speaking seigneuries, and twenty-five French-speaking parishes.

SOURCES: Nominative censuses of 1831 and 1842.

54. Occupational Structure, Rural Seigneuries and Townships, 1831 and 1842

	1831		1842	
Montreal seigneuries		%		%
professionals	44	0.48	58	0.68
businessmen	195	2.11	199	2.34
tradesmen	744	8.05	793	9.34
farmers	5,739	62.06	5,393	63.52
labourers	2,034	22.00	1,492	17.57
other	491	5.30	556	6.55
total	9,247	100.00	8,491	100.00
Quebec seigneuries				
professionals	39	0.72	47	0.77
businessmen	131	2.43	200	3.26
tradesmen	552	10.23	745	12.13
farmers	3,919	72.64	4,198	68.38
labourers	596	11.05	885	14.42
other	158	2.93	64	1.04
total	5,395	100.00	6,139	100.00
Montreal townships				
professionals	20	0.85	22	1.00
businessmen	63	2.68	104	4.74
tradesmen	323	13.76	321	14.62
farmers	1,675	71.37	1,342	61.11
labourers	202	8.61	233	10.61
other	64	2.73	174	7.92
total	2,347	100.00	2,196	100.00

SOURCES: Calculated from nominative censuses of 1831 and 1842.

55. Land Distribution, 1831 (number of landowners)

	Quebec District		Montreal District	
		%		%
50 *arpents* and less	3,260	24	8,718	35
51-100	5,213	39	10,434	42
101-200	3,649	27	4,555	18
201 and over	1,361	10	1,151	5
total	13,483	100	24,858	100

SOURCE: Calculated from nominative census of 1831.

56. Land Distribution: Rural Montreal District Seigneuries, 1831 and 1842
(number of landowners)

	1831		1842	
		%		%
50 *arpents* and less	2,668	40	2,922	46
51-100	2,550	38	2,065	33
101-200	1,228	19	1,081	17
201 and over	218	3	240	4
total	6,664	100	6,308	100

SOURCES: Nominative censuses of 1831 and 1842.

57. Votes for William Grant, 1792
(Quebec Upper Town)

	French-speaking		English-speaking		total
		%		%	
professionals	4	4.2	5	4.6	9
businessmen	31	32.3	60	55.6	91
tradesmen	43	44.8	20	18.5	63
labourers and carters	13	13.5	6	5.6	19
other	5	5.2	17	15.7	22
total	96	100.0	108	100.0	204

SOURCES: PAC: Young Papers; poll book.

58. Votes in Quebec Upper Town, 1816

	Fletcher		Vanfelson*		Dénéchaud	
	French-speaking	English-speaking	French-speaking	English-speaking	French-speaking	English-speaking
professionals	2	2	10	1	10	0
businessmen	4	26	77	27	79	14
tradesmen	17	18	109	17	103	7
labourers and carters	10	3	26	1	17	1
other	4	58	22	21	21	7
total	37	107	244	67	230	29

*Vanfelson was the son of a German father and a French-Canadian mother, was Catholic, and had a French-Canadian wife.
SOURCE: ASQ, Viger-Verreau Collection.

59. French-speaking Vote for a French-speaking Candidate, 1824 and 1827 (Quebec Upper Town)

	vote for Canadian Party		vote for French-speaking candidate	
1824		%		%
professionals	49	83	15	51
businessmen	258	79	100	50
tradesmen	283	64	166	56
labourers	110	82	77	57
other	90	62	37	51
total	790	71	395	53
1827				
professionals			54	76
businessmen			237	84
tradesmen			454	77
labourers			168	83
other			80	81
total			993	80

SOURCE: APQ, poll books, Quebec Upper Town, 1824 and 1827.

60. French-speaking Vote for a French-speaking Candidate, 1829 (by-election, Quebec Upper Town)

	Duval		Vanfelson	
		%		%
professionals	23	79	6	21
businessmen	80	77	23	23
tradesmen	179	73	65	27
labourers	77	72	29	28
other	42	76	13	24
total	401	74	136	26

SOURCE: APQ, poll book, Quebec Upper Town, 1829.

61. Vote by Ethnic Groups, Montreal West By-election, 1832

	Daniel Tracey		Stanley Bagg		Total
		%		%	
French-Canadian	500	84	93	15	593
Irish	150	71	60	29	210
American	11	9	106	91	117
English and Scottish	30	7	428	93	458
total	691		687		

SOURCES: Statistics for this by-election are from those made by J. Viger from the poll book, which has disappeared. ASQ, Viger-Verreau Collection; House of Assembly inquiry, JHALC, 1832-1833.

62. Vote by Occupation, Montreal West By-election, 1832

	Tracey	Bagg	French Canadians for Bagg
	%	%	%
professionals	4.0	5.1	8.6
businessmen	21.7	31.4	15.05
tradesmen	34.8	29.7	27.9
labourers	10.2	2.4	8.6
other	28.7	31.1	39.7

SOURCES: Same as for Table 61.

63. French-speaking Vote, Quebec Lower Town, 1832

	Vanfelson		McCulloch	
		%		%
professionals	11	100	0	—
businessmen	101	84	19	16
tradesmen	164	78	44	22
labourers	17	60	11	40
other	18	85	3	15
total	308	80	77	20

SOURCE: APQ, poll book, Quebec Lower Town, 1832.

64. Vote for Neilson by Ethnic Groups, Quebec, 1827 and 1834

	1827 French-speaking		1827 English-speaking		total	1834 French-speaking		1834 English-speaking		total
		%		%			%		%	
professionals	12	92	1	8	13	2	22	7	78	9
businessmen	84	77	24	23	108	2	5	35	95	37
tradesmen	119	83	23	17	142	2	18	10	82	12
farmers	210	86	32	14	242	47	39	72	61	119
labourers	24	96	1	4	25	3	100	0	—	3
other	27	84	5	16	32	19	46	22	54	41
total	476	84	86	16	562	75	34	146	66	221

SOURCE: APQ, poll books, Quebec, 1827 and 1834.

65. Property Values by Ethnic Groups, Quebec Upper Town, 1825 and 1835 (averages)

	1825 French-speaking		1825 English-speaking		1835 French-speaking		1835 English-speaking	
		£		£		£		£
professionals	29	101	14	129	51	85	25	96
businessmen	102	47	47	130	135	39	66	85
tradesmen	247	15	37	27	279	11	50	24
labourers	106	10	7	13	109	8	11	9
other	37	56	31	76	45	51	44	96
total	521		136		619		195	

SOURCE: City of Quebec Archives, assessment rolls, Upper Town, 1825 and 1835 (statistics from B. Foster, student research paper).

66. French-Canadian Vote, Quebec Upper Town, 1834

	Stuart		Fr.-speaking candidates		total
		%		%	
professionals	5	9	55	91	60
businessmen	0	—	238	100	238
tradesmen	15	3	508	97	523
labourers	5	3	169	97	174
other	7	9	66	91	73
total	32	3	1,036	97	1,068

SOURCE: APQ, poll book, Quebec Upper Town, 1834.

67. Vote Showing Local Community Partiality, Hampshire (Portneuf), 1827*

	candidates from east of riding		candidates from west of riding	
		%		%
Pte-aux-Trembles	217	86	52	14
Ste-Anne de la Pocatière	20	3	768	97
Les Grondines	20	7	295	93
Cap-Santé	761	90	79	10
Les Ecureuils	104	100	0	—
Deschambault	144	42	197	58
St-Patrick	92	91	10	9
Lorette	114	92	10	8
St-Augustin	307	84	58	16
Ste-Foy	6	—	0	—
St-Ambroise	2	—	0	—
Lachevrotière	2	—	2	—
total	1,889	56	1,471	44

*The 1826 poll book yields similar statistics.
SOURCE: APQ, poll book, Hampshire (Portneuf), 1827.

68. Vote Showing Local Community Partiality, Saguenay, 1832 and 1833

	1832				1833			
	Simon		Fraser		Tessier		Harvey	
		%		%		%		%
Les Éboulements	137	91	13	9	4	13	27	87
Baie-St-Paul	264	99	2	—	225	70	96	30
Petite-Rivière	3	—	0	—	7	78	2	22
Île-aux-Coudres	45	100	0	—	0	—	65	100
La Malbaie	202	42	268	58	232	74	78	26
total	651	69	283	31	468	63	268	37

SOURCE: APQ, poll book, Saguenay, 1832, 1833.

69. Vote Showing Urban and Rural Partiality, Quebec, 1833

	urban vote for Besserer		rural vote for Rainville	
		%		%
professionals	24	100	0	—
businessmen	159	94	11	73
tradesmen	346	94	85	92
farmers	14	87	455	95
labourers	61	87	19	100
other	28	87	1	—
total	632		571	

SOURCE: APQ, poll book, Quebec, 1833.

70. Vote by Parish, Lotbinière, 1830

	Lachevrotière		Noël		Méthot	
		%		%		%
St-Antoine	3	0.5	332	50.5	323	49
St-Louis	302	43	47	7	351	50
Ste-Croix	69	13	184	36	260	51
St-Jean	43	36	17	14	60	50
St-Gilles	0	—	2	—	2	—
total	417	21	582	29	996	50

SOURCE: APQ, poll book, Lotbinière, 1830.

71. Vote by Parish, Beauce, 1834

	A.-C. Taschereau		P.-E. Taschereau		G. Desbarats		W. De Lery	
		%		%		%		%
Ste-Marie	468	48	488	50	9	1	4	1
St-Joseph	160	51	142	45	11	4	3	—
St-François	248	86	25	9	6	2	9	3
St-Georges	1	—	0	—	0	—	0	—
Ste-Claire	128	34	4	1	5	1	245	64
Ste-Marguerite	42	40	34	32	28	26	2	2
Frampton	77	43	0	—	103	57	0	—
Cranbourne	5	50	0	—	5	50	0	—
Jersey	3	60	1	20	0	—	1	20
Kennebec Road	15	54	13	46	0	—	0	—
total	1,147	45	707	28	410	16	279	11

SOURCE: APQ, poll book, Beauce, 1834.

72. Vote by Parish, Dorchester, 1834

	Bouffard		P. Lageux		Beaudoin	
		%		%		%
Pointe-Lévy	201	37	183	33	162	30
St-Anselme	210	52	9	2	188	46
St-Charles	8	36	1	5	13	59
St-Nicolas	243	47	219	42	59	11
St-Jean	72	19	260	67	53	14
St-Isidore	65	36	28	16	86	48
St-Henri	265	44	37	6	306	50
Québec	6	55	2	18	3	27
total	1,070	40	739	28	870	32

SOURCE: APQ, poll book, Dorchester, 1834.

73. Economic Status of Voters, Orléans, 1834 Election

	average voter for Plante, English party moderate	average voter for Godbout, *patriote*
arpents occupied	145	123
arpents cultivated	86	64
wheat (*minots*)	116	89
oats (*minots*)	117	86
potatoes (*minots*)	193	87
cattle (head)	13	10
hogs (head)	5	4
sheep (head)	16	13

SOURCES: Economic data is from 1831 census. Since the agricultural sector had deteriorated by 1834, the averages shown are probably higher than they actually were at that date. APQ, poll book, Orléans, 1834.

74. Vote by Locality, Megantic (Township), 1834

	Layfield		Clapham	
		%		%
Broughton	47	92	4	8
Leeds	154	81	36	19
Halifax	2	4	43	96
Inverness	100	38	158	62
Ireland	9	7	113	93
Wolfstown	0	—	3	—
Nelson	3	—	2	—
Tring	7	—	0	—
total	322	47	359	53

SOURCE: APQ, poll book, Megantic, 1834.

75. Vote by Ethnic Groups and Occupations, Quebec Upper Town, 1836

| | French-speaking vote | | | | English-speaking vote | | | |
	A. Stuart	%	J. Painchaud	%	A. Stuart	%	J. Painchaud	%
professionals	4	25	12	75	36	94	2	6
businessmen	2	3	65	97	126	98	2	2
tradesmen	10	7	152	93	107	94	6	6
labourers	5	11	42	89	19	100	0	—
other	2	9	21	91	57	98	1	2
total	23	8	292	92	345	96	11	4

SOURCE: APQ, poll book, Quebec Upper Town, 1836.

76. English-speaking Vote, Quebec Upper Town, 1824 and 1827*

| | 1824 | | | | 1827 | | | |
	"Canadian" candidates	%	English-speaking candidates	%	patriote candidates	%	English-speaking candidates	%
professionals	22	73	15	50	13	19	52	77
businessmen	81	63	74	57	60	25	160	68
tradesmen	52	35	95	65	85	32	184	69
labourers	4	18	16	72	22	38	44	77
other	38	53	42	59	36	18	140	72
total	197	49	242	60	216	26	580	71

*Some "Canadian" and patriote candidates were English-speaking.
SOURCES: APQ, poll books, Quebec Upper Town, 1824 and 1827.

77. English-speaking Vote, Quebec, 1827*

	patriote candidates	%	English-speaking candidates	%
professionals	2	40	4	80
businessmen	46	65	48	68
tradesmen	41	47	68	79
farmers	39	54	65	90
other	13	38	26	76
total	143	50	224	79

*Some patriote candidates were English-speaking.
SOURCE: APQ, poll book, Quebec, 1827.

78. English-speaking Vote, Quebec Upper Town, 1829 and 1834

	1829 (by-election)				1834						
	Vanfelson	%	Duval	%	Caron (patriote)	%	Berthelot (radical patriote)	%	Stuart (English party)	%
professionals	9	70	4	30	20	30	1	2	45	68
businessmen	85	76	27	24	76	32	2	1	156	67
tradesmen	99	87	15	13	65	31	21	10	121	59
labourers	22	74	8	26	4	15	8	31	14	54
other	61	84	12	16	19	20	1	1	75	79
total	276	81	66	19	184	29	33	5	411	66

SOURCE: APQ, poll book, Quebec Upper Town, 1829 and 1834.

79. English-speaking Vote, Quebec Lower Town, 1832

	Vanfelson (*patriote*)		Dubord (*patriote*)		McCulloch (English party)	
		%		%		%
professionals	3	75	0	—	1	25
businessmen	15	23	0	—	50	77
tradesmen	25	23	0	—	82	77
labourers	3	13	0	—	19	87
other	7	41	0	—	10	59
total	53	24	0	—	162	76

SOURCE: APQ, poll book, Quebec Lower Town, 1832.

80. Agricultural Production, Nicolet, 1831-40
(annual averages, *minots*)

	wheat	oats	peas	barley	rye
1831-35	20,514	17,602	2,080	676	112
1836-40	9,724	17,836	2,288	1,144	728

SOURCES: AAQ, reports of the parish priest to the Quebec bishop. See F. Ouellet, *Éléments*, 80-3. Total production has been estimated by multiplying the tithe by 26.

81. Agricultural Production, Yamachiche, 1830-39 (*minots*)

	wheat	oats	peas	barley	rye	buckwheat
*1831-35	26,406	48,140	4,222	2,685	246	1,321
*1836-39	16,620	42,784	2,776	4,312	159	1,121
**1831	24,797	48,432	3,375	3,597	485	2,542
***1831	24,261	44,348	3,746	3,176	430	2,008
1832	25,987	45,814	5,879	3,725	178	1,519
1833	28,373	58,081	5,472	2,643	109	1,205
1834	22,559	43,299	2,699	1,375	216	812
1835	30,851	49,190	3,314	2,509	298	1,063
1836	26,374	49,192	2,732	3,237	244	610
1837	19,878	35,928	1,815	2,854	97	581
1838	12,407	45,959	3,652	5,478	202	1,375
1839	7,821	39,914	2,906	5,682	96	1,921

*Annual averages calculated from Yamachiche tithe book, which registers the tithe paid by each producer.

**From 1831 census.

***Total production is estimated by multiplying all tithe data by 26. Results show a 6.3% under-reporting in tithe receipts when compared to census data for the 1831 crop year: 77,969 and 83,238 *minots* respectively for all crops (except potatoes). This point was missed in the table in F. Ouellet, *Le Bas-Canada*, 425.

SOURCES: Yamachiche tithe book, 1831-39, Yamachiche parish archives; nominative census for 1831, JHALC, 1831-32, appendix.

82. Wheat and Oats Producers by Production Volume, Yamachiche, 1831-39 (number of producers)

	1-50 *minots*	%	51-100 *minots*	%	101-200 *minots*	%	201 and over	%	total
wheat									
1831-35	139	41	106	31	78	23	18	5	341
1836-39	129	49	87	32	46	17	6	2	268
oats									
1831-35	78	23	78	23	103	30	81	24	340
1836-39	44	16	63	23	85	32	77	29	269

SOURCE: Parish of Yamachiche archives, tithe book, 1831-39.

83. Agricultural Producers at Yamachiche, 1831-39
(number of producers)

	wheat	oats	peas	barley	buckwheat	rye
*1831	392	420				
**1831	321	337	160	123	118	17
1832	348	345	214	139	87	13
1833	350	335	191	94	66	5
1834	332	312	115	62	48	10
1835	319	299	122	89	58	8
1836	280	269	103	94	38	13
1837	287	273	104	95	36	6
1838	284	298	146	145	65	9
1839	226	243	141	153	90	5

SOURCES: *PAC, nominative census of 1831; **calculated from Yamachiche tithe book, parish of Yamachiche archives. See Table 81 (notes).

84. François Lesieur's Harvest, 1831-39
(*minots*)

	wheat	oats	peas	barley	buckwheat	rye
1831	611	949		169	52	
1832	806	1,040		221		
1833	754	1,495		104		
1834	455	663				
1835	598			130	26	
1836	585	611		91		
1837	468	988		143	26	
1838	195	1,274	13	130		26
1839	156	1,118	13	130	39	

SOURCE: The tithe paid by Lesieur to the parish priest has been multiplied by 26. See Yamachiche tithe book.

85. Population Growth and Wheat Production, 1730-1851

	population	wheat production (*minots*)	production per capita (*minots*)
*1730-39	38,388	551,811	14.3
1827	471,875	2,921,240	6.1
1831	511,917	3,404,756	6.6
1844	697,084	942,829	1.3
1851	890,261	3,073,943	3.4

*Annual average calculated on a six-year period. See also Tables 11, 12, 21, and 86.
SOURCES: Lunn, *Economic Development in New France, 1713-1760*, 443-4. Reproduced in J. Hamelin (ed.), *Histoire du Québec*, 196. See census of 1871, vol. IV; JHALC, 1831-32, appendix.

86. Origin of Wheat Exports, Port of Quebec, 1801-31

	Upper Canada and United States	Lower Canada	total
	%	%	%
1801-02	7	93	100
1806-07	24	76	100
1817-21	68	32	100
1822-26	61	39	100
1827-31	92	8	100

SOURCES: Appendices to JHALC. See also Tables 11, 12, 21, and 85.

87. Grain Producers by Yield, Parish of Montreal, 1831
(number of producers)

yield per *arpent*	French-speaking		English-speaking	
		%		%
1-12 *minots*	81	69	21	32
13 *minots* and over	36	31	43	68
total	117	100	64	100

SOURCE: Nominative census of 1831.

88. Agricultural Production, Parish of Montreal, 1831
(average per producer)

	French-speaking	English-speaking
wheat (*minots*)	141.0	97.1
oats (*minots*)	147.6	161.3
peas (*minots*)	44.0	47.8
barley (*minots*)	55.5	189.2
buckwheat (*minots*)	28.2	32.5
rye (*minots*)	34.7	39.8
potatoes (*minots*)	478.9	1,116.2
corn (*minots*)	30.4	53.6
cattle (head)	8.4	12.9
horses (head)	4.2	4.0
sheep (head)	10.5	14.8
hogs (head)	4.9	12.1

SOURCE: Nominative census of 1831.

CHAPTER NOTES

NOTES TO THE INTRODUCTION

1. F. Ouellet, *Histoire économique et sociale du Québec 1760-1850* (1966), 1-148, 539-96.
2. D.G. Creighton, *The Empire of the St. Lawrence* (1956), 1-174; E.E. Rich, *The Fur Trade and the Northwest to 1857* (1957), ch. 8, 9, 10; H. Innis, *The Fur Trade in Canada* (1962).
3. P. Tousignant, "La Genèse et l'avènement de la constitution de 1791" (unpublished Ph.D. thesis, Université de Montréal, 1971), 394.
4. I. Caron, *La Colonisation de la Province de Québec* (1923), I, app. 8: 281-7.
5. *Ibid.*, app. 7: 275-80.
6. Creighton, *The Empire of the St. Lawrence*, 103.
7. Cited by Tousignant, "La Genèse et l'avènement," 426.
8. M. Wade, *The French Canadians, 1760-1947* (1968), 47.
9. DC, 1759-91, 275 [retranslation of original English quote given in French].
10. Caron, *La Colonisation*, I, 121-6.
11. Survey by J.M. Clemens, student research paper.
12. DC, 1759-91, 758ff.; 929ff.
13. Cited by Tousignant, "La Genèse et l'avènement," 320.
14. *Ibid.*, 319.
15. F. Ouellet, *Éléments d'histoire sociale du Bas-Canada* (1972), 251f.
16. Document provided by P. Tousignant.
17. DC, 1759-91, 710 [retrans.].
18. Cited by Tousignant, "La Genèse et l'avènement," 428.
19. *Ibid.*, 311; list of signatories, 447.
20. Cited *Ibid.*, 315.
21. *Ibid.*, 328.
22. L. Villat, *La Révolution et l'empire* (1947), I, 61-73.
23. N. Gash, *Politics in the Age of Peel* (1953), 31ff.
24. F. Ouellet, "La Sauvegarde des patrimoines dans le district de Québec durant la première moitié du XIXe siècle," RHAF (1973), 319-74.
25. APQ, poll books, Quebec Upper Town and Lower Town.
26. *Ibid.*
27. *Ibid.*, Quebec.
28. Cited by J. Garner, *The Franchise and Politics in British North America, 1755-1867* (1969), 157.
29. JHALC, 1832-33, appendix.
30. APQ, poll book, Quebec Upper Town.
31. F.-J. Audet, *Les Députés du premier parlement du Bas-Canada* (1946).
32. G.P. Judd, *Members of Parliament, 1734-1832.*

NOTES TO CHAPTER ONE

1. T. Chapais, *Cours d'histoire du Canada* (1917-34), II, 41-43.

2. L.-J. Papineau—Julie Papineau, 7 February 1825, RAPQ (1953-55), 222f.

3. Innis, *The Fur Trade*, 232.

4. Creighton, *The Empire of the St. Lawrence*, 131-7.

5. Innis, *The Fur Trade*, 267.

6. For a description of the effort to extend the economic space to the Pacific and Arctic Oceans, as exemplified by Mackenzie's explorations, see E.E. Rich, *The Fur Trade in the Northwest to 1857* (1957), 163-94.

7. *Ibid.*, 188.

8. F. Crouzet, *L'Économie britannique et le blocus continental* (1958), I, 97.

9. F. Ouellet, "L'Agriculture bas-canadienne vue à travers les dîmes et la rente en nature," *Éléments*, 37-88; "Sauvegarde," RHAF (1973), 319-74; Caron, *La Colonisation*, I, appendices: tithe report for 1784 and population report for 1790; Reports on... Crown Lands (1821-4): birth, baptismal, and burial statistics for the districts of Quebec and Trois-Rivières, JHALC (1824), app. F.

10. H.U. Faulkner, *Histoire économique des Etats-Unis d'Amérique* (1958), 170-4 [French trans.].

11. J. Boucher, "Les Aspects économiques de la tenure seigneuriale au Canada," *Recherches d'histoire économique* (1964), 149-219.

12. Cited by J.-M. Deneault, "Les Vues du gouverneur Prescott sur les problèmes canadiens, 1796-99" (unpublished M.A. thesis, Université d'Ottawa, 1966-67), 20 [quote given in English].

13. *Ibid.*, 103.

14. Cited by Caron, *La Colonisation*, II, 136.

15. G.F. McGuigan, "Administration of Land Policy," CHAR (1963), 65-7.

16. Caron, *La Colonisation*, II, 140, 228.

17. JHALC (1795).

18. Ouellet, *Éléments*, 177-202.

19. Milnes—Portland, 1 September 1800, DC, 1791-1818, 239f.

20. Mgr Hubert, Memorial, 20 May 1790, H. Têtu and C.-O. Gagnon (eds.), *Mandements, lettres pastorales et circulaires des évêques de Québec* (1887), II, 429ff.

21. Sermon, 1799.

22. Sermon, 1810.

23. Sermon, 1799. On this subject see also C. Galarneau, *La France devant l'opinion canadienne, 1760-1815* (1970), 144-56.

24. T.S. Webster, "Ira Allen in Paris, 1800: Planning a Canadian Revolution," CHAR (1963), 74-80.

25. Sewell—Prescott, 12 May 1797, PACR (1891), 76.

26. For facts relating to these incidents, see W. Kingsford, *History of Canada* (1887-98), VII, 354-406; Chapais, *Cours*, II, 106-28; Galarneau, *La France devant l'opinion canadienne*, 228-50.

27. L. Labadie—Neilson, 4 May 1797, PAC, Neilson Papers, I, 63. See also letters (14 January 1798 and 23 January 1799) in which he speaks of the rejoicing on the occasion of victories won by Admirals Duncan and Nelson. "You will send me a newspaper I can show to [the lads of] the Royal Verchères who have shared my joy." *Ibid.*, 121, 143.

28. Chapais, *Cours*, II, 58-76.

29. *Ibid.*, 79 [retrans.].

30. Cited by Deneault, "Les Vues du gouverneur Prescott" [retrans.].

31. Cited by Caron, *La Colonisation*, II, 62 [retrans.].

32. Cited by F. Ouellet, "Joseph Papineau et le régime parlementaire," BRH (1955), 71.

33. Cited by J. and M. Hamelin, *Les Moeurs électorales dans le Québec de 1791 à nos jours* (1962), 32.

NOTES TO CHAPTER TWO

1. Cited by H.T. Manning, *The Revolt of French Canada, 1800-1835* (1962), 57.

2. *Le Canadien*, 9 October 1809.

3. *Ibid.*, 18 November 1809.

4. *Quebec Gazette*, 21 June 1810.

5. Creighton, *Empire*, 145.

6. Innis, *Fur Trade*, 267.

7. *Ibid.*, 263.

8. *Quebec Gazette*, 1 January 1807.

9. Timber seems not to have played a role comparable to that of cotton in the American economy in the period 1815-60. See D.C. North, *The Economic Growth of the United States, 1790-1860* (1966).

10. L.-M. Deschênes, "William Price, 1810-1850," (unpublished thesis, Université Laval, 1964); Deschênes, "Les enterprises de William Price," *Histoire sociale* (1968), 16-52.

11. A. Dubuc, "Problems in the Study of the Stratification of the Canadian Society from 1760 to 1840," CHAR (1965), 13-29.

12. F. Ouellet, *Histoire de la Chambre de Commerce de Québec, 1809-1959* (1959).

13. Creighton, *Empire*, 145.

14. *Le Canadien*, 22 November 1806.

15. Milnes—Mgr Hubert, 1 March 1802, R. Christie, *Interesting Public Documents and Official Correspondence Illustrative of and Supplementary to the History of Lower Canada*, vol. VI of *History of the Late Province of Lower Canada, 1791-1841* (6 vols., 1848-55), 67. Hereafter cited as Christie, *Interesting Public Documents*.

16. Chapais, *Cours*, II, 179-85.

17. Mountain—Milnes, 6 June 1803, PACR (1893), 20.

18. Mgr Plessis—Grand Vicar Bourret, 10 and 15 May 1807, ASQ, Saberdache bleue, XI, 291-325.

19. *Ibid.*

20. Plessis, sermon, 6 April 1815, BRH (1929), 161-72.

21. Plessis, sermon, 10 January 1799.

22. Plessis, sermon, 6 April 1815, BRH (1929), 161-72.

23. Plessis, sermon, 10 January 1799.

24. Plessis, sermon, 1 April 1810.

25. Plessis—curé of Lislet, 30 December 1815, AAQ, letters.

26. Plessis, sermon, 10 January 1799.

27. Plessis—Lartigue, 13 September 1823, AAQ, letters, XI.

28. Abbé J. Boucher—Plessis, 28 March 1810, *ibid.*, VI, 52.

29. Plessis—Grand Vicar Roux, 4 December 1809, *ibid.*, VII.

30. Plessis—Bishop of Saldas, 23 March 1810, *ibid.*

31. Plessis—Bourret, 10 and 15 May 1807, ASQ, Saberdache bleue, XI, 291-325. "This letter contains much that I should be most vexed to have revealed, but it has appeared essential to me that you be advised of things which you will be negotiating. I pray you to destroy it."

32. Abbé F.-J. Deguise—Plessis, 29 March 1810, RAPQ (1932-33), 67.

33. Plessis—Coadjutor, 23 March 1810, RAPQ (1928-29), 273.

34. Plessis, Memorial, 15 May 1812, *Mandements*, III, 85ff.

35. Plessis—Bathurst, 16 September 1819, RAPQ (1928-29), 128f.

36. Curé Boucher—Plessis, 28 March 1810, AAQ, VI, 52.

37. *Le Canadien*, 22 August 1807.

38. Manning, *The Revolt of French Canada*, 54.

39. Regulations for pupils, College of Ste-Anne de la Pocatière, 27 September 1829, AAQ, K, 106ff.

40. Curriculum, 1790, Seminary of Quebec, ASQ, Viger-Verreau Coll., 16:10.

41. P. Hasard, *La Pensée européenne au XVIIIe siècle* (1946), I, 259-62.

42. M. Lebel, "L'Enseignement de la philosophie au Séminaire de Québec," RHAF (1964), 405-24.

43. *Ibid.* (1965), 582-95; *ibid.* (1966), 106-28; P. Savard, "Les Débuts de

l'enseignement de l'histoire et de la géographie au Séminaire de Québec," RHAF (1962), 509-25; *ibid.* (1963), 43-62.

44. College of Nicolet graduates, 1803-23: 31.7% became priests, 31.4% professionals, 6.6% merchants, 21.6% farmers and 8.4% took other vocations. Plessis, Memorial on the diocese, 14 September 1814, RAPQ (1932-33), 102.

45. *Le Canadien*, 17 January 1807.

46. *Ibid.*, 5 December 1807; *ibid.*, 19 December 1807.

47. *Ibid.*, 23 January 1808.

48. *Ibid.*

49. *Ibid.*, 29 November 1806.

50. *Ibid.*, 1 August 1807.

51. *Ibid.*, 28 November 1807.

52. L.A. Smith, "Le Canadien and the British Constitution, 1806-1810," CHR (1957), 93-108 [retrans.].

53. *Le Canadien*, 28 November 1807.

NOTES TO CHAPTER THREE

1. A.R.M. Lower, *Colony to Nation* (1949), 153ff.

2. Caron, *La Colonisation*, II, 272.

3. Portland—Milnes, 6 January 1801, in W.P.M. Kennedy (ed.), *Documents of the Canadian Constitution* (1918), 244; DC, 1791-1818, 255.

4. Milnes—Portland, 18 June 1801, DC, 1791-1818, 255, n.2.

5. *Ibid.*, 1 November 1800, in Kennedy, *Documents*, 241.

6. *Ibid.*, 242.

7. Because of the attitudes of certain curés, the governor wanted to have control of their appointment.

8. Cited by Chapais, *Cours*, II, 144.

9. Milnes — Portland, 1 November 1800, in Kennedy, *Documents*, 243.

10. Craig-Liverpool, 1 May 1810, in Kennedy, *Documents*, 258.

11. J. Viger—Abbé J. Demers, 15 March 1810, ASQ, Saberdache bleue, I, 249-55.

12. Cited by Chapais, *Cours*, II, 176ff. [retrans.].

13. Bédard—Neilson, 26 June 1817, PAC, Neilson Papers, III, 96f.

14. J.-M. Mondelet—J. Voyer, 14 December 1809, ASQ, Saberdache bleue, I, 240-3.

15. J.-P. Wallot traces this quarrel in a series of articles, RHAF (June 1960-March 1961), 61-86, 259-76, 395-407, 559-82.

16. *Ibid.*, June 1960, 74f.

17. *Quebec Mercury*, 10 March 1806.

18. Manning, *The Revolt of French Canada*, 58-76.

19. J. Viger—J. Demers, 15 March 1810, ASQ, Saberdache bleue, I, 249-55.

20. Bédard—Neilson, 23 November 1814, PAC, Neilson Papers, II, 411-4.

21. J. Papineau—L.-J. Papineau, 22 February 1810, RAPQ (1951-3), 174.

22. M. Viger—J. Viger, 7 December 1808, ASQ, Saberdache bleue, I, 94; see also *ibid.*, 3 January 1809, I, 131.

23. F.-J. Audet, *Députés*, 25-37.

24. Bédard—Neilson, 4 November 1814, PAC, Neilson Papers, II, 398f.

25. F.-J. Audet, *Députés*, 27.

26. Bédard—Neilson, 17 November 1814, PAC, Neilson Papers, II, 408-11.

27. *Ibid.*

28. *Ibid.*, 8 March 1815, II, 463.

29. *Ibid.*, 17 November 1814, II, 408-11.

30. *Ibid.*, 5 March 1803, I, 412; see also *ibid.*, 18 January 1804, I, 466.

31. F.-J. Perreault—Neilson, 7 August 1807; *ibid.*, II, 45.

32. Bédard—Neilson, 11 November 1813, *ibid.*, II, 310.

33. Mondelet—J. Voyer, 14 December 1809, ASQ, Saberdache bleue, I, 243.

34. Bédard—Neilson, 27 August 1817, PAC, Neilson Papers, III, 101f.

35. *Ibid.*, 11 August 1825, V, 149ff.

36. *Ibid.*, 18 January 1828, VI, 20.

37. *Ibid.*, 11 August 1825, V, 149ff.

38. *Ibid.*, 21 June 1814, II, 364.

39. *Ibid.*, 12 January 1815, II, 427ff.

40. Mémoire des habitants du Bas-Canada, November 1814, in Christie, *Interesting Public Documents*, 315-24. In *The Revolt of French Canada*, H.T. Manning attributes this document to Bédard but admits not having found proof of authorship. Bédard — Neilson, 3 March 1814, indicates that it was drafted from notes by Bédard. PAC, Neilson Papers, II, 391-4.

41. A. Dunham, *Political Unrest in Upper Canada, 1815-1836* (1963), 153-7.

42. *Le Canadien*, 24 January 1807.

43. *Ibid.*, 31 January 1807.

44. Manning, *Revolt*, 69.

45. *Le Canadien*, 31 January 1807.

46. Mémoire des habitants, November 1814, in Christie, *Interesting Public Documents*, 315; see also 319-21.

47. *Ibid.*

48. On this question see F.-J. Audet, *Députés*, 95-153.

49. Manning, *Revolt*, 77.

50. Chapais, *Cours*, II, 186ff.

51. Bédard — Neilson, 20 December 1817, PAC, Neilson Papers, III, 135f.

52. *Ibid.*, 25 September 1814, II, 378.

53. *Ibid.*, 11 January 1828, VI, 9ff.

54. DC, 1791-1818, 348.

NOTES TO CHAPTER FOUR

1. A.L. Burt, *The United States, Great Britain and British North America from the Revolution to the Establishment of Peace after the War of 1812* (1940), 210.

2. Crouzet, *L'Économie britannique*, 209f.

3. *Ibid.*, 856.

4. *Ibid.*, 72.

5. Burt, *The United States, Great Britain and British North America*, 222.

6. *Ibid.*, 223.

7. Crouzet, *L'Économie britannique*, 810-36.

8. C.P. Nettels, *The Emergence of a National Economy, 1775-1815* (1962); North, *Economic Growth of the United States*.

9. Burt, *The United States, Great Britain and British North America*, 323f.

10. Crouzet, *L'Économie britannique*, 308, 371, 387.

11. *Ibid.*, 387.

12. B. Perkins, *The Causes of the War of 1812. National Honor or National Interest?* (1962), 71-85.

13. *Ibid.*, 84.

14. *Ibid.*, 71.

15. *Ibid.*, 114.

16. Burt, *The United States, Great Britain and British North America*, 310.

17. Mandement, 22 April 1813, *Mandements*, II, 101.

18. Cited by J.-P. Wallot, "Une Émeute à Lachine contre la 'conscription'," RHAF (1964), 225f.

19. Plessis, circular letter, 21 March 1810, *Mandements*, II, 45; Lartigue, sermon, 21 March 1812, RHAF (1968), 304.

20. Lartigue, sermon, 22 August 1812, *ibid.*

21. Grand Vicar Roux, mandement, 3 July 1812, *Mandements*, 89.

22. Plessis, mandement, 29 October 1812, *ibid.*, 95.

23. Roux, mandement, *ibid.*, 87.

24. Lartigue, sermon, 12 July 1812, RHAF (1968), 306.

25. *Ibid.*, 304.

26. *Ibid.*, 306f.

27. Philippe Aubert de Gaspé notes this distinction between Catholic belief and sociological Catholicism: "I would have been very sensitive to the slightest jibe at Catholicism, for even in my years of apathy, I might even say 'unbelief,' I would never have passively suffered an insult to the creed of my forefathers and the religion in which I was raised." *Mémoires* (1886), 501.

28. L.-M. Le Jeune, *Dictionnaire général... du Canada*, 2 vols. (1931).

29. *Le Canadien*, 17 December 1808.

30. D.-B. Viger, *Considérations sur les effets qu'ont produit en Canada la conservation des établissements du pays, les moeurs, l'éducation, etc.... de ses habitants* (1809), 7.

31. *Ibid.*, 47.

32. *Le Canadien,* 4 November 1809.

33. Aubert de Gaspé, *Mémoires,* 496.

34. *Le Canadien,* 17 December 1808.

35. Mémoire des habitants, November 1814, in Christie, *Interesting Public Documents,* 315-41.

36. *Ibid.,* 322.

37. *Ibid.,* 323.

38. *Ibid.*

39. *Ibid.,* 322f.

40. R.J. Strachan, *A Discourse on the Character of King George the Third* (1810); see also J.-P. Wallot and J. Hare, *Les Imprimés dans la Bas-Canada, 1801-1810* (1967).

41. S. Wise and R.C. Brown, *Canada Views the United States...* (1967), 16-30.

42. Creighton, *Empire,* 175-85.

43. Cited by Wallot, "Emeute," RHAF (1964), 225ff.

44. Christie, *Interesting Public Documents,* 330.

45. *Ibid.,* 331.

46. Prevost—Ryland, 7 November 1811, *ibid.,* 281.

47. *Ibid.*

48. Manning, *Revolt,* 100.

49. Prevost—Ryland, 7 November 1811, in Christie, *Interesting Public Documents,* 281.

50. Prevost—Bathurst, 4 September 1814, DC, 1791-1818, 468, 467, 466, 468, 467.

51. Manning, *Revolt,* 98f.

52. *Le Canadien,* 23 July 1808.

53. Prevost—Bathurst, 18 March 1814, DC, 1791-1818, 462.

54. Plessis, Mémoire faisant connaître au gouverneur ..., *Mandements,* III, 92.

55. J.M. Hitsman, *The Incredible War of 1812: A Military History* (1965), 29f.

56. Crouzet, *L'Economie britannique,* 836-42.

57. Plessis, circular letter, *Mandements,* III, 92.

58. *Ibid.,* 115.

59. *Ibid.,* 127-32.

60. Cited by Hitsman, *The Incredible War,* 243-9.

61. Ouellet, *Histoire économique,* 229.

62. Wallot, "Emeute," RHAF (1964), 125, 227.

63. *Ibid.,* 229.

64. M. Zaslow (ed.), *The Defended Border: Upper Canada and the War of 1812* (1964), 12.

65. Hitsman, *The Incredible War,* 163; Zaslow, *The Defended Border,* 61-5.

66. Hitsman, *The Incredible War,* 163.

67. *Ibid.,* 164-7.

68. *Ibid.,* 215-31; Manning, *Revolt,* 103-8.

69. Hitsman, *The Defended Border,* 231.

70. Chapais, *Cours,* II, 268.

NOTES TO CHAPTER FIVE

1. G. Paquet and J.-P. Wallot, "Crise agricole et tensions socio-ethniques dans le Bas-Canada, 1802-1812; éléments pour une ré-interprétation," RHAF (1972), 213, 234; Paquet and Wallot, "The Agricultural Crisis in Lower Canada, 1802-1812: mise au point. A Response to T.J.A. Legoff, " CHR (1975), 134-68; F. Ouellet, "Le Mythe de l'habitant sensible au marché. Commentaires sur la controverse Legoff-Wallot et Paquet," *Recherches sociographiques* (1976), 115-32.

2. T.J.A. Legoff, "The Agricultural Crisis in Lower Canada, 1802-1812: A Review of a Controversy," CHR (1974), 1-31.

3. JHALC, 1823, app. G: Agricultural Society report.

4. Blondeau—Commissioners, 10 February 1806, APQ, Jesuit Estates, correspondence of the seigneurial agent.

5. Since parish tithes were set at one twenty-sixth of harvests, production volumes of those crops subject to tithing (wheat, oats, barley, rye, buckwheat, and peas) can be estimated from the curés' tithe reports. With due allowance for the fact that these reports were made following pastoral visits, not annually, in the case of wheat the statistics obtainable show close correspondence between production and exports, as do those derived from the records of la Quête de l'Enfant-Jésus. Other useful sources are parish censuses, seigneurial dues and mill revenues paid in wheat, and the records of certain farms belonging to the Quebec Seminary. See Ouellet, "Agriculture ... dîmes et rente," Eléments, 37-88.

6. W.H. Parker, "A New Look at Unrest in Lower Canada in the 1830's," CHR (1959), 209-18.

7. Quebec Gazette, 2 August 1819.

8. Ibid.

9. Ibid., 18 October 1821.

10. Blondeau—Commissioners, APQ, Jesuit Estates, correspondence of the seigneurial agent.

11. Quebec Gazette, 3 September 1821.

12. Montreal Gazette, 4 May 1789.

13. P. Savard (ed.), Paysans et ouvriers canadiens d'autrefois (1968), 48-51.

14. Anonymous, Canada: courte esquisse de sa position géographique, ses productions, son climat (1860).

15. APQ, Fraser Papers, seigneurial agent's reports.

16. APQ, Jesuit Estates, seigneurial agent's quarterly reports.

17. RAPQ (1943-44), 243, 387.

18. JHALC (1832-33), app. PP.

19. Quebec Gazette, 7 August 1821.

20. R.C. McIvor, Canadian Monetary, Banking and Fiscal Development (1958).

21. JHALC (1830), app. N; ibid. (1831), app. M.

22. W.T. Easterbrook and H.G.J. Aitken, Canadian Economic History (1956), 254-67.

23. G.P. Glazebrook, A History of Transportation in Canada (1964), I, 67-72.

24. JHALC (1835).

25. Ibid. (1827).

26. Ibid. (1835), application for incorporation, St Lawrence Co.

27. The Champlain and St Lawrence Railway, completed by 1837.

28. In the summer of 1833 there were eighty-three days of rain; in 1835, ninety days. JHALC (1835-36).

29. For figures on revenues, expenditures, borrowing, and investment in canals in Upper Canada, see JHALC (1847), app. KKK.

30. Ibid.

31. R.M. Martin, History, Statistics and Geography of Upper Canada and Lower Canada (1838).

NOTES TO CHAPTER SIX

1. Cited by G. Filteau, Histoire des Patriotes (1938-39), I, 103.

2. P. Goubert, Beauvaisis et le Beauvaisis de 1600 à 1730 (1960), 1-83.

3. La Minerve, 18 June 1832.

4. J. Papineau—Rosalie Papineau, 19 June 1832, RAPQ (1951-53), 275.

5. J. Papineau—D.-B. Papineau, 21 June 1832, ibid., 277.

6. Ibid.

7. Minutes of the Standing Committee of the House, JHALC (1832-33), app.

Cited in M. Armstrong, student research paper.

8. J. Papineau—D.-B. Papineau, 21 June 1832, RAPQ (1951-53), 276.

9. L.-J. Papineau—Julie Papineau, 1 January 1833, ibid., 328.

10. Montreal Gazette, 21 August 1832.

11. Winter—Duvernay, 20 July 1832, APQ, Duvernay Coll., 132.

12. Third Report on Crown Lands (1821), 133.

13. Testimony, Hall and Duchesnay,

ibid., 129, 137.
14. Testimony, W.B. Felton, *ibid.*, 131.
15. Testimony, Isaac Man, *ibid.*, 125.
16. Testimony, Skeene, *ibid.*, 140.
17. Testimony, Felton, *ibid.*, 132.
18. Testimony, John Neilson, Seventh Report on Crown Lands (1824), 71f.
19. *Ibid.*, 80.
20. Ouellet, "Sauvegarde," RHAF (1972), 319-74.
21. Seventh Report on Crown Lands (1824), 65.
22. First Report on Crown Lands (1821), 22.
23. Second Report on Crown Lands (1821), 14.
24. Seventh Report on Crown Lands (1824), 66.
25. *Ibid.*, 22.
26. First Report on Crown Lands (1821), 150.
27. JHALC (1832-33), app. NN.
28. First Report on Crown Lands (1821), 17.
29. Second Report on Crown Lands (1821), 47.
30. JHALC (1832-33), app. NN.
31. *Ibid.*
32. *Ibid.*, 30.
33. *Ibid.*, 46.

34. *Ibid.*, 27.
35. *Ibid.*
36. *Ibid.*, 21.
37. *Ibid.*
38. *Ibid.*
39. Ouellet, *Histoire économique*, 352.
40. First Report on Crown Lands (1821), 18ff.
41. F. Ouellet, *Papineau: textes choisis*, (1959), 70.
42. *Ibid.*, 68.
43. Second Report on Crown Lands (1821), 33.
44. DC, 1819-28, 348-51.
45. Chapais, *Cours*, IV, 47f.
46. J. Hamelin and F. Ouellet, "Les Rendements agricoles dans les seigneuries et les cantons, 1800-1850," in C. Galarneau and E. Lavoie (eds.), *France et Canada français du XVIe au XXe siècle* (1966), 81-145.
47. Second Report on Crown Lands (1821), 38.
48. *Ibid.*, 127.
49. JHALC, 1831, app. F.
50. DC, 1819-28, 132.
51. Second Report on Crown Lands (1821), 122.
52. *Ibid.*, 48-56.

NOTES TO CHAPTER SEVEN

1. F. Ouellet, *Histoire de la Chambre de Commerce de Québec, 1809-1959* (1959).
2. Ouellet, "Sauvegarde," RHAF (1972), 319-74.
3. The censuses of 1831 and 1842, based on the number of occupants of each house, are preserved in the Public Archives of Canada. Despite certain gaps, particularly for 1842, the record covers the cities and most of the rural areas, and is the source of most of the figures used in this chapter. See also Ouellet, *Eléments*, 110-202; "Sauvegarde," RHAF (1972), 319-74.
4. Cited by L.-P. Audet, *Le Système scolaire de la Province de Québec* (5 vols., 1950-55), III, 148.

5. R.G. Bouliane, "The French Canadians and the Schools of the Royal Institution for the Advancement of Learning," *Social History* (1972), 158ff.
6. L. Lemieux, *L'Etablissement de la première province ecclésiastique au Canada, 1783-1843* (1967).
7. *Ibid.*, 178.
8. G.-E. Baillargeon, *La Survivance du régime seigneurial à Montréal* (1968), 16-50.
9. PAC, Dalhousie Papers.
10. F. Ouellet, "L'Enseignement primaire: responsabilité des églises ou de l'état?, " *Eléments*, 259-77.
11. Cited by L.-P. Audet, *Système scolaire*, IV, 58.
12. *Ibid.*

13. *Ibid.*, v, 79f. On Perreault's plan, see J.-J. Jolois, *Jean-François Perreault et les origines de l'enseignement laïque au Bas-Canada* (1969), 99-121.

14. Cited by L.-P. Audet, *Système scolaire*, iv, 132. On these questions see R. Chabot, *Le Curé de campagne et la contestation locale au Québec de 1791 aux troubles de 1837-38* (1975).

15. Cited by Ouellet, *Eléments*, 271f.

16. *Ibid.*, 272.

17. Chabot, *Le Curé*.

18. Ouellet, *Eléments*, 184.

19. J. Vallée (ed.), *Tocqueville au Bas-Canada* (1973), 103.

20. *Ibid.*, 1048.

21. *Ibid.*, 88.

22. Ouellet, *Papineau: textes*, 71.

23. Théophile Bruneau—Papineau, 17 December 1831, APQ, P-B, T. Bruneau letters.

24. Papineau—Viger, 31 December 1831, ASQ, Saberdache bleue, IX, 109.

25. Morin—Duvernay, 28 December 1831, APQ, Duvernay Coll., 107.

26. Perreault—Fabre, 22 February 1836, APQ, Fabre Papers.

27. Vallée, *Tocqueville*, 87.

28. Ouellet, *Papineau: textes*, 73f.; *Eléments*, 329-31.

29. APQ, Duvernay Coll.

30. Rodier—Duvernay, 2 January 1834, *ibid.*

31. Vallée, *Tocqueville, 100*.

32. Parent—Duvernay, 10 December 1833, APQ, Duvernay Coll., 198.

33. *La Minerve*, 8 December 1834.

34. *Ibid.*, 6 November 1834.

35. *Ibid.*, 21 November 1831.

36. Ouellet, *Eléments*, 177; "Sauvegarde," RHAF (1972), 358.

37. J.-C. Robert, "Un Seigneur entrepreneur: Barthélémy Joliette et la fondation du village de l'Industrie (1822-1850)," RHAF (1972), 375-95.

38. *Ibid.*, 394.

39. Vallée, *Tocqueville, 102*.

40. *Ibid.*, 101.

NOTES TO CHAPTER EIGHT

1. R.S. Neale, *Class and Ideology in the Nineteenth Century* (1972), 34.

2. *Ibid.*, 80.

3. G.M. Craig (ed.), *Lord Durham's Report* (1963), 22, 24, 25f., 26, 23.

4. Vallée, *Tocqueville*, 91, 109.

5. R. de Roquebrune, "M. de Pontois et la rébellion des Canadiens français," *Nova Franca* (1927-28), 247f.

6. F. Elliott—Henry Taylor, 24 October 1835, PACR (1883), 161f.

7. E. Mailhot—Duvernay, 19 October 1839, APQ, Duvernay Coll., 354.

8. Bédard—Neilson, 25 September and 3 November 1814, PAC, Neilson Papers, II, 378.

9. J. Viger—Demers, 15 March 1810, ASQ, Saberdache bleue, I, 249-55.

10. Cited in English by Manning, *Revolt*, 259.

11. *La Minerve*, 17 February 1831.

12. Vallée, *Tocqueville*, 101.

13. J. Viger—wife, 4 March 1817, ASQ, Saberdache bleue, v, 120.

14. Bédard — Neilson, 29 September 1814, PAC, Neilson Papers, II, 384f.

15. *Ibid.*, 3 November 1814, II, 391-4.

16. *Ibid.*, 12 March 1815, III, 12ff.

17. Rosalie Papineau—Benjamin Papineau, 1 March 1807, PAC, Papineau Papers, 44ff.

18. F. Ouellet, *Papineau: un être divisé*, Canadian Historical Association Booklets; "L.-J. Papineau (1786-1871)," *Eléments*, 319-47.

19. Cited by Ouellet, *Eléments*, 322.

20. Vallée, *Toqueville*, 101.

21. Bédard—Neilson, 21 June 1814, PAC, Neilson Papers, II, 364.

22. *Ibid.*, 18 February 1815, II, 441.

23. *Ibid.*, 27 February 1818, III, 188ff.

24. *Le Canadien*, 17 January 1818.

25. *Ibid.*, 10 October 1817.

26. APQ, P-B., 16n.

27. L.-J. Papineau—Julie Papineau, 7 January 1821, RAPQ (1953-55), 195.

28. *Le Canadien*, 28 February 1821.

29. L.-J. Papineau—Julie Papineau, 27 February 1821, RAPQ (1953-55), 199.

30. Bédard—Neilson, 4 February 1818, PAC, Neilson Papers, III, 176ff.

31. *Le Canadien*, 28 February 1821.

32. *Quebec Gazette*, 16 February 1818 [reported in English].

33. *Ibid.*, 26 January 1815.

34. Neilson—D.-B. Viger, 9 September 1824, PAC, Neilson Papers.

35. For more information on this strife-ridden election (during which bribery was used liberally by both sides—a common practice in hotly-contested elections), see Bédard—Neilson, 24 August 1817, PAC, Neilson Papers; *ibid.*, 26 June, 29 July, and 3 August 1817, 14 March, 11 April, and 27 May 1818, PAC, Neilson Papers, III, 97-110; JHALC, 1818, app. D.

36. L.-J. Papineau—Julie Papineau, 11 February 1821, RAPQ (1953-55), 196.

37. *Quebec Gazette*, 10 July 1820.

38. Bédard—Neilson, 4 February 1818, PAC, Neilson Papers, III, 176ff.

39. *Quebec Gazette*, 2 April 1818.

40. Cited by H. Brun, *La Formation des institutions parlementaires québécoises, 1791-1838* (1970), 240f. [retrans.].

41. PAC, Neilson Papers, III, 462-5.

42. L. Moquin—Neilson, 28 March 1820, PAC, Neilson Papers, III, 441ff.

43. J. Viger—H. Heney, 15 February 1821, ASQ, Saberdache bleue, V, 226f.

44. *Le Canadien*, 8 August 1821.

45. L.-J. Papineau—D.-B. Papineau, 15 July 1822, APQ, P-B, 141.

46. L. de Salaberry—J. Viger, 22 January 1823, ASQ, Saberdache bleue, VI, 50f.

47. J. Bélanger—Neilson, 22 January 1823, PAC, Neilson Papers, IV, 198f.

48. L.-J. Papineau—Neilson, 18 November 1822, APQ, P-B, 502a.

49. *Ibid.*

50. Manning, *Revolt*, 161.

51. L.-J. Papineau and Neilson—Wilmot, 10 May 1823, JHALC (1823), app. K.

52. L.-J. Papineau—Neilson, 16 December 1822, PAC, Neilson Papers, IV, 72.

53. Neilson—L.-J. Papineau, 5 December 1822, *ibid.*, misc., 18, 46.

54. L.-J. Papineau—Neilson, 9 November 1822, *ibid.*, IV, 54.

55. L.-J. Papineau—Julie Papineau, 27 June 1823, RAPQ (1953-55), 208.

56. *Ibid.*, 209.

57. *Ibid.*

58. Heney—J. Viger, 13 January 1823, ASQ, Saberdache bleue, VI, 43f.

59. D.-B. Viger—Neilson, 2 November 1826, PAC, Neilson Papers, V, 402f; 10 November 1825, V, 195f.

60. JHALC (1825).

61. ASQ, Saberdache bleue, VII, 10f.

62. Heney—J. Viger, 8 January 1825, *ibid.*, 13f.

63. L.-J. Papineau—Julie Papineau, 8 January 1825, RAPQ (1953-55), 213.

64. Bédard—Neilson, 26 March 1824, PAC, Neilson Papers, IV, 369f.

65. A. Beaulieu and J. Hamelin, *La Presse québécoise des origines à nos jours* (1973), I, 14-100.

66. L.-J. Papineau—Julie Papineau, 28 February 1825, RAPQ (1953-55), 225.

67. APQ, poll books, Quebec and Upper Town, 1827.

68. *La Minerve*, 23 August 1829.

69. *Ibid.*, 13 September 1827.

70. *Ibid.*, 3 August 1827.

71. L.-J. Papineau—D.-B. Papineau, 20 August 1827, APQ, P-B, 61.

72. Mondelet—D.-B. Viger, 23 April 1828, PAC, Viger Coll., I, 500ff.

73. Select Committee on the State of Civil Government in Canada, 1828, in Kennedy, *Documents*, 349.

74. Bidwell—Neilson, 21 November 1829, PAC, Neilson Papers, VI, 512ff.

75. Mackenzie—Neilson, 7 December 1829, *ibid.*, 519ff.

76. L.-J. Papineau—Neilson, 21 December 1829, *ibid.*, 546ff.

NOTES TO CHAPTER NINE

1. B. Foster, student research paper.

2. L.-J. Papineau—Neilson, 12 Novem-

ber 1829, PAC, Neilson Papers, VI, 506ff.

3. L.-J. Papineau—Julie Papineau, 9 March 1829, RAPQ (1953-55), 273.

4. Bédard—Neilson, 8 March 1829, PAC, Neilson Papers, VI, 395f.

5. Brun, *La Formation des institutions,* 248ff.

6. L.-J. Papineau—Neilson, 21 December 1829, PAC, Neilson Papers, VI, 546ff.

7. Bélanger — Neilson, 10 February 1823, *ibid.,* 218ff.

8. L.-J. Papineau—Neilson, 21 December 1829, *ibid.,* 546ff.

9. House of Assembly instructions to envoys, 6 February 1828, *ibid.,* 53-61.

10. L.-J. Papineau—Julie Papineau, 8 January 1829, RAPQ (1953-55), 262, 268.

11. *La Minerve,* 27 February 1834.

12. *Ibid.,* 3 March 1834.

13. Lacroix—Duvernay, 6 September 1833, APQ, Duvernay Coll., 190.

14. Morin—Duvernay, 22 February 1831, *ibid.,* 86.

15. L.-J. Papineau—Julie Papineau, 25 March 1830, RAPQ (1953-55), 301.

16. *La Minerve,* 17 March 1836.

17. *Ibid.,* 24 January 1833.

18. *Ibid.,* 17 February 1831.

19. *Ibid.,* 24 March 1834.

20. *Ibid.,* 3 March 1834.

21. *Ibid.,* 18 February 1834.

22. *Ibid.,* 17 March 1836.

23. *Ibid.,* 6 February 1834.

24. *Ibid.,* 24 March 1834.

25. L.-J. Papineau—Julie Papineau, 23 December 1835, RAPQ (1953-55), 375.

26. *La Minerve,* 24 January 1833.

27. *Ibid.,* 21 January 1833.

28. *Ibid.*

29. *Ibid.,* 24 January 1833.

30. *Ibid.*

31. *Ibid.,* 18 February 1834.

32. *Ibid.,* 24 January 1833.

33. *Ibid.,* 4 December 1834.

34. *Ibid.,* 17 March 1836.

35. *Ibid.,* 17 February 1834.

36. *Ibid.,* 24 January 1833.

37. *Ibid.,* 17 March 1836.

38. *Ibid.,* 18 February 1834.

39. *Ibid.,* 3 March 1831.

40. *Ibid.,* 1 February 1836.

41. *Ibid.,* 18 March 1830.

42. *Ibid.,* 18 August 1837.

43. *Ibid.,* 22 January 1834 [reported in English].

44. *Ibid.,* 29 November 1832.

45. Demers—Neilson, PAC, Neilson Papers, VII, 413ff.

46. *La Minerve,* 3 March 1834.

47. *Ibid.,* 4 December 1834.

48. *Ibid.,* 13 February 1832.

49. *Ibid.,* 24 January 1832.

50. *Ibid.,* 17 March 1836.

51. L.-J. Papineau—Julie Papineau, 8 March 1831, RAPQ (1953-55), 316.

52. *La Minerve,* 24 January 1833.

53. *Ibid.*

54. *Ibid.,* 3 March 1831.

55. *Ibid.,* 14 January 1833.

56. APQ, Duvernay Coll.

57. *La Minerve,* 18 March 1830.

58. Neilson—L.-J. Papineau, 20 November 1830, PAC, Neilson Papers, corr. 1815-66, 25ff.

59. *Ibid.,* 4 August 1830, 29ff.

60. ASQ, Saberdache bleue, VIII, 302f.

61. Morin — Gosselin, 18 December 1831, APQ, Duvernay Coll., 106.

62. *La Minerve,* 13 February 1832.

63. E. McKenna, student research paper.

64. *Ibid.*

65. *La Minerve,* 3 February 1834.

66. *Ibid.,* 24 May 1832.

67. McKenna, research paper.

68. *Ibid.*

69. APQ, P-B.

70. Glackmeyer — Neilson, 21 April 1833, PAC, Neilson Papers, VIII, 39.

71. *La Minerve,* 24 January 1833.

72. *Ibid.,* 24 March 1834.

73. Curé Viau — Duvernay, August 1832, APQ, Duvernay Coll., 141.

74. Abbé L.-M. Brassard—Duvernay, 21 August 1832, *ibid.,* 144.

75. Lartigue—D.-B. Viger, 5 June 1832, PAC, Viger Coll., III, 1404f.

76. *Ibid.,* 15 April 1834, IV, 2106.

77. *Ibid.*

78. L.-J. Papineau—Julie Papineau, 9 March 1835, RAPQ (1953-55), 357.

79. McKenna, research paper.
80. Neilson—de Lotbinière, 31 May 1834, PAC, Neilson Papers, 12.
81. Neilson—Denison, 26 June 1835, *ibid.*
82. L.-J. Papineau—Julie Papineau, 21 January 1833, RAPQ (1953-55), 332.
83. *La Minerve*, 18 February 1834.
84. L.-J. Papineau—Julie Papineau, 11 February 1833, RAPQ (1953-55), 333.
85. Mackenzie—Neilson, 7 February 1834, PAC, Neilson Papers, VIII, 216f.
86. L.-J. Papineau—Julie Papineau, 21 January 1834, RAPQ (1953-55), 343.
87. J. Viger—wife, 3 March 1834, ASQ, Saberdache bleue, IX, 270.
88. Debartzch—J. Viger, 24 February 1834, *ibid.*, 258-60.
89. J. Viger—wife, 21 February 1834, *ibid.*, 255.
90. De Lotbinière—Neilson, 21 March 1834, PAC, Neilson Papers, VIII, 224ff.
91. Foster, research paper.
92. ASQ, Viger-Verreau Coll.
93. Foster, research paper.
94. *Ibid.*
95. *Quebec Gazette*, 22 October 1834.
96. *La Minerve*, 4 December 1834.
97. *Ibid.*
98. *Ibid.*
99. *Ibid.*
100. *Ibid.*
101. Cited by B. Dufebvre, "Une Drôle d'élection en 1834," *Revue de l'Université Laval* (1953), 604.
102. APQ, Duvernay Coll.
103. Dufebvre, "Une Drôle d'élection," 606.
104. *Ibid.*, 607.

105. G. Maffre, student research paper.
106. Morin—Duvernay, 31 December 1832, APQ, Duvernay Coll., 173.
107. APQ, poll book, Beauce, 1841.
108. *Ibid.*, Dorchester, 1827 and 1830.
109. C. Kaine, student research paper [cited in English].
110. *Ibid.*
111. APQ, poll books, Dorchester, 1832 and 1834.
112. *Ibid.*, Mégantic, 1832.
113. D. Smith, student research paper.
114. *Ibid.*
115. *La Minerve*, 4 December 1834.
116. Mackenzie—Neilson, 18 November 1835, PAC, Neilson Papers, VIII, 487f.
117. *La Minerve*, 14 February 1832.
118. *Ibid.*, 23 November 1835.
119. L.-J. Papineau—Julie Papineau, 23 December 1835, RAPQ (1953-55), 376.
120. Legendre—Neilson, 10 April 1836, PAC, Neilson Papers, IX, 64.
121. *La Minerve*, 4 December 1834.
122. *Ibid.*
123. L.-J. Papineau—Julie Papineau, 30 November 1835, RAPQ (1953-55), 347.
124. *La Minerve*, 18 August 1837.
125. Cited by Ouellet, *Eléments*, 327.
126. *La Minerve*, 19 March 1836.
127. *Ibid.*, 4 December 1834.
128. L.-J. Papineau—Julie Papineau, 1 February 1836, RAPQ (1953-55), 385.
129. Boucher-Belleville—Duvernay, 4 April 1835, APQ, Duvernay Coll.
130. Perreault — Fabre, 23 February 1836, APQ, Fabre Papers.

NOTES TO CHAPTER TEN

1. *La Minerve*, 14 February 1831.
2. Elliott—Henry Taylor, 24 October 1835, PACR (1883), 166-70.
3. A. Garon, "La Fonction politique et sociale des Chambres hautes canadiennes, 1791-1841," *Histoire sociale* (1971), 66-87.
4. Sherbrooke—Bathurst, DC, 1791-1818, 300.

5. Manning, *Revolt*, 124-48.
6. *Ibid.*, 132.
7. DC, 1819-28, 139.
8. *Ibid.*
9. *Ibid.*, 136.
10. *Ibid.*, 148.
11. *Ibid.*, 224.
12. Manning, *Revolt*, 141.

13. Foster, research paper [cited in English].

14. DC, 1819-28, 404.

15. Aylmer—Franks, 2 December 1830, CO, 387:9, 5f.

16. Aylmer — Goderich, 17 January 1831, *ibid.*, 7, 1.

17. *Ibid.*, 26 August 1831, 7, 9f.

18. Aylmer—Heney, 10 October 1832, *ibid.*, 8, 54.

19. Aylmer — Goderich, 17 January 1831, *ibid.*, 7, 2.

20. Aylmer—Glenelg, 30 January 1833, *ibid.*, 7, 71f.

21. Aylmer—Spring-Rice, 19 August 1834, *ibid.*, 7, 131.

22. *Ibid.*, 7 November 1834, 7, 144.

23. Aylmer—Hay, 14 December 1834, *ibid.*, 7, 160ff.

24. Aylmer—Kempt, 2 April 1831, *ibid.*, 8, 12.

25. Aylmer—Goderich, 16 June 1832, *ibid.*, 7, 25.

26. *Ibid.*, 17 October 1832, 7, 45.

27. *Ibid.*, 29 November 1832, 7, 54.

28. Stephen—Aberdeen, 19 September 1834, BM, Aberdeen Papers, 43236: 96-120.

29. Aberdeen—Aylmer, 28 February 1835, *ibid.*, 282ff.

30. *Ibid.*, 11 March 1835, 284ff.

31. Stephen—Aberdeen, 19 September 1834, *ibid.*, 96-120.

32. *La Minerve*, 21 February 1831.

33. *Ibid.*, 28 January 1833.

34. *Ibid.*, 5 March 1835.

35. *Ibid.*

36. *Ibid.*, 3 March 1834.

37. *Ibid.*

38. *Ibid.*, 5 March 1835.

39. Stephen—Aberdeen, 19 September 1834, BM, Aberdeen Papers, 43236: 96-120.

40. Foster, research paper.

41. *La Minerve*, 5 June 1837.

42. Stephen—Aberdeen, 19 September 1834, BM, Aberdeen Papers, 43236: 96-120.

43. Heney—Neilson, 27 March 1835, PAC, Neilson Papers, VIII, 344.

44. *Ibid.*, 324-42.

45. *La Minerve*, 14 March 1836.

46. *Ibid.*, 8 May 1837 [retrans.].

47. PAC, Imperial Blue Books, VII, 0.3, 9.

48. *La Minerve*, 4 May 1837.

49. *Ibid.*, 1 May 1837.

50. *Ibid.*

51. *Ibid.*, 4 May 1837.

52. Gosford—Glenelg, 2 September 1837, PAC, Q 238-1.

53. *Ibid.*

NOTES TO CHAPTER ELEVEN

1. Julie Papineau—L.-J. Papineau, 17 February 1836, APQ, P-B, 659.

2. Julie Papineau-Dessaulles—L.-J. Papineau, October 1836, APQ, P-B.

3. JHALC (1836), app. T.

4. See Ouellet, "Agriculture... dîmes et rente," *Eléments*, 37-88; Ste-Anne de Yamachiche parish archives, tithe book, which gives all the farmers' payments to the curé in the minutest detail.

5. PAC, Neilson Papers, IX, 361f.

6. Casgrain—Neilson, 1 January 1839, *ibid.*, 377f.

7. Ouellet, *Histoire économique*, 418ff.

8. APQ, QBT, minute book, 1832-42.

9. Cited by D.G. Creighton, "The Economic Background of the Rebellion of 1837," in W.T. Easterbook and M.H. Watkins (eds.), *Approaches to Canadian Economic History* (1967), 234.

10. J. Papineau — Amédée Papineau, 27 April 1838, RAPQ (1953-55), 290.

11. APQ, QBT, minute book, 1832-42.

12. Cited by Ouellet, *Histoire économique*, 421.

13. *Ibid.*, 424.

14. Legendre—Neilson, 22 December 1838, PAC, Neilson Papers, IX, 361f.

15. *La Minerve*, 13 April 1837.

16. The three wills are preserved in APQ, P-B.

17. Kimber—Lafontaine, 22 November 1837, *ibid.*

18. Cited by Ouellet, *Éléments*, 353. Papineau admitted having asked associates to destroy important documents.

19. Journal d'un Fils de la Liberté, APQ, P-B.

20. Marchesseault—wife, 1838, APQ, Boucher de Labruyère Papers, 8.

21. Filteau, *Histoire des Patriotes*, II, 84.

22. Journal d'un Fils de la Liberté, APQ, P-B.

23. Cited by Filteau, *Histoire des Patriotes*, II, 111.

24. Deposition, N. Duchesneau, APQ, E. 1837-38, 845.

25. Dep., R. Hall confirmed by J.W. Roberts, *ibid.*, 607.

26. Dep., A. Loiselle, *ibid.*, 849.

27. Dep., T. Danis, *ibid.*, 807.

28. Dep., D. Mitchell, *ibid.*, 847.

29. Dep., J. Choquette, *ibid.*, 784.

30. Dep., E. Sabourin, *ibid.*, 771, 767, 775.

31. *Ibid.*, 771.

32. Dep., A. Danis, *ibid.*, 808.

33. Journal d'un Fils de la Liberté, APQ, P-B.

34. Dep., P. Hébert, L. Héon, and J. Prince, APQ, E. 1837-38, 247; see also 235, 323.

35. Dep., L. Lanoville, *ibid.*, 249; see also 229.

36. Dep., L. Thonin dit Roc, *ibid.*, 846.

37. Dep., J. Dodelin, *ibid.*, 345.

38. Dep., A. Foisie, *ibid.*, 346.

39. Dep., L. Holmes, *ibid.*, 529.

40. Dep., A. Brisebois, *ibid.*, 1651.

41. Dep., P. Nichols, *ibid.*, 1741.

42. Dep., H. Guérin, *ibid.*, 32; confirmed by Hart, 86.

43. Cited by Chapais, *Cours*, IV, 78.

44. *Ibid.*, 186.

45. Journal d'un Fils de la Liberté, APQ, P-B.

46. Dep., C. Lemoine, APQ, E. 1837-38, 704.

47. Dep., P. Martin, *ibid.*, 17.

48. Dep., A. Weindenbacker, *ibid.*, 11.

49. Dep., A. Bonning and A. Leggo, *ibid.*, 183, 184.

50. Journal d'un Fils de la Liberté, APQ, P-B.

51. Anonymous, Mémoire d'un prisonnier politique, PAC, Viger Coll; VI, 2777.

52. Julie Papineau—Lactance Papineau, 17 October 1837, APQ, P-B.

53. Dep., Drolet and Duvert, APQ, E. 1837-38, 45, 46.

54. Dep., J. Vivien, *ibid.*, 842.

55. Dep., T. Franchères, *ibid.*, 48.

56. Dep., A. Brodeur and L. Beauchamp, *ibid.*, 40-41.

57. Mémoire d'un prisonnier politique, PAC, Viger Coll; VI, 2777.

58. Cited by Ouellet, *Éléments*, 356.

59. Ouellet, *Papineau: textes*, 81f.

60. Dep., T. Franchères, APQ, E. 1837-38, 49.

61. Dep., E. Cheval, *ibid.*, 776.

62. Dep., D. Joanette, *ibid.*, 615.

63. Dep., W.H. Scott, *ibid.*, 571.

64. Cited by Ouellet, *Éléments*, 363.

65. Dep., E. Babin, APQ, E. 1837-38, 135.

66. Dep., M. Marchesseault, *ibid.*, 497.

67. Cited by Ouellet, *Éléments*, 362.

68. Report of the Canada (Province) commission of inquiry on seigneurial tenure in Lower Canada, submitted 4 October 1843, printed 1844.

69. Dep., R. Beswick, APQ, E. 1837-38, 1341.

70. Dep., J. Palardie, *ibid.*, 1543.

71. Dep., A. Clark, *ibid.*, 124.

72. Dep., R. Lattmer, *ibid.*, 119.

73. Dep., W.H. Scott, *ibid.*, 743.

74. Dep., J. Lacoste and P. Morin, *ibid.*, 1478.

75. Dep., A. Dupuis, *ibid.*, 125.

76. Dep., E. Rocque, *ibid.*, 1409.

77. Dep., J. Trudel, father and son, *ibid.*, 227, 228.

NOTES TO CHAPTER TWELVE

1. Cited by Filteau, *Histoire des Patriotes*, II, 232.

2. Lartigue—Signay, 29 July 1837, RAPQ (1944-45), 247.

3. Cited by Chapais, *Cours*, IV, 173.

4. *Ibid.*, 74.

5. Dep., A. Blanchet, APQ, E. 1837-38, 1100.

6. Dep., E. Couillard Després, *ibid.*, 889.

7. Dep., I. Marchesseault, *ibid.*, 885; see also 881.

8. Cited by Filteau, *Histoire des Patriotes*, II, 186.

9. Cited by F. Ouellet, "Le Mandement de Mgr Lartigue et la réaction libérale," BRH (1952), 99, 100, 101.

10. Cited by L. Groulx, *Notre maître, le passé* (1936), II, 105.

11. Dep., S. Marchesseault, APQ, E. 1837-38, 844.

12. Dep., A. Michon, *ibid.*, 1520.

13. Dep., M. Brodeur, *ibid.*, 457; see also 341.

14. Anonymous letter from political prisoners to Mgr Lartigue, APQ, P-B.

15. *La Minerve*, 30 October 1837.

16. Dep., Casimir de Montigny, APQ, E. 1837-38, 567.

17. Lartigue—Gosford, 5 May 1837, RAPQ, 1944-45, 240. This request was to be repeated later, stressing the role played by the clergy during the rebellion period.

18. Dep., Casimir de Montigny, APQ, E. 1837-38, 567.

19. Gosford, dispatch, 8 September 1837, PACR (1923), 337.

20. APQ, E. 1837-38, 3206a.

21. Cited by Filteau, *Histoire des Patriotes*, II, 205ff.

22. Cited by Ouellet, *Papineau: textes*, 81f.

23. Dep., A. Labadie, APQ, E. 1837-38, 843.

24. Journal d'un Fils de la Liberté, APQ, P-B.

25. Dep., J. Poet, APQ, E. 1837-38, 988.

26. Dep., Catherine Dufresne, *ibid.*, 995.

27. Mémoire d'un prisonnier politique, PAC, Viger Coll., VI, 2777.

28. Dep., L.-A. Lefebvre, APQ, E. 1837-38, 1838.

29. Dep., S.-T. Lesperance, *ibid.*, 292.

30. Dep., M. Roy, *ibid.*, 328.

31. Dep., L. Étier, *ibid.*, 346a.

32. Dep., M. Vilbon, *ibid.*, 355.

33. Dep., S.-T. Lesperance, *ibid.*, 291.

34. Dep., L. Etier, *ibid.*, 356a.

35. Dep., J. Couvillon, *ibid.*, 354.

36. Mémoire d'un prisonnier politique, PAC, Viger Coll., 2777.

37. Dep., O. Lussier, APQ, E. 1837-38, 353.

38. Dep., J.-B. Tétro, *ibid.*, 136.

39. Dep., F. Darche, *ibid.*, 1433.

40. *Ibid.*

41. R.-L. Séguin, *Le Mouvement insurrectionnel dans la presqu'île de Vaudreuil* (1955), 28ff.

42. APQ, E. 1837-38, 3888.

43. Dep., W. Kell, *ibid.*, 116.

44. Dep., J. Renny, *ibid.*, 633.

45. Dep., P. Brazeau, *ibid.*, 805.

46. Dep., N. Duchesneau, *ibid.*, 810.

47. Dep., G. Spinard, *ibid.*, 767.

48. Dep., F. Paquin, *ibid.*, 766.

49. H. Aquin (ed.), *M. Globensky. La Rébellion de 1837 à St-Eustache* (1974), 53.

50. Dep., A. Foisie, APQ, E. 1837-38, 719.

51. Dep., A. Rochon, *ibid.*, 687.

52. Dep., J. Danis, *ibid.*, 744.

53. Duvernay—J. Robitaille, 7 April 1838, *Canadian Antiquarian* (1909), 98.

54. Mailhot—Duvernay, 9 August 1839, APQ, Duvernay Coll., 322.

55. Dep., J. Martin, APQ, E. 1837-38, 621.

56. Dep., E. Richard, *ibid.*, 1053.

57. Dep., L. Piché, *ibid.*, 622.

58. Dep., J. Miron, *ibid.*, 568.

59. Dep., J. Lavoie, *ibid.*, 1091.

60. Dep., A. Berthiaume, dep., J. Champagne and A. Cloutier, *ibid.*, 322, 232.

61. McDermott's report, *ibid.*, 3210.

62. Dep., F. Hart, *ibid.*, 1789.

63. Cited by F. Ouellet, "Papineau dans la révolution de 1837-38," CHAR (1958), 27.

64. *Ibid.*

65. L.-J. Papineau—Amédée Papineau, 16 December 1837, APQ, P-B, 241a.

66. Dep., J. Hunter, APQ, E. 1837-38, 590.

67. C.-H.-O. Côté—Duvernay, 26 Jan-

uary 1838, *Canadian Antiquarian* (1909), 10.

68. Cited by Ouellet, "Papineau dans la révolution," 27.

69. Julie Papineau—L.-J. Papineau, 4 March 1839, APQ, P-B, 676.

70. L.-J. Papineau—Julie Papineau, 1 February 1838, *ibid.*, 396.

71. APQ, P-B.

72. Dep., J.B.E. Fratelin, APQ, E. 1837-38, 2598.

73. Anonymous letter to Durham, *ibid.*, 3321.

74. Cited by Ouellet, *Éléments*, 343.

75. Mailhot—Duvernay, 6 April 1838, *Canadian Antiquarian* (1909), 93ff.

76. Dep., J. Bourdon, APQ, E. 1837-38, 963.

77. Mailhot—Duvernay, 4 June 1838, *Canadian Antiquarian* (1909), 156.

78. Dep., M. Meunier, APQ, E. 1837-38.

79. Dep., T. Gagnon, *ibid.*, 1655.

80. Dep., N. Guertain, *ibid.*, 2758.

81. Dep., J.B.E. Fratelin, *ibid.*, 2958.

82. Dep., T. Gagnon, *ibid.*, 1655.

83. Dep., J.-D. Hébert, *ibid.*, 2437.

84. Dep., M. Tremblay, *ibid.*, 2051.

85. Dep., L. Duteau, *ibid.*, 2450.

86. Dep., A. Vien, *ibid.*, 1665.

87. Dep., N. Boyer, *ibid.*, 2046.

88. Dep., J. Gariépy, *ibid.*, 978.

89. Dep., P. Colette, *ibid.*, 1462.

90. Dep., J. Bourdon, *ibid.*, 963.

91. Dep., W. Brewster, *ibid.*, 1159.

92. Dep., Guillaume dit Lescarbeau, *ibid.*, 1443.

93. Dep., L. Remillard, *ibid.*, 2719.

94. Dep., F. Robichaud, *ibid.*, 1552.

95. Dep., T. Legrand, *ibid.*, 1816.

96. Dep., E. Lavoie, *ibid.*, 1834.

97. Dep., T. Gagnon, *ibid.*, 1655.

98. *Ibid.*

99. Dep., J. Menard, *ibid.*, 2741.

100. Dep., E. Ford, *ibid.*, 2901.

101. Dep., N. Guertain, *ibid.*, 2758.

102. *Ibid.*

103. Dep., A. Courtemanche, *ibid.*, 2761.

104. Dep., P. Fillion, *ibid.*, 2622.

105. Dep., T. Legrand dit Dufresne, *ibid.*, 1816.

106. Dep., P. Pinsonnault and A. Lanctot, *ibid.*, 2802.

107. Dep., S. Pinsonnault and B. Cligny, *ibid.*, 2607, 2617.

108. Dep., I. Carpentier, *ibid.*, 1654.

109. Dep., L. Odell, *ibid.*, 2440.

110. Dep., F. Bourassa the elder, *ibid.*, 1262.

111. Dep., L. Défaillette, *ibid.*, 2712.

112. Dep., L. Lussier, *ibid.*, 2723.

113. Dep., L. Odell, *ibid.*, 2440.

114. Dep., J.-B. Lukin, *ibid.*, 2536.

115. Dep., N. Bruyère, *ibid.*, 2246.

116. Dep., M. Tremblay, *ibid.*, 2051.

117. Dep., J.-O. Manthet, *ibid.*, 3438.

118. W. Ormsby (ed.), "Crisis in the Canadas, 1838-39," *The Grey Journals and Letters* (1964), 151.

119. *Ibid.*, 165.

120. APQ, E. 1837-38, 2958, 2961, 3310, 3312, 3314, 3316, 3317, 3318.

121. Dep., J. Demers, *ibid.*, 2864.

122. Dep., C. Allard, *ibid.*, 1566.

123. Dep., R. North, *ibid.*, 1982.

124. Bourget—Signay, 21 February 1840, RAPQ (1945-46), 216.

125. Dep., T. Étier and J.-B. Richer, APQ, E. 1837-38, 2920, 2922.

126. Globensky—Murdoch, 9 March 1840, *ibid.*, 2923.

127. Dep., T. Prévost, *ibid.*, 13310.

128. Dep., I. Carpentier, *ibid.*, 1654.

NOTES TO CHAPTER THIRTEEN

1. F. Ouellet, "Dualité économique et changement technologique au Québec, 1760-1790," *Histoire sociale* (1976), 256-96.

2. F. Ouellet, "Propriété seigneuriale et groupes sociaux dans la vallée du Saint-Laurent, 1663-1840," in P. Savard (ed.), *Mélanges d'histoire du Canada français offerts au Professeur Marcel Trudel* (1978), 183-213.

3. Mackenzie—O'Callaghan, 16 September 1844, PAC, O'Callaghan Papers.

SELECT BIBLIOGRAPHY

In order to keep this bibliography brief, I have included here only those sources consulted and books and articles published since compilation in 1966 of the bibliography for my *Histoire économique et sociale du Québec*, which contains an analytical bibliography of sources referred to therein. For other relevant bibliographies see: D.G. Creighton, *The Empire of the St. Lawrence* (Toronto, 1960); H.T. Manning, *The Revolt of French Canada, 1800-1835* (Toronto, 1962); A.R.M. Lower, *Colony to Nation* (3rd. ed., Toronto, 1957); E. McInnis, *Canada, A Political and Social History* (Toronto, 1947); T. Chapais, *Cours d'histoire du Canada* (8 vols., Quebec, 1917-34); and L. Groulx, *Lendemains de conquête* (Montreal, 1920).

1. SOURCES

A. The Economy

Prices

Price movements may be traced through newspapers, account records of religious communities, parishes, and merchants, and official documents. On the problems of assembling information on prices for farm produce in urban centres, see J. Hamelin and F. Ouellet, "Le Mouvement des prix agricoles dans la province de Québec," in C. Galarneau and E. Lavoie (eds.), *France et Canada français du XVIe au XXe siècle* (Quebec, 1966), 35-48.With invaluable assistance from R. Chabot, we are beginning to have a fairly accurate idea of the evolution of agricultural prices in rural areas, for which parish account books are the principal source. Professors Wallot and Paquet have brought to light the monthly reports of the market clerk for the city of Quebec, an important source (PAC, MG 11, Series Q); see G. Paquet and J.-P. Wallot, "Aperçu sur le commerce international et les prix domestiques dans le Bas-Canada, 1793-1812," RHAF (1967), 461-8.

Agricultural Production

The volume and evolution of agricultural production are more difficult to determine because of the lack of periodic census records on harvests. The census of 1784 provides the amount of wheat sown and the size of livestock herds, but nothing about production. After 1760 the earliest comprehensive figures are for 1827. The 1831 census gives production and herd data not only for parishes and seigneuries, but also for individual producers. That of 1842, although not as complete as regards territory covered, likewise gives figures for individual producers. This has made it possible to compile agricultural statistics for some 85,000 rural families, using six variables. The 1844 census, however, again gives only parish and seigneury data. The original nominative censuses are found at the Public Archives of Canada, reel no. c 719-33.

For the period 1784-1827, for which there are no production records, it is necessary to use other direct and indirect harvest indicators. Account books kept by parish priests have been invaluable to this end. Since the tithe was one twenty-sixth of grain harvested, the size of harvests can be ascertained from the tithes collected. Unfortunately, few tithe books have been preserved, but among them are those of the parish of Ste-Anne de Yamachiche for the years 1831-39, which have been thoroughly analyzed. In compensation for the dearth of other books, curés' reports to the bishops of Quebec and Montreal are an extremely important source. See F. Ouellet, "L'Agriculture bas-canadienne vue à travers la dîme et la rente en nature," *Histoire sociale* (1971), 5-44. Less direct indicators: the seigneurial *rente* (*censitaires'* annual land rents) paid in kind; the *banalité*, or toll, paid in wheat for use of the seigneur's mill, which, being a proportion of grain milled, reveals valuable production data; the voluntary Quête de l'Enfant-Jésus on which we have data for some one hundred parishes; and certain qualitative sources, such as comments by travellers and newspapers on the size and condition of harvests.

Land Ownership

Changes in land ownership can be examined in two categories, namely, holdings by seigneurs and by *censitaires*. For the seigneurial category, see especially P.-G. Roy, *Inventaire des concessions en fief et seigneurie, foi et hommage, et aveux et dénombrements, conservés aux Archives de la province de Québec* (6 vols., Beauceville, 1923-36). See also F. Ouellet, "Propriété seigneuriale et groupes sociaux dans la vallée du Saint-Laurent (1663-1840)," in P. Savard (ed.), *Mélanges d'histoire du Canada français offerts au Professeur Marcel Trudel* (Ottawa, 1978), 183-213. The abridged *cadastre* (land titles register) of 1854 is also an important source. For the study of seigneurial revenues, a necessary source is the *censiers* preserved in the archives of religious communities and especially the Archives of the Province of Quebec. Land ownership by *censitaires* may be analyzed from certain basic records: the *aveux et dénombrements* (English régime) for the period 1784-90; the abridged *cadastre* of 1854; certain *terriers*, such as that for the seigneurie of Laprairie; most important, the nominative censuses of 1831 and 1842, which have yielded an inventory of about 85,000 lots of land. For land situated in the townships, the essential source is the enormous number of records in the Archives of the Province of Quebec and the Public Archives of Canada. See also J.-C. Langelier, *List of Lands Granted by the Crown in the Province of Quebec from 1793 to 31st December 1890* (Quebec, 1891).

Import-Export Data

Import-export movements at the various ports (Quebec, St-Jean, Gaspé, Côteau-du-Lac, Ste-Marie de Beauce, Stanstead), as well as traffic through the Lachine and Rideau canals, can be determined readily from the *Journals of the House of Assembly of Lower Canada* and their appendices. See also Imperial Blue Books on Affairs Relating to Canada (1824-41), 6 vols., PAC, RG 1, and Report on Inland Navigation (1839), PAC, RG 1, E 12, vol. 3. Difficulty in obtaining complete records for certain products has been partially overcome through data from Naval Officers' Records, PAC, RG 5. The problem has since been resolved with the publication of these series by G. Paquet and J.-P. Wallot in "Aperçu sur le commerce international et les prix domestiques dans le Bas-Canada (1793-1812)," RHAF (1967), 451-7.

Shipbuilding

The evolution of shipbuilding can be traced statistically from the JHALC and appendices. The *Quebec Mercury* of 11 February 1840 gives statistics beginning with 1818, including the number of workmen employed each year. *Le Journal de Québec* of 21 February 1867 contains statistics beginning with 1787 and indicating the number of ships built by category, according to size.

Public Finance and Financial Institutions

The appendices to the JHALC provide figures on public finance and the annual reports of banks, sometimes with lists of shareholders. For a partial study of the civil list, see G. Paquet and J.-P. Wallot, "La Liste civile du Bas-Canada (1794-1812): un essai d'histoire économique," RHAF (1969), 225-7.

Qualitative Sources

The appendices to the JHALC are invaluable for contemporary data revealing various problems, economic and otherwise. Enormous numbers of reports of public and private bodies and committees of inquiry provide an accurate view of conditions in all segments of the economy. The agricultural and land problems emerge with striking clarity.

B. Demography

The censuses of 1784, 1790, 1822, 1827, 1831, 1842, and 1844 are essential to population study, for they provide data on age structure, geographic distribution, matrimonial status, growth, etc. With less consistency they also indicate religion and ethnicity. Birth, marriage, and death statistics are contained in the *Annuaire statistique de la Province de Québec* (1914), 87, and in G. Langlois, *Histoire de la population canadienne-française* (Montréal, 1935). The same data for each parish of the Quebec and Trois-Rivières districts appears in one of the numerous House of Assembly land reports (1823-25). For further detailed figures by locality, see the appendices to the JHALC, which also give British immigration figures from 1815 onward. For the latter, see also H. Cowan, *British Immigration to British North America* (Toronto, 1961).

C. Social Structure, Ethnic Conflict

The 1831 and 1842 censuses enable ethnic and occupational classification of individuals, and this has been done for the cities and rural districts at both dates in this book. For the city of Quebec there are also Plessis's censuses of 1792, 1795, 1798, and 1805 (taken when Plessis was its parish priest). These are published in the *Annual Report of the Archivist of the Province of Quebec, 1948-49*, 9-250. Also consulted were the Quebec and Montreal *Directories* for 1819 to 1845 and the city of Quebec evaluation rolls. The evolution of certain social groups, such as the professionals, may be traced through the *Quebec Almanac*, published from 1792 to 1840. See also PAC, Trade Licences, RG 4, B 28, vols. 110-55; Tavern Licences, Peddlars' Licences, Shop Licences, *ibid.*, 59-105; Notaries' and Advocates' Commissions, *ibid.*, 1-27; and Medical Licences and Certificates, *ibid.*, 47-55. For the social aspect of the insurrections of 1837-38, the APQ collection, Les Evénements de 1837-38, is the prime source; it enables quantification of the participants in the revolutionary movement, identification of component groups, and analysis of motivations and ideology.

The PAC has a parallel collection, Rebellion Records, 1837-39, RG 4, B 14, 24 and 37.

D. Politics

For analysis of political events, some fifty poll books are available for years ranging from 1792 to 1841. In this sampling, while the Montreal region seems poorly represented, the Quebec region is adequately covered, both in diversity of ridings and number of elections. The poll books give each elector's name and occupation, his status as property owner or tenant, and the nature of his vote or votes. The components of the electorate can be distinguished according to ethnicity, social and economic status, family ties, and locality, especially if the nominative censuses and evaluation rolls are used along with the poll books.

Social analysis of the elected politicians as a group requires examination of very diverse sources, among which F.-J. Audet's publications and his personal papers (PAC) are indispensable. We have traced the family history of 386 out of 415 individuals elected to the House of Assembly. For a study of legislative councillors see A. Garon, "La Fonction politique et sociale des Chambres hautes canadiennes, 1791-1841," *Histoire sociale* (1970), 66-87.

Comprehension of the political conflicts and climate has required the use of A.G. Doughty and D.A. MacArthur (eds.), *Documents Relating to the Constitutional History of Canada, 1792-1818* (Ottawa, 1914); and A.G. Doughty and N. Story (eds.), *ibid., 1819-1828* (Ottawa, 1935). Even more useful are general correspondence and certain major manuscript collections. The Neilson Papers (PAC) are essential for the period 1810 to 1830. The Papineau (PAC) and Papineau-Bourassa (APQ) Collections are valuable, particularly for the period subsequent to 1820. The Duvernay Collection (APQ) provides good coverage of the decade 1830 to 1840, as does the correspondence of C.-O. Perreault, which is included in the Lafontaine Papers (APQ). The D.-B. Viger Papers (PAC) and La Saberdache bleue (APQ) are good complements to the above records. The Archives of the Quebec and Montreal Boards of Trade are also useful.

Contemporary newspapers such as *Le Canadien, La Minerve, Quebec Mercury, Montreal Herald, Spectateur canadien,* and *Vindicator,* to name only the most important, contain a mass of information on all subjects, and politics in particular; debates in the House of Assembly are abundantly reported and commented on.

2. RECENT BOOKS AND ARTICLES

Aquin, H. (ed.) *Maximilien Globensky. La Rebellion de 1837 à St-Eustache.* Montreal, 1974.

Baillargeon, G.-E. *La Survivance du régime seigneurial à Montréal: un régime qui ne veut pas mourir.* Montreal, 1968.

Beaulieu, A. and Hamelin, J. *La Presse québécoise des origines à nos jours,* I: 1764-1859. Quebec, 1973.

Beaulieu, A. and Morley, W.F.E. *Histoires locales et régionales canadiennes des origines à 1950.* Toronto, 1971.

Boucher, J. "Les Aspects économiques de la tenure seigneuriale au Canada," *Recherches d'histoire économique* (Paris, 1964), 149-219.

Bouliane, R.G. "The French Canadians and the Schools of the Royal Institution for the Advancement of Learning," *Social History* (1972), 144-64.

Bourque, G. *Classes sociales et question nationale au Québec, 1760-1840.* Montreal, 1970.

Brun, H. *La Formation des institutions parlementaires québecoises, 1791-1838.* Quebec, 1970.

Chabot, R. *Le Curé de campagne et la contestation locale au Québec de 1791 aux troubles de 1837-38.* Montreal, 1975.

Deschênes, L. "Les Entreprises de William Price," *Histoire sociale* (1968), 16-52.

Dubuc, A. "Problems in the Study of the Stratification of the Canadian Society from 1760 to 1840," CHAR (1965), 13-29.

Galarneau, C. *La France devant l'opinion canadienne, 1760-1815.* Quebec, 1970.

Galarneau, C. and Lavoie, E. (eds.) *France et Canada français du XVIe au XXe siècle.* Quebec, 1966. 35-48, 81-120, 159-76.

Garon, A. "La Fonction politique et sociale des Chambres hautes canadiennes, 1791-1841," *Histoire sociale* (1970), 66-87.

―――― "Le Conseil législatif du Canada uni: révision constitutionnelle et composante socio-ethnique," *Histoire sociale* (1971), 61-83.

Hare, J. "La Population de la ville de Québec, 1795-1805," *Histoire sociale* (1974), 23-47.

Hitsman, J.M. *The Incredible War of 1812: A Military History.* Toronto, 1965.

Jolois, J.-J. *Jean-François Perreault (1753-1844) et les origines de l'enseignement laïque au Bas-Canada.* Montreal, 1969.

Lebel, M. "L'Enseignement de la philosphie au Séminaire de Québec," RHAF (1964), 405-24; (1965), 582-95; (1966), 106-28.

Legoff, T.J.A. "The Agricultural Crisis in Lower Canada, 1802-1812; a Review of a Controversy," CHR (1974), 1-31.

Lemieux, L. *L'Etablissement de la première province ecclésiastique au Canada, 1783-1844.* Montreal, 1967.

Linteau, P.-A. and Robert, J.-C. "Propriété foncière et societé à Montréal: une hypothèse," RHAF (1974), 45-67.

Neatby, H. *Quebec: the Revolutionary Age, 1760-1791.* Toronto, 1966.

Ormsby, W. (ed.), *The Grey Journals and Letters.* Toronto, 1964.

Ouellet, F. "La Sauvegarde des patrimoines dans le district de Québec durant la première moitié du XIXe siècle," RHAF (1972), 319-74.

―――― *Histoire économique et sociale du Québec, 1760-1850.* Montreal, 1966.

―――― *Elements d'histoire sociale du Bas-Canada.* Montreal, 1972.

―――― "Dualité économique et changement technologique au Québec, 1760-1790," *Histoire sociale* (1976), 256-96.

―――― "Le Mythe de l'habitant sensible au marché. Commentaires sur la controverse Legoff-Wallot et Paquet," *Recherches sociographiques* (1976), 115-32.

Paquet, G. and Wallot, J.-P. *Patronage et pouvoir dans le Bas-Canada, 1794-1812.* Montreal, 1973.

―――― "Le Bas-Canada au début du XIXe siècle: une hypothèse," RHAF (1971), 39-61.

―――― "Crise agricole et tensions socio-ethniques dans le Bas-Canada, 1802-1812: éléments pour une ré-interprétation," RAHF (1972), 185-237.

―――― "Groupes sociaux et pouvoir: le cas canadien au début du XIXe siècle," RHAF (1974), 509-64.

―――― "The Agricultural Crisis in Lower Canada, 1802-1812: mise au point. A Response to T.J.A. Legoff," CHR (1975), 134-68.

Rich, E.E. *The Fur Trade and the North West to 1857.* Toronto, 1957.

Robert, J.-C. "Un Seigneur entrepreneur: Barthélémy Joliette et la fondation du village de l'Industrie, 1822-1850," RHAF (1972), 375-95.

Roy, J.-L. *Edouard-Raymond Fabre: Libraire et patriote canadien, 1799-1854.* Montreal, 1974.

Ryerson, S. *Unequal Union: Confederation and the Roots of Conflict in the Canadas, 1815-1873.* Toronto, 1968.

Savard, P. "Les Débuts de l'enseignement de l'histoire et de la géographie au Séminaire de Québec," RHAF (1962), 509-25; (1963), 43-62.

_____ (ed.) *Mélanges d'histoire du Canada français offerts au Professeur Marcel Trudel.* Ottawa, 1978.

Séguin, M. *La Nation canadienne et l'agriculture, 1760-1850.* Trois-Rivières, 1970.

Tousignant, P. "La Genèse et l'avènement de la constitution de 1791," Doctoral thesis, Université de Montréal, 1971.

_____ "Problématique pour une nouvelle approche de la constitution de 1791," RHAF (1973), 181-234.

Vallée, J. (ed.) *Tocqueville dans le Bas-Canada.* Montreal, 1973.

Vincent, J.R. *How Victorians Voted.* Cambridge, U.K., 1968.

Wallot, J.-P. *Un Québec qui bougeait.* Trois-Rivières, 1973.

_____ "Le Régime seigneurial et son abolition au Canada," CHR (1969), 367-93.

Wallot, J.-P. and Hare, J. *Les Imprimés dans le Bas-Canada, 1801-1810.* Montreal, 1967.